The American Madness

Jack S. Romine
Merritt College

Nancie Piper Hughes
Formerly of West Valley College

Houghton Mifflin Company • **Boston**
New York • Atlanta • Geneva, Illinois • Dallas • Palo Alto

Preface

The title of this book demands some explanation, for its many possible interpretations underlie the choice of essays presented here. The term *madness* refers generally to incongruities, absurdities, and paradoxes which are apparent in American society; *madness* is also used as another name for hypocrisy, vulgarity, extremism, injustice, apathy, insincerity, and violence. Although these deviations from the golden mean are certainly not unique to this country, we Americans display a distinctive set of symptoms. The manifestations of these symptoms have been the subject of many essays and treatises, old and new. Thus, we have chosen to focus on this American madness, the peculiar nature of the American character and American society.

The title may also be read as a pun: those elements of our society that we could call sick or mad generate anger and indignation among men of conscience. If we or they chose merely to present accusations of madness, our effort would be boring at best, destructive at worst. But madness expressed as anger or indignation can act as a catharsis and provide a base for constructive change. Many of our authors have used the energy generated by indignation to probe and analyze social problems, some to exercise private demons. Many offer an element of hope either for the individual or the group, provided that the individual assumes his responsibility to make the effort towards change. We concur with Irwin Edman, who says, "human intelligence accompanied by human goodwill may profoundly improve the life of mankind."

We have held the apparatus to a minimum. Instead of confronting a student with tiresome dictionary work, we wish to speed him along towards a pleasurable absorption in ideas. Within each selection we have footnoted the words which are most difficult, most uncommon, most essential for comprehension. These are defined in context as simply as possible. When we have supplied a title for an article, we have so indicated in a footnote. The footnotes we have added are numbered; those appearing in an article as it was originally published have been retained and are indicated by an asterisk (*).

J.S.R.
N.P.H.

Berkeley, California

Contents

229 # *Prognosis*

A symptom is a sign or token of something else. An alteration in bodily function may indicate the presence of disease, and an aberration in behavior may be a sign of emotional or spiritual disorder. Every man in a society is a potential set of symptoms, for by his behavior, his language, and his choices, he reflects the influence on him of his family, his friends, and his group. Europeans often regard the collective traits of American behavior and attitude as ''the American madness,'' asserting that as a nation we have a peculiar style, a unique set of symptoms. Any list of these would be as numerous and varied as the number of observers. The eleven authors in this section chart the current manifestations of that chronic condition known as madness and reveal the toll it takes among Americans.

We begin with Wolfe's description of a demolition derby, an American innovation which for its appeal relies on mass destruction of automobiles in a display of deliberate, aggressive collisions and rammings. What the

Symptoms

demolition derby reveals about us is probably more than a need to give vent to our aggressions, for as Baker points out, guns are a more direct way of doing that. It is shocking how frequently Americans kill each other. Rosenthal asks us to consider which is more pathologic—that one man could brutally kill another or that thirty-eight citizens could watch it happen and not try to intervene. Even worse than physical violence, perhaps, is the mutilation of children's spirits which, according to Kozol, is sometimes accomplished in the name of public education.

The American madness reveals itself not only as man against man, but as man against nature. Ten years ago Miss Carson warned us that we were, often unwittingly, polluting and destroying some of our most precious resources. The trend continues: some men are even capable of malicious, irreversible destruction, as Roueché discovered in Texas.

Man against himself is the worst manifestation of our disorder. Hard-drug users such as Dom Abruzzi have become dropouts from society and from productive living. After documenting the widespread use of drugs and pills among adults of all classes, Jackson concludes that drugs have become a permanent feature of the American scene. In a dramatic withdrawal from society almost without parallel, thousands of middle class youth became hippies in protest against the sterile philosophy of their status-seeking parents. Yet as Harris reconstructs it, this movement contained the seeds of its own dissolution. At the end of the sixties, alienation from one's self and from one's society remains a predominant theme.

2

DOGGIE!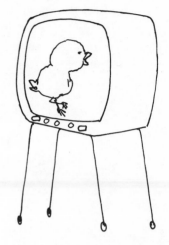

CHICKIE!

HORSIE!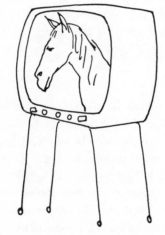

KITTY!

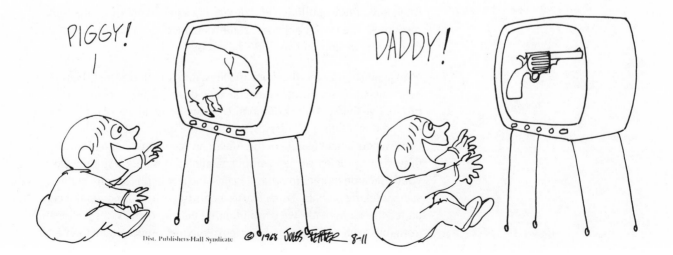

PIGGY!

DADDY!

Clean Fun at Riverhead

TOM WOLFE

The inspiration for the demolition derby came to Lawrence Mendelsohn one night in 1958 when he was nothing but a spare-ribbed twenty-eight-year-old stock-car driver halfway through his 10th lap around the Islip, L.I., Speedway and taking a curve too wide. A lubberly[1] young man with a Chicago boxcar haircut came up on the inside in a 1949 Ford and caromed him 12 rows up into the grandstand, but Lawrence Mendelsohn and his entire car did not hit one spectator.

"That was what got me," he said, "I remember I was hanging upside down from my seat belt like a side of Jersey bacon and wondering why no one was sitting where I hit. 'Lousy promotion,' I said to myself.

"Not only that, but everybody who *was* in the stands forgot about the race and came running over to look at me gift-wrapped upside down in a fresh pile of junk."

At that moment occurred the transformation of Lawrence Mendelsohn, racing driver, into Lawrence Mendelsohn, promoter, and, a few transactions later, owner of the Islip Speedway, where he kept seeing more of this same underside of stock car racing that everyone in the industry avoids putting into words. Namely, that for every purist who comes to see the fine points of the race, such as who is going to win, there are probably five waiting for the wrecks to which stock car racing is so gloriously prone.

[1] awkward or clumsy

Reprinted with the permission of Farrar, Straus & Giroux, Inc. from **The Kandy-Kolored Tangerine Flake Streamline Baby** by Tom Wolfe. Copyright © 1963 by the Herald Tribune, Inc.

The pack will be going into a curve when suddenly two cars, three cars, four cars tangle, spinning and splattering all over each other and the retaining walls, upside down, right side up, inside out and in pieces, with the seams bursting open and discs, rods, wires and gasoline spewing out and yards of sheet metal shearing off like Reynolds Wrap and crumpling into the most baroque[2] shapes, after which an ash-blue smoke starts seeping up from the ruins and a thrill begins to spread over the stands like Newburg sauce.

So why put up with the monotony between crashes?

Such, in brief, is the early history of what is culturally the most important sport ever originated in the United States, a sport that ranks with the gladiatorial games of Rome as a piece of national symbolism. Lawrence Mendelsohn had a vision of an automobile sport that would be all crashes. Not two cars, not three cars, not four cars, but 100 cars would be out in an arena doing nothing but smashing each other into shrapnel. The car that outrammed and outdodged all the rest, the last car that could still move amid the smoking heap, would take the prize money.

So at 8:15 at night at the Riverhead Raceway, just west of Riverhead, L.I., on Route 25, amid the quaint tranquility of the duck and turkey farm flatlands of eastern Long Island, Lawrence Mendelsohn stood up on the back of a flat truck in his red neon warmup jacket and lectured his 100 drivers on the rules and niceties of the new game, the "demolition derby." And so at 8:30 the first 25 cars moved out onto the raceway's quarter-mile stock car track. There was not enough room for 100 cars to mangle each other. Lawrence Mendelsohn's dream would require four heats. Now the 25 cars were placed at intervals all about the circumference of the track, making flatulent[3] revving noises, all headed not around the track but toward a point in the center of the infield.

Then the entire crowd, about 4,000, started chanting a countdown, "Ten, nine, eight, seven, six, five, four, three, two," but it was impossible to hear the rest, because right after "two" half the crowd went into a strange whinnying wail. The starter's flag went up, and the 25 cars took off,

[2] irregular or having grotesque ornamentation; in art, a 16th and 17th century style characterized by heavy and contorted forms and an exaggeration of ornamental and pictorial effects
[3] marked by or affected with gases generated in the intestine or stomach

4   roaring into second gear with no mufflers, all headed toward that same point in the center of the infield, converging nose on nose.

The effect was exactly what one expects that many simultaneous crashes to produce: the unmistakable tympany[4] of automobiles colliding and cheap-gauge sheet metal buckling; front ends folding together at the same cockeyed angles police photographs of night-time wreck scenes capture so well on grainy paper; smoke pouring from under the hoods and hanging over the infield like a howitzer cloud; a few of the surviving cars lurching eccentrically on bent axles. At last, after four heats, there were only two cars moving through the junk, a 1953 Chrysler and a 1958 Cadillac. In the Chrysler a small fascia[5] of muscles named Spider Ligon, who smoked a cigar while he drove, had the Cadillac cornered up against a guard rail in front of the main grandstand. He

[4] the resonance given off by percussion instruments
[5] a sheet of connective tissue covering or binding together body structures

dispatched it by swinging around and backing full throttle through the left side of its grille and radiator.

By now the crowd was quite beside itself. Spectators broke through a gate in the retaining screen. Some rushed to Spider Ligon's car, hoisted him to their shoulders and marched off the field, howling. Others clambered over the stricken cars of the defeated, enjoying the details of their ruin, and howling. The good, full cry of triumph and annihilation rose from Riverhead Raceway, and the demolition derby was over.

That was the 154th demolition derby in two years. Since Lawrence Mendelsohn staged the first one at Islip Speedway in 1961, they have been held throughout the United States at the rate of one every five days, resulting in the destruction of about 15,000 cars. The figures alone indicate a gluttonous appetite for the sport. Sports writers, of course, have managed to ignore demolition derbies even more successfully than they have ignored stock car racing and drag racing. All in all, the new automobile sports have shown that the sports pages, which on the surface appear to hum with life and earthiness, are at bottom pillars of gentility. This drag racing and demolition derbies and things, well, there are too many kids in it with sideburns, tight Levis and winkle-picker boots.

Yet the demolition derbies keep growing on word-of-mouth publicity. The "nationals" were held last month at Langhorne, Pa., with 50 cars in the finals, and demolition derby fans everywhere know that Don McTavish, of Dover, Mass., is the new world's champion. About 1,250,000 spectators have come to the 154 contests held so far. More than 75 per cent of the derbies have drawn full houses.

The nature of their appeal is clear enough. Since the onset of the Christian era, i.e., since about 500 A.D., no game has come along to fill the gap left by the abolition of the purest of all sports, gladiatorial combat. As late as 300 A.D. these bloody duels, usually between men but sometimes between women and dwarfs, were enormously popular not only in Rome but throughout the Roman Empire. Since then no game, not even boxing, has successfully acted out the underlying motifs of most sport, that is, aggression and destruction.

Boxing, of course, is an aggressive sport, but one contestant has actually destroyed the other in a relatively small percentage of matches. Other games are progressively more sublimated[6] forms of sport. Often, as in the case of football, they are encrusted with oddments of passive theology and metaphysics[7] to the effect that the real purpose of the game is to foster character, teamwork, stamina, physical fitness and the ability to "give-and-take."

But not even those wonderful clergymen who pray in behalf of Congress, expressway ribbon-cuttings, urban renewal projects and testimonial dinners for ethnic aldermen would pray for a demolition derby. The demolition derby is, pure and simple, a form of gladiatorial combat for our times.

As hand-to-hand combat has gradually disappeared from our civilization, even in wartime, and competition has become more and more sophisticated and abstract, Americans have turned to the automobile to satisfy their love of direct aggression. The mild-mannered man who turns into a

[6] having directed the energy of an impulse from its primitive aim (here, violence and destruction) to a socially acceptable or constructive level
[7] loosely, philosophy

bear behind the wheel of a car—i.e., who finds in the power of the automobile a vehicle for the release of his inhibitions—is part of American folklore. Among teen-agers the automobile has become the symbol, and in part the physical means, of triumph over family and community restrictions. Seventy-five per cent of all car thefts in the United States are by teen-agers out for "joy rides."

5

"The Demolition derby is, pure and simple, a form of gladiatorial combat for our times."

The symbolic meaning of the automobile tones down but by no means vanishes in adulthood. Police traffic investigators have long been convinced that far more accidents are purposeful crashes by belligerent drivers than they could ever prove. One of the heroes of the era was the Middle Eastern diplomat who rammed a magazine writer's car from behind in the Kalorama embassy district of Washington two years ago. When the American bellowed out the window at him, he backed up and smashed his car again. When the fellow leaped out of his car to pick a fight, he backed up and smashed his car a third time, then drove off. He was recalled home for having "gone native."

The unabashed, undisguised, quite purposeful sense of destruction of the demolition derby is its unique contribution. The aggression, the battering, the ruination are there to be enjoyed. The crowd at a demolition derby seldom gasps and often laughs. It enjoys the same full-throated participation as Romans at the Colosseum. After each trial or heat at a demolition derby, two drivers go into the finals. One is the driver whose car was still going at the end. The other is the driver the crowd selects from among the 24 vanquished on the basis of his courage, showmanship or simply the awesomeness of his crashes. The numbers of the cars are read over loudspeakers, and the crowd chooses one with its cheers. By the same token, the crowd may force a driver out of competition if he appears cowardly or merely cunning. This is the sort of driver who drifts around the edge of the battle avoiding crashes with the hope that the other cars will eliminate one another. The umpire waves a yellow flag at

". . . Americans have turned to the automobile to satisfy their love of direct aggression."

6 him and he must crash into someone within 30 seconds or run the risk of being booed off the field in dishonor and disgrace.

The frank relish of the crowd is nothing, however, compared to the kick the contestants get out of the game. It costs a man an average of $50 to retrieve a car from a junk yard and get it running for a derby. He will only get his money back—$50 —for winning a heat. The chance of being smashed up in the madhouse first 30 seconds of a round are so great, even the best of drivers faces long odds in his shot at the $500 first prize. None of that matters to them.

Tommy Fox, who is nineteen, said he entered the demolition derby because, "You know, it's fun. I like it. You know what I mean?" What was fun about it? Tommy Fox had a way of speaking that was much like the early Marlon Brando. Much of what he had to say came from the trapezii,[8] which he rolled quite a bit, and the forehead, which he cocked, and the eyebrows, which he could bring together expressively from time to time. "Well," he said, "you know, like when you hit 'em, and all that. It's fun."

Tommy Fox had a lot of fun in the first heat. Nobody was bashing around quite like he was in his old green Hudson. He did not win, chiefly because he took too many chances, but the crowd voted him into the finals as the best showman.

"I got my brother," said Tommy. "I came in from the side and he didn't even see me."

His brother is Don Fox, thirty-two, who owns the junk yard where they both got their cars. Don likes to hit them, too, only he likes it almost too much. Don drives with such abandon, smashing into the first car he can get a shot at and leaving himself wide open, he does not stand much chance of finishing the first three minutes.

For years now sociologists have been calling upon one another to undertake a serious study of America's "car culture." No small part of it is the way the automobile has, for one very large segment of the population, become the focus of the same sort of quasi-religious[9] dedication as art is currently for another large segment of a higher social order. Tommy Fox is unemployed, Don Fox runs a junk yard, Spider Ligon is a maintenance man for Brookhaven Naval Laboratory, but to categorize them as such is getting no closer to the truth than to have categorized William Faulkner in 1926 as a clerk at Lord & Taylor, although he was.

Tommy Fox, Don Fox and Spider Ligon are acolytes[10] of the car culture, an often esoteric[11] world of arts and sciences that came into its own after World War II and now has believers of two generations. Charlie Turbush, thirty-five, and his son, Buddy, seventeen, were two more contestants, and by no stretch of the imagination can they be characterized as bizarre[12] figures or cultists of the death wish. As for the dangers of driving in a demolition derby, they are quite real by all physical laws. The drivers are protected only by crash helmets, seat belts and the fact that all glass, interior handles, knobs and fixtures have been removed. Yet Lawrence Mendelsohn claims that there have been no serious injuries in 154 demolition derbies and now gets his insurance at a rate below that of stock car racing.

*T*he sport's future may depend in part on word getting around about its relative safety. Already it is beginning to draw contestants here and there from social levels that could give the demolition derby the cachet[13] of respectability. In eastern derbies so far two doctors and three young men of more than passable connections in eastern society have entered under whimsical *noms de combat*[14] and emerged neither scarred nor victorious. Bull fighting had to win the same social combat.

All of which brings to mind that fine afternoon when some high-born Roman women were out in Nero's box at the Colosseum watching this sexy Thracian carve an ugly little Samnite up into prime cuts, and one said, darling, she had an inspiration, and Nero, needless to say, was all for it. Thus began the new vogue of Roman socialites fighting as gladiators themselves, for kicks. By the second century A.D. even the Emperor Commodus was out there with a tiger's head as a helmet hacking away at some poor dazed fall guy. He did a lot for the sport. Arenas sprang up all over the empire like shopping center bowling alleys.

The future of the demolition derby, then, stretches out over the face of America. The sport draws no lines of gender, and post-debs may reach Lawrence Mendelsohn at his office in Deer Park.

---

[8] large flat triangular muscles on each side of the back
[9] seemingly religious
[10] followers; minor attendants at a religious ceremony
[11] limited to a small circle, and designed for or understood by only the specially initiated
[12] odd or eccentric
[13] seal
[14] French for fictitious names used in fighting or competition. The author is trading on the more familiar *noms de plumes*, meaning pen names.

Unexpected Rewards of Virtue

FRED J. COOK

On March 10, 1961, Douglas William Johnson, a fifty-year-old Negro janitor in Los Angeles, a man who had felt the pinch of poverty, drove to an apartment house under construction to see if he could get the job of cleaning up the debris. With him was his wife, Helen, thirty-eight. The superintendent whom he had to see about the debris-cleaning chore wasn't at the site, and so Johnson climbed back into his station wagon and started home. He had driven only a short distance when he happened to see, lying in the street in front of his car, a bulky canvas bag. Thinking it might contain something useful, Johnson stopped, picked it up and tossed it into the back of the station wagon.

As he got behind the wheel and drove off, his wife, possessed by curiosity, turned around and began to examine the bag. It was sealed, but it bore a tag. The tag said that the bag contained $240,000 in $10 and $20 bills.

"Do you know what you've picked up?" Mrs. Johnson asked her husband. "There's $240,000 in that bag'"

"No!" he said—and started to shake all over.

Explaining his reaction later, Johnson told reporters: "I was knocked off my feet. I never dreamed I'd have my hands on anything like that."

Here certainly was king-sized temptation. Bills of relatively small denominations are not easily traced, and Johnson—the part-time maintenance man, father of three sons—had $240,000 worth of those bills at his finger tips. What to do?

"I thought if I kept that money I'd never be able to look my three kids in the face again," Johnson explained, using the simplistic[1] imagery of a

[1] reduced to false or misleading simplicity

From **The Corrupt Society** by Fred J. Cook in **The Nation,** June 1–8, 1963. Reprinted by permission of the author.

bygone age when man had stature[2] and was supposed to be responsible for his acts.

So Johnson acted according to the dictates of pure and simple honesty. As soon as he reached home, he telephoned a friend, a former Chicago policeman, to find out whom he should notify about the money; the friend advised him to call the FBI. He did. In minutes, four FBI agents were at his door, recovering the money bag that had fallen from the rear of a passing Brinks truck. The truck had traveled for some distance before the $240,000 loss was discovered, and scores of police and FBI agents had begun to search along the truck's route when Johnson telephoned that he had the missing money.

Brinks paid Johnson a $10,000 reward for his honesty, but this wasn't the end of the story. A little more than a month later, on April 21, 1961, the press of the nation recorded the sad and revealing sequel. Johnson's life had been made utterly miserable; the strictly honest deed that should have made him the most admired of men had made him instead the most despised, ridiculed and harassed.

Crackpots wrote obscene letters to him, neighbors ridiculed him, fellow workers needled him, schoolmates taunted his sons. The universal theme was that Johnson had proven himself to be the world's greatest boob by returning that $240,000 once he had it in his hands. The taunts became too much for his oldest son, Richard, sixteen, who finally ran away from home, returning after a few days, hungry and disillusioned. "The kids kept saying things to me," he explained. "All the time, they were saying my father was dumb, and a fool and stupid. . . . I just couldn't stand it."

Johnson himself said it was "nice" that Brinks had given him a $10,000 reward, but he added:

"I can't leave the house to get work without someone throws it all up to me and calls me a fool. Can't be on the job without someone says, 'Why you need work? You had 240,000.' And now it's hurting my boys.

"I wish I'd never seen any of it. I wish we'd let that money sit in the street and rot. I wish we'd thrown it down a sewer or burned it.

"That money? It's not worth anything. It has made me a poor man."

. . . In a monied[3] society, Douglas Johnson had committed the cardinal[4] sin; acting on honest impulse, he had returned a fortune that he might have kept.

[2] moral standing
[3] wealthy
[4] principal, chief

Dom Abruzzi

JEREMY LARNER

I guess it was sort of a lark. At that time anyway, we were all off on a kick. I was sixteen years old exactly, and I was walking with one friend on Henry Street, and he asked me, have you ever smoked pot before? I didn't know what pot was, and I had to ask him, so he told me it was marijuana and I almost fell with shock. But then he talked about it, and he explained to me it was nothing to worry about, and three days later I was smoking my first weed. Three months afterward, I started snorting heroin. I got in on that because it was so cheap—a dollar and a half apiece to split a three-dollar bag—and everybody was getting so high and seemed so happy. I just indulged, I put in my dollar and a half, and the first time I got high on horse I was sick as a pig. I couldn't see, I kept vomiting all over the place, and a few months after that I took my first shot. That was a skin-pop,[1] and followed a week later by a mainline.[2] But for the first few years I would say I was an oddity, because I kept myself in check; I didn't get a habit. I was going out with a very wonderful girl at the time, and I wanted to marry her. But in the next few years that followed, I got arrested once, then a second time, and the girl and I broke up. After we broke up, we had money in the bank, in a joint account. I took it all out and spent it on dope, and that's how I acquired my first habit.

I didn't even know I was hooked. I was sitting on a bench right here in the Vladeck project, I was yawning and tearing and a friend came over to me and started talking to me, and said, Dom, you know you're sick. And for the first time I realized I was actually addicted. I had the habit and I had to have it. So from then on it was every day, and when I ran out of the bank money, I began bor-

[1] injection under the skin
[2] injection directly into a vein

From **The Addict in the Street,** edited by Jeremy Larner from tape recordings collected by Ralph Tefferteller. Reprinted by permission of Grove Press, Inc. Copyright © 1964 by Grove Press, Inc.

rowing. At that time, the first few years, your parents don't know anything about your taking dope and everything is so easy; money is much easier to get than when everyone knows you're a drug addict. So I did get arrested again—that was 1956—that was the third time and I went into Riverside Hospital. I spent seven months undergoing psychiatric treatment, but it was all a falsity because I wasn't really undergoing it, I was pretending my way through. I wasn't really trying to help myself. The seven months I was there I was thinking about just one thing: going home and taking that first shot of dope. In fact, all of us there were thinking the same thing. Nobody wanted to help themselves, or so it seemed to me. So I got out in April, 1957, and the first day I was out, I was out two hours, I took my first shot of dope.

And it went on for the next few months; I got another habit, and I saw I couldn't support my habit just by running around borrowing money or trying to steal money, and I started pushing.[3] I made a lot of money pushing. I was supporting my habit. I wasn't looking to make money, but it just so happened a stroke of if-you-want-to-call-it luck, I made a lot of money. I could support my habit, I could buy clothes, I even bought a car, and odd as it may seem I was working. I had the dope, and I could work. So it was no worry about going to work every morning, just so long as I had my tools—my needle, my eye-dropper and my heroin. I would take a shot maybe three times a day while I was at work, come home and continue selling the dope. That went on for seven or eight months.

I was young and I was a small scale, actually; I guess I coulda went deeper into it, but I was scoring in weight an eighth, and it was costing me fifty dollars an eighth. And I would buy one eighth or two, or I would get a quarter, the equivalent of two eighths. An eighth is one-eighth of an ounce. Half of it I would use for myself because I had to, and the other half I would sell, I would turn over, and it would bring me back three times the amount I paid for it. I did no cutting,[4] the heroin I was getting was considered very good. Now it could have been cut a number of times, I could have made much more money, but I guess I just didn't want to cut it. I wanted to leave it just as good as it was. The quality was terrific and I just didn't want to be bothered. I was just thinking of my habit. I would presume it was cut before I got it with mannite or milk sugar. But consid-

[3] selling narcotics
[4] diluting by mixing with other substances

ering the quality of the stuff they got today, it wasn't cut much. Today the same dope would turn over an enormous amount of money, because you don't find the same stuff anymore.

To buy my heroin, I could go to any part of the city. At that time, I knew some people on the west end of Greenwich Village. Another time I knew some people in the Bronx. Another time it was at the east end of Harlem; it was the Spanish-Italian section. It's all according to who you know at the time.

After seven-eight months of dealing I stopped it. I was really fed up. I went to a Dr. W. on 47th Street, who supposedly will take you off the habit by lowering the shots every day. The price was sixty dollars a week, double for two weeks. But it didn't help, and the disadvantage of it was that I stopped dealing, and I found myself in a hole with money and everything. I lost my car, I lost my job, and I was back in the street with holes in my pockets and seven days of beard on my face. But it is possible for an addict to kick while living at home if he wants to do it. I did it once by staying up for seven days with a friend. I told the friend ahead of time that if I want to get out of here, don't let me out. And for seven days he

didn't let me out. That means I lay in bed with convulsions, jerking to and fro, and after seven days I felt very good. In fact the seventh day was on a Sunday, and I got up and to my surprise I went to church. I had to go to church because that's how good I felt. But to just show you the complete change of mind, the next day I took another shot and I was back on the road.

There is one substitute for dope you can take to help you kick without kicking cold turkey.[5] A lot of dope addicts will try to buy them; in a drugstore with a prescription they might cost $1.75 for a bottle of a hundred. But a drug addict would give you a dollar for one pill. Because they help. I've taken them when I was trying to kick and they did help, I wasn't sick. You have to take them before you're sick and sporadically every three-four hours. I kicked my habit that way also. But being out in the street, as soon as I kicked my habit I took it for granted I'm healthy again—which wasn't true—the next day I'd be taking dope again. I guess being out in the street and being surrounded by drugs and drug addicts and this way of life, I had to take that shot.

[5] abruptly, unaided

White-Collar Pill Party

BRUCE JACKSON

There was a thing called Heaven; but all the same they used to drink enormous quantities of alcohol. . . . There was a thing called the soul and a thing called immortality. . . . But they used to take morphia and cocaine. . . . Two thousand pharmacologists and bio-chemists were subsidized in A.F. 178. . . . Six years later it was being produced commercially. The perfect drug. . . . Euphoric,[1] narcotic, pleasantly hallucinant. . . . All the advantages of Christianity and alcohol; none of their defects. . . . Take a holiday from reality whenever you like, and come back without so much as a headache or a mythology.

ALDOUS HUXLEY, *Brave New World,* 1932

Drugs, like chewing gum, TV, oversize cars, and crime, are part of the American way of life. No one receives an exemption.

This was made particularly clear to me recently by my four-year-old son, Michael, who came into the kitchen one evening and asked me to go out and buy a certain brand of vitamin pills for him. Since he is quite healthy and not observably hypochondriac,[2] I asked why he wanted them. "So I can be as strong as Jimmy down the block."

"There isn't any Jimmy down the block," I said, whereupon he patiently explained that the clown on the 5 P.M. TV program he watches every day had *told* him the pills would make him stronger than Jimmy, and his tone gave me to understand that the existence of a corporeal[3] Jimmy was irrelevant: the truehearted clown, the child's friend, had advised the pills, and any four-year-old knows a clown wouldn't steer you wrong.

For adults the process is modified slightly. An afternoon TV commercial urges women to purchase a new drug for their "everyday headache" (without warning them that anyone who has a headache every day should certainly be consulting a GP or a psychiatrist); a Former Personality with suggestive regularity tells you to keep your bloodstream pure by consuming buffered aspirin for the headache you are supposed to have, and another recommends regular doses of iron for your "tired blood." (It won't be long before another screen has-been mounts the TV commercial podium with a pill that doesn't do anything at all; it just keeps your corpuscles company on the days you ate liver and forgot to have a headache.)

One result of all the drug propaganda and the appalling faith in the efficacy[4] of drugs is that a lot of people take a lot more pills than they have any reason to. They think in terms of pills. And so do their physicians: you fix a fat man by giving him a diet pill, you fix a chronic insomniac by giving him a sleeping pill. But these conditions are frequently merely symptoms of far more complicated disorders. The convenient prescription blank solves the problem of finding out what the trouble really is—it makes the symptom seem to go away.

[1] bringing a feeling of well-being
[2] a person with a morbid concern for his health who often suffers from imaginary illnesses
[3] bodily, material
[4] power to produce a desired effect

Think for a moment: how many people do you know who cannot stop stuffing themselves without an amphetamine and who cannot go to sleep without a barbiturate (over *nine billion* of those produced last year) or make it through a workday without a sequence of tranquilizers? And what about those six million alcoholics, who daily ingest[5] quantities of what is, by sheer force of numbers, the most addicting drug in America?

The publicity goes to the junkies, lately to the college kids, but these account for only a small portion of the American drug problem. Far more worrisome are the millions of people who have become dependent on commercial drugs. The junkie *knows* he is hooked; the housewife on amphetamine and the businessman on meprobamate hardly ever realize what has gone wrong.

Sometimes the pill-takers meet other pill-takers, and an odd thing happens: instead of using the drug to cope with the world, they begin to use their time to take drugs. Taking drugs becomes *something to do.* When this stage is reached, the drugtaking pattern broadens: the user takes a wider variety of drugs with increasing frequency. For want of a better term, one might call it the white-collar drug scene.

I first learned about it during a party in Chicago last winter, and the best way to introduce you will be to tell you something about that evening, the people I met, what I think was happening.

*T*here were about a dozen people in the room, and over the noise from the record player scraps of conversation came through:

"Now the Desbutal, if you take it with this stuff, has a peculiar effect, contraindication,[6] at least it did for me. You let me know if you . . ."

"I don't have one legitimate prescription, Harry, not *one!* Can you imagine that?" "I'll get you some tomorrow, dear."

". . . and this pharmacist on Fifth will sell you all the leapers [amphetamines] you can carry—just like that. Right off the street. I don't think he'd know a prescription if it bit him." "As long as he can read the labels, what the hell."

"You know, a funny thing happened to me. I got this green and yellow capsule, and I looked it up in the Book, and it wasn't anything I'd been using, and I thought, great! It's not something I've

[5] take in for or as if for digestion
[6] In this context, taking two drugs together has produced an undesirable effect.

built a tolerance to. And I took it. A couple of them. And you know what happened? *Nothing!* That's what happened, not a goddamned thing."

The Book—the *Physicians' Desk Reference*, which lists the composition and effects of almost all commercial pharmaceuticals produced in this country—passes back and forth, and two or three people at a time look up the contents and possible values of a drug one of them has just discovered or heard about or acquired or taken. The Book is the pill-head's *Yellow Pages:* you look up the effect you want ("Sympathomimetics" or "Cerebral Stimulants," for example), and it tells you the magic columns. The pillheads swap stories of kicks and sound like professional chemists discussing recent developments; others listen, then examine the *PDR* to see if the drug discussed really could do that.

Eddie, the host, a painter who has received some recognition, had been awake three or four days, he was not exactly sure. He consumes between 150 and 200 milligrams of amphetamine a day, needs a large part of that to stay awake, even when he has slipped a night's sleep in somewhere. The dose would cause most people some difficulty; the familiar diet pill, a capsule of Dexamyl or Eskatrol, which makes the new user edgy and over-energetic and slightly insomniac the first few days, contains only 10 or 15 milligrams of amphetamine. But amphetamine is one of the few central nervous system stimulants to which one can develop a tolerance, and over the months and years Ed and his friends have built up massive tolerances and dependencies. "Leapers aren't so hard to give up," he told me. "I mean, I sleep almost constantly when I'm off, but you get over that. But everything is so damned boring without the pills."

I asked him if he knew many amphetamine users who have given up the pills.

"For good?"

I nodded.

"I haven't known anybody that's given it up for good." He reached out and took a few pills from the candy dish in the middle of the coffee table, then washed them down with some Coke.

The last couple to arrive—a journalist and his wife—settled into positions. The wife was next to me on the oversize sofa, and she skimmed through the "Product Identification Section" of the *PDR*, dozens of pages of pretty color photos of tablets and capsules. "Hey!" she said to no one in particular. Then, to her husband, "Look at the

12 pretty hexagonal. George, get the Source to get some of them for me." George, across the table, near the fire, nodded.

I had been advised to watch him as he turned on. As the pills took effect something happened to the muscles of his face, and the whole assembly seemed to go rubbery. His features settled lower and more loosely on the bones of his head. He began to talk with considerably more verve.

A distractingly pretty girl with dark brown eyes sat at the edge of our group and ignored both the joint making its rounds and the record player belching away just behind her. Between the thumb and middle finger of her left hand she held a pill that was blue on one side and yellow on the other; steadily, with the double-edged razor blade she held in her right hand, she sawed on the seam between the two halves of the pill. Every once in a while she rotated it a few degrees with her left index finger. Her skin was smooth, and the light from the fireplace played tricks with it, all of them charming. The right hand sawed on.

I got the Book from the coffee table and looked for the pill in the pages of color pictures, but before I found it, Ed leaned over and said, "They're Desbutal Gradumets. Abbott Labs."

I turned to the "Professional Products Information" section and learned that Desbutal is a combination of Desoxyn (methamphetamine hydrochloride, also marketed as Methedrine) and Nembutal, that the pill the girl sawed contained 15 milligrams of the Desoxyn, that the combination of drugs served "to both stimulate and calm the patient so that feelings of depression are overcome and a sense of well-being and increased energy is produced. Inner tension and anxiety are relieved so that a sense of serenity and ease of mind prevails." Gradumets, the Book explained, "are indicated in the management of obesity, the management of depressed states, certain behavioral syndromes,[7] and a number of typical geriatric[8] conditions," as well as "helpful in managing psychosomatic[9] complaints and neuroses," Parkinson's disease, and a hangover.

The girl, obviously, was not interested in all of the pill's splendid therapeutic promises; were she, she would not have been so diligently sawing

[7] groups of signs and symptoms that occur together and characterize an abnormality
[8] of or pertaining to aged persons
[9] relating to a physical disorder that is caused by or notably influenced by the person's emotional state

along that seam. She was after the methamphetamine, which like other amphetamines "depresses appetite, elevates the mood, increases the urge to work, imparts a sense of increased efficiency, and counteracts sleepiness and the feeling of fatigue in most persons."

After what seemed a long while the pill split into two round sections. A few scraps of the yellow Nembutal adhered to the Desoxyn side, and she carefully scraped them away. "Wilkinson's the best blade for this sort of thing," she said. I asked if she didn't cut herself on occasion, and she showed me a few nicks in her left thumb.
"But a single edge isn't thin enough to do it neatly."

She put the blue disk in one small container, the yellow in another, then from a third took a fresh Desbutal and began sawing. I asked why she kept the Nembutal, since it was the Desoxyn she was after.

"Sometimes I might want to sleep, you know. I might *have* to sleep because something is coming up the next day. It's not easy for us to sleep, and sometimes we just don't for a couple or three days. But if we have to, we can just take a few of these." She smiled at me tolerantly, then returned to her blade and tablet.

When I saw Ed in New York several weeks later, I asked about her. "Some are like that," he said; "they like to carve on their pills. She'll sit and carve for thirty or forty minutes."

"Is that sort of ritual an important part of it all?"

"I think it is. She seems to have gotten hung up on it. I told her that she shouldn't take that Nembutal, that I have been cutting the Nembutal off my pills. It only takes about thirty seconds. And she can spend a good half hour at it if she has a mind to. I told her once about the effect of taking a Spansule; you know, one of those big things with sustained release [like Dexamyl, a mixture of dextroamphetamine sulfate and amobarbital designed to be effective over a twelve-hour period]. What you do is open the capsule and put it in a little bowl and grind up the little pellets until it's powder, then stuff all the powder back in the pill and take it, and it all goes off at once. I'll be damned if I haven't seen her grinding away like she was making matzo meal. That's a sign of a fairly confirmed head when they reach that ritual stage."

Next to the candy dish filled with Dexedrine, Dexamyl, Eskatrol, Desbutal, and a few other

". . . instead of using the drug to cope with the world, they begin to use their time to take drugs. Taking drugs becomes something to do."

14 products I hadn't yet learned to identify, near the five-pound box of Dexedrine tablets someone had brought, were two bottles. One was filled with Dexedrine Elixir, the other with Dexamyl Elixir. Someone took a long swallow from the latter, and I thought him to be an extremely heavy user, but when the man left the room, a lawyer told me he'd bet the man was new at it. "He has to be. A mouthful is like two pills, and if he was a real head, he'd have a far greater tolerance to the Dexedrine than the amobarbital, and the stuff would make him sleepy. Anyhow, I don't like to mess with barbiturates much anymore. Dorothy Kilgallen died from that." He took a drink from the Dexedrine bottle and said, "And this tastes better. Very tasty stuff, like cherry syrup. Make a nice cherry Coke with it. The Dexamyl Elixir is bitter."

Someone emptied the tobacco from a Salem and filled the tube with grass; he tamped it down with a Tinkertoy stick, crimped the tip, then lighted it and inhaled noisily. He immediately passed the joint to the person on his left. Since one must hold the smoke in one's lungs for several seconds to get the full effect, it is more economical for several people to turn on at once. The grass was very good and seemed to produce a quiet but substantial high. One doesn't notice it coming on, but there is a realization that for a while now the room has been a decidedly pleasant one, and some noises are particularly interesting for their own sake.

I leaned back and closed my eyes for a moment. It was almost 5 A.M., and in three hours I had to catch a plane at O'Hare. "You're not going to *sleep* are you?" The tone implied that this group considered few human frailties truly gauche,[10] but going to sleep was surely one of them. I shook my head no and looked to see who had spoken. It was Ed's wife; she looked concerned. "Do you want a pill?" I shook my head no again.

Then, just then, I realized that Ed—who knew I was not a pill-user—had not once in the evening offered me one of the many samples that had been passed around, nor had anyone else. Just the grass, but not the pills. His wife suggested a pill not so that I might get high, but merely so that I could stay awake without difficulty.

"I'm not tired," I said, "just relaxing." I assured her I wouldn't doze off. She was still concerned, however, and got me a cup of coffee from the kitchen and offered some Murine from her purse.

The front door opened, and there was a vicious blast of winter off Lake Michigan. Ed kicked the door closed behind him and dumped an armful of logs by the fireplace, then went back into the kitchen. A moment later he returned and passed around a small dish of capsules. And this time it was handed to me. They looked familiar. "One a Days," he said. I had learned enough from the Book to see the need for them: the amphetamine user often does not eat for long periods of time (some days his only nourishment is the sugar in the bottles of soda which he drinks to wash down the pills and counter their side effect of dehydration of the mouth), and he not only tends to lose weight but also risks vitamin deficiencies. After a while, the heavy user learns to force-feed himself or go off pills every once in a while in order to eat without difficulty and to keep his tolerance level down.

Later, getting settled in the plane, I thought, What a wild party that was. I'd never been to anything quite like it, and I began making notes about what had gone on. Not long before we came into Logan, it suddenly struck me that there had been nothing wild about the party at all, nothing. There had been women there, some of them unaccompanied and some with husbands or dates, but there had been none of the playing around and sexual hustling that several years of academic and business world parties had led me to consider a correlative[11] of almost any evening gathering of more than ten men and women; no meaningful looks, no wisecracks, no "accidental" rubbing. No one had spoken loudly, no one had become giggly or silly, no one had lost control or seemed anywhere near it. Viewed with some perspective, the evening seemed nothing more than comfortable.

There are various ways to acquire the pills, but the most common is also the most legal: prescriptions. Even though there is now a federal law requiring physicians and pharmacists to maintain careful records regarding prescriptions for drugs like Dexamyl, many physicians are careless about prescribing them, and few seem to realize that the kind of personality that needs them is often the kind of personality that can easily acquire an overwhelming dependency on them. Often a patient will be issued a refillable prescription; if the pa-

---

[10] lacking social graces, awkward

[11] an action which implies or involves a second one in a mutual relation

tient is a heavy user, all he needs to do is visit several physicians and get refillable prescriptions from each. If he is worried that a cross-check of druggists' lists might turn up his name, he can easily give some of his doctors false names.

There are dealers, generically[12] called the Source, who specialize in selling these drugs; some give them away. They do not seem to be underworld types but professional people in various capacities who, for one reason or another, have access to large quantities of them. If one is completely without connections, the drugs can be made at home. One young man I know made mescaline, amphetamine, methamphetamine, LSD, and DET and DMT (diethyl- and dimethyl-tryptamine, hallucinogens of shorter duration and greater punch than LSD) in his kitchen. In small lots, dextroamphetamine sulfate costs him about 50 cents a gram; a pound costs him about $30 (the same amounts of Dexedrine at your friendly corner druggist's would cost, respectively, about $10 and $4200).

In some areas, primarily those fairly distant from major centers of drug distribution, the new law has begun to have some significant effect. In one medium-sized city, for example, the price of black-market Dexamyl and Eskatrol Spansules has risen from 15 cents to 50 cents a capsule, when one can connect for them at all.

In the major cities one can still connect, but it is becoming more difficult. The new law will inhibit, but there may be complications. It would be unfortunate if the price should be driven up so high that it would become profitable for criminal organizations to involve themselves with the traffic, as was the case with opiates in the 1940s and 1950s and alcohol in the 1920s.

There was talk in Manhattan last winter, just before the new law took effect, that some LSD factories were closing down, and I know that some sources stopped supplying. For a short time the price of LSD went up; then things stabilized, competition increased, a new packaging method developed popularity (instead of the familiar sugar cubes, one now takes one's dose on a tiny slip of paper; like a spitball, only you don't spit it out), and now the price for a dose of LSD is about 20 percent *less* than it was a year ago.

Since most of the pillheads I'm talking about are middle-class and either professional or semi-professional, they will still be able to obtain their drugs. Their drugs of choice have a legitimate use, and it is unlikely that the government's attempt to prevent diversion will be more than partially successful. If our narcotics agents have been unable to keep off the open market drugs which have no legitimate use at all—heroin and marijuana—it hardly seems likely that they will be able to control chemicals legitimately in the possession of millions of citizens. I asked one amphetamine head in the Southwest how local supplies had been affected by the new law. "I heard about that law," he said, "but I haven't seen anybody getting panicked." Another user tells me prices have risen slightly, but not enough yet to present difficulties.

There are marked differences between these drug-users and the ones who make the newspapers. They're well educated (largely college graduates), are older (25 to 40), and middle-class (with a range of occupations: writers, artists, lawyers, TV executives, journalists, political aides, housewives). They're not like the high school kids who are after a kick in any form (some of them rather illusory, as one psychosomatic gem reported to me by a New Jersey teen-ager: "What some of the kids do is take a cigarette and saturate it with perfume or hairspray. When this is completely soaked in and dry, they cup the cigarettes and inhale every drag. Somehow this gives them a good high"), or college students experimenting with drugs as part of a romantic program of self-location. The kids take drugs "because it's cool" and to get high, but when you talk to them you find that most ascribe the same general high to a wide range of drugs having quite diverse effects; they're promiscuous[13] and insensitive. There is considerable evidence to suggest that almost none of the college drug-users take anything illegal after graduation, for most of them lose their connections and their curiosity.

It is not likely that many of the thousands of solitary amphetamine abusers would join these groups. They take drugs to *avoid* deviance—so they can be fashionably slim, or bright and alert and functional, or so they can muster the *quoi que*[14] with which to face the tedium of housework or some other dull job—and the last thing they want is membership in a group defined solely by one clear form of rule-breaking behavior. Several of the group members were first turned on by physicians, but a larger number were turned on by

12 generally, or as a group

13 indiscriminate
14 wherewithal

16 friends. Most were after a particular therapeutic effect, but after a while interest developed in the drug for its own sake and the effect became a cause, and after that the pattern of drug-taking overcame the pattern of taking a specific drug.

Some of the socialized amphetamine-users specialize. One takes Dexedrine and Dexamyl almost exclusively; he takes other combinations only when he is trying to reduce his tolerance to Dexamyl. Though he is partly addicted to the barbiturates, they do not seem to trouble him very much, and on the few occasions when he has had to go off drugs (as when he was in California for a few months and found getting legal prescriptions too difficult and for some reason didn't connect with a local Source), he has had no physiological trouble giving them up. He did, of course, suffer from the overwhelming depression and enervation that characterize amphetamine withdrawal. Most heads will use other drugs along with amphetamine—especially marijuana—in order to appreciate the heightened alertness they've acquired; some alternate with hallucinogens.

". . . all the college students and all the junkies account for only a small portion of American drug abuse. The adults, the respectable grown-ups, the nice people . . . present a far more serious problem."

To the heroin addict, the square is anyone who does not use heroin. For the dedicated pillhead there is a slightly narrower definition: the square is someone who has an alcohol dependency; those who use nothing at all aren't even classified. The boozers do bad things, they get drunk and lose control and hurt themselves and other people. They contaminate their tubes, and whenever they get really far out, they don't even remember it the next day. The pillhead's disdain is sometimes rather excessive. One girl, for example, was living with a fellow who, like her, was taking over 500 milligrams of amphetamine a day. They were getting on well. One night the two were at a party, and instead of chewing pills, her man had a few beers; the girl was furious, betrayed, outraged. Another time, at a large party that sprawled

through a sprawling apartment, a girl had been on scotch and grass and she went to sleep. There were three men in the room, none of them interested in her sexually, yet they jeered and wisecracked as she nodded off. It was 4 or 5 A.M. of a Sunday, not too unreasonable a time to be drowsy. When they saw she was really asleep—breaking the double taboo by having drunk too much scotch and been put to sleep by it—they muttered a goddamn and went into another room; she was too depressing to have around.

There is an important difference in the drug-use patterns of the pillhead and opiate dependent: the latter is interested only in getting his drug and avoiding withdrawal; the former is also interested in perceiving his drugs' effects. I remember one occasion attended by someone who had obtained a fairly large mixed bag. In such a situation a junkie would have shot himself insensible; this fellow gave most of his away to his friends. With each gift he said something about a particular aspect of the drug which he found interesting. The heroin-user is far less social. His stuff is too hard to get, too expensive, his withdrawal too agonizing. But the pillhead is an experimenter. Often he seems to be interested as much in observing himself experiencing reactions as he is in having the reactions.

A large part of the attractiveness may be the ritual associated with this kind of group drug abuse: the *PDR* (a holy book), the Source (the medicine man whose preparations promise a polychromatic[15] world of sensory and mystical experiences), the sharing of proscribed[16] materials in a closed community, the sawing and grinding, the being privy to the Pythian secrets[17] of colors and milligrams and trade names and contraindications and optimum[18] dosages. And, of course, using drugs is something of a fad.

But there are costs. Kicks are rarely free in this world, and drugs are no exception. One risks dysfunction;[19] one can go out of one's head; one may get into trouble with the police. Though the users are from a socioeconomic class that can most likely beat a first offense at almost anything, there is the problem that legal involvement of any kind,

[15] characterized by many colors
[16] forbidden
[17] referring to the ancient Greek priestess of Apollo, Pythia, who, when seated on a tripod over the rock sacred to the god, was believed by him and to utter his prophecies
[18] giving the best results
[19] inability of the body to function properly

whether successfully prosecuted or not, can cause considerable embarrassment; an arrest for taking drugs may be negligible to a slum dweller in New York, but it is quite something else for a lawyer or reporter. And there is always the most tempting danger of all: getting habituated to drugs to such a degree that the drugs are no longer something extra in life but are instead a major goal.

One user wrote me, "Lately I find myself wishing not that I might kick the lunatic habit—but simply that our drug firms would soon develop something NEW which might refresh the memory of the flash and glow of that first voom-voom pill." I had asked him why take them at all, and he wrote, "I don't know. Really. Why smoke, drink, drive recklessly, sunbathe, fornicate, shoot tigers, climb mountains, gamble, lie, steal, cheat, kill, make war—and blame it all largely on our parents. Possibly to make oneself more acceptable to oneself."

Many of the pillheads are taking drugs not *only* to escape but also to have an experience that is entirely one's own. There is no one else to be propitiated,[20] there are no explanations or excuses needed for what happens inside one's own head when one is turned on; words won't do, and that is as much a benefit as a disadvantage, because if you cannot describe, then neither can you discuss or question or submit to evaluation. The benefit and the risk are entirely one's own. Indiana University sociologist John Gagnon pointed out at a drug symposium held at Antioch College last year, "I'd like to argue that possibly in our attempt to protect people, we have underrepresented the real payoff for drug-taking as an experience, at a risk people want to run."

You select your own risks—that's what living is all about. For some of these drug-users, the risks currently being marketed do not have very much sales appeal: going South for the summer with SNCC is out because they feel that they are too old and that ofays[21] aren't much wanted anyhow; going to Vietnam for Lyndon is absurd. So they go inside. A scarier place, but no one else can muddle around with it.

There is nothing *wrong* with using chemicals to help cope with life. That is one of the things science is supposed to do, help us cope, and the business of living can be rough at times. And we have the requisite faith: I am sure that far more Americans believe in the efficacy of a pill than believe in God. The problem arises when one's concern shifts so that life becomes an exercise in coping with the chemicals.

I think there has been an unfortunate imbalance in the negative publicity. For years the press has printed marvelous tales about all the robberies and rapes performed by evil beings whose brain tissue had been jellied by heroin. But it has rarely printed stories that point out that opiates make even the randiest[22] impotent, or that alcohol, which has five hundred times as many addicts, is an important factor in sex offenses and murders.

Lately, attention has been focused on drug abuse and experimentation among college students. Yet all the college students and all the junkies account for only a small portion of American drug abuse. The adults, the respectable grown-ups, the nice people who cannot or will not make it without depending on a variety of drugs, present a far more serious problem. For them the drug experience threatens to disrupt or even destroy life patterns and human relationships that required many years to establish.

And the problem is not a minor one. Worse, it seems to be accelerating. As Ed advised one night, "You better research the hell out of it because I'm convinced that the next ruling generation is going to be all pillheads. I'm convinced of it. If they haven't dysfunctioned completely to the point where they can't stand for office. It's getting to be unbelievable. I've never seen such a transformation in just four or five years. . . ."

[22] most lecherous

[20] appeased; to make amends for some offense committed against another person
[21] a derogatory term for white men

Gunsmoke

RUSSELL BAKER

One of the many extraordinary aspects of American life is the frequency with which people shoot people. To answer the question, why do they do it?, Curiosity Associates, an unknown research organization, assembled a typical group of people shooters for a panel discussion. Following is a transcript of their remarks:

Moderator: Would you kick things off, Mr. B. J., by telling us why you shoot people?

A. Clumsiness mostly. I'll be sitting around the house caressing one of my guns and before I know it, bang! The thing goes off and I've shot somebody again.

Q. Mr. M. O., do you find that clumsiness is a factor with you in shooting people?

A. Not a bit. I never shoot anybody unless I mean to. See this telescopic sight? Accurate up to 10,000 yards. When I want to shoot people I put it on the old rifle, tote the whole thing up to some place nice and high and pop them off like sitting ducks.

Q. But why do you do it?

A. A lot of reasons. Sometimes I feel rejected and want attention. Other times I get frustrated and have to let off steam. You can get a lot of attention and let off a good bit of steam by shooting people.

Q. I'll bet you can. How about you, Mr. K. S., do you find that shooting people is therapeutic?

A. No sir. With me it's strictly business. If you want some people shot, just give me their names and if your price is right I do the shooting.

Q. A tribute to the ingenuity with which you have met the challenge of the Free Enterprise System, Mr. K. S. Would you ever consider shooting people for a living, Mr. D. L.?

A. Frankly, I consider shooting people for profit a reprehensible perversion of the constitutional right to operate an arsenal. I never shoot people except for real gut reasons on the spur of the moment.

Q. Would you elaborate?

A. I see another man with my wife and lose my temper. Bang! On the spur of the moment I'm a people shooter. When people get on the bus and step on my toes on days when I'm feeling out of sorts, I pull out the old .38 and shoot them.

Q. Perhaps Mr. R. W. will tell us why he shoots people?

A. Gladly. With me, shooting people is a matter of principle. I've never shot any people insincerely. If peoples' politics are, in my best judgment, dangerous to this wonderful country of ours, I shoot them. If people violate the sanctity of private property, I shoot them, too. In addition, I also shoot people whose color is a threat either to our traditional American way of life or to my security.

And you, Mr. A. C., what is your reason for shooting people?

A. Because they're there.

Q. Mr. A. C., would you please put down your shotgun? Mr. A. C.!

At this point the transcript terminates without explanation.

Study of the Sickness Called Apathy

A. M. ROSENTHAL

It happens from time to time in New York that the life of the city is frozen by an instant of shock. In that instant the people of the city are seized by the paralyzing realization that they are one, that each man is in some way a mirror of every other man. They stare at each other—or, really, into themselves—and a look quite like a flush of embarrassment passes over the face of the city. Then the instant passes and the beat resumes and the people turn away and try to explain what they have seen, or try to deny it.

The last 35 minutes of the young life of Miss Catherine Genovese became such a shock in the life of the city. But at the time she died, stabbed again and again by a marauder in her quiet, dark but entirely respectable, street in Kew Gardens, New York hardly took note.

It was not until two weeks later that Catherine Genovese, known as Kitty, returned in death to cry the city awake. Even then it was not her life or her dying that froze the city, but the witnessing of her murder—the choking fact that 38 of her neighbors had seen her stabbed or heard her cries, and that not one of them, during that hideous half-hour, had lifted the telephone from the safety of his own apartment to call the police and try to save her life. When it was over and Miss Genovese was dead and the murderer gone, one man did call—not from his own apartment but from a neighbor's, and only after he had called a friend and asked her what to do.

The day that the story of the witnessing of the death of Miss Genovese appeared in this newspaper became that frozen instant. "Thirty-eight!" people said over and over. "Thirty-eight!"

It was as if the number itself had some special meaning, and in a way, of course, it did. One person or two or even three or four witnessing a murder passively would have been the unnoticed symptom of the disease in the city's body and again would have passed unnoticed. But 38—it was like a man with a running low fever suddenly beginning to cough blood; his friends could no longer ignore his illness, nor could he turn away from himself.

At first there was, briefly, the reaction of shared guilt. Even people who were sure that they certainly would have acted differently felt it somehow. "Dear God, what have we come to?" a woman said that day. "We," not "they."

For in that instant of shock, the mirror showed quite clearly what was wrong, that the face of mankind was spotted with the disease of apathy—all mankind. But this was too frightening a thought to live with and soon the beholders began to set boundaries for the illness, to search frantically for causes that were external and to look for the carrier.

There was a rash of metropolitan masochism.[1] "What the devil do you expect in a town, a jungle, like this?" Sociologists and psychiatrists reached for the warm comfort of jargon—"alienation of the individual from the group," "megalopolitan[2] societies," "the disaster syndrome."[3]

People who came from small towns said it could never happen back home. New Yorkers, ashamed, agreed. Nobody seemed to stop to ask whether there were not perhaps various forms of apathy and that some that exist in villages and towns do not exist in great cities.

Guilt turned into masochism, and masochism, as it often does, became a sadistic search for a target. Quite soon, the target became the police.

There is no doubt whatsoever that the police in New York have failed, to put it politely, to instill a feeling of total confidence in the population. There are great areas in this city—fine parks as well as slums—where no person in his right mind would wander of an evening or an early morning. There is no central emergency point to receive calls for help. And a small river of letters from citizens to this newspaper testifies to the fact that patrols are often late in answering calls and that

[1] pleasure derived from being hurt or abused
[2] characterized by enormous urban complexes
[3] a group of signs and symptoms that occur together and characterize a particular abnormality

20 policemen on desk duty often give the bitter edge of their tongues to citizens calling for succor.

There is no doubt of these things. But to blame the police for apathy is a bit like blaming the sea wall for springing leaks. The police of this city are more efficient, more restrained and more responsive to public demands than any others the writer has encountered in a decade of traveling the world. Their faults are either mechanical or a reflection of a city where almost every act of police self-protection is assumed to be an act of police brutality, and where a night-club comedian can, as one did the other night, stand on a stage for an hour and a half and vilify[4] the police as brutes, thieves, homosexuals, illiterates and "Gestapo agents" while the audience howls in laughter as it drinks Scotch from bootleg bottles hidden under the tables.

There are two tragedies in the story of Catherine Genovese. One is the fact that her life was taken from her, that she died in pain and horror at the age of 28. The other is that in dying she gave every human being—not just species New Yorker—an opportunity to examine some truths about the nature of apathy and that this has not been done.

Austin Street, where Catherine Genovese lived, is in a section of Queens known as Kew Gardens. There are two apartment buildings and the rest of the street consists of one-family homes—red-brick, stucco or wood-frame. There are Jews, Catholics and Protestants, a scattering of foreign accents, middle-class incomes.

On the night of March 13, about 3 A.M., Catherine Genovese was returning to her home. She worked late as manager of a bar in Hollis, another part of Queens. She parked her car (a red Fiat) and started to walk to her death.

Lurking near the parking lot was a man. Miss Genovese saw him in the shadows, turned and walked toward a police call box. The man pursued her, stabbed her. She screamed, "Oh my God, he stabbed me! Please help me! Please help me!"

Somebody threw open a window and a man called out: "Let that girl alone!" Other lights turned on, other windows were raised. The attacker got into a car and drove away. A bus passed.

The attacker drove back, got out, searched out Miss Genovese in the back of an apartment building where she had crawled for safety, stabbed her again, drove away again.

The first attack came at 3:15. The first call to the police came at 3:50. Police arrived within two minutes, they say. Miss Genovese was dead.

That night and the next morning the police combed the neighborhood looking for witnesses. They found them, 38.

Two weeks later, when this newspaper heard of the story, a reporter went knocking, door to door, asking why, why.

Through half-opened doors, they told him. Most of them were neither defiant nor terribly embarrassed nor particularly ashamed. The underlying attitude, or explanation, seemed to be fear of involvement—any kind of involvement.

"I didn't want my husband to get involved," a housewife said.

"We thought it was a lovers' quarrel," said another woman. "I went back to bed."

"I was tired," said a man.

"I don't know," said another man.

"I don't know," said still another.

"I don't know," said others.

On March 19, police arrested a 29-year-old business-machine operator named Winston Moseley and charged him with the murder of Catherine Genovese. He has confessed to killing two other women, for one of whose murders police say they have a confession from another man.

Not much is said or heard or thought in the city about Winston Moseley. In this drama, as far as the city is concerned, he appeared briefly, acted his piece, exited into the wings.

A week after the first story appeared, a reporter went back to Austin Street. Now the witnesses no longer wanted to talk. They were harried, annoyed; they thought they should keep their mouths shut. "I've done enough talking," one witness said. "Oh, it's you again," said a woman witness and slammed the door.

The neighbors of the witnesses are willing to talk. Their sympathy is for the silent witnesses and the embarrassment in which they now live.

Max Heilbrunn, who runs a coffee house on Austin Street, talked about all the newspaper publicity and said his neighbors felt they were being picked on. "It isn't a bad neighborhood," he said.

And this from Frank Facciola, the owner of the neighborhood barber shop: "I resent the way these newspaper and television people have hurt us. We have wonderful people here. What happened could have happened any place. There is no question in my mind that people here now

---

[4] degrade or abuse

only in response to certain reflexes or certain beliefs will a man step out of his shell toward his brother.

To say this is not to excuse, but to try to understand and in so doing perhaps eventually to extend the reflexes and beliefs and situations to include more people. To ignore it is to perpetuate myths that lead nowhere. Of these the two most

would rush out to help anyone being attacked on the street."

Then he said: "The same thing [failure to call the police] happens in other sections every day. Why make such a fuss when it happens in Kew Gardens? We are trying to forget it happened here."

A Frenchwoman in the neighborhood said: "Let's forget the whole thing. It is a quiet neighborhood, good to live in. What happened, happened."

Each individual, obviously, approaches the story of Catherine Genovese, reacts to it and veers away from it against the background of his own life and experience, and his own fears and shortcomings and rationalizations.

It seems to this writer that what happened in the apartments and houses on Austin Street was a symptom of a terrible reality in the human condition—that only under certain situations and

futile philosophically are that apathy is a response to official ineptitude[5] ("The cops never come on time anyway"), or that apathy is a condition only of metropolitan life.

Certainly police procedures must be improved—although in the story of Miss Genovese all indications were that, once called into action, the police machine behaved perfectly.

As far as is known, not one witness has said that he remained silent because he had had any unpleasant experience with the police. It is a pointless point; there are men who will jump into a

[5] incompetence

river to rescue a drowner; there are others who will tell themselves that a police launch will be cruising by or that, if it doesn't, it should.

Nobody can say why the 38 did not lift the phone while Miss Genovese was being attacked, since they cannot say themselves. It can be assumed, however, that their apathy was indeed of a big-city variety. It is almost a matter of psychological survival, if one is surrounded and pressed by millions of people, to prevent them from constantly impinging on you and the only way to do this is to ignore them as often as possible. Indifference to one's neighbor and his troubles is a conditioned reflex of life in New York as it is in other big cities. In every major city in which I have lived—in Tokyo and Warsaw, Vienna and Bombay—I have seen, over and over again, people walk away from accident victims. I have walked away myself.

Out-of-towners, and sometimes New Yorkers themselves, like to think that there is something special about New York metropolitan apathy. It is special in that there are more people here than any place else in the country—and therefore more people to turn away from each other.

For decades, New York turned away from the truth that is Harlem or Bedford-Stuyvesant in Brooklyn. Everybody knew that, in the Negro ghettoes, men, women and children lived in filth and degradation. But the city, as a city, turned away with the metropolitan brand of apathy. This, more simply, consists of drowning the person-to-person responsibility in a wave of impersonal social action.

Committees were organized, speeches made, budgets passed to "do something" about Harlem or Bedford-Stuyvesant—to do something about the communities. This dulled the reality, and still does, that the communities consist of individual people who ache and suffer in the loss of their individual prides. Housewives who contributed to the N.A.A.C.P. saw nothing wrong in going down to the daily shape-up of domestic workers in the Bronx and selecting a maid for the day after looking over the coffle[6] to see which "girl" among the Negro matrons present looked huskiest.

Now there is an acute awareness of the problems of the Negroes in New York. But, again, it is an impersonal awareness, and more and more, it is tinged with irritation at the thought that the

[6] a chain of slaves or animals fastened together

integration movement will impinge on the daily personal life of the city.

Nor are the Negroes in the city immune from apathy—toward one another or toward whites. They are apathetic toward one another's right to believe and act as they please; one man's concept of proper action is labeled with the group epithet "Uncle Tom." And, until the recent upsurge of the integration movement, there was less action taken within the Negro community to improve conditions in Harlem than there was in the all-white sections of the East Side. It has become fashionable to sneer at "white liberals"—fashionable even among Negroes who for years did nothing for brothers even of their own color.

". . . only under certain situations and only in response to certain reflexes or certain beliefs will a man step out of his shell toward his brother."

In their own sense of being wronged, some Negroes of New York have become totally apathetic to the sensitivities of all other groups. In a night club in Harlem the other night, an aspiring Negro politician, a most decent man, talked of how the Jewish shopkeepers exploited the Negroes, how he wished Negroes could "save a dollar like the Jews," totally apathetic toward the fact that Jews at the table might be as hurt as he would be if they talked in clichés of the happy-go-lucky Stepin Fetchit Negro. When a Jew protested, the Negro was stunned—because he was convinced he hated anti-Semitism. He did, in the abstract.

Since the Genovese case, New Yorkers have sought explanations of their apathy toward individuals. Fear, some say—fear of involvement, fear of reprisal from goons, fear of becoming "mixed up" with the police. This, it seems to this writer, is simply rationalization.

The self-protective shells in which we live are determined not only by the difference between big cities and small. They are determined by economics and social class, by caste and by color, and by religion, and by politics.

If I were to see a beggar starving to death in rags on the streets of Paris or New York or London

23

I would be moved to take some kind of action. But many times I have seen starving men lying like broken dolls in the streets of Calcutta or Madras and have done nothing.

I think I would have called the police to save Miss Genovese but I know that I did not save a beggar in Calcutta. Was my failing really so much smaller than that of the people who watched from their windows on Austin Street? And what was the apathy of the people of Austin Street compared, let's say, with the apathy of non-Nazi Germans toward Jews?

Geography is a factor of apathy. Indians reacted to Portuguese imprisoning Goans, but not to Russians killing Hungarians.

Color is a factor. Ghanaians reacted toward Frenchmen killing Algerians, not toward Congolese killing white missionaries.

Strangeness is a factor. Americans react to the extermination of Jews but not to the extermination of Watusis.

There are national as well as individual apathies, all inhibiting the ability to react. The "mind-your-own-business" attitude is despised among individuals, and clucked at by sociologists, but glorified as pragmatic[7] national policy among nations.

Only in scattered moments, and then in halting embarrassment, does the United States, the most involved nation in the world, get down to hard cases about the nature of governments with which it deals, and how they treat their subject citizens. People who believe that a free government should react to oppression of people in the mass by other governments are regarded as fanatics or romantics by the same diplomats who would react in horror to the oppression of one single individual in Washington. Between apathy, regarded as a moral disease, and national policy, the line is often hard to find.

There are, it seems to me, only two logical ways to look at the story of the murder of Catherine Genovese. One is the way of the neighbor on Austin Street—"Let's forget the whole thing."

The other is to recognize that the bell tolls even on each man's individual island, to recognize that every man must fear the witness in himself who whispers to close the window.

[7] related to matters of fact or practical affairs, often to the exclusion of intellectual or artistic matters

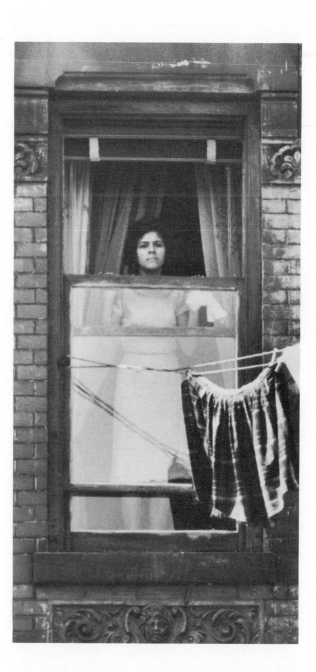

Nature Fights Back

RACHEL L. CARSON

To have risked so much in our efforts to mold nature to our satisfaction and yet to have failed in achieving our goal would indeed be the final irony. Yet this, it seems, is our situation. The truth, seldom mentioned but there for anyone to see, is that nature is not so easily molded and that the insects are finding ways to circumvent[1] our chemical attacks on them.

"The insect world is nature's most astonishing phenomenon," said the Dutch biologist C. J. Briejèr. "Nothing is impossible to it; the most improbable things commonly occur there. One who penetrates deeply into its mysteries is continually breathless with wonder. He knows that anything can happen, and that the completely impossible often does."

The "impossible" is now happening on two broad fronts. By a process of genetic selection, the insects are developing strains resistant to chemicals. This will be discussed in the following chapter. But the broader problem, which we shall look at now, is the fact that our chemical attack is weakening the defenses inherent in the environment itself, defenses designed to keep the various species in check. Each time we breach these defenses a horde of insects pours through.

From all over the world come reports that make it clear we are in a serious predicament. At the end of a decade or more of intensive chemical control, entomologists[2] were finding that problems they had considered solved a few years earlier had returned to plague them. And new problems had arisen as insects once present only in insignificant numbers had increased to the status of serious pests. By their very nature chemical con-

trols are self-defeating, for they have been devised and applied without taking into account the complex biological systems against which they have been blindly hurled. The chemicals may have been pretested against a few individual species, but not against living communities.

In some quarters nowadays it is fashionable to dismiss the balance of nature as a state of affairs that prevailed in an earlier, simpler world—a state that has now been so thoroughly upset that we might as well forget it. Some find this a convenient assumption, but as a chart for a course of action it is highly dangerous. The balance of nature is not the same today as in Pleistocene times, but it is still there: a complex, precise, and highly integrated system of relationships between living things which cannot safely be ignored any more than the law of gravity can be defied with impunity[3] by man perched on the edge of a cliff. The balance of nature is not a *status quo*; it is fluid, ever shifting, in a constant state of adjustment. Man, too, is part of this balance. Sometimes the balance is in his favor; sometimes—and all too often through his own activities—it is shifted to his disadvantage.

Two critically important facts have been overlooked in designing the modern insect control programs. The first is that the really effective control of insects is that applied by nature, not by man. Populations are kept in check by something the ecologists[4] call the resistance of the environment, and this has been so since the first life was created. The amount of food available, conditions of weather and climate, the presence of competing or predatory species, all are critically important. "The greatest single factor in preventing insects from overwhelming the rest of the world is the internecine[5] warfare which they carry out among themselves," said the entomologist Robert Metcalf. Yet most of the chemicals now used kill all insects, our friends and enemies alike.

The second neglected fact is the truly explosive power of a species to reproduce once the resistance of the environment has been weakened. The fecundity[6] of many forms of life is almost beyond our power to imagine, though now and then we have suggestive glimpses. I remember from student days the miracle that could be wrought in

[1] get around; defeat strategically
[2] scientists who specialize in the study of insects

From **Silent Spring** by Rachel Carson. Reprinted by permission of Houghton Mifflin Company.

[3] freedom from harm
[4] scientists who study the relations between organisms and their environment
[5] mutually destructive
[6] fertility, productiveness

a jar containing a simple mixture of hay and water merely by adding to it a few drops of material from a mature culture of protozoa. Within a few days the jar would contain a whole galaxy of whirling, darting life—uncountable trillions of the slipper animalcule,[7] *Paramecium,* each small as a dust grain, all multiplying without restraint in their temporary Eden of favorable temperatures, abundant food, absence of enemies. Or I think of shore rocks white with barnacles as far as the eye can see, or of the spectacle of passing through an immense school of jellyfish, mile after mile, with seemingly no end to the pulsing, ghostly forms scarcely more substantial than the water itself.

We see the miracle of nature's control at work when the cod move through winter seas to their spawning grounds, where each female deposits several millions of eggs. The sea does not become a solid mass of cod as it would surely do if all the progeny of all the cod were to survive. The checks that exist in nature are such that out of the millions of young produced by each pair only enough, on the average, survive to adulthood to replace the parent fish.

Biologists used to entertain themselves by speculating as to what would happen if, through some unthinkable catastrophe, the natural restraints were thrown off and all the progeny of a single individual survived. Thus Thomas Huxley a century ago calculated that a single female aphis (which has the curious power of reproducing without mating) could produce progeny in a single year's time whose total weight would equal that of the inhabitants of the Chinese empire of his day.

Fortunately for us such an extreme situation is only theoretical, but the dire results of upsetting nature's own arrangements are well known to students of animal populations. The stockman's zeal for eliminating the coyote has resulted in plagues of field mice, which the coyote formerly controlled. The oft repeated story of the Kaibab deer in Arizona is another case in point. At one time the deer population was in equilibrium with its environment. A number of predators—wolves, pumas, and coyotes—prevented the deer from outrunning their food supply. Then a campaign was begun to "conserve" the deer by killing off their enemies. Once the predators were gone, the deer increased prodigiously and soon there was not enough food for them. The browse line on the

trees went higher and higher as they sought food, and in time many more deer were dying of starvation than had formerly been killed by predators. The whole environment, moreover, was damaged by their desperate efforts to find food.

The predatory insects of field and forests play the same role as the wolves and coyotes of the Kaibab. Kill them off and the population of the prey insect surges upward.

No one knows how many species of insects inhabit the earth because so many are yet to be identified. But more than 700,000 have already been described. This means that in terms of the number of species, 70 to 80 per cent of the earth's creatures are insects. The vast majority of these insects are held in check by natural forces, without any intervention by man. If this were not so, it is doubtful that any conceivable volume of chemicals —or any other methods—could possibly keep down their populations.

The trouble is that we are seldom aware of the protection afforded by natural enemies until it fails. Most of us walk unseeing through the world, unaware alike of its beauties, its wonders, and the strange and sometimes terrible intensity of the lives that are being lived about us. So it is that the activities of the insect predators and parasites are known to few. Perhaps we may have noticed an oddly shaped insect of ferocious mien[8] on a bush in the garden and been dimly aware that the praying mantis lives at the expense of other insects. But we see with understanding eye only if we have walked in the garden at night and here and there with a flashlight have glimpsed the mantis stealthily creeping upon her prey. Then we sense something of the drama of the hunter and the hunted. Then we begin to feel something of that relentlessly pressing force by which nature controls her own.

The predators—insects that kill and consume other insects—are of many kinds. Some are quick and with the speed of swallows snatch their prey from the air. Others plod methodically along a stem, plucking off and devouring sedentary[9] insects like the aphids. The yellowjackets capture soft-bodied insects and feed the juices to their young. Muddauber wasps build columned nests of mud under the eaves of houses and stock them with insects on which their young will feed. The horseguard wasp hovers above herds of grazing

[7] animal of microscopic smallness

[8] outward appearance
[9] fixed, remaining in one place

cattle, destroying the blood-sucking flies that torment them. The loudly buzzing syrphid fly, often mistaken for a bee, lays its eggs on leaves of aphis-infested plants; the hatching larvae then consume immense numbers of aphids. Ladybugs or lady beetles are among the most effective destroyers of aphids, scale insects, and other plant-eating insects. Literally hundreds of aphids are consumed by a single ladybug to stoke the little fires of energy which she requires to produce even a single batch of eggs.

Even more extraordinary in their habits are the parasitic insects. These do not kill their hosts outright. Instead, by a variety of adaptations they utilize their victims for the nurture of their own young. They may deposit their eggs within the larvae or eggs of their prey, so that their own developing young may find food by consuming the host. Some attach their eggs to a caterpillar by means of a sticky solution; on hatching, the larval parasite bores through the skin of the host. Others, led by an instinct that simulates foresight, merely lay their eggs on a leaf so that a browsing caterpillar will eat them inadvertently.

Everywhere, in field and hedgerow and garden and forest, the insect predators and parasites are at work. Here, above a pond, the dragonflies dart and the sun strikes fire from their wings. So their ancestors sped through swamps where huge reptiles lived. Now, as in those ancient times, the sharp-eyed dragonflies capture mosquitoes in the air, scooping them in with basket-shaped legs. In the waters below, their young, the dragonfly nymphs, or naiads, prey on the aquatic stages of mosquitoes and other insects.

Or there, almost invisible against a leaf, is the lacewing, with green gauze wings and golden eyes, shy and secretive, descendant of an ancient race that lived in Permian[10] times. The adult lacewing feeds mostly on plant nectars and the honeydew of aphids, and in time she lays her eggs, each on the end of a long stalk which she fastens to a leaf. From these emerge her children—strange, bristled larvae called aphis lions, which live by preying on aphids, scales, or mites, which they capture and suck dry of fluid. Each may consume several hundred aphids before the ceaseless turning of the cycle of its life brings the time when it

[10] pertaining to the latest period in the Paleozoic era, marked by the rise of reptiles and modern insects (210 to 185 million years ago)

will spin a white silken cocoon in which to pass the pupal stage.

And there are many wasps, and flies as well, whose very existence depends on the destruction of the eggs or larvae of other insects through parasitism. Some of the egg parasites are exceedingly minute wasps, yet by their numbers and their great activity they hold down the abundance of many crop-destroying species.

All these small creatures are working—working in sun and rain, during the hours of darkness, even when winter's grip has damped down the fires of life to mere embers. Then this vital force is merely smoldering, awaiting the time to flare again into activity when spring awakens the insect world. Meanwhile, under the white blanket of snow, below the frost-hardened soil, in crevices in the bark of trees, and in sheltered caves, the parasites and the predators have found ways to tide themselves over the season of cold.

The eggs of the mantis are secure in little cases of thin parchment attached to the branch of a shrub by the mother who lived her life span with the summer that is gone.

The female *Polistes* wasp, taking shelter in a forgotten corner of some attic, carries in her body the fertilized eggs, the heritage on which the whole future of her colony depends. She, the lone survivor, will start a small paper nest in the spring, lay a few eggs in its cells, and carefully rear a small force of workers. With their help she will then enlarge the nest and develop the colony. Then the workers, foraging ceaselessly through the hot days of summer, will destroy countless caterpillars.

Thus, through the circumstances of their lives, and the nature of our own wants, all these have been our allies in keeping the balance of nature tilted in our favor. Yet we have turned our artillery against our friends. The terrible danger is that we have grossly underestimated their value in keeping at bay a dark tide of enemies that, without their help, can overrun us.

*T*he prospect of a general and permanent lowering of environmental resistance becomes grimly and increasingly real with each passing year as the number, variety, and destructiveness of insecticides grows. With the passage of time we may expect progressively more serious outbreaks of insects, both disease-carrying and crop-destroy-ing species, in excess of anything we have ever known.

"Yes, but isn't this all theoretical?" you may ask. "Surely it won't really happen—not in my life-time, anyway."

But it is happening, here and now. Scientific journals had already recorded some 50 species involved in violent dislocations of nature's bal-ance by 1958. More examples are being found every year. A recent review of the subject contained ref-erences to 215 papers reporting or discussing unfavorable upsets in the balance of insect popu-lations caused by pesticides.

"... we have turned our artillery
against our friends. . . .
we have grossly underestimated
their value in keeping at bay
a dark tide of enemies that,
without their help, can overrun us."

Sometimes the result of chemical spraying has been a tremendous upsurge of the very insect the spraying was intended to control, as when black-flies in Ontario became 17 times more abundant after spraying than they had been before. Or when in England an enormous outbreak of the cabbage aphid—an outbreak that had no parallel on record —followed spraying with one of the organic phosphorus chemicals.

At other times spraying, while reasonably effec-tive against the target insect, has let loose a whole Pandora's box of destructive pests that had never previously been abundant enough to cause trou-ble. The spider mite, for example, has become practically a worldwide pest as DDT and other insecticides have killed off its enemies. The spider mite is not an insect. It is a barely visible eight-legged creature belonging to the group that in-cludes spiders, scorpions, and ticks. It has mouth parts adapted for piercing and sucking, and a prodigious appetite for the chlorophyll that makes the world green. It inserts these minute and stiletto-sharp mouth parts into the outer cells of leaves and evergreen needles and extracts the chlorophyll. A mild infestation gives trees and

shrubbery a mottled or salt-and-pepper appear-ance; with a heavy mite population, foliage turns yellow and falls.

This is what happened in some of the western national forests a few years ago, when in 1956 the United States Forest Service sprayed some 885,000 acres of forested lands with DDT. The intention was to control the spruce budworm, but the fol-lowing summer it was discovered that a problem worse than the budworm damage had been cre-ated. In surveying the forests from the air, vast blighted areas could be seen where the magnifi-cent Douglas firs were turning brown and drop-ping their needles. In the Helena National Forest and on the western slopes of the Big Belt Moun-tains, then in other areas of Montana and down into Idaho the forests looked as though they had been scorched. It was evident that this summer of 1957 had brought the most extensive and spectac-ular infestation of spider mites in history. Almost all of the sprayed area was affected. Nowhere else was the damage evident. Searching for prece-dents, the foresters could remember other scourges of spider mites, though less dramatic than this one. There had been similar trouble along the Madison River in Yellowstone Park in 1929, in Colorado 20 years later, and then in New Mexico in 1956. *Each of these outbreaks had followed forest spraying with insecticides.* (The 1929 spraying, occurring before the DDT era, employed lead arsenate.)

Why does the spider mite appear to thrive on insecticides? Besides the obvious fact that it is relatively insensitive to them, there seem to be two other reasons. In nature it is kept in check by various predators such as ladybugs, a gall midge, predaceous mites and several pirate bugs, all of them extremely sensitive to insecticides. The third reason has to do with population pressure within the spider mite colonies. An undisturbed colony of mites is a densely settled community, huddled under a protective webbing for concealment from its enemies. When sprayed, the colonies disperse as the mites, irritated though not killed by the chemicals, scatter out in search of places where they will not be disturbed. In so doing they find a far greater abundance of space and food than was available in the former colonies. Their enemies are now dead so there is no need for the mites to spend their energy in secreting protective webbing. Instead, they pour all their energies into

28 producing more mites. It is not uncommon for their egg production to be increased threefold— all through the beneficent effect of insecticides.

In the Shenandoah Valley of Virginia, a famous apple-growing region, hordes of a small insect called the red-banded leaf roller arose to plague the growers as soon as DDT began to replace arsenate of lead. Its depredations had never before been important; soon its toll rose to 50 per cent of the crop and it achieved the status of the most destructive pest of apples, not only in this region but throughout much of the East and Midwest, as the use of DDT increased.

The situation abounds in ironies. In the apple orchards of Nova Scotia in the late 1940's the worst infestations of the codling moth (cause of "wormy apples") were in the orchards regularly sprayed. In unsprayed orchards the moths were not abundant enough to cause real trouble. . . .

*I*n America, farmers have repeatedly traded one insect enemy for a worse one as spraying upsets the population dynamics of the insect world. Two of the mass-spraying programs recently carried out have had precisely this effect. One was the fire ant eradication program in the South; the other was the spraying for the Japanese beetle in the Midwest.

When a wholesale application of heptachlor was made to the farmlands in Louisiana in 1957, the result was the unleashing of one of the worst enemies of the sugarcane crop—the sugarcane borer. Soon after the heptachlor treatment, damage by borers increased sharply. The chemical aimed at the fire ant had killed off the enemies of the borer. The crop was so severely damaged that farmers sought to bring suit against the state for negligence in not warning them that this might happen.

The same bitter lesson was learned by Illinois farmers. After the devastating bath of dieldrin recently administered to the farmlands in eastern Illinois for the control of the Japanese beetle, farmers discovered that corn borers had increased enormously in the treated area. In fact, corn grown in fields within this area contained almost twice as many of the destructive larvae of this insect as did the corn grown outside. The farmers may not yet be aware of the biological basis of what has happened, but they need no scientists to tell them they have made a poor bargain. In trying to get rid of one insect, they have brought on a scourge of a much more destructive one. Accord-

ing to Department of Agriculture estimates, total damage by the Japanese beetle in the United States adds up to about 10 million dollars a year, while damage by the corn borer runs to about 85 million. . . .

All these examples concern insects that attack agricultural crops. What of those that carry disease? There have already been warnings. On Nissan Island in the South Pacific, for example, spraying had been carried on intensively during the Second World War, but was stopped when hostilities came to an end. Soon swarms of a malaria-carrying mosquito reinvaded the island. All of its predators had been killed off and there had not been time for new populations to become established. The way was therefore clear for a tremendous population explosion. Marshall Laird, who has described this incident, compares chemical control to a treadmill; once we have set foot on it we are unable to stop for fear of the consequences.

In some parts of the world disease can be linked with spraying in quite a different way. For some reason, snail-like mollusks seem to be almost immune to the effects of insecticides. This has been observed many times. In the general holocaust that followed the spraying of salt marshes in eastern Florida, aquatic snails alone survived. The scene as described was a macabre[11] picture— something that might have been created by a surrealist brush. The snails moved among the bodies of the dead fishes and the moribund[12] crabs, devouring the victims of the death rain of poison.

But why is this important? It is important because many aquatic snails serve as hosts of dangerous parasitic worms that spend part of their life cycle in a mollusk, part in a human being. Examples are the blood flukes, or schistosoma, that cause serious disease in man when they enter the body by way of drinking water or through the skin when people are bathing in infested waters. The flukes are released into the water by the host snails. Such diseases are especially prevalent in parts of Asia and Africa. Where they occur, insect control measures that favor a vast increase of snails are likely to be followed by grave consequences.

And of course man is not alone in being subject to snail-borne disease. Liver disease in cattle, sheep, goats, deer, elk, rabbits, and various other warm-blooded animals may be caused by liver

[11] gruesome, ghastly
[12] dying

flukes that spend part of their life cycles in fresh-water snails. Livers infested with these worms are unfit for use as human food and are routinely condemned. Such rejections cost American cattlemen about 3½ million dollars annually. Anything that acts to increase the number of snails can obviously make this problem an even more serious one.

Over the past decade these problems have cast long shadows, but we have been slow to recognize them. Most of those best fitted to develop natural controls and assist in putting them into effect have been too busy laboring in the more exciting vineyards of chemical control. It was reported in 1960 that only 2 per cent of all the economic entomologists in the country were then working in the field of biological controls. A substantial number of the remaining 98 per cent were engaged in research on chemical insecticides.

Why should this be? The major chemical companies are pouring money into the universities to support research on insecticides. This creates attractive fellowships for graduate students and attractive staff positions. Biological-control studies, on the other hand, are never so endowed—for the simple reason that they do not promise anyone the fortunes that are to be made in the chemical industry. These are left to state and federal agencies, where the salaries paid are far less.

This situation also explains the otherwise mystifying fact that certain outstanding entomologists are among the leading advocates of chemical control. Inquiry into the background of some of these men reveals that their entire research program is supported by the chemical industry. Their professional prestige, sometimes their very jobs depend on the perpetuation of chemical methods. Can we then expect them to bite the hand that literally feeds them? But knowing their bias, how much credence can we give to their protests that insecticides are harmless?

Amid the general acclaim for chemicals as the principal method of insect control, minority reports have occasionally been filed by those few entomologists who have not lost sight of the fact that they are neither chemists nor engineers, but biologists.

F. H. Jacob in England has declared that "the activities of many so-called economic entomologists would make it appear that they operate in the belief that salvation lies at the end of a spray nozzle . . . that when they have created problems of resurgence or resistance or mammalian tox-icity, the chemist will be ready with another pill. That view is not held here . . . Ultimately only the biologist will provide the answers to the basic problems of pest control."

"Economic entomologists must realize," wrote A. D. Pickett of Nova Scotia, "that they are dealing with living things . . . their work must be more than simply insecticide testing or a quest for highly destructive chemicals." Dr. Pickett himself was a pioneer in the field of working out sane methods of insect control that take full advantage of the predatory and parasitic species. The method which he and his associates evolved is today a shining model but one too little emulated. Only in the integrated control programs developed by some California entomologists do we find anything comparable in this country.

Dr. Pickett began his work some thirty-five years ago in the apple orchards of the Annapolis Valley in Nova Scotia, once one of the most concentrated fruit-growing areas in Canada. At that time it was believed that insecticides—then inorganic chemicals—would solve the problems of insect control, that the only task was to induce fruit growers to follow the recommended methods. But the rosy picture failed to materialize. Somehow the insects persisted. New chemicals were added, better spraying equipment was devised, and the zeal for spraying increased, but the insect problem did not get any better. Then DDT promised to "obliterate the nightmare" of codling moth outbreaks. What actually resulted from its use was an unprecedented scourge of mites. "We move from crisis to crisis, merely trading one problem for another," said Dr. Pickett.

At this point, however, Dr. Pickett and his associates struck out on a new road instead of going along with other entomologists who continued to pursue the will-o'-the-wisp of the ever more toxic chemical. Recognizing that they had a strong ally in nature, they devised a program that makes maximum use of natural controls and minimum use of insecticides. Whenever insecticides are applied only minimum dosages are used—barely enough to control the pest without avoidable harm to beneficial species. Proper timing also enters in. Thus, if nicotine sulphate is applied before rather than after the apple blossoms turn pink one of the important predators is spared, probably because it is still in the egg stage.

Dr. Pickett uses special care to select chemicals that will do as little harm as possible to insect parasites and predators. "When we reach the point of using DDT, parathion, chlordane, and other new insecticides as routine control measures in the same way we have used the inorganic chemicals in the past, entomologists interested in biological control may as well throw in the sponge," he says. Instead of these highly toxic, broad-spectrum insecticides, he places chief reliance on ryania (derived from ground stems of a tropical plant), nicotine sulphate, and lead arsenate. In certain situations very weak concentrations of DDT or malathion are used (1 or 2 ounces per 100 gallons—in contrast to the usual 1 or 2 pounds per 100 gallons). Although these two are the least toxic of the modern insecticides, Dr. Pickett hopes by further research to replace them with safer and more selective materials.

How well has this program worked? Nova Scotia orchardists who are following Dr. Pickett's modified spray program are producing as high a proportion of first-grade fruit as are those who are using intensive chemical applications. They are also getting as good production. They are getting these results, moreover, at a substantially lower cost. The outlay for insecticides in Nova Scotia apple orchards is only from 10 to 20 per cent of the amount spent in most other apple-growing areas.

More important than even these excellent results is the fact that the modified program worked out by these Nova Scotian entomologists is not doing violence to nature's balance. It is well on the way to realizing the philosophy stated by the Canadian entomologist G. C. Ullyett a decade ago: "We must change our philosophy, abandon our attitude of human superiority and admit that in many cases in natural environments we find ways and means of limiting populations of organisms in a more economical way than we can do it ourselves."

BERTON ROUECHÉ

The highway ran on and on between two walls of
trees. The trees were mainly white oak and beech
and loblolly pine, with here and there a Southern
magnolia, and they rose from the roadside sixty,
eighty, a hundred feet into the hot blue morning
sky. This was the Big Thicket of East Texas. It
was the remains of a bog-and-bayou wilderness
that once—before sawmills and oil wells and pipe-
lines and subdivisions and water-ski resorts—
spread over more than three million acres of land
in the counties of Polk, Tyler, Hardin, and Liberty.
At the urging of local conservationists, the National Park Service had recently proposed that
some thirty-five thousand acres of this remainder
be preserved as a National Monument, and we—
Ernest Borgman, superintendent of Padre Island
National Seashore, at Corpus Christi, and I—had
driven up to spend a day in that part of the
Thicket.

The wall of woods moved back from the highway, and an old frame house appeared on the left,
and then, on the right, a field of grazing cattle
with cattle egrets[1] following underfoot. At the
edge of the field was a sign: "Saratoga." Saratoga
(pop. 806), a village founded by a nostalgic up-
state New Yorker, lies close to the heart of the Big
Thicket, and it was here that we had arranged to
pick up our guide, a local naturalist named Lance
Rosier. The highway became a street. There was a
Texaco station on one side of the street and a Fina
station on the other. Then came a block of houses,
and then a block of one-story buildings with covered sidewalks: "Crouch Coca-Cola Gro.,"
"Wimpy's Carnation Fresh Milk Gro. & Mkt.,"
"Crawford's Have-a-Pepsi Café," a barbershop
with a wooden barber pole, a Gulf station, a brick

[1] herons which flock in pastures, feeding on insects

post office. Rosier was waiting for us on a bench in front of the post office. He was a small man with a big nose and big ears, and he had on a faded blue work shirt and a little cotton golf hat. Borgman pulled in to the curb, and Rosier got up and came across to the car. He looked to be about seventy. He gave us each a limp, country handshake, and got into the back seat and sat there with his hands folded in his lap.

"Well, Lance?" Borgman said.

"Sir?" Rosier said.

"Where to?" Borgman said. "Where do we start?"

"Do you know the old Ghost Road?" Rosier said.

"I've heard of it," Borgman said. He swung the car around, and we headed back out of town. "It's on the way to Big Sandy and Tight-Eye and all up there."

"Yes, sir," Rosier said. "Turn right, please."

We turned off the highway and onto a narrow sandy road. It ran between fields of grazing cattle and greening corn for half a mile, and then the woods rose up and we were back in the Thicket. The woods were deep and dense and dark, and there was standing water under most of the trees. In the water along the roadside were spiky clumps of scrub palmetto. Up ahead, a buzzard hung over the road. It was a spooky-looking place.

"This must be the Ghost Road," I said.

"Yes, sir," Rosier said. "It is. And do you notice how straight it runs? It runs as straight as an arrow for nine miles—all the way to Bragg. Bragg is a ghost now, too. This used to be a branch line of the Gulf, Colorado & Santa Fe Railway. They tore up the tracks in 1934. But that's only partly why they call this the Ghost Road. There's supposed to be a ghost in here. A man was jacking deer in here one night, and he was drinking and he got himself drunk. So he lay down on the railroad tracks to rest. He was still laying there when the train come along, and it cut off his head. The ghost is his lantern. People still see it burning here at night."

"Have you ever seen it, Lance?" Borgman said.

"No, sir," Rosier said. "Now, do you notice that right along here you don't see any hardwood? The lumber company—one of them—sprayed about seven thousand acres to kill off the hardwood and get a pure stand of pine for lumber. It was a hormone spray, and they did it from a helicopter. That was about three years ago. So you don't see any hardwood at all. Or any birds, either."

We drove on down an endless aisle of loblolly pine. After a couple of miles, the woods deepened and darkened, and another buzzard hung over the road. We were out of the pine desolation. Rosier leaned forward. There was something moving on the road ahead. The movement took form—a big brown sow and eight tumbling little pigs. But a glimpse was all I got. There was another commotion, and they all were gone.

Rosier laughed. "Now you know we're out of the sprayed area," he said. "Those wild pigs are a sure sign. They live on acorns. They live right well, too. They can get up to three and four hundred pounds. There are all kinds of animals gone feral[2] in the Thicket. There are pigs like those, and cats and goats, and even some cattle. And about a year ago a man I know got tired of a herd of jackasses he had, and he turned them loose in here. I believe there were twenty-six of them. They're all in here somewhere."

"What about real wild animals?" I said.

"Yes, sir," he said. "We have those, too. Including rattlesnakes and copperheads and water moccasins. We've got deer and coons and possums and skunks and otters and foxes and flying squirrels and bobcats and cougars, and there used to be some jaguars. I know there are still some bear—black bear. I've seen them. And there are plenty of armadillos. I don't know about alligators. I think the poachers have just about killed them all. But there may be a few still left in places where even those fellows don't like to go."

"Don't forget the ivorybill, Lance," Borgman said.

"The ivory-billed woodpecker?" I said. "I thought that was supposed to be extinct."

"Yes, sir," Rosier said. "That's what everybody thought. But it isn't. There are still a few of them here in the Thicket. That's one reason why I'd like to see the Monument go through. You have to go deep to find them, though. The first confirmed sighting in many years was a couple of years ago, and there have been several more since then. They tell about one fellow that saw one, and to prove it he shot it and brought it in. I don't know how true that is."

[2] wild

"No," Borgman said. "But I do know there are people like that."

The Ghost Road came out on a gravel highway. Beyond the highway was the main line of the Gulf, Colorado & Santa Fe, and on a siding were six flatcars loaded with loblolly logs. The logs were the length of telephone poles and at least two feet in diameter. Beyond the railroad tracks the Thicket began again.

"Turn left, please," Rosier said. He cleared his throat. "You know, this is right nice. I'm right happy to go out with you fellows today. I always like to get back in the Thicket. It's where I've spent most of my life. I started when I was just a boy. I never was big enough to play ball or anything, so I took to going back in the Thicket. I wanted to learn what was there—what was growing there. The other fellows, they called me crazy. They called me sissy, too. That's the way it was in those days. If a man even planted a rosebush in his front yard they called him henpecked. But I didn't pay any mind to that. I used to leave home—I was living with my auntie then—with a bag for specimens and a sweet potato in my pocket for lunch, and spend the day in the Thicket. I liked wild flowers, but I didn't know but a very few. There weren't any books—any field guides—in those days. What I did was this. When I found a flower I didn't know, I'd wrap it up and send it off to one of the colleges, and by and by they would write me back and give me the name—both names—for it. There are over a thousand species of flowering plants in the Thicket, and I learned them all, and that's the way I did it. I learned them the hard way."

"The best way," Borgman said.

"Yes, sir," Rosier said. "I think so, too. Now, if you'll turn right, please—at that little dirt road up there. I want to show you one of the most historic spots in East Texas. Then we'll go on to Big Sandy."

The dirt road took us across the railroad tracks and into another deep woods. A cardinal blazed out of the trees and down the edge of the road. But that was only the first one. This was a haven for cardinals. In not much more than a mile, I counted eleven of them. It was also a garden of wild flowers. The roadside grass was bright with crimson clover and blue vervain and yellow but-

tercups. Even the air was sweet with some rich and blossomy scent. I looked back at Rosier.

"Hawthorn," he said.

We crossed a little brown creek on a bridge of old crossties. A column of dust rose up ahead, and we came up behind a heavy truck.

"That looks like a well-pulling rig," Borgman said.

"Yes, sir," Rosier said. "They've got a lot of oil fields around in here, and he's probably going in to pull out some wells that have given out and gone dry. You'll see where he's going directly. You can't very well miss it. And if you listen you can hear a power saw over yonder. That's some of what's happening to the Big Thicket. They tell me the Thicket is going at the rate of fifty acres a day."

We dropped back out of the dust and followed the truck at a distance. We followed it for a couple of miles. Then the road took a turn, and when we came around the bend the truck was gone. And so were the woods. On both sides of the road lay a waste of mud and puddles and rotting stumps and a few palmetto saplings. This was the remains of an oil field. It covered forty or fifty acres, and off to the right, through a screen of skeleton trees, I could see the scar of a second field and the truck moving on toward another.

"What did all that?" I said. "Spilled oil?"

"No, sir," Rosier said. "They don't waste anything that valuable. It's the salt water they have to pump out of the wells that does the damage. It does a right good job, too. They abandoned this field at least five years ago."

"It's gone," Borgman said.

I looked at the poisoned land. It couldn't be helped: this was the look of the twentieth century. I supposed it couldn't be helped. But it made me feel sick, and I was thankful when the woods sprang up from the ruins and we were back again in the green of the Thicket.

Rosier leaned forward. "Here we are," he said. "Pull over, please—up there by that big sweet gum. This is the history I want to show you. I'm going to take you back in the woods and show you the Keyser Burnout."

Borgman pulled off the road and under the big gum tree. We got out, and Rosier led the way across the road and onto an overgrown wagon-track trail. The trees arched and mingled over-head, and some of them were hung with pink-flowered honeysuckle. It was hot and damp and dim and still, and there were mosquitoes everywhere. And birds. The birds were hidden in the trees, but I could hear them calling—a crow, a cardinal, a white-eyed vireo, a warbler of some kind, a Carolina wren.

"The Keyser Burnout goes back to the War Between the States," Rosier said. "The first residents of the Big Thicket were what they called jayhawkers. They were draft evaders. They were people who didn't own no slaves, so they didn't see no reason to fight, and to keep from being drafted they hid out in here. There were whole families of them. I don't know exactly how many. Different people tell it different. But there must have been anyway two hundred. They lived very careful. They split up into two groups, and each group had its own well, and they came and went through the Thicket without even breaking a twig. But they lived right well. They lived on game and wild honey. They didn't need for anything but coffee and tobacco, and they traded game for that. The government was against them, of course, and finally it sent a man named Captain Keyser up from Galveston to root them out. He come up the Trinity River with his troops and sent word into the Thicket that they either give up or he would burn them out. The jayhawkers wouldn't give up, but there are two different stories about what happened next. One story is that when Captain Keyser set the woods on fire, the jayhawkers all run off and he never did find them. The other story is that they all burned up in the fire. The only thing I ever heard people agree on about the jayhawkers was where Mr. Lilly was shot. Mr. Lilly wasn't a jayhawker, but he was out in the Thicket hunting one day, and Captain Keyser's soldiers mistook him for one, and they shot him. The bullet hit him right where his galluses[3] crossed."

"He must have been running away," Borgman said.

"Yes, sir," Rosier said. "I reckon he was scared." He slapped a mosquito. "And this is where the Keyser Burnout starts. You notice here on the right the woods is all slash pine. That's where the Burnout was. It's all pine for over two hundred acres."

*T*here was a crossroads up ahead, and Borgman slowed the car. Just beyond the crossing, in a clearing on the left, was a little white store with a big red sign: "Williams Dr Pepper Gro." A dirt track led around the store and across the clearing and into the woods behind. A man on a horse came out of the woods. But it wasn't a horse. He was riding a saddled mule.

"This is Segno," Rosier said. "If you want to see Big Sandy Creek, we can park right here and walk in. It isn't but a couple of miles."

We left the car near the store and walked up the track. It climbed through the woods and around the slope of a hill to an open grove of big magnolia trees. There was a long, low building under the trees with a corrugated-iron roof and a sign above the door: "Welcome to Magnolia Hill Assembly of God Church." On one side of the church were three long, rickety picnic tables.

"My God," Borgman said. "Look at those old tables. They really bring back memories."

"They used to have a saying," Rosier said. " 'Dinner on the ground, preaching all around.' "

"I never heard that," Borgman said. "But that sure is the way it was."

We walked on beyond the church and down past a burying ground. Pink phlox and bluebonnets were growing together between the gravestones, and I could see bees working among the flowers. There was still wild honey in the Thicket. Magnolia Hill was the end of the track. Beyond the burying ground was a limp barbed-wire fence, and then the woods began again. It was an open woods of beech and loblolly pine, and it was cut by deep cattle trails. We walked single file down a downhill trail. Some of the beeches were as big as New England village elms, but there was very little underbrush and very few understory trees, and almost no grass at all. That was the work of grazing cattle.

"I don't know," Borgman said. "This doesn't look too bad. It's all been cut over and it's all been overgrazed, but I'm hopeful. The Monument could save it. It can still come back."

"It's better on down by the creek," Rosier said. "It's wilder down there in the bottom. But these woods are still alive. Hear that over yonder? Hear that paup-paup-paup? That's a pileated woodpecker sounding off. He isn't quite as shy as the ivorybill, but he's another bird that only likes deep woods."

"I think he's worth saving, too," Borgman said.

The cattle trail led down and down. The underbrush began to thicken, and the trees reached high overhead. We were in the creek bottom now. The

---

[3] suspenders

air was hot and heavy, and there were puddles here and there in the mud of the trail. We skirted a grove of bony cypresses standing knee-deep in a black bayou. A little black skink twisted across the trail, and behind us a bullfrog croaked and gulped. Rosier stopped and looked around. We left the trail and broke through a stand of brush and briar and came out on the bank of Big Sandy Creek. It looked like a spring-fed creek. The water was brown and clear, and the sandy bottom was orange in the sunlight. I squatted down and put in my hand. I could feel the tug of the current, and the water was as cold as spring water.

"Big Sandy Creek," Borgman said. "You were right, Lance. This is real great. I like this rough topography. I certainly want to see some of this in the Monument."

"It's a right nice creek," Rosier said. "That hole down yonder is always full of channel cat. Big ones, too. They'll average two or three pounds."

"What about mushrooms?" Borgman said. "There ought to be mushrooms in here."

"Yes, sir," Rosier said. "There are—plenty of them. Every kind there is, almost. Or so they tell me. Mushrooms are something I never did learn. I tried one time. I sent away for a book. It cost me twenty-five dollars, and when it came I went out in the Thicket down near home, and I searched around, and pretty soon I found a nice-looking mushroom. It was a big old thing, and I remember it was all white. I dug it up as careful as I could and started home, and I hadn't got very far when I began to feel sick to my stomach. And then my head began to ache. I thought my head was going to bust open. But I finally got home and got out my book and looked up my mushroom, and I found it there, and I read what it said, and it said this was a mushroom that had a smell that would make a man sick. That was the end of me and mushrooms. I even gave up eating mushroom soup."

"I wonder what kind it was," Borgman said.

"I don't remember," Rosier said. "I gave the book away."

We walked on along the bank of the creek. I looked down into the catfish hole, but I couldn't see any fish. They were probably back under the bank. We followed the wandering course of the creek for about a hundred yards and then turned off. The undergrowth was too much. We cut across the bottom and found another cattle trail and started back up the hill. We came through a patch of mulberry brush and into a glade of flow-ers and soaring, pairing, mating butterflies. They were brown with bright-blue dots on the wingtips —mourning cloaks. The flowers were mostly the usual flowers of the Thicket, but there were some I didn't know. One was a little white flower with a fresh, old-fashioned look. I pointed it out to Rosier.

"That's a sundew," he said. "*Drosera rotundifolia*. It's a pretty little thing. Look at those little hairs on the leaves. Look how they shine. You'd swear they were drops of dew. They even fool the bugs. A bug comes along and he sees that shining dew and he comes down to have himself a drink of water. But the hairs aren't dew, and they stick to him and he can't get away. He's caught. And then the sundew eats him."

*I*t was one o'clock when we got back to the Williams Gro., and time we had some lunch. There was no place to eat but where we were, and we bought what we could—yellow cheese, Vienna sausages, bread, Dr Pepper—from a barefooted woman in the store, and took it outside and ate at a table in the shade of a live-oak tree. It was good to sit down, and somewhere up in the tree a mockingbird whistled like a cardinal and called like a wren. The ground under the table was paved with a thousand bottle caps—soda-pop caps. This was a bone-dry county.

We finished lunch, and Borgman lighted a thick cigar. "I guess we ought to get going," he said. "I'd like to take a look at Tight-Eye before we call it a day."

"I'd like to show it to you," Rosier said. "I'll take you in and show you the Witness Tree. Maybe you've heard of it. The Witness Tree is a big magnolia tree that marks the corner where Liberty County and Hardin County and Polk County all meet. The experts say it's a thousand years old. I want you to see it."

"Why do they call it Tight-Eye?" I said.

"I reckon because it's so thick," he said. "You can't walk through it with your eyes wide open. The branches and brambles would put them out. It's the thickest part of the Thicket."

We dropped the remains of our lunch in a box in front of the store and got in the car and circled back to the crossroads and headed down another gravel highway. There was a big "No Dumping" sign on the right, and piles of trash and garbage, and the trees for a hundred yards around were plastered with windblown papers. We passed the

endless gash of a pipeline right-of-way. We passed two miles of forest marked with the sky-blue blaze of a lumber company, and then a mile blazed in orange. We passed a billboard: "Model Homes." We passed a sudden pasture and a fallen-down log cabin. Then we turned off the highway and onto a narrow, potholed asphalt road. The trees came together high overhead, and the asphalt road gave way to sandy mud. We were well into Tight-Eye now. We drove for another ten or fifteen minutes. The only car we met was a station wagon with Louisiana plates.

Rosier sat up and cleared his throat. "I reckon this will do," he said. "We'll get out here and walk in to the famous Witness Tree."

A track that had once been a logging road led into the Tight-Eye woods. The track was over-grown with red oak and sweet-gum saplings, and hedged with broomstick pine. It wasn't much more than a crack in the forest wall.

"This is real Thicket," Borgman said. "This is the best I've seen today. This is what we want for the Monument."

"Yes, sir," Rosier said. "And we'll be right in the middle of it in just about a minute. This track doesn't go where we're going." He had his eyes on the trees ahead on the right. He hesitated, moved on again, and stopped. "This is it," he said. "There's the old survey blaze. We go across country now."

We broke off the track and into the flanking woods. It *was* real Thicket—a forest floor of fallen trees swamped with brush and briar, an under-story of holly and dogwood and gum and oak and maple and hawthorn trailing vines and Spanish moss, and a soaring, pillared canopy of beech and magnolia and loblolly pine. There was no sky, no sun, no sense of direction. We climbed over logs and circled sloughs and ducked under hanging branches, and every log and every slough and every branch looked very much like the last. There were no landmarks. There were only the double welts of the old blazes. We picked our way from blaze to blaze—missing a blaze and circling back and finding it and moving on to the next. We walked for a mile and a half. Then a kind of clearing appeared. It was a grassy clearing with a big gray stump full of woodpecker holes and a tumble of big vine-covered logs. Rosier stopped and kicked around in the grass at the edge of the clearing and uncovered a wooden stake—an ironclad boundary stake.

"Here we are," he said. "This is the county corner. Ernest is standing in Hardin County, and you're in Polk County, and I'm over here in Liberty County." He turned and pointed at the stump. "And that's the famous and historic Witness Tree."

"That *stump?*" I said. It was a very big stump. It was fifty feet high and at least four feet in diameter. But still it was just a stump. "That stump is the Witness Tree?"

Borgman was staring at it, too. "What happened, Lance?" he said.

"They poisoned it three years ago," Rosier said. "They pumped it full of lead arsenate. I can show you the holes they bored to put in the poison. I came in with the experts that made the investigation. We found the holes stopped up with little wooden pegs."

"But why?" I said. "Why would anybody do a thing like that?"

"It sounds crazy," Borgman said.

"Yes, sir," Rosier said. "But there isn't any mystery about it. They did it for a warning. They were some of the folks that don't want the Monument."

The Pursuit of Status

VANCE PACKARD

Before the present era of great material abundance in America began, it was assumed that prosperity would eliminate, or greatly reduce, class differences. If everybody enjoyed the good things of life, as defined by mass merchandisers, it was thought the meanness of class distinctions would disappear. Unfortunately, the theory didn't work. Today, instead of being indifferent to outward evidences of rank and affluence, millions of prosperous Americans are becoming anxious status seekers.

Many of us seek possessions as status symbols. We draw social lines to try to prove our own superior status. We rate acquaintances on whether it is smart or not smart to be seen with them, and we are rated in turn. In so doing, we are intensifying social stratification in the United States.

One place where this status seeking is most vividly apparent is in the thousands of new, one-layer suburbs where many Americans are establishing homes. The home, as shrewdly merchandised today, is much more than a family nest. It is becoming the nation's prime status symbol, the most favored way to stake a status claim. A Chicago mass builder advises prospective buyers that purchasing one of his $28,500 houses "means they have arrived." He is an enthusiast of the motivational approach to selling. One of his conclusions is that most of his prospects are "striving, frightened people." He cheerfully plays upon both of these traits in his selling.

Some home builders employ the mass-selling strategies perfected in the automotive field. They give their products rich status meanings. Note, as an example, this advertisement of a Roslyn,

L. I., developer: "An unbelievably lavish, hand-crafted manorial estate for a very limited number of affluent families of good taste . . . $47,900."

The home, the builders have concluded, has far greater potentialities as a status symbol than the automobile. It can cost more, and it is easier to surround the home with high-status cultural overtones (antiques, books, art, high-fidelity music equipment).

At a recent convention of home builders in Chicago, a consultant reported that he had conducted 411 "depth interviews" to find what modern home buyers really want in a home. In a great many cases, he reported, they want a symbol of success. He discussed strategies for giving a home "snob appeal." One strategy, he said, is to use French phrases in your selling. Soon thereafter, we began seeing "the French touch" in advertisements. One, penned by a developer in Manetto Hills, L. I., exclaimed: "C'est Magnifique! . . . Une maison Ranch très originale avec 8 rooms, 2½ baths . . . 2-Cadillac garage . . . $21,900 . . . No cash for veterans." A mass builder in Florida began running his entire ad in French as he announced, "Une Autre Maison Contemporaine de Floride."

Tiny slivers of earth available for purchase also receive the up-grading treatment. They become in announcements "Huge One-Third Acre Estate Sites" and unbelievably large "Full 10,000-square-feet Estate Sites" (10,000 feet is slightly less than one-quarter acre). According to one rule of thumb cited by a building consultant, any lot larger than one-fourth acre can reasonably be termed an "estate" site and anything larger than half an acre can be labeled a "farm."

Both home builders and home buyers have given considerable thought to finding symbols of higher status in extra touches that will provoke gasps of admiration. Examples: push-button-controlled draperies, "His and Her" bathrooms, television sets installed in bedroom ceilings. One highly successful builder northwest of Chicago showed me a gold-plated faucet in the guest bathroom of one of his houses. He said that this feature has proved to be so popular that he is introducing it as an optional accessory in his $40,000 houses. The gold faucet, he explained, is "a little $500 extra" that not only impresses the neighbors, but that also adds to the resale value of the house.

Symbols suggesting that the homeowner has ties going far back into American history are also growing in popularity. The gaslight is such a symbol. One of the new vogues is the installation of flickering gaslights outside higher-priced homes. A large development firm in the Detroit area now promotes its new "estates" with expensively printed brochures illustrated with such Early American symbols as hitching posts, spinning wheels, muskets, horseshoes, old lanterns and town crier's bells. It places gray-haired hostesses in period costumes in its model homes and transports prospects about the projected development in horse-drawn carriages.

Richard Doan of Newtown, Conn., who until recently was a dealer in antiques, says that many of the persistent buyers of antiques are "definitely trying to give themselves background." He relates that he and his wife had a pair of eighteenth-century portraits hanging in their living room, until they decided to sell them. Sometime later, Doan was surprised to learn that the man to whom the paintings now belong was modestly explaining to visitors that the portraits were not of his family but were of his wife's ancestors.

"Membership shares in the River Oaks Country Club of Houston have sold for as high as $17,500. . . . 'It's the cost of getting on the team.'"

Another indication of growing status consciousness is our preoccupation with having a proper address. In earlier days, when everybody knew who was who in a community, little attention was paid to the "right" address. There was more desire to keep our roots in a family homestead we had come to love. Today, the importance people attach to address can be seen in an item involving Long Island. A builder in Manhasset, in promoting his houses, declared: "Most important—your address is Munsey Park; and Munsey Park in Manhasset is more than an address, it is a symbol of tradition and prestige—a supreme achievement in luxurious suburban living."

A Fairfield County, Conn., builder relates that an advertising executive from New York admired a $38,000 home in a town bordering Darien, Conn. The executive and his wife balked at buying, however, because they were anxious to have a Darien address. Their resistance melted when the builder shrewdly pointed out that they could buy themselves a post-office box in Darien.

Each U.S. community has its own way of deciding where the elite of today can be found. With many, elevation is the principal factor. As you wind your way up Lookout Mountain bordering Chattanooga, Tenn., the homes become more and more costly. Hollywood movie and TV people live in the area of Beverly Hills north of Santa Monica Boulevard. As you drive up the slope starting at the boulevard, you note that, with each passing block, the yards become wider and the homes larger. By the time you reach the white, sprawling homes of Jack Benny and Desi Arnaz, the yards have become very wide and very large indeed.

In some towns, nearness to water is the ruling factor determining eliteness. This is true for example along the North Shores of both Chicago and Boston. In places such as Lancaster, Pa., Wichita Falls, Texas, and Bel Air, Calif., many of the most prized home sites face the golf course.

One of the most successful real-estate agents in southwestern Connecticut is the astute wife of a businessman. She sells address rather than home. Regardless of the particular house she plans to show a prospect, she manages to get there by a route which passes the country club. She waves to her fellow members and chats in familiar terms about the more notable members. Her commissions typically run around $25,000 a year.

Approximately 30,000,000 Americans change their address each year. And millions of these movers strive in their home hopping to upgrade themselves socially with each hop. These highly mobile citizens are also the nation's prize consumers. They not only try to upgrade their home with each move, but, market studies show, they have a tremendous "upgrading urge" when it comes to the extras. If they move into an area where the neighbors have clothes driers or air conditioners, they feel they must have them, too, and quickly. Experts on consumer motives find they are ripe for any goods sold to them as "keys to social acceptance."

This code of acceptance is also applied to socializing. The people who ask us to dinner are almost always those who regard us as their equals in social prestige (or slightly higher). The stratification of socialized patterns is most vividly seen in those towns which are dominated by a military base or a university or by one industry. In towns where a major corporation dominates the local economic life, the families of management personnel will, rather compulsively, confine their socializing almost entirely to other families from

the company management. And often there will be unwritten rules of protocol.[1] Except for the courtesy calls, a wife may invite only families where the husband has the approximate rank of her own husband. When a friend's husband is promoted, socializing should stop.

At one military base, the wife in her more ambitious ventures in entertaining must follow exquisite rules of procedure. Seating is likely to be by date of rank. If it is a large affair where both tea and coffee are to be poured, the husband of the lady invited to pour coffee must outrank the husband of the lady invited to pour tea.

The wife of an ex-Air Force lieutenant has concluded that wives of officers are more likely to wear their rank than their husbands. The colonel's wife, she relates, expected the rest of the officers' wives waiting in line at the commissary to give way whenever she appeared. My informant had the misfortune to become pregnant at approximately the same date as the colonel's wife. As the delivery dates approached, she found that her appointment to see a base doctor always fell on the same day as that of the colonel's wife. The colonel's wife invariably went directly into an inner office whenever she appeared, and was promptly checked over. The lieutenant's wife waited.

In college towns, faculty members—for all their presumed broadmindedness—are as careful about observing rank in social matters as the most anxious corporate executive trainee. Some time ago, while visiting Pennsylvania State University, I was escorted to a party by a dean. I mentioned to him that I had heard at the University of Michigan that deans were expected to arrive last and leave first. He laughed and said they didn't believe in that sort of fancy protocol at Penn State. He went on to say, however, that at some colleges where he had served, they had frightful unwritten rules of etiquette regulating social intercourse. (Associate professors would not invite full professors to their home: full professors would not invite deans, etc.)

When we arrived, the party was in full progress. I noted that no guest arrived after we did. We had been at the party for what seemed a short time when the dean said he was ready to leave any time I was. There were about 60 people present. We were the first to go.

In most sections of the U.S., opinions as to what constitutes a good party vary according to the social status of the participants. The most ambitious hostesses are not at the top of the social scale. In fact, parties near the top tend to be either jovial, informal gatherings or quietly proper gatherings. A wealthy party giver of Dallas and Southampton was questioned by reporters about the secret of her success. She responded, "Why, I just give them peanuts and whiskey."

The straining to make an impression by the display of unusual foods (preferably imported) and fancy decorations is more likely to be encountered at what I call the semiupper level (junior executives, etc.). Lower down the scale, at the butcher or carpenter level, the emphasis is more on proving one's respectability and "niceness" at a party. Further down the social ladder, most socializing is done with kinfolk or very near neighbors, and is quite random. The social clique—a pack of people running together—which is found at all the higher levels, disappears at the working-class level. And at the lower level, there is much more tendency for men and women at a party to segregate by sex.

One interesting indication of social status is the manner in which two married couples sit in an automobile. Let's assume they are on their way, together, to some festivity. If they are from the lower part of the social scale, the men will most likely climb into the front seat and the women will get into the back. If they are from the middle part of the scale, where respectability is cherished, each man will sit beside his own wife. If they are from the upper part of the scale, each husband will get in gallantly with the other man's wife.

The status consciousness of Americans in their socializing reveals itself, too, in their fondness for joining prestige-giving clubs. With the national rise in opulence[2] plumbers can drive limousines, foot doctors can buy mansions. The private club consequently looks more and more attractive to status-minded people as a place to draw lines. In a private club, you can sit, as in a fortress, in judgment on pretender-applicants. They can pound on the walls in vain, if you have your blackball and a good sound membership committee in front of you to do the preliminary screening.

Most of the elite country clubs surrounding one city I surveyed excluded Jewish residents from membership. The leading Gentile citizens were quick to deny there was any significant relationship between club membership and their success

---

[1] a code of diplomatic or military etiquette

[2] wealth, affluence, plenty

in business. The clubs, they said, were "just social." And most of them saw no handicap to Jewish businessmen who were barred. In other remarks, however, they revealed that their club memberships made an important contribution to their own business effectiveness. One of the city's leading bankers said, "An active banker belongs to every club in town. It's a part of the game."

Some country clubs try to make, or keep, themselves exclusive by charging a staggering membership fee. Membership shares in the River Oaks Country Club of Houston have sold for as high as $17,500. A Texas millionaire who explained this situation to me said simply, "It's the cost of getting on the team."

Many private schools, aware of their highly important role in screening future members of "the team," scrutinize the parents' social standing when application is made. The ideal father should have a high-status business or professional position. A fashionable address is usually important. And the father's membership in clubs may unofficially be weighed in the balance.

The U.S. now has more than 3,000 private schools (day or boarding). And most of the schools have more applicants than they can manage. The boarding schools cost parents about $2,000 a year; the day schools average close to $650.[3] In addition, the parents pay taxes to support the free public schools in their community.

E. Digby Baltzell, University of Pennsylvania sociologist and himself a graduate of elite St. Paul's School, has made a study of the role of private schools in American life. He concludes that the private schools—along with the Ivy League universities—"serve the sociological function of differentiating the upper class in America from the rest of the population." They train "the members of the younger generation, especially those not quite to the manner born, into an upper-class style of life." The growing importance in some areas of going to a proper private school is coming to loom larger than the family coat of arms, Baltzell says, in determining whether a young person is qualified to be accepted in the real upper circle. Many prospering higher-status families in the

Northeast and South feel impelled to turn to the private school. In contrast, virtually all the upper-income families on the North Shore above Chicago send their youngsters to the very fine local public schools.

A team of American-Canadian sociologists studying a suburban town reports this comment from one mother: She said she planned to send her daughter to a private school, even though the teaching standards were "much higher" at the local public schools. The best system, she decided from talking with friends, was to let your child get a "good academic grounding" in the public schools and then "finish at a private school and get the social graces." She confessed that she planned to switch to the private school, "not because I think it is better for her, but because I think it is socially necessary."

The corporate hierarchy[4] of America is the final area I will cite where status consciousness has become conspicuous. The *Wall Street Journal* recently concluded that, "at an increasing number of concerns, the corporate caste system is being formalized and rigidified." Increased attention is being paid to the trappings and privileges of corporate rank. In a small company, everybody knows who is who and where power resides. But in a large corporation, the management man feels a need for highly visible signs of his authority.

In a typical corporation, the head of the hierarchy gets the corner office with the nicest view, and the offices of his subordinates branch out from his corner in descending order of rank. Desks, also, are categorized by rank. Mahogany outranks walnut, and walnut outranks oak. The man who is entitled to wall-to-wall carpeting is likely to have such additional prerogatives as the water carafe, the leather desk set and the red-leather couch. All are symbols of flag rank. An executive with a two-pen set, of course, outranks a man with a one-pen set.

The private washroom in many companies is reserved for vice-presidents and up. At a Midwestern oil firm, a fine line is drawn. The vice-presidents, like the president, have private washrooms; but they are literally that. Only the president's washroom has a toilet.

An invitation to use the executive dining room is another prerogative that comes only when the employee passes a certain level. At a steel plant near Pittsburgh, there are two executive dining

---

[3] In 1968, costs had risen considerably. Private boarding schools for boys, tuition and incidental expenses, ran as follows: at Eaglebrooke, in Deerfield, Massachusetts, $3,250; at St. Mark's, in Southboro, Massachusetts, $2,850 ($1,450 for day school only). At Bryn Mawr School (a day school for girls) in Baltimore, Maryland, tuition and incidental expenses varied from $760 to $1,185. At Anna Head School (a day school for girls) in Oakland, California, the costs ranged from $900 to $1,400.

[4] arrangement of persons into a graded series of importance

rooms side by side for different levels of executives.

Perhaps the most precise status symbols in corporations—certainly the most visible to the general public—are the cars companies assign employees. Some auto assignments are so highly codified[5] as to make, model and accessories that knowledgeable townspeople can get a pretty clear idea of a man's rank and income by the car assigned to him. One major oil company divides its management people into five levels for the purpose of distributing all sorts of privileges, including company cars. A Class V person (salesman, etc.) is confined in his choice of car to certain popular low-priced models. A Class I person (division managers, etc.) is assigned a limousine.

Status awareness is by no means confined to corporate hierarchy. It is, for example, equally predominant on the secretarial level. The $150-a-week secretary does not usually associate socially with the $70-a-week secretary. And neither one of them will have anything to do with the girl in the secretarial pool.

Ironically, while our status consciousness has increased, the opportunity for millions of Americans to make any real gains in status has decreased. The one factor that establishes our status more than any other is our productive role in life, our occupation. And the great majority of people working for large companies today have, in actuality, only limited opportunities to rise above their established level.

The old-fashioned type of U.S. hero, the two-fisted laborer who pushes his way to the top of a great company, is becoming more and more of a rarity. Today, management trainees are usually drawn from the ranks of young men just out of college. As a result, a Diploma Elite is emerging in industrial America. Yet we pretend that precisely the opposite is occurring. We consign tens of millions of people without higher education to fixed roles where any large aspiration (at least in the big organization) is usually futile. And we keep telling them that "those who have the stuff" will rise to the top. We don't even allow them the satisfaction of feeling secure, dignified and creative in their modest status. When people, either in large organizations or elsewhere, have been trained to have aspirations that are unrealistic, the strain shows.

In a society requiring as great a variety of skills as our own, status distinctions are inevitable. The problem is not to try to wipe them out—which

would be impossible—but to achieve a reasonably happy society within their framework. In that context, much can be done to promote contentment, mutual respect and life satisfaction.

One way is to generate more understanding and intermingling among people of the various socio-economic groupings in our society. Most of us have become too confined in our social and professional contacts. A second approach, and this seems imperative, is to widen the gates of opportunity. If we are going to make education the main basis for deciding who should be considered for high-status positions, we should assure access to higher education for all with unusual potentialities. Too much of our talent is wasted. In one study, it was found that half the high-school graduates with the highest IQ's did not go on to college.

They fail to go, first of all, because of the high cost of college. (Costs can vary from around $1,000 a year at a state school to as much as $3,000 at a private college.[6]) A more important deterrent, however, appears to be lack of motivation. Students have not been reared in an atmosphere where the importance of a college education has been made clear to them.

If the American Dream is to have real meaning for the majority of our young people, they must be encouraged to do their best. They must be *assured* that if they do their best, they will be considered for the big opportunities of the nation. Those with natural talent must be identified and inspired to qualify for the higher roles in our economy. This is a challenge that deserves the earnest attention of our business leaders, our government leaders and our educational leaders.

Finally, I think we must learn to transcend the pettiness of scrambling for the symbols of status. We should recognize the true strength that lies in being individuals who think for themselves and are independent in mind and spirit. We would all lead more contented and satisfying lives if we judged people not by the symbols they display, but by their individual worth.

[5] systematized, reduced to a code
[6] In 1968, costs at Kansas University ranged from $1,550 to $1,650 a year for residents or $2,100 to $2,300 for non-residents. At Yale University, costs totalled $3,600 for tuition and board and room. For the 1969–70 year, Yale's inclusive fee (tuition, room and board, and other fees) is $3,900.

The Flowering of the Hippies

MARK HARRIS

The hippie "scene" on Haight Street in San Francisco was so very visual that photographers came from everywhere to shoot it, reporters came from everywhere to write it up with speed, and opportunists came from everywhere to exploit its drug addiction, its sexual possibility, and its political or social ferment.[1] Prospective hippies came from everywhere for one "summer of love" or maybe longer, some older folk to indulge their latent[2] hippie tendencies, and the police to contain, survey, or arrest. "Haight"—old Quaker name—rhymed with "hate," but hippies held that the theme of the street was love, and the best of hippies, like the best of visitors and the best of the police, hoped to reclaim and distill the best promise of a movement which might yet invigorate American movement everywhere. It might, by resurrecting the word "love," and giving it a refreshened definition, open the national mind, as if by the chemical LSD, to the hypocrisy of violence and prejudice in a nation dedicated to peace and accord.

It was easier to see than understand: the visual came first, and the visual was so discordant that tourists drove with their cars locked and an alarmed citizenry beseeched the police to clean it out.

It was easy to see that the young men who were hippies on Haight Street wore beards and long hair and sometimes earrings and weird-o granny eye-glasses, that they were barefoot or in sandals, and that they were generally dirty. A great many

[1] activity, agitation
[2] undeveloped

of the young men, by design or by accident, resembled Jesus Christ, whose name came up on campaign pins or lavatory walls or posters or bumper stickers. *Are You Bombing With Me, Baby Jesus. Jesus Is God's Atom Bomb.*

The script was "psychedelic." That is to say, it was characterized by flourishes, spirals, and curlicues in camouflaged tones—blues against purples, pinks against reds—as if the hippie behind the message weren't really sure he wanted to say what he was saying. It was an item of hippie thought that speech was irrelevant. *You Don't Say Love You Do It. Those Who Speak Don't Know Those Who Know Don't Speak.* But it was also my suspicion that hippies would speak when they could; meanwhile, their muteness suggested doubt. In one shop the wall was dominated by an old movie advertisement—Ronald Reagan and June Travis in *Love Is in the Air* (Warner Brothers), their faces paper-white, blank, drained. I asked the hippie at the counter why it was there, but she didn't trust herself to try. "It's what you make of it," she said.

It was easy to see that the young women who were hippies were draped, not dressed; that they, too, were dirty from toe to head; that they looked unwell, pale, sallow hair hung down in strings unwashed. Or they wore jeans, men's T-shirts over brassieres. When shoes were shoes the laces were missing or trailing, gowns were sacks, and sacks were gowns. *If You Can't Eat It Wear It.*

A fashion model was quoted in a newspaper as saying, "They don't really exist," who meant to say, of course, "I *wish* they didn't." The young ladies were experimenting in drugs, in sexual license, living in communal quarters furnished with mattresses. *Praise The Pill. Bless Our Pad.* Girls who might have been in fashion were panhandling.[3] "Sorry, I've got to go panhandle," I heard a hippie lady say, which was not only against the law but against the American creed, which holds that work is virtue, no matter what work you do. Hippie girls gave flowers to strangers, and they encouraged their dirty young men to avoid the war in Vietnam. *Thou Shalt Not Kill This Means You. Caution: Military Service May Be Hazardous To Your Health.*

The shops of the "hip" merchants were colorful and cordial. The "straight" merchants of Haight Street sold necessities, but the hip shops smelled of incense, the walls were hung with posters and paintings, and the counters were laden with thousands of items of nonutilitarian nonsense—metal

[3] begging

jewelry, glass beads, dirty pictures, "underground" magazines, photographs of old-time movie stars, colored chalk, dirty combs, kazoos, Halloween masks, fancy matchboxes, odd bits of stained glass, and single shoes. Every vacant wall was a bulletin board for communication among people not yet quite settled ("Jack and Frank from Iowa leave a message here").

The music everywhere was rock 'n' roll out of Beatles, folk, African drums, American pop, jazz, swing, and martial.

Anybody who was anybody among hippies had been arrested for something, or so he said—for "possession" (of drugs), for "contributing" (to the delinquency of a minor), for panhandling, for obstructing the sidewalk, and if for nothing else, for "resisting" (arrest). The principal cause of their conflict with the police was their smoking marijuana, probably harmless but definitely illegal. Such clear proof of the failure of the law to meet the knowledge of the age presented itself to the querulous[4] minds of hippies as sufficient grounds to condemn the law completely.

Hippies thought they saw on Haight Street that everyone's eyes were filled with loving joy and giving, but the eyes of the hippies were often in fact sorrowful and frightened, for they had plunged themselves into an experiment they were uncertain they could carry through. Fortified by LSD (*Better Living Through Chemistry*), they had come far enough to see distance behind them, but no clear course ahead. One branch of their philosophy was Oriental concentration and meditation; now it often focused upon the question "How to kick" (drugs).

The ennobling idea of the hippies, forgotten or lost in the visual scene, diverted by chemistry, was their plan for *community*. For *community* they had come. What kind of community, upon what model? Hippies wore brilliant Mexican *chalecos*, Oriental robes, and red-Indian headdress. They dressed as cowboys. They dressed as frontiersmen. They dressed as Puritans. Doubtful who they were, trying on new clothes, how could they know where they were going until they saw what fit? They wore military insignia. Among bracelets and bells they wore Nazi swastikas and the German Iron Cross, knowing, without knowing much more, that the swastika offended the Establishment, and no enemy of the Establishment could be all bad. They had been born, give or take a year or two, in the year of Hiroshima.

[4] disposed to complaining

Once the visual scene was ignored, almost the first point of interest about the hippies was that they were middle-class American children to the bone. To citizens inclined to alarm this was the thing most maddening, that these were not Negroes disaffected[5] by color or immigrants by strangeness but boys and girls with white skins from the right side of the economy in all-American cities and towns from Honolulu to Baltimore. After regular educations, if only they'd want them, they could commute to fine jobs from the suburbs, and own nice houses with bathrooms, where they could shave and wash up.

Many hippies lived with the help of remittances from home, whose parents, so straight, so square, so seemingly compliant, rejected, in fact, a great portion of that official American program rejected by the hippies in psychedelic script. *The 19th Century Was A Mistake The 20th Century Is A Disaster.* Even in arrest they found approval from their parents, who had taught them in years of civil rights and resistance to the war in Vietnam that authority was often questionable, sometimes despicable. George F. Babbitt, forty years before in Zenith, U.S.A., declared his hope, at the end of

[5] alienated

45

a famous book, that his son might go farther than Babbitt had dared along lines of break and rebellion.

When hippies first came to San Francisco they were an isolated minority, mistrustful, turned inward by drugs, lacking acquaintance beyond themselves. But they were spirited enough, after all, to have fled from home, to have endured the discomforts of a cramped existence along Haight Street, proud enough to have endured the insults of the police, and alert enough to have identified the major calamities of their age.

". . . hippies were Puritan Americans, gorged with moral purpose, and loath to confess that their captivation was basically the pursuit of pleasure."

In part a hoax of American journalism, known even to themselves only as they saw themselves in the media, they began at last, and especially with the approach of the "summer of love," to assess their community, their quest, and themselves.

They slowly became, in the word that seemed to cover it, polarized,[6] distinct in division among themselves between, on one hand, weekend or summertime hippies, and on the other, hippies for whom the visual scene was an insubstantial substitute for genuine community. The most perceptive or advanced among the hippies then began to undertake the labor of community which could be accomplished only behind the scene, out of the eye of the camera, beyond the will of the quick reporter.

*T*he visual scene was four blocks long on Haight Street. Haight Street itself was nineteen, extending east two miles from Golden Gate Park, through the visual scene, through a portion of the Negro district known as the Fillmore, past the former campus of San Francisco State College, and flowing at its terminus into Market Street, into the straight city, across the Bay Bridge, and into that wider United States whose values the hippies

[6] divided

were testing, whose traditions were their own propulsion in spite of their denials, and whose future the hippies might yet affect in singular ways unimagined by either those States or those hippies. From the corner of Haight and Ashbury Streets it was three miles to Broadway and Columbus, heart of North Beach, where the Beats had gathered ten years before.

The Haight-Ashbury district is a hundred square blocks of homes and parks. One of the parks is the Panhandle of Golden Gate, thrusting itself into the district, preserving, eight blocks long, a green and lovely relief unimpaired by prohibitions against free play by children or the free promenade of adults along its mall. Planted in pine, maple, redwood, and eucalyptus, its only serious resistance to natural things is a statue honoring William McKinley, but consigned to the farthest extremity, for which, in 1903, Theodore Roosevelt broke the ground.

The Panhandle is the symbolic and spiritual center of the district, its stay against confusion. On March 28, 1966, after a struggle of several years—and by a single vote of the San Francisco Supervisors—the residents of the Haight-Ashbury district were able to rescue the Panhandle from the bulldozer, which would have replaced it with a freeway assisting commuters to save six minutes between downtown and the Golden Gate Bridge.

In one of the few triumphs of neighborhood over redevelopment the power of the district lay in the spiritual and intellecutal composition of its population, which tended toward firm views of the necessity to save six minutes and toward a skeptical view of the promise of "developers" to "plant it over" afterward. Apart from the Panhandle controversy, the people of the district had firm views clustering about the conviction that three-story Tudor and Victorian dwellings are preferable to skyscrapers, that streets should serve people before automobiles, that a neighborhood was meant for living as well as sleeping, that habitation implies some human dirt, that small shops foster human acquaintance as department stores don't, and that schools which are integrated are more educational than schools which are segregated.

One of the effects of the victory of the bulldozer would have been the obliteration of low-cost housing adjacent to the Panhandle, and therefore the disappearance of poorer people from the district. But the people of the Haight-Ashbury failed of enthusiasm. "Fair streets are better than silver," wrote Vachel Lindsay, leading hippie of Springfield, Illinois, half a century ago, and considered that part of his message central enough to carry it in psychedelic banners on the end pages of his *Collected Poems*:

> Fair streets are better than silver.
> Green parks are better than gold.
> Bad public taste is mob law.
> Good public taste is democracy.
> A crude administration is damned already.
> A bad designer is to that extent a bad citizen.
> Let the best moods of the people rule.

The Haight-Ashbury—to give it its San Francisco sound—had long been a favorite residential area for persons of liberal disposition in many occupations, in business, labor, the arts, the professions, and academic life. It had been equally hospitable to avant-garde[7] expression, to racial diversity, and to the Okies and Arkies who came after World War II. Its polyglot[8] population, estimated at 30,000, was predominantly white, but it included Negroes and Orientals in sizable numbers and general distribution, and immigrants of many nations. Here William Saroyan and Erskine Caldwell had lived.

During the decade of the sixties it was a positive attraction to many San Franciscans who could easily have lived at "better addresses" but who chose the Haight-Ashbury for its congeniality and cultural range. Here they could prove to anyone who cared, and especially to their children, the possibilities of racial integration. The Haight-Ashbury was the only neighborhood in the nation, as far as I know, to send its own delegation—one white man, one Negro woman—to the civil rights March on Washington in 1963.

Wealth and comfort ascended with the hills in the southern portion of the district. In the low, flat streets near the Panhandle, where the hippies lived, the residents were poorer, darker, and more likely to be of foreign extraction. There, too, students and young artists lived, and numbers of white families who had chosen the perils of integration above the loss of their proximity to the Panhandle. With the threat of the freeway many families had moved away and many stores had become vacant, and when the threat had passed, a vacuum remained.

[7] the most advanced and daring
[8] speaking several languages

The hippies came, lured by availability, low rents, low prices, and the spirit of historic openness. The prevailing weather was good in a city where weather varied with the contours of hills. Here a hippie might live barefoot most of the months of the year, lounge in sunswept doorways slightly out of the wind, and be fairly certain that political liberals, bedeviled Negroes, and propertyless whites were more likely than neighbors elsewhere to admit him to community.

The mood of the Haight-Ashbury ranged from occasional opposition to the hippies to serene indifference, to tolerance, to interest, and to delight. As trouble increased between hippies and police, and as alarm increased elsewhere in the city, the Haight-Ashbury kept its head. It valued the passions of the young, especially when the young were, as hippies were, nonviolent. No doubt, at least among liberals, it saw something of its own earlier life in the lives of hippies.

Last March the Haight-Ashbury Neighborhood Council, formed in 1957 to meet a crisis similar to the Panhandle controversy, committed itself to a policy of extended patience. It declared that "we particularly resent the official position of law-enforcement agencies, as announced by [Police] Chief Cahill, that hippies are not an asset to the community. The chief has not distinguished among the many kinds of citizens who comprise the hippie culture. . . . War against a class of citizens, regardless of how they dress or choose to live, within the latitude of the law, is intolerable in a free society. We remember the regrettable history of officially condoned crusades against the Chinese population of San Francisco whose life style did not meet with the approval of the established community and whose lives and property were objects of terrorism and persecution."

If any neighborhood in America was prepared to accommodate the hippies, it was the Haight-Ashbury. On the heights and on the level rich and poor were by and large secure, open, liberal, pro-civil-rights, and in high proportion anti-war. Its U.S. congressman was Philip Burton, a firm and forthright liberal, and its California assemblyman was Willie Brown, a Negro of unquestioned intellect and integrity. Here the hippies might gain time to shape their message and translate to coherence the confusion of the visual scene. If the hippies were unable to make, of all scenes, the Haight-Ashbury scene, then there was something wrong with *them*.

The principal distinction between the hippies and every other endeavor in utopian[9] community was LSD, which concentrated upon the liver, produced chemical change in the body, and thereby affected the brain. Whether LSD produced physical harm remained an argument, but its most ardent advocates and users (not always the same persons) never denied its potentially dangerous emotional effects. Those effects depended a great deal on the user's predisposition. Among the hippies of San Francisco, LSD precipitated suicide and other forms of self-destructive or antisocial behavior. For some hippies it produced little or nothing, and was therefore a disappointment. For many, it precipitated gorgeous hallucinations, a wide variety of sensual perceptions never before available to the user, and breathtaking panoramic visions of human and social perfection accompanied by profound insights into the user's own past.

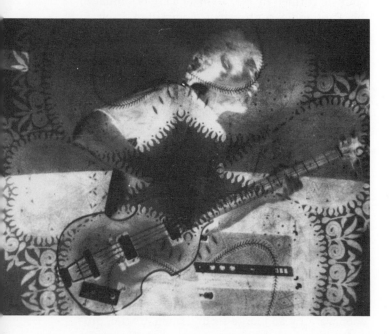

It could be manufactured in large quantities by simple processes, like gin in a bathtub, easily carried about, and easily retained without detection. In liquid it was odorless and colorless; in powder it was minute. Its administration required no needles or other paraphernalia, and since it was taken orally, it left no "tracks" upon the body.

[9] ideal

Technically it was nonaddictive, but it conspicuously induced in the user—the younger he was, the more so—a strong desire for another "trip": the pleasures of life under LSD exceeded the realities of sober perception. More far-reaching than liquor, quicker for insights than college or psychiatry, the pure and instant magic of LSD appeared for an interesting moment to capture the mind of the hippies. Everybody loved a panacea.[10]

Their text was *The Psychedelic Experience*, by Leary, Metzner, and Alpert, "a manual based on the Tibetan Book of the Dead," whose jacket assured the reader that the book had been completed free of academic auspices.[11] It was likely that the hippies' interest in the book lay, in any case, rather in its use as "manual" than in its historical reference.

Bob Dylan, favorite of many hippies, told in a line of song, "To live outside the law you must be honest." But hippies were Puritan Americans, gorged with moral purpose, and loath to confess that their captivation was basically the pursuit of pleasure. They therefore attached to the mystique of LSD the conviction that by opening their minds to chemical visions they were gaining insights from which society soon should profit.

Hippies themselves might have profited, as anyone might, from LSD in a clinical environment, but the direction of their confidence lay elsewhere, and they placed themselves beneath the supervision mainly of other hippies. Dialogue was confined among themselves, no light was shed upon the meaning of their visions, and their preoccupation became LSD itself—what it did to them last time, and what it might do next. Tool had become symbol, and symbol principle. If the hippie ideal of community failed, it would fail upon lines of a dull, familiar scheme: the means had become the end.

Far from achieving an exemplary[12] community of their own, with connections to existing community, the hippies had achieved only, in the language of one of their vanguard,[13] "a community of acid-heads." If LSD was all the hippies talked about, the outlying community could hardly be blamed for thinking this was all they were. Visions of community seen under LSD had not been imparted to anyone, remaining visible only to hip-

[10] cure-all
[11] guidance
[12] model
[13] the front runners of a movement

pies, or entering the visual scene only in the form of commentary upon LSD itself, jokes and claims for its efficacy growing shriller with the increase of dependence. But the argument had been that LSD inspired transcendence,[14] that it was, as one hippie phrased it, "a stepping-stone to get out of your environment and look at it."

Under the influence of LSD hippies had written things down, or drawn pictures, but upon examination the writings or the pictures proved less perfect than they had appeared while the trip was on. Great utterances delivered under LSD were somehow unutterable otherwise. Great thoughts the hippies had thought under LSD they could never soberly convey, nor reproduce the startling new designs for happier social arrangements.

Two years after the clear beginnings of the hippies in San Francisco, a date established by the opening of the Psychedelic Shop, hippies and others had begun to recognize that LSD, if it had not failed, had surely not fully succeeded. ("We have serious doubts," said a Quaker report, "whether drugs offer the spiritual illumination which bears fruit in Christlike lives.") Perhaps, as some hippies claimed, their perceptions had quickened, carrying them forward to a point of social readiness. It had turned them on, then off.

Whatever the explanation, by the time of the "summer of love" their relationship with the surrounding community had badly deteriorated. The most obvious failure of perception was the hippies' failure to discriminate among elements of the Establishment, whether in the Haight-Ashbury or in San Francisco in general. Their paranoia[15] was the paranoia of all youthful heretics. *Even Paranoids Have Real Enemies.* True. But they saw all the world as straight but them; all cops were brutes, and everyone else was an arm of the cops. Disaffiliating with all persons and all institutions but themselves, they disaffiliated with all possible foundations of community.

It was only partly true, as hippies complained, that "the Establishment isn't listening to us." The Establishment never listened to anyone until it was forced to. That segment of the Establishment known as the Haight-Ashbury, having welcomed the hippies with friendliness and hope, had listened with more courtesy to hippies than hippies had listened to the Haight-Ashbury.

Hippies had theories of community, theories of work, theories of child care, theories of creativity. Creative hippies were extremely creative about things the city and the district could do for them. For example, the city could cease harassing hippies who picked flowers in Golden Gate Park to give them away on Haight Street. The city replied that the flowers of Golden Gate Park were for all people—were *community* flowers—and suggested that hippies plant flowers of their own. Hippies imagined an all-powerful city presided over by an all-powerful mayor who, said a hippie, "wants to stop human growth." They imagined an all-powerful Board of Supervisors which with inexhaustible funds could solve all problems simultaneously if only it wanted to.

Their illusions, their unreason, their devil theories, their inexperience of life, and their failures of perception had begun to persuade even the more sympathetic elements of the Haight-Ashbury that the hippies perhaps failed of perception in general. The failure of the hippies to communicate reasonably cast doubt upon their reliability as observers, especially with respect to the most abrasive of all issues, their relationship with the police.

Was it merely proof of its basic old rigidity that the Haight-Ashbury believed that community implied social relief, that visions implied translation to social action? *Squares Love, Too: Haight-Ashbury For All People.* So read an answering campaign pin as friction increased. But the hippies, declining self-regulation, aloof, self-absorbed, dumped mountains of garbage on the Panhandle. The venereal rate of the Haight-Ashbury multiplied by six. (The hippies accused Dr. Ellis Sox of the health department of sexual repression.) The danger grew alarmingly of rats, food poisoning, hepatitis, pulmonary tuberculosis, and of meningitis caused by overcrowded housing. "If hippies don't want to observe city and state laws," said Dr. Sox, "let them at least observe a few natural laws."

Hippies behaved so much like visitors to the community that their neighbors, who intended to live in the district forever, questioned whether proclamations of community did not require *acts* of community. Hippies had theories of love, which might have meant, at the simplest level, muting music for the benefit of neighbors who must rise in the morning for work. Would the Haight-Ashbury once again, if the emergency arose, expend years of its life to retain a Panhandle for hippies

---

[14] going beyond the limits of normal experience
[15] mental disorder characterized by delusions of persecution

50 to dump their garbage on? Or would it abandon the hippies to the most primitive interpretations of law, permit their dispersion, and see their experiment end without beginning?

At no point was the hippies' failure to seek community so apparent as with relation to the Negroes of the district. With the passage of the civil rights movement from demonstrations to legal implementation excellent opportunities existed for the show of love. What grand new design in black and white had hippies seen under LSD? If Negroes were expected to share with hippies the gestures of love, then hippies ought to have shared with Negroes visions of equal rights.

The burdens of the Negroes of the district were real. Negro tenants *desired* the attention of the health department, *desired* the attention of agencies whom hippies monopolized with appeals for food and housing for the "summer of love." The needs of the Negroes, especially for jobs, appeared to Negroes a great deal more urgent than the needs of white middle-class hippies who had dropped out of affluence to play games of poverty in San Francisco. "Things should be given away free," said a Negro man in a public debate, "to people that *really* need them."

One afternoon, on Masonic Street, a hundred feet off Haight, I saw a Negro boy, perhaps twelve years old, repairing an old bicycle that had been repaired before. His tools lay on the sidewalk beside him, arranged in a systematic way, as if according to an order he had learned from his father. His face was intent, the work was complicated. Nearby, the hippies masqueraded. I mentioned to a lady the small boy at work, the big boys at play. "Yes," she said, "the hippies have usurped the prerogatives of children—to dress up and be irresponsible."

THE POLARIZATION OF THE HIPPIES

A hippie record is entitled *Notes From Underground.* The hippie behind the counter told me that "underground" was a hippie word. He had not yet heard of Dostoevsky, whose title the record borrowed, or of the antislavery underground in America, or of the World War II underground in France. A movement which thought itself the world's first underground was bound to make mistakes it could have avoided by consultation with the past, and there was evidence that the hippies had begun to know it.

Nobody asked the hippies to accept or acknowledge the texts of the past. Their reading revealed their search for self-help, not conducted among the traditional books of the Western world but of the Orient—in *I Ching* and *The Prophet,* and in the novels of the German Hermann Hesse, especially the "Oriental" *Siddhartha.* Betrayed by science and reason, hippies indulged earnestly in the occult,[16] the astrological, the mystical, the horoscopic, and the Ouija. Did hippies know that Ouija boards were a popular fad not long ago?

Or did they know that *The Prophet* of Kahlil Gibran, reprinted seventy-seven times since 1923, lies well within the tradition of American self-help subliterature? No sillier book exists, whose "prose poetry," faintly biblical, offers homiletic[17] advice covering one by one all the departments of life (On Love, On Marriage, On Children, On Giving, On Eating and Drinking, On Work—on and on) in a manner so ambiguous as to permit the reader to interpret all tendencies as acceptable and to end by doing as he pleases, as if with the sanction of the prophet.

Hesse was a German, born in 1877, who turned consciously to romantic expression after age forty, but the wide interest of the hippies in *Siddhartha* is less conscious than Hesse's. To the hero's search for unity between self and nature they respond as German youth responded to Hesse, or as an earlier generation of Americans responded to the spacious, ambiguous outcry of Thomas Wolfe.

Inevitably, they were going through all these things twice, unaware of things gone through before. Inherent in everything printed or hanging in the visual scene on Haight Street was satirical rejection of cultural platitudes,[18] but in the very form and style of the platitudes themselves. Children of television, they parodied it, spoofing Batman, as if Batman mattered. The satire in which they rejoiced was television's own artistic outpost. The walls of Haight Street bore, at a better level, the stamp of *Mad* magazine or collages satirizing the chaos of advertising: but anyone could see the same who turned the pages of *Reader's Digest* fast.

Of all the ways in which hippies began to polarize toward work their withdrawal from the visual scene was most astute.[19] They had begun to learn, after flight, rebellion, and the pleasures of

---

[16] the magical arts and practices
[17] sermon-like
[18] commonplace or trite statements, ideas, or patterns of behavior
[19] shrewd

satirizing things they hoped they could reject, that work requires solitude and privacy, and that to work well means to resist the shaping influence of the media, abandoning the visual scene to those whom it gratifies.

The ideal of work—not simply jobs, but meaningful work, work as service—had been a hippie ideal from the outset. The apprehension of quiet, positive acts as meaningful, requiring time and *liaison*,[20] was a more difficult act than parading the streets in costume. The act of extending community beyond oneself, beyond other hippies, beyond the comfort of drugs to the wider community of diverse color and class was nearer than hippies had thought to the unity of self and nature.

At the start, it was frightening to undertake. Finally, it was instructive and exalting. To share *community*, to arrive finally at the meaning of one's own world, was to feel life from a point of view formerly hidden from oneself, and only partly revealed by mystical reading. Self-regulation was more satisfying than regulation by the police, and conformity to enduring objectives more liberating finally than chemical visions.

The hippies patrolled their garbage—the "sweep-in"—and modulated their music. If such acts were this side millennium,[21] they were nevertheless gestures of community reflecting an emergence of the hippies from the isolation of their first two years in San Francisco. Acquaintance with the straight community increased as work and work projects proliferated. Acquaintance produced degrees of trust and accurate identity. Generalizations failed. Not all straights were pure straight, even as hippies differed one from another.

*T*he life of the hippie community began to reveal a history of its own. It had evolved through flight, drugs, and conflict, and back into the straight world, which it now knew in a manner different from before. To direct the Hip Job Co-op, the Free Store, public feedings in the Panhandle, to produce even one memorable edition of the *Oracle* (Volume I, Number 7, preserving the essence of hippie theory in debate among Ginsberg, Leary, Snyder, and Watts) required a pooling of skills, resources, and confrontation with the straight

community. It meant, even, coming face to face with the telephone company, and it meant, as well, the ironic recognition that necessary work invited imitation of the very processes hippies had formerly despised. To purchase houses to shelter hippies, food to feed them, required compromise with the community, a show of dependable intentions. In the language of Leonard Wolf, San Francisco State College professor who organized formal instruction among hippies, it required "coming to terms with the ethical quandary[22] of money." Projects with long-range implications, such as the purchase of rural sites for hippie communities, required leadership, planning, authority, discipline, and more or less continuous sobriety.

At some moments the process of learning was almost visible. "The American passion is murder," said a hippie spokesman, challenging a straight audience of physicians, lawyers, teachers, and others, including police officers, to rise and shout him down. None of his listeners betrayed alarm—some feared that his words were too true. "I would like to see the American Establishment give more examples of love, and fewer pronouncements." He appeared suddenly to be aware that he had heard these sentiments before, and indeed it was a complaint some members of the Establishment had made forever and ever. Hippies were scarcely the first to discover hypocrisy.

A hippie said, at the same meeting, "The American empire is driving our sons and daughters to Haight Street. All America knows is profit and property. We all know . . ."—that is, we all just this minute realized; that was to say, *he* just this minute realized—"we all know all we need to know to act, but we don't act. Everyone knows what's wrong . . ." perceiving in that moment a straight community which shared with him, among other things, its powerlessness. It, too, had fought its battles with authority, and he saw it now in its diversity, rather than as monolith.[23]

At such moments of meeting hippies knew sensations of reconciliation and escape from their own isolation. They learned, as American minorities before them had learned, that nothing was more instructive about human life than to have been a minority group, and to have emerged. Acquaintance clarified: straights had not so much

---

[20] relationship or connection with people or agencies
[21] a period of happiness and prosperity

[22] predicament
[23] single, large, uniform block

52 opposed drugs or dirt as their inefficiency; runaway children broke real hearts; plagues of rats, by the agreement of mankind, were unaesthetic; straights, too, resisted work, yearned for varieties of love, and found the balance. Frank Kavanaugh, teacher at a Catholic high school, resident of the Haight-Ashbury for fourteen years, summarized the positive aspects of polarization in a public statement widely applauded. He wrote in part:

I would estimate that even though there have been many unwelcome incidents occasioned by both the old and new community, there has still arisen an area of understanding and mutual appreciation. I would describe it in this fashion. The new community by its rejection of certain middle-class attitudes of comfort, security, position, and property has pointed out to us our exaggerated concern for these material distractions. In their effort to create new life styles based on personalism and simple awareness of the basic joys of sensible creation, they make us more aware of the overlooked pleasures of colors, sounds, trees, children, smiles. Yet I think that they have learned much from us too. They have learned that the neighborhood in which they have chosen to demonstrate their rejection of middle-class conformity is not such a bad neighborhood after all. If they have been the victims of generalized attitudes by authority, they have also been the perpetrators of generalized attitudes themselves. Not all middle-class people are squares. Generally speaking, upon the close, personal examination of any square by any hippie, the sharp corners soften considerably and the image of a human being appears. . . . Given more time and the absence of undue friction, the dialogue could bear rich fruit. The old and new could form one community, unique and rich in human resources, a community that could demonstrate that such a neighborhood could flourish despite the system; indeed, one that could bear the seed for a joyous revolution of attitudes in the entire city and produce a large urban community based on the real needs of its inhabitants.

The hippies had come for help. The freedom of cities had always attracted a significant segment of every generation seeking to resolve American dilemmas unrestrained by commitments to family obligations in home communities. New York and Chicago had always known waves of hippies fleeing Winesburg, Ohio. In San Francisco, as hippies engaged in public dialogue, they forced the city to examine and modify standing practices. Laws governing marijuana became exposed for their paradoxes. Accurate information on drugs be-

came an objective. Police methods were reviewed. Perhaps the most useful debate involved new and imaginative uses of public facilities: a city which could entertain and amuse immense conventions, sporting crowds, providing for visitors luxurious frivolities of every kind, could, for example, release Kezar Stadium, site of professional football during certain seasons, to the tents of hippies for their "summer of love." Haight-Ashbury Assemblyman Willie Brown, in a letter to the Supervisors, placed in perspective the nature of the conflicting forces: "It appears to me that you are in danger of making a very fundamental mistake concerning both your own identity and that of the young people who are coming to us. *They* are not some horde of invading foreigners. They are our children, yours and mine, exercising their right to move freely about a country which will soon be very much their own. You for your part are not some select group of medieval chieftains who can, at will, close up your town and withdraw behind the walls of your own closed society. The City of St. Francis deserves better from you. Whether we like or dislike, agree or disagree with the 'Hip' community is not the issue here. The issue *is* whether you can by fiat[24] declare a minority unwelcome in our community. If you declare against these young people today, what minority is going to bear the brunt of your discrimination tomorrow?"

THE COP'S DIRECTIVE

Somewhat forgotten among general fears was the hippies' unwavering adherence to the ideal of nonviolence. Miraculously, they retained it in a community and in a world whose easiest tendency was guns. For that virtue, if for no other, they valuably challenged American life. If they did not oppose the war in Vietnam in the way of organized groups, they opposed it by the argument of example, avoiding violence under all circumstances. They owned no guns. By contrast, the manner in which the major Establishment of San Francisco approached the hippies chillingly suggested the basis of American failure abroad: never questioning its own values, lacking the instinct for difficult dialogue, it sought to suppress by exclusion; exclusion failing, it was prepared to call the police.

The trouble on the visual scene was drugs, and drugs brought cops; the trouble was runaway children (some as young as ten years old) lost among

[24] positive, authoritative order

hippies, and runaway children brought cops; dirty books brought cops. The trouble was hazardous housing, which brought the health department, and in the wake of the health department, cops.

The trouble with the police, from the point of view of the hippies, was false arrest, illegal arrest, incitement to arrest, cops with swinging clubs, obscene cops diseased by racial hatred, and the tendency of any appearance by police to stimulate excitement where none had been. They accused cops of accepting bribes from drug peddlers and then arresting users, and they singled out a few officers whose zeal for the enforcement of standard morality exceeded reason. The cop was the enemy-visible in a marked car, whom hippies

viewed as the living symbol of all the vice and hypocrisy of the Establishment.

The San Francisco cop had never lived in the Haight-Ashbury. Now, by and large, he lived in the Richmond, the Sunset, or within the thirty-mile suburban radius established by law, in a house with a patch of grass and a garage with an oil-proof floor he might live long enough to pay for. He earned $9000 for a forty-nine-week year, and he would receive a pension at age sixty-five, of after thirty years of service. He read his Hearst newspaper and watched television and went to church and Candlestick Park. He hated the sound of sirens: his occupational hazard was heart failure at an early age from too many surges of adrenalin.

54   For the San Francisco cop the sixties had been, said one, "the age of riots," not food riots, not labor strikes, for objectives or upon principles he understood, but disorders emanating from obscure causes and upheld for their justice by those elements of the community the cop had always associated with normal process and quietude. Said the same cop: "I am caught in the bind of history."

The first significant confrontation of the decade between police and the new antagonist occurred on Friday, May 13, 1960, in the rotunda of city hall, where several hundred persons had gathered to attend, in a spirit of protest, a hearing of a House Committee on Un-American Activities. Denied admission to the hearing room, the crowd sang, chanted, and appeared to represent potential violence. Four hundred policemen, a contingent larger than the gathering itself, dispersed the crowd with clubs and fire hoses, jailed more than fifty persons, brought one to trial (a Berkeley student)—and failed to convict him.

But to the astonishment of the cop, in so clear a case, instead of commendation from a grateful public for having quelled a disorder, he was abused for his "brutality." The next day thousands of persons gathered at various points of the city to protest not only the continued presence of the subcommittee, but also the cop, the two causes becoming one. In the years which followed, all issues were to be repeatedly merged with the issue of police action: the cop himself became an issue.

The San Francisco Police Department, between 1960 and 1967, undertook liberal reforms never dramatic enough to please its critics. Its leadership had always been proud of the department's flexibility, its openness to innovation. It was the *servant* of the city. Now, in a new climate, it intended to acquaint itself with new problems, especially the problems of racial or temperamental minorities.

The creation in 1962 of a Community Relations Unit, which grew from two members to thirteen, was an experiment of remarkable promise and frequent achievement. Its goal was to anticipate commotion rather than to react in panic, to understand the aims of dissident groups, and to survey rather than to arrest. The role of the unit was to provide "feedback" between police and public, often by sponsoring or attending public meetings where dialogue might ensue between citizen and cop, who had never before met.

The unit wore no uniform, made no arrests, and identified itself wherever it went. Honorably, it never carried back hard information to the department. It had somewhat the aspect of the intellectual wing of the police asking *why*, never *who*, though the position was relative, and in the short run it was a long way down the line from the new, informed, even theoretical cop to the rank-and-file cop in the car, riding scared, feeling himself surrounded by alien and sinister forces, feeling eyes of contempt and hatred upon him, anxious for his own safety, and moved finally to rely upon the same old weapons he still treasured above all sociology, all theory, and all goodwill.

He was a better-informed, more feeling cop than he had been eight years before, but he could never quite remain abreast of history. He had learned to accept the aspirations of Negroes, but he was now confronted by hippies, who were patently and undeniably breaking laws for reasons beyond the cop's comprehension. The Beats, who were the forerunners of the hippies, had obstructed the sidewalks of North Beach and offended cops by their strange untidiness, but they had gathered in a traditional bohemian quarter, and they were *beat,* they admitted it, prepared to flee.

The instinct of the cop was ancient: break the law, be punished. Typical of the citizenry of San Francisco, his heart the repository of all populist values, the cop would uphold the law at every stage of its interpretation. In the main, he transcended his emotions. He waited to see whether the hippies would triumph over their visual scene, whether their shift from street to community would occur before the Haight-Ashbury or the city beyond arrived at last at disenchantment. If the Haight-Ashbury abandoned the hippies the mood of the city at large would be released in the direction of his own gut responses. Then the anxiety of the cop would be shared by all powers, the nervous system of the cop, the city, and the Haight-Ashbury would vibrate upon one note. Then the directive of the cop would be clear. Then the cop *would* move in.

Death
at an Early Age

JONATHAN KOZOL

Someday, maybe," Erik Erikson has written, "there will exist a well-informed, well-considered and yet fervent[1] public conviction that the most deadly of all possible sins is the mutilation of a child's spirit."

If that day ever comes, American educators may be able to reflect with some horror upon the attitudes and procedures that have been allowed to flourish within a great many urban public schools.

It is a commonplace by now to say that the urban school systems of America contain a higher percentage of Negro children each year. More than anywhere else, it is here within these ghetto systems that the mutilation of which Erikson speaks becomes apparent. My own experience took place in Boston, in a segregated fourth-grade classroom. The Boston school system is not perhaps the worst offender, but it provides a clear example of the kind of education being offered the disadvantaged children of many cities. There are, admittedly, in Boston a cluster of unusually discouraging problems, chief among them the school administration's refusal for a great many years to recognize that there *was* any problem. Only slightly less troubling has been the exceptional virulence[2] of the anti-Negro prejudice, both among teachers and the general public. Yet Boston's problems are not much different from those of other cities, and the solutions here as elsewhere will have to await a change in attitude at all levels of society.

Stephen is an eight-year-old pupil in the Boston public schools. A picture of him standing in front of a bulletin board on Arab bedouins shows a little light-brown person staring with unusual concentration at a chosen spot upon the floor. Stephen is tiny, desperate, unwell. Sometimes he talks to himself, or laughs out loud in class for no apparent reason. He is also an indescribably mild and unmalicious child. He cannot do any of his schoolwork very well. His math and reading are poor. In third grade his class had substitute teachers much of the year. Most of the year before that he had substitute teachers too. He is in the fourth grade now, but his work is barely at the level of the second.

Nobody has complained about Stephen's situation because he does not have a real family. Stephen is a ward of the Commonwealth of Massachusetts, and as such has been placed in the home of some very poor people who do not want him now that he is not a baby anymore. He often comes to school badly beaten. If I ask him about it, he is apt to deny it because he does not want us to know what a miserable time he has. He lied to me first when I asked him how his eye got battered, claiming that it was an accident. Later, he admitted that his foster mother had flung him out onto the porch.

Although Stephen did poorly in his schoolwork, there was one thing he could do well: he made delightful drawings. They were not neat and orderly and organized, but random and casual, messy, somewhat unpredictable. For these drawings Stephen received terrific and steady embarrassment from the art teacher.*

The art teacher was a lady no longer very young who had a number of fixed opinions about children and teaching. Her most common technique of instruction was to pass out mimeographed designs, which the pupils then were asked to color according to a dictated or suggested plan. An alternate approach was to stick up on the wall or the blackboard some of the drawings that had been done in previous years by predominantly white classes. These drawings, neat and ordered and very uniform, would serve as models for the

[1] intense, burning
[2] infectiousness, poison

From **Death at an Early Age** by Jonathan Kozol. Reprinted by permission of Houghton Mifflin Company.

* Our school was assigned a number of experts in different subject areas, which was the result of our participation in the Boston version of a compensatory program for Negro children. The compensation involved was, in fact, of a questionable nature. When Boston lost $2 million in federal aid for compensatory education, the reason given was that the federal government did not consider Boston's program to be offering any kind of legitimate compensation. It should be added, of course, that experts, teachers, and administrators described in this article are composites.

56 children. The neatest and most accurate reproductions would receive the greatest applause.

Stephen was unable to cope with a teacher of this sort. He turned off his signals when she was speaking and withdrew into his own private world. With a pencil, frequently stubby and bitten, he would scribble and fiddle, and he would cock his head and whisper to himself. After a while, he would push aside his little drawing and try the paint and paper that he had been given, usually using the watercolors freely and a little defiantly, and he would produce paintings that were very full of his own nature.

". . . Irish children were once whipped by Yankee teachers . . . Jewish children, in turn, by Irish. . . . corporal punishment today is being used by whites on Negroes, and being used in too many cases to act out, on a number of persuasive pretexts, a deeply seated racial hate."

If Stephen began to fiddle around during a lesson, he and I and the children near him would prepare for trouble. The art teacher would rush at his desk and would shriek at him, "Give me that! You've made a mess! Look what he's done! He's mixed up the colors! I don't know why we waste good paper on this child!" Then: "Garbage! Junk! He gives me garbage and junk! And garbage is one thing I will not have!"

I do not know a great deal about painting, but the art teacher did not know much about it either, and furthermore, she did not know or care at all about the way a human being can be destroyed. Stephen, in many ways already dying, died many more times before her anger.

Much of Stephen's life, inwardly and outwardly, involved a steady, and as it turned out, losing, battle to survive. Like many defenseless humans, he had to use whatever little weapons came to hand. Acting-up at school was part of it. He was granted so little attention that he must have panicked repeatedly about the possibility that with a few slight mistakes, he might simply stop existing or being seen at all. This is why, I imagine, he seemed so often to invite a tongue-lashing or whipping. Outside school, he might pull a fire-alarm lever and then have the satisfaction of hearing the sirens and seeing the fire engines, and knowing that it was all his doing, so that at least he could have proof in this way that his hands and arm muscles and his mischievous imagination did count for something measurable in the world. It must have seemed better than not having any use at all.

One time, seeing him curled up in one of the corners, I tried to get him to look up at me and smile and talk. He refused, and remained shriveled and silent, and so I said to him: "Stephen, if you curl up like that and will not even look up at me, it will just seem as if you want to make me think you are a little rat." He looked down at himself hurriedly, and then up at me, chuckled grotesquely, and said, with a pitiful little smile: "I *know* I couldn't be a rat, Mr. Kozol, because a rat has got to have a little tail."

When I later repeated this to a child psychiatrist, he suggested that the absence of a tail was all that remained to convince Stephen that he had not yet become a rat. Although this comment might smack a bit of psychiatric dogmatism,[3] I do not really think it carried the point too far. For Boston schoolteachers for years have been speaking of their Negro children as "animals" and the school building that houses them as a "zoo." The repercussions of this attitude probably affected Stephen more than other children, but the price it exacted was paid ultimately by every child, and in the long run, I am convinced that it was paid by every teacher too.

*S*tephen's misery at school was only partially caused by the psychological harassment that I have been describing, for Stephen was also subjected to corporal[4] punishment regularly, in spite of the fact that he was obviously mentally unstable and had very little control over his behavior. Corporal punishment is still sanctioned in the Boston public schools and takes the form of beatings on the hand with a thin bamboo whip or rattan.

I don't know exactly how many times Stephen underwent these whippings, but unquestionably

[3] arrogant assertion of beliefs, perhaps not sufficiently tested by evidence
[4] physical

they occurred at least as often as once a month, and probably more often, closer to once or twice a week. They happened frequently when the class was having math instruction, and this, I came to believe, was connected with the unfriendliness that the math teacher felt toward Stephen. She spoke of it on more than one occasion, yet she was also aware of his mental instability, and she was the first to acknowledge it.

I remember when she discussed this with me, snapping out the words with sureness: "The child's not in his right mind." When I asked her whether she had thought of recommending psychiatric help for him, she replied that it was no use, since he would only tell the psychiatrist that all the teachers were prejudiced. A few days after this conversation, Stephen was sent to the cellar for another rattaning, and her comment, in accusation, not diagnosis or sympathy, was that he was "not in his right mind."

I would like to describe how Stephen behaved when he went downstairs to take his beating. I have said how little he was. Sixty pounds isn't very heavy, and he couldn't have been more than four feet tall. He had terrified tiny hopeless eyes. He had on a Red Sox baseball jersey, baggy corduroy pants, and baseball sneakers which looked a few sizes too large. His hair had oil in it, and it had been shaved down almost to the scalp. He was standing near the men's smoke room. Above were the pipes of the cellar ceiling, nearby the door to the basement boys' toilet. Out of that doorway came the stink of urine. His elbows froze at his sides. The teacher who administered the whipping gave the order to hold out his hands. He wouldn't respond. Again the teacher, standing above him, passed down the order. To no effect. The teacher, now losing patience, ordered it a third time. And still he wouldn't answer or comply. A fourth time. Still this frozen terror. So the decision is made: he will get it twice as many times.

He can't hold out forever. Finally he breaks down and stops resisting. The teacher who gives the beating may, in all other instances, seem a decent man. Even in giving this beating he may do it absolutely as he is supposed to. Yet, properly done or not, and whatever the man's intent, the tears still come, and the welts are formed upon the light-brown hand.

One obvious question immediately comes to mind. Why would *any* teacher whip a child for acts that the teacher has already acknowledged, both to himself and to others, to be beyond the child's ability to prevent? Perhaps a partial explanation lies in the fact that segregated schools seem to require this kind of brutal discipline because of the bitter feelings which are so often present in the air. The children—enough of them anyway—are constantly smoldering with a generally unrecognized awareness of their own degradation. The resulting atmosphere is deeply threatening to teachers and administrators.

Possibly in most cases, this is the entire story. Thinking of some of the teachers, however, I am convinced that something else was happening at times, and once you had watched it, you would know exactly what it was and would never deny that it was there. "This hurts me," goes the saying, "more than it hurts you." Yet there are moments when the visible glint of gratification becomes unmistakable in the white teacher's eyes.

White Bostonians sometimes argue that corporal punishment did not begin with Negro children,

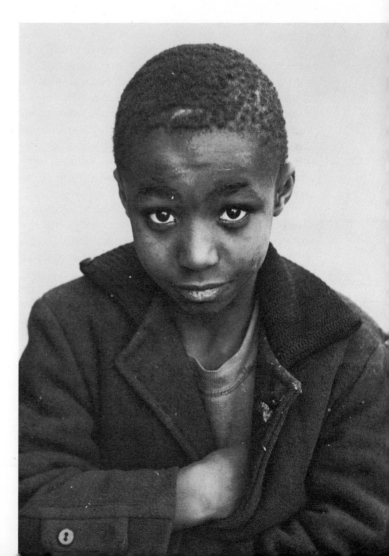

58 that it is, in fact, a very old tradition within the school system. I have never found this a convincing argument. The fact that a crime might have been committed with impunity[5] in the past may make it seem more familiar and less gruesome, but surely does not give it any greater legitimacy. Whether Irish children were once whipped by Yankee teachers, or Jewish children, in turn, by Irish, is immaterial. What does matter is that corporal punishment today is being used by whites on Negroes, and being used in too many cases to act out, on a number of persuasive pretexts, a deeply seated racial hate.

If just any tough teen-ager is beaten on the fingers by his teacher, one can assume that school officials will be able to pass it off as discipline. But when a sixty-pound mentally ill fourth-grader is whipped for acts that are manifestly crazy, and when the teacher who prepares the punishment has, not ten days before, been speaking calmly of the niggers down South, or the little bastards causing trouble up there in Room Four, then even the administrators of the system are going to have to admit that something has gone wrong.

*T*he room in which I taught my fourth grade was not really a room at all, but the corner of an auditorium. Three or four blackboards, two of them unstable, made the area seem a little bit set apart. The first time I approached that classroom I noticed a huge torn stage curtain, a couple of broken windows, and about thirty-five bewildered-looking children, most of whom were Negro. At the other end of the auditorium there was a classroom similar to mine.

The room was relatively quiet during the first hour of the morning. Not until ten o'clock did the bad cross fire start. By ten thirty it attained such a crescendo that the children in the back rows of my section couldn't hear my questions, and I couldn't hear their answers. The room, being large and wooden, echoed every sound. Sometimes the other fourth-grade teacher and I would stagger the lessons in which our classes had to recite aloud. But this makeshift method meant that one class had to be induced to maintain an unnatural rule of silence during major portions of the day. We couldn't always do it anyway, and usually the

only solution was to try to outshout each other, so that both of us often left school hoarse or wheezing.

Hours were lost in this manner, yet that was not the worst. Soon after I came into that auditorium, I discovered that our two fourth grades were also going to have to share the space with the glee club, with play rehearsals, special reading, special arithmetic, and at certain times a third- or fourth-grade phonics class. I began to make head counts of the numbers of pupils:

Seventy children from the two regular fourth grades before the invasion.

Then ninety with the glee club and remedial arithmetic.

One hundred and seven with the play rehearsal.

One day the sewing class came in with their sewing machines, and then that became a regular practice in the hall. Once I counted one hundred and twenty people, all talking, singing, yelling, laughing, reciting. Before the Christmas break it became apocalyptic. Not more than half of the planned lessons took place throughout that time.

One day a window whose frame had rotted was blown right out of its sashes by a strong gust of wind. I had noticed several times before that it was in bad condition, but so many other things were broken in the school building that I had not said anything about it. The principal and custodians and other people had been in that building for a long time before me. I felt they must have known the condition of the window. If anything could have been done, I assumed they would have done it.

First there was a cracking sound, then a burst of icy air. The next thing I knew, a child was saying: "Mr. Kozol—look at the window!" As I turned, it was starting to fall in. I was standing by coincidence, only about four or five feet off and was able to catch it. But the wind was so strong that it nearly blew right out of my hands. A couple of seconds of good luck kept glass from the desks of six or seven children and very possibly saved several of them from being injured. I soon realized that I was not going to be able to hold the thing up by myself, and I was obliged to ask one of the stronger boys in the class to give me a hand. Meanwhile, as the children beneath us shivered in the icy wind, and as the two of us now shivered also since the mercury was hovering close to zero, I asked one of the children in the front row to run down and fetch the janitor.

[5] freedom from punishment

When he asked me what he should tell him, I said, "Tell him the house is falling in." The children laughed. It was the first time I had ever said anything like that when the children could hear me. I am sure my reluctance to speak out more often must appear odd to many readers, for at this perspective it seems odd to me as well.

Certainly plenty of things were wrong within that school building, and there was enough we could have joked about. The truth, however, is that I very seldom talked like that, nor did many of the other teachers. Unless a teacher was ready to buck the system utterly, it would become far too difficult to teach in an atmosphere of that kind of honesty. It was a great deal easier to pretend as much as possible that everything was OK.

Some teachers carried out this posture with so much eagerness, in fact, that their defense of the school ended up as something like a hymn of praise. "You children should thank God and feel blessed with good luck for all you've got. There are so many little children in the world who have been given so much less." The books are junk, the paint peels, the cellar stinks, the teachers call you nigger, the windows fall in on your heads. "Thank God that you don't live in Russia or Africa Thank God for all the blessings that you've got"

After the window blew in on us, the janitor finally came up and hammered it shut with nails so that it would not fall in again, but also so that it could not be opened. A month passed before anything was done about the missing glass. Children shivered a few feet away from it. The principal walked by frequently and saw us. So did the various lady experts who traveled all week from room to room within our school. At last one day the janitor came up with a piece of cardboard and covered over about one quarter of that lower window so that no more wind could come in, but just that much less sunshine too. I remember wondering what a piece of glass cost in Boston, and thought of going out and buying some and trying to put it in myself. That rectangle of cardboard covered our nailed-shut window for half of the term, and it was finally removed only because a television station was going to visit in the building and the school department wanted to make the room look more attractive. But it was winter when the window broke, and the repairs did not take place until the middle of the spring.

Other schools in the ghetto were no better than my own, and some were worse. One of the most

unfortunate, according to those who made comparisons, was the Endicott School, also heavily imbalanced. Endicott, I learned, had become so overcrowded that in some classes the number of pupils exceeded the number of desks and the extra pupils had to sit in chairs behind the teacher. A child absent one day commonly came back the next and found someone else sitting at his desk. These facts had been brought out in the newspaper, but nothing had been done. When the parents of the Endicott children pressed the school department to take action, a series of events transpired which told a large part of the story of segregation in a very few words.

The school department offered, in order to resolve the problem, to buy a deserted forty-year-old Hebrew school and allot about $7000 to furnish it with desks and chairs. Aside from the indignity of getting everybody else's castoffs (the Negroes already lived in former Jewish tenements and bought in formerly Jewish stores), to buy and staff this old Hebrew school with about a dozen teachers would cost quite a lot more than to send the children down the street a couple of miles to a white school which had space. The Hebrew school was going to cost over $180,000. To staff it and supply it with books and equipment would cost $100,000 more a year. To send the children into available seats in nearby white classrooms (no new teachers needed) would have cost $40,000 to $60,000 for the year. The school department was willing to spend as much as an extra $240,000 in order to put the Negro children into another segregated school.

As it happened, the school committee debated the issue in so many directions that most of the school year passed before anything of a final nature was decided. Meanwhile, the children in the Endicott classrooms had lost another year from their lives.

In my own school there was another bad situation in the third of the three fourth grades. This class had been subjected for most of the year to a highly unstable teacher—a man of goodwill and mild disposition, who, however, had been dismissed from another position within the Boston system after serious trouble of a psychiatric nature. It was readily apparent that he was in no emotional condition to handle the problems posed by a crowded ghetto class. Beginning in October and continuing through March, his teaching had brought little to the children besides unending noise and chaos. Yet all the complaints of the bewildered Negro parents and even the stated dissatisfaction of the principal had not been able to effect a change.

At last in early April, after about six months of agony, the man was leaving. But the school administration did not have the competence or insight to assign a better-qualified person in his place. Instead of a confident or experienced instructor, a bashful and quite terrified young lady took over the class, and then, after her departure,

A chart on the wall gave some measure of the situation by keeping a record of math and spelling grades. The math average of the class for weeks had remained, almost without exception, below the point of failing—for certain stretches of time, as much as 30 points below. The spelling and writing had fluctuated around the third-grade level. Reading levels were a year, and often two

a string of substitute teachers, who seemed at times truly to have been grabbed off the street at seven thirty, knocked over the head, handed a twenty-dollar bill, and shipped over to our schoolhouse in a taxi. Some of them were nice people, but few had any kind of real qualifications.

One fellow, I remember, did not even get there until about ten thirty because he had been out driving a cab the night before, and he announced within about forty-five minutes that he would certainly not be coming back. The consequence of all this in academic terms was an overall retardation of almost the entire class.

years, beneath the national norm. All of these subject failures were major tragedies because in many respects and for a number of the children the stunting of their learning at such an early age was likely to prove almost irreversible.

But the setbacks in math and spelling and writing were not as serious for them as the lack of continuity in their work in social studies. For at least in the basic subjects, no matter how poorly they were doing, the children had had some continuity of material. In geography and history, there had been no continuity, but rather a frantic shifting of focus almost every day.

One morning a substitute teacher, groping for a way to kill an hour, would have the children read aloud to him about India. The next day, another teacher, not knowing what had been done before, and having a special fondness for another country, Holland perhaps, would tell the class to flip back a hundred pages and read about dikes and wooden shoes. Then someone would appear long enough to get some help from one of the full-time teachers, and the children would get two or three abortive sessions on the desert, but the day after that they would be doing India over again; then off to Lima, Peru; suddenly to American cotton production, or the corn belt, or coal production—or then, with the arrival of a new teacher, back to dikes and wooden shoes. It is not surprising that with a crazy arrangement of this sort, the children would frequently start out by lying to a new substitute and would do their best to break him down. Nor is it surprising that their sense of place and time soon grew to be disastrously confused. They could make no distinction, even in the most tentative and general manner, between a city, town, state, or country, or even between a continent or island. Words like Yangtze River, hemisphere, Himalayas, pyramid were all mixed up in their minds. A question about what one could get from rushing streams in Switzerland might elicit such an answer as "population" or "migration," and a question about what "self-evident" meant, or "created equal," would easily bring back from the class such answers as "Red Coats," "transportation," or "white coal."

Seven different teachers in the course of ten days became the final catastrophe of this classroom. The children grew wild, and the atmosphere from day to day grew more explosive. At this point, on the morning of the third of May, the principal called me into her office and asked me if I would agree to take the class for the remainder of the year. With the assurance that my own students would not be getting a string of substitutes, I agreed to make the transfer.

Consider what it is like to go into a new classroom and to see before you suddenly, and in a way you cannot avoid recognizing, the dreadful consequences of a year's wastage of so many lives. You walk into a narrow and old wood-smelling classroom and see thirty-five curious, cautious, and untrusting children, aged nine to thirteen, of whom about two thirds are Negro. Lifetime records of seven of them are missing, symptomatic and emblematic at once of the chaos of the teacher changes. On the first math test the class average is 36. The children tell you with

embarrassment that it has been like that since fall.

You check around the classroom. Of forty desks five have tops with no hinges. You lift a desktop to fetch a paper, and you find the top has fallen off. There are three windows: one can't be opened. A sign on it written in the messy scribble of some custodial person warns: "Do Not Unlock This Window It Is Broken." The general look of the room is that of a bleak-light photograph of a mental hospital. Above the one poor blackboard, gray rather than really black, and hard to write on, hangs from one tack, lopsided, a motto attributed to Benjamin Franklin: "Well begun is half done." So much within this classroom seems to be a mockery of itself.

Into this grim scenario,[6] drawing on your own pleasures and memories, you do what you can to bring some kind of life. You bring in some cheerful and colorful paintings by Joan Miró and Paul Klee. While the paintings by Miró do not arouse much interest, the ones by Klee become an instantaneous success. One picture in particular, entitled *Bird Garden,* catches the imagination of the entire class. You slip it out of the book and tack it on the wall beside the doorway, and it creates a traffic jam every time the children have to file in or file out. You discuss with your students some of the reasons why Klee may have painted the way he did, and you talk about the things that can be accomplished in a painting which cannot be done in a photograph. None of this seems to be above the children's heads. Despite this you are advised flatly by the art teacher that your naïveté has gotten the best of you, and that the children cannot possibly appreciate these drawings.

For poetry, instead of the materials recommended by the course of study, you decide to introduce a poem of William Butler Yeats. The poem that you select is "The Lake Isle of Innisfree." The children do not go crazy about it at first, but a number of them seem to like it as much as you do, and you tell them how once, two years before, you were living in England and you helped a man in the country to make his home from wattles[7] and clay. Many of them grow more curious than they appeared at first. Here again, however, you are advised by older teachers that you are making a mistake: Yeats is too difficult for children. They can't enjoy it, won't appreciate it, wouldn't like it.

---

[6] outline of a dramatic plot
[7] a frame of twigs woven together

On a number of other occasions, the situation is repeated. The children are offered something new and lively. They respond to it energetically, and their attention doesn't waver. For the first time in a long while, perhaps, there is actually some real excitement and some growing and some thinking going on within that room. In each case, however, you are advised sooner or later that you are making a mistake. Your mistake, in fact, is to have impinged[8] upon the standardized condescension[9] upon which the entire administration of the school is based. To hand Paul Klee's pictures to the children of a ghetto classroom, particularly in a twenty-dollar volume, constitutes a threat to the school system. The threat is handled by a continual underrating of the children. In this way many students are unjustifiably held back from a great many experiences that they might come to value, and are pinned down instead to books the teacher knows, and tastes that she can handle easily.

My own feeling was that it was precisely the familiar material which had so deadened the previous three years of schooling and which had been so closely identified with the misery and chaos and intellectual aridity[10] of this most recent year. To attempt to revive or reawaken a child's curiosity long gone dead or long sedated by use of the same poison that had laid him low seemed futile. Only by introducing new and totally fresh materials did there seem a chance to make a difference. Although the poems and pictures I brought in did not appeal to every student, there is no doubt at all of the degree to which the will to learn, as well as the most simple will to laugh or speak or smile or joke, reappeared among the children.

The change in attitude carried over, curiously, into utterly unrelated areas. One teacher of an older grade, who had little fondness for me, felt impelled, nevertheless, to come upstairs and offer me a compliment. "Everyone has been so impressed," she said, "by the way your children have been filing in the stairways." In an odd way, I felt pleased by what she had told me. I couldn't have cared less how my pupils were filing in the stairways, but it was a source of satisfaction to me to think that they were doing something which,

within the context of this school, was so much to their advantage.

A more serious measure of the impact of these changes came to light when I started testing the class on the intensive work we had been doing in math and English. In less than a month, the math average went up to a median well above grade level. Test score averages over the course of three weeks began at 36, rose to 60, and leveled off at 79.

There was no unusual expertise at work within the classroom. There was, in fact, total professional naïveté as well as considerable technical incompetence. One thing *was* present, however, and this was the personal motivation of the children. It was there, unused and wholly unawakened, but very much in evidence as soon as it was looked for and believed in. To care about their work, the children asked only a few grains of faith and expectation, a small degree of fun, a mood of relaxation, and an open understanding between their teacher and themselves that the things that had been going on that year were not their fault.

" 'You children should thank God and feel blessed with good luck for all you've got . . . Thank God that you don't live in Russia or Africa! Thank God for all the blessings that you've got!' "

A great deal has been written in recent years about the purported lack of motivation in the children of the Negro ghettos. Little in my experience supports this, yet the phrase has been repeated endlessly, and the blame in almost all cases is placed somewhere outside the classroom. Boston's former deputy superintendent, in putting forward the aims of the compensatory program, presented it in this way:

It is our hope through this program to raise the achievement of these pupils closer to their potentials, which have for too long been submerged by parental lack of values.

Such language belies a sense of failure on the part of those who run these schools. The suggestion is made that the child will be offered a certain

---

[8] infringed, struck
[9] manifesting an attitude of conscious lowering of oneself to inferiors
[10] dryness, barrenness

amount of compassion, just so long as it is made absolutely clear ahead of time that the heart of the problem is the lack of values of his family. Unquestionably, there are Negro children whose school careers give testimony to the problems that plague their parents' lives. Both Stephen's original and foster parents are pertinent examples. But the greater number of Negro parents whom I have known in Boston do not lead lives lacking in real values. Faced with the particular nature of the deputy superintendent's rhetoric, we have to ask whose values we are talking about—and deprived in the eyes of whom. To say that Negroes in Boston are deprived of rights would be an honest statement. It would also be honest to say that they are deprived of good schools, and at least to that degree, of a fair chance for democracy, for opportunity, and all the things these words are supposed to mean. But to say that they are deprived culturally, in the face of the present school administration and in the face of the profound callousness and cynicism of the entire system, seems to me meaningless.

Glimmerings of a personal understanding of these points and of the ironies involved in them can sometimes be perceived among the teachers. I recall a conversation I had with an unusually frank red-neck teacher in my school. "They talk about the Negroes being culturally deprived," he said with an unembarrassed smile, "I'm the one who's been goddamn culturally deprived, and I don't need anyone to tell me. I haven't learned a thing, read a thing that I wished I'd read or learned since the day I entered high school, and I've known it for years, and I tried to hide it from myself, and now I wish I could do something about it, but I'm afraid it's just too late."

The same teacher confided to me on another occasion that he had been beaten around and treated rough and whipped by his parents and by his Yankee schoolmasters when he was a child. To him, this seemed to clear the field for beating others around today. The attitude of many people in Boston and other cities has been consistent with this view: "We had a hard time of it, so why shouldn't they?" This less than gentle attitude seems characteristic of a less than gentle society, in which the prevailing viewpoint of those who are moderately successful is too likely to be that they have got theirs, and the others can damn well wait a while before they get the same.

How serious is this American illness, and how shall we interpret the symptoms everywhere apparent? The authors in this section undertake the process of determining the nature and circumstances of the diseased condition.

In a satirical assessment of the "turned-on," "super-sincere" generation, Todd says that thousands of Californians are practicing a contrived innocence, nourished not so much by LSD as by the heady language of soul. In a more objective vein, Bradbury also focuses attention on a shift in language and perceives one reason for the communication gap between generations. Without changing the moral vocabulary, young people have replaced old meanings and values with new ones.

We are all well aware of those who view the current student rebellion as a sure sign of social degeneration. Cleaver argues that we should not be alarmed. Yes, he says, white youth have repudiated their heritage, but in doing so they have also become the first generation of

Diagnosis

whites worthy of the black man's respect. Gray puts the whole issue into a larger philosophical perspective, explaining that students wish only to escape a meaningless life: they are working out the age-old conflict between individual freedom and social authority.

Not all concern is reserved for new movements of the radical young. Cox finds that *Playboy's* adolescent concept of sexuality appeals equally to middle-aged men and teen-aged boys. Lobsenz opens his psychiatric files on the pleasure neurotic, an extreme product of the traditional emphasis on work and salvation, who is filled with anxiety at the prospect of leisure. Rovere recounts the McCarthy era of the 1950's, explaining how it was possible for a politician like Senator Joseph McCarthy to acquire almost dictatorial powers practically overnight, and he leaves us wondering if it is possible for a new demagogue or a new threat to our national security to reactivate another wave of anti-intellectualism. Krutch and Fitch warn us that when we search for social causes we must look at the individual man. His willingness—or unwillingness—to accept responsibility for his actions or to maintain his own sense of integrity determines what kind of society we have. For reassurance we can turn to Kouwenhoven, who finds in American culture an open-endedness, a flexibility, which makes possible a continuing development in response to our environment. It may well be that the disturbing aspects of American life are an inevitable part of the process whereby society changes to meet the new requirements of the age.

BILLIE CAME OVER TO ME IN THE MORNING AND SAID YOU PROMISED TO TAKE ME TO THE ZOO TODAY, DADDY. AND I SAID I'M SORRY BILLIE-BOY BUT DADDY HAS GOT SOMETHING ELSE HE MUST DO TODAY.

AND BILLIE'S MOMMA SAID NOW YOU STOP BOTHERING YOUR DADDY, BILLIE-BOY. AND I SAID DON'T SCOLD THE BOY, CHARLOTTE. I KNOW JUST THE WAY HE FEELS BECAUSE I STILL REMEMBER WHAT IT WAS LIKE WHEN MY DADDY DISAPPOINTED ME.

AND CHARLOTTE HUGGED ME AND CALLED ME HER HONEY-BEAR AND SAID YOU'RE TOO GENTLE FOR YOUR OWN GOOD, DANNY. AND I SAID IT'S A BAD THING WHEN A FATHER HAS TO BREAK A PROMISE TO HIS SON. THAT'S THE WAY A CHILD CAN TURN SOUR.

AND CHARLOTTE SAID NO CHILD OF OURS WILL TURN SOUR SO LONG AS A MAN LIKE YOU IS AROUND. AND I HUGGED HER AND SAID YOU'RE MY LITTLE GIRL. THEN I PICKED UP MY BAT AND I SAID I'D BEST BE ON MY WAY. I'M LATE AS IT IS.

HIT ONE FOR ME, CHARLOTTE YELLED. AND FOR ME TOO, DADDY, BILLIE-BOY YELLED. AND I YELLED BACK DON'T YOU WORRY ABOUT ME. I'LL DO FINE.

AND THEN I DROVE DOWN-TOWN TO THE CIVIL RIGHTS DEMONSTRATION.

Turned-On and Super-Sincere in California

RICHARD TODD

At 3:30 P.M. he said: "I feel terribly strange." Tom handed him a small toy animal he had played with as an infant. Charley cuddled the toy, kissed it, and said: "There's something very reassuring about this." . . . Charley lay with a peaceful look on his face, cuddling the toy animal. Tom lay down outside on a deck adjoining the bedroom and his face, too, filled with peacefulness.

San Francisco Chronicle, May 30, 1966.

Charley, the thirty-six-year-old man cuddling the toy, has taken LSD. He is acting strangely, but his trip will end in a few hours and with luck he will be back to normal. He arouses only your casual interest as you leaf through the *Chronicle,* in which LSD is as much a staple as recipes and rape. But you might listen more carefully to Tom, his observer and "guide," who has not had any acid and is speaking in his own voice:

It was a wonderful few moments for me. I felt very much at one with Charley and I knew he was living for a while as a five-year-old child. . . . The guide grows in this experience of giving. What a privilege it is to be with another person in this way! No words can describe it.

These few lines represent with splendid typicality a way of talking that is not at all unusual at the moment here in California. The new idiom is characterized by self-revelation and utter seriousness. It places highest value on private emotions and "interpersonal relations," and considers restraint in talking about these intimate matters a signal of hypocrisy. The remarks of the LSD guide are faithful to these assumptions, and include some lesser, but important notions: for example, that childhood and simplicity are ideal states of being.

If the LSD milieu[1] is particularly conducive to such innocence, the phenomenon is by no means confined to the drug set. Californians of many sorts are in its grip. Bulletins from the soul fill the air; all manner of private data is yours without asking. Telephone-talk-show callers crowd the switchboards for a chance to talk about their personal commitments; young marrieds eagerly discuss the state of their relationship; everyone will share with you the latest information on his "growth." Are you curious about anything? That fourteen-year-old playmate in bell-bottomed hip-huggers lolling down Sunset on the arm of a Beatlesque Older Man—do you wonder what her parents think? She will let you in on her hang-ups with them. Do you find it odd that the strapping Santa Cruz surfer has peroxided his hair into golden fleece? Talk to him; he will at least let you know that he uses Lady Clairol. The Berkeley girl

[1] environment, setting

scenities, "indeeds," and the music of Bobby Dylan, who is taunting some hapless middle-class lady for not being turned on: "Something is happening and you don't know what it is, do you, Mrs. Jones?" Talking over this din, you find yourself in an unexpectedly serious conversation with your host. He has taken LSD lately and, though you are not pressing him, he is anxious to tell you about it. The first time was up on the mountain, just after a rain. They went walking and . . . "The dripping leaves," he repeats, "the dripping leaves. It was so beautiful and it was sufficient . . . the forest seemed vast." But words are running out; the expression on his face suggests that it was an experience for which no words were necessary at the time and few are available now. He explains that they have taken LSD many times since, but always indoors. They sit on the sofa and talk. "It lasts for about twelve hours, and we talk the whole time. It has brought us much closer together than we have ever been before. We've been able to say things about our relationship that I wouldn't have thought possible. It's deepened our love . . ."

There is no adequate response for this kind of speech, delivered in a conversational way by a casual acquaintance, nothing perhaps, except a similar disclosure. Yet you realize that if there is embarrassment in the silence that follows, it is entirely your own, and you suspect yourself of undue squeamishness. After all, what's wrong with saying what you feel?

For some, to be sure, openness in speech is more than an occasional matter, even more than a habit: it is a code. The code not only prohibits indirection, but frowns on the use of the conventional language of social deceit. A successful California dinner party may suddenly swerve into failure with the conventional closing lines: "It was nice to see you." Suddenly everyone is on edge, a social blunder has occurred: the offender was speaking artificially, not of the self.

*S*ometimes a believer will explain the code in clear and vehement[3] terms. You are on the top floor of a San Francisco apartment house on the edge of the Haight-Ashbury district—the West Coast, if not the world-wide center for psychedelic experiences. Cigarette smoke, only lightly

will tell you that she smokes nickel cigars, lived with her boy friend first semester, works hard, and that "I feel this growing . . . I guess I'm building my own truth."

Even where you would look for exceptions, you discover that the California language of soul holds sway: the academic community and its intellectual suburbs practice the new idiom without a blush. To a surprising degree, California intellectuals, particularly young ones, have forsaken traditional ironic speech, with its insistence on a certain distance between the speaker and his inner self. As a result, self-deprecation, wit, insouciance[2]—all the cherished intellectual habits— are out of fashion here. If anything, they are taken as a badge of hated phoniness.

A listener unaccustomed to this attitude can experience some discomfort. You go to a party at the house of a young Stanford couple; he is a Ph.D. candidate and teacher. You don't know them well; as you arrive you note that since you saw them last his hair, once a shaggy pompadour, is now combed *à la mode*, draping forehead, ears, and neck. The party is distinctly academic: the air, which smells of beer and wine, is full of ob-

---

[2] indifference, carefree attitude

[3] ardent, violent

laced with pot, thickens the air. Through the lone window at the end of the room, you can see the orange lights of the Golden Gate Bridge. Across the table from you is an authentic Haight-Ashbury denizen,[4] a bearded Dane, swathed in corduroy, his head a torrent of hair. His wife is next to him, a Roger Vadim girl, with pouting insolent lips. When the Dane speaks, his English is immaculate, so perfect that his accent seems an affectation. But the Dane does not speak often. Indeed, he has sat, silent, sullen, but intense, for most of the evening. Suddenly, despite the late hour and the general grogginess, he whirls upon you. You have made an error, filling in a silence with an empty remark about the hour, the distance home, the necessity of a departure. The Dane exclaims, "Stop playing games. We do not know each other. We could sit here saying these polite things for a century and we would not know each other. Why don't you tell me what you think of me? Of course, you dislike me. But suppose I did not wear my beard; then you would like me, would you not? Tell me your opinion of me, and I will be candid with you, and perhaps we can get to know one another, but no more of this game."

"The game of truth," his wife exclaims, "the game of truth. Let's play the game of truth."

Now the game of truth is not about to become a favorite parlor game, and people like the Dane are easy enough to dismiss. At best they are trying to substitute a new and clumsy set of manners for the ones that have served fairly well to protect people from one another for centuries. At worst, they are "going through a phase." Taken alone, they are simply a curiosity. And yet they are not an isolated example; if there are few people who would express the code with equal vehemence, there are many who believe in it. They are impatient not just with "polite" language, but with all the old forms of literate speech, which they see as a barrier to feeling.

Could this be a hopeful development? Might the emergence of youthful minds willing to speak with directness suggest the bright prospect of mental energies not wasted on self-defense?

One popular observer (*Look* Magazine) thinks so. For *Look,* the "turned-on Californian" is playing "a new game," whose rules include a "surprising openness in personal relations, a new intensity of personal commitment, a radical shift

in the morally admissible, an expanded definition of education . . ." As these futurists get more adept at their game, *Look* says, "Relations between people will gain a new depth and subtelty."

". . . the possibility of a good trip, a voyage to simplicity, a glorious regression to the imagination's childhood, is considered worth the risks."

You think of the B.'s and you wonder. They are not native Californians, but unequivocal[5] Californians: "When we came here, we threw away our clocks. We eat when we want to, sleep when we want to, write when we want to, make love when we want to. It's wonderful." Martin B. is jack-of-all-sophisticated-trades: he has earned exotic degrees in technological fields, has held postdoctoral fellowships and rich jobs in California industry, but has turned, with equal success, to art: won creative writing fellowships, written a novel, is now rumored to be working on a play of outrageous political satire. Debby B. bakes more than two hundred kinds of bread. The B.'s are always talking about making love, and once said they practice the act each night. You sense that their preoccupation is an emblem of a larger concern: their contemporaneity,[6] their freedom. The B.'s rid themselves of property each two years in a "pot-latch." They have disposed of all books except reference matter, though they make voracious[7] use of the public library. Their house, free of photographs or mementos, furnished entirely in beige and teak, is a monument to the present.

For the B.'s, whom you see from time to time, you suspect that you are a curiosity, and this is what they are to you. You listen to their exuberant conversation, which has a theme with limitless variations. On a night in June you hear them speak of the musicology of the Beatles, the intra-uterine device, their friends ("we like anyone who's open . . . people who can share"), the Nike X, the Grand Tetons ("a wonderful place to make

[4] inhabitant

[5] unquestionable, clear
[6] here, the state of being "with it," or current with the temper of the times
[7] greedy, insatiable

70 love"), model trains, childbirth, and plant chromosomes. Nothing out of the ordinary here.

You are caught off guard, however, when, on the porch as you are leaving, Martin remarks with no lapse in his ebullience,[8] "We feel so close to you people "

Outside in the air, you discover that you have a distinctly uncomfortable feeling, as if you had been kissed against your will. What Martin said is certainly not true. You do not feel close to the B.'s, it seems preposterous that they could feel close to you; you are somewhat annoyed by the imposition of the remark, which demands a response it is impossible to give. If there is a naïveté to their behavior, it is an insidious sort of naïveté, because it encumbers you, however briefly, in its untidy emotions.

This odd quality of contrived innocence is not limited to private lives; in California it is institutionalized. Experiments in human behavior abound: family therapy, group therapy, "movement therapy" (no one says a word), industrial "think-tanks," Joan Baez's Institute for the Study of Non-Violence.

The Esalen Institute flourishes at Big Sur—a handsome well-endowed cluster of buildings overlooking the sea, which swirls about the rocks in beautiful subtleties of blue, white, and green. The Institute is dedicated to the "potentialities of human existence." It believes "People can change. Their institutions can change. All can change for the better, not just superficially, but deep down." Here you can come and participate in enterprises of self-improvement led by psychiatrists and therapists, for a cost of $67 (for a weekend) or $170 (for five days). Recent seminars included "Psychodrama and the Body" and "Bio-Energetic Analysis," also an arts-and-crafts event called "Down Home with Staff Members." (One of the staff is described as "potter, printmaker, and sometime breakfast cook," and of another it is said, "In addition to his jewelry and sculpture, he is well-known on the West Coast as a sandal-maker.")

There is that sound again: what is there about it that can simultaneously amuse and annoy? We all know that sandalmakers are respectable, and there is no real reason to suspect that "Bio-Energetic Analysis" is not on the up-and-up. And yet somehow these phrases seem inadequate to the exploration of "human potentialities." Perhaps it is the easy assurance, that certain chumminess ("sometime breakfast cook") with the confident implication that all within earshot are believers, that everyone agrees that we can push back the frontiers of human experience this weekend.

*I*t is the same happy assumption that accompanies the activity that has inspired so many contemporary idioms—drugs. The use of drugs, it should be repeated, does not account for the phenomenon in question; not all the "turned-on" Californians are turned-on in the literal way. Yet it is true that drugs are widely used in California, that they are never far from intellectual circles, and that they define the hip personality, the man who has, as Timothy Leary prescribes, dropped out to turn on. And while drugs are more a symptom than a cause, the function they appear to serve may offer a clue to the way minds are working here. From pot to LSD, all are used for the same ostensible reason: they "expand the mind."

"The music."

"Wo-ow."

"The levels, so many levels."

"I'm up here."

"Don't talk about it; you'll bring it down."

"Did you hear that? 'You'll bring it down.' Oh fantastic."

This conversation—as the joint (of marijuana) is passed around—is not so much an intimation[9] of perceptions as an attempt to keep aloft the mystical communion. The most important effect of pot is evident less in the words that are spoken than in the looks on the faces of the smokers, who are most likely to assume a gentle, abstracted, beneficent, open expression; to let down their guard. The mind is expanded, to be sure; it is made large enough to hold in harmony elements of one's life that are in conflict when the high ends. Pot, like bourbon or nutmeg, is used to simplify, not to complicate experience. That the experience can become very complicated indeed when stronger drugs are used does not mean that the goal is different. The air is full of tales of bad trips, the flesh melting away, etc. (One peyote-mescaline-LSD veteran recalled his first experience: "I thought I was all right until I saw a gorilla at the urinal.") The significant point is that the possi-

---

[8] exuberance, bubbling over

[9] hint, indirect suggestion

bility of a good trip, a voyage to simplicity, a glorious regression to the imagination's childhood, is considered worth the risks. One of the *Chronicle's* LSD subjects said of his experience, "I never get insanity or hallucinations anymore—just peace—and I feel love for everybody who is here." Another put the matter precisely, "I found I was young, about fifteen, walking down the streets of Rome. I was an Italian boy with no complicated emotions."

"No complicated emotions" says it well. After the drug scene has died out, been confined to the laboratory or legalized into dullness, the item of enduring interest will be that—for a short time anyway—simplicity of feeling was elevated to the level of an heroic ideal. It is what everyone, not just the acid head, seems to be striving for. You hope, half the time you believe (if you are a par-

ticipant in this euphoric[10] sensibility), that emotional prosperity is just around the corner. In the meantime, though, you must prime the pump with LSD. Or—the more frequent alternative—you must rely on the symbol instead of the sensation, on the easy, "open" speech that marks you as a man of feeling.

When a society wears its heart on its sleeve, something curious is likely to happen. Berkeley is as good a place as any to search for these consequences. It is, of course, a magnificent place: after Berkeley nearly every other campus feels like Slippery Rock. There is turmoil, controversy, intellectual energy, a fervid unleashing of the mind. There is local color. It is no doubt true that Berkeley suffers from a tendency to appreciate the

[10] characterized by a feeling of buoyancy and well-being

"When a society wears its heart on its sleeve, something curious is likely to happen."

72   defiant act in any form, but these are usually harmless. (No one seriously worries about the activities, say, of the East Bay Sexual Freedom League—including a nude wade-in in San Francisco last year.) Berkeley's present danger is probably not extremism but . . . contentment.

Contentment is a paradoxical word for the university that supported the Free Speech Movement. Any day of the week rows of tables display the trophies and causes of the moment, advertise open-air speakers and a hundred diversions, including the "Cinema Psychedelica." But if you linger, around the Plaza, you are likely to discover the peculiar kind of joy that is the result of self-absorption. The happiness of those who roam about the campus, sit dangling their feet in the fountain, or even harangue[11] each other, is the solid pleasure of the craftsman content in his work. You stroll through Sather Gate and take the pamphlet that is modestly proffered. It addresses itself to whether or not God is dead, and ends with the assurance, "We welcome any questions about life."

This is a nice complacency, which says not so much that we will answer your questions, but simply that we are *here,* and you are out there, and you don't dare laugh at us. This sense of rightness perhaps explains the familiar hip gesture of making non-jokes. You are sitting, to give an example, in the kitchen of an apartment on Grove Street. Its old tongue-in-groove boards were painted pink long ago and are now peeling to reveal green. There is almost nothing in the place: a few cans of garbanzo beans on the shelves, some milk and Vichy water in the icebox. You are having breakfast, Cheerios, with Walter, who lives there. The stairs to the apartment above lead through Walter's kitchen and the two tenants from upstairs appear: Blossom and Manny. Manny eyes the Cheerios box on the table, chuckles, and points, "Look." Blossom looks, shakes her head, and murmurs, "Fantastic." Manny chuckles, "Cheerios," and shakes his head. Exit. This routine is easily done with any object, the more ordinary the better: a radio, a toy (a plastic Jesus would be excessively obvious). You just stare at the thing in apparent wonder, as if you could see the absurdity of the whole civilization contained within it. You remain wordless, or utter a "fantastic," that word that hippies reserve almost entirely for the banal.[12]

This air of sureness about the world has a kind of charm on the antic level, but it presents certain difficulties when the discourse moves to a higher plane. Think of all those fresh-faced girls who repeat the new categorical imperative with such artless confidence, "I believe anything's moral as long as it doesn't hurt someone else." The ease with which that remark dismisses tradition's offer of advice and asserts its faith in one's ability to weigh the implications of every act—these qualities can find their way beneath the skin. And when this kind of mind turns to matters of life and death, unnatural results can be expected.

A recent issue of the weekly Berkeley *Barb* contained a front-page elegy for a nineteen-year-old boy who died while on an LSD trip. The piece, entitled "Vernon P. Cox: an Elegy—HE DIDN'T QUITE MAKE IT," described the author's relationship with the boy (friends, fellow poets), appraised his talent (real, prolific, sometimes seventy poems a day), and, of course, lamented his death.

It reads in part:

His name is Vernon P. Cox, and he didn't quite make it. A very decent human being, came from a good family of Stillwater, Oklahoma. (What a fitting name, what a still place. Cattle grazing, oil wells, fraternities. Devoid of original thought. Plain, every day Stillwater.) . . .

So they come to Berkeley. Shaggy Dog adopted Sanders, who shared their two mattresses for a couple of nights. English from N. Y. and two-three girls were also guests there. Pot, nutmeg, always near, a refrigerator with some peanut butter—and nothing else —pregnant fifteen-year-olds, the beat scene. That's where he lived and wrote, and, a shame to say, didn't quite make it . . .

He has his first LSD trip in company: Shaggy Dog as usual lay down, softly singing to himself. Their two other companions were busy and happy in themselves. Vernon free and exulted beyond belief suddenly realized, that the trip to Europe he desired, but was afraid of, is a must. Packed his things to start then and there. His companions argued with, restrained him, and for a while he was quiet. Then knowing that for him nothing is impossible, that physical laws

---

[11] address at length in loud and vehement speech   [12] ordinary, common, hackneyed

don't bind him, not bothering to use the door he walked through the window-pane. No one there was quick enough to block his way. He fell three stories. . . . It wasn't suicide; he only started for Europe and didn't quite make it.

The truth about this elegy is that it is comic. It is horrible, unconscious comedy, slapstick, a Charlie Chaplin movie rendered in earnest prose. It manages, through the tandem devices of undoubted sincerity and total mindlessness, to make an already senseless death almost irredeemably absurd.

And yet, it is not likely that the *Barb's* elegy—whatever wretchedness it might have caused the boy's Stillwater, Oklahoma, family—disturbed many Berkeley readers. It asserts, after all, unassailable notions: that youth, sensitivity, poetry, love, and freedom are good things. It only disregards the necessity for a double vision; it makes no attempt to imagine this tragedy as it might look to another time, another town, a parent, to the author himself a few years (months?) later. It only fails to throw a sop to a world in which walking through a window to one's death, with the illusion of going on a European tour, qualifies as a bizarre act. It speaks with absolute assurance, an assurance that is oddly justified by the complacency of its audience.

*T*he "elegy," of course, is a grotesque, a heightened version of unreality—but, like other grotesques, it has its instructive value. In one sense it can be taken as the careless remarks of a young writer, but in another sense it is the product of a culture as well; if ordinary restraints were operating the elegy would not likely have been written; certainly it would not be received with equanimity.[13] In its painful assumptions that you need only feel, be straight, put down hypocrisy, say what you mean, it is utterly faithful to the unchallenged ideas of the intelligent people whose voice rules this coast.

If this intellectual style is not explicable, it at least is somewhat appropriate to the state whose residents—from hippies to systems men—share, if they share anything, a devotion to the moment. What California seems to need is what it clearly wants least: a past. It is possible to grow obsessed with this prescription, perhaps because every-

thing looks like spilt milk. The land is always wrenchingly visible; from the heart of Berkeley, from the midsts of the most hysterical freeway, you can always see the brown hills, their contours too subtle to accept a building gracefully, waiting to be defiled by another onslaught of tract houses.

If your mood is right, of course, you can be bemused, even exhilarated, by the hodgepodge, as you can by its intellectual concomitants.[14] But your mood can change, as quickly as the passing of the sun can transform the landscape itself—surely no place is as ugly as California on a cloudy day—and you are pushed toward visions of a distinctly hideous future for this state.

Whatever is to become of the place, it is no hopeful sign that so many bright voices are celebrating the self and the now and that much of the state is on a sentimental trip; high, indeed out-of-its-mind—not on LSD, but on language: oldest, strongest drug of them all.

[14] accompaniments

[13] calmness, composure

McCarthyism

RICHARD ROVERE

The late Joseph R. McCarthy, a United States Senator from Wisconsin, was in many ways the most gifted demagogue[1] ever bred on these shores. No bolder seditionist[2] ever moved among us—nor any politician with a surer, swifter access to the dark places of the American mind.

The major phase of McCarthy's career was mercifully short. It began in 1950, three years after he had taken his seat in the Senate, where he had seemed a dim and inconsiderable figure. It ended in 1954, when the Senate passed a resolution of censure against him. That was three years before his death at the age of forty-eight. Both his rise and his fall were accomplished with breath-taking speed. At the start of 1950, he was a jackstraw[3] in Washington. Then he discovered Communism —almost by inadvertence, as Columbus discovered America, as James Marshall discovered California gold. By the spring of the year, he was a towering figure, and from then on, except for a few brief weeks early in that summer, no man was closer than he to the center of American consciousness or more central to the world's consciousness of America. . . .

His decline was more difficult to account for than his ascent. He suffered defeats but not destruction. Nothing of a really fatal consequence had happened. He was in a long and sweaty rumble before television cameras in the spring; in the late summer, a Senate committee recommended that he be censured; and in the winter he was censured—or, in the language of the reso-

[1] one who leads the people by playing on their ignorance and fears and prejudices
[2] one who attempts to overthrow the existing government
[3] man unworthy of consideration or lacking influence

Title supplied by editors. From **Senator Joe McCarthy,** © 1959, by Richard H. Rovere. Reprinted by permission of Harcourt, Brace & World, Inc.

lution, "condemned" for conduct that "tended to bring the Senate into dishonor and disrepute." But other Senators, less powerful than he, had been censured and gone on to greater triumphs— among them, an earlier Senator from Wisconsin, Robert M. La Follette, whose son and namesake McCarthy had defeated in 1946. (In the year of McCarthy's death, the Senate voted the elder and censured La Follette one of the five greatest men ever to grace the chamber, the other four being Henry Clay, Daniel Webster, John C. Calhoun, and Robert A. Taft.) Still he had five years on stage, and he was at stage center almost all of that time. He walked, then, with a heavy tread over large parts of the Constitution of the United States, and he cloaked his own gross figure in the sovereignty it asserts and the powers it distributes. He usurped executive and judicial authority whenever the fancy struck him. It struck him often. . . .

*A*t the start of 1950, McCarthy was an empty vessel to the general public outside Wisconsin. There he was known as a cheap politician of vulgar, flamboyant ways and a casual approach to the public interest. It is unlikely that one in a hundred Americans knew of his existence. He was a voice making no sound in the wilderness. Then, on February 9, 1950, he made a speech in Wheeling, West Virginia, in the course of which he said that the Department of State was full of Communists and that he and the Secretary of State knew their names. Later there was some dispute (there was always dispute whenever he said anything) as to whether he had stated that there were 205, 81, 57, or "a lot" of Communists, but the number was of slight importance alongside what he insisted was the fact that Communists "known to the Secretary of State" were "still working and making policy." A Senate committee was immediately appointed to look into his startling assertions. It was the first of five investigations, held by four different committees, to be concerned exclusively with the problem of whether Senator McCarthy was telling the truth about others or, *mutatis mutandis,*[4] others were telling the truth about Senator McCarthy. In the spring of 1950, only the first question was considered. Through March and April and May,

[4] the necessary changes having been made

when Communist power in the Far East was being mobilized for the war in Korea, life in Washington, political life in the United States, seemed largely a matter of determining whether American diplomacy was in the hands of traitors.

Little of importance was learned except that McCarthy had little of importance to say. He had been talking through his hat; if there were Communists in the State Department, he did not know who they were. Nevertheless, he had cued himself in. The lights played over him. Eyes were upon him. The show was his. Within a matter of weeks, his name was known and heard everywhere, and his heavy, menacing countenance was familiar to newspaper readers, to moviegoers, to television viewers everywhere. Henceforth it would be hard to find anyone who was *unaware* of him.

And he became, quickly, an eponym.[5] Barely a month after Wheeling, "McCarthyism" was coined by Herbert Block, the cartoonist who signs himself "Herblock" in the Washington *Post*. The word was an oath at first—a synonym for the hatefulness of baseless defamation, or mudslinging.

[5] one whose name is so prominently connected with something as to be a figurative designation for it; a name associated with a period in history or an administration

(In the Herblock cartoon, "McCarthysim" was crudely lettered on a barrel of mud, which teetered on a tower of ten buckets of the stuff.) Later it became, for some, an affirmation. The term survives both as oath and as affirmation—not very usefully as either, one is bound to say—and has far broader applications than at first. Now it is evocative[6] of an almost undifferentiated evil to a large number of Americans and of a positive good to a somewhat smaller number. To the one, whatever is illiberal, repressive, reactionary, obscurantist,[7] anti-intellectual, totalitarian, or merely swinish will for some time to come be McCarthyism, while to the other it means nothing more or less than a militant patriotism. "To many Americans, McCarthyism is Americanism," Fulton Lewis, Jr., a radio commentator and the official McCarthyite muezzin,[8] said. Once the word caught on, McCarthy himself became intrigued with it. "McCarthyism is Americanism with its sleeves rolled," he told a Wisconsin audience in 1952, and, sure enough, there was the eponym, with his hairy arms bare to the biceps. That year he published a book of snippets from his speeches and his testimony before committees, and it bore the modest title of *McCarthyism: The Fight for America*. There is injustice as well as imprecision in both meanings; if patriotism can hardly be reduced to tracking down Marxists in the pastry kitchens of the Pentagon or the bindery of the Government Printing Office, neither is the late Senator's surname to be placed at the center of all the constellations of political unrighteousness. He was not, for example, totalitarian in any significant sense, or even reactionary. These terms

[6] calling forth to re-create imaginatively
[7] serving to confuse the issues
[8] in Islam, a crier who calls the faithful to prayer

apply mainly to the social and economic order, and the social and economic order didn't interest him in the slightest. If he was anything at all in the realm of ideas, principles, doctrines, he was a species of nihilist;[9] he was an essentially destructive force, a revolutionist without any revolutionary vision, a rebel without a cause.

It is pointless, though, to quarrel with words. They acquire a life and a history of their own, and we have little choice but to accept them and seek understanding. It is simply a measure of McCarthy's impact on our society that he stamped with his name a whole cluster of tendencies in American life—some of them as distant as the stars from any concern or responsibility of his. Once, Brooks Atkinson, the theater critic of the New York *Times*, held McCarthy and McCarthyism responsible for a bad season on Broadway. He said McCarthy had driven all good playwrights to silence or triviality. And in the New York *Herald Tribune* for May 25, 1952, at the height of that green season in which college boys are in the habit of laying siege to college girls' dormitories, the following headline appeared:

RABBI BLAMES MC CARTHYISM IN COLLEGE RAIDS
He Says Danger of Voicing Dissent on
Big Issues Makes Campus Restless

This was madness, of course, and if it can be said that the Rabbi in question would have been the sort to blame the rape of the Sabines on the lack of outing clubs, bowling alleys, ceramics classes, and square dances in Alba and Lavinium, it was nevertheless a tribute to McCarthyism's actual force and impact that this divine conceived his extraordinary theory. It was an even greater tribute to it that such a newspaper as the *Herald Tribune* would regard this particular sermon as worthy of notice in its sober pages.

In time, the whole world took notice of Senator McCarthy. "In all countries they know of him, and in all tongues they speak of him," Adlai Stevenson said after a trip to almost all countries in 1953. In Western Europe as well as in Eastern, in much of Asia and Africa, in Latin America and the Antipodes, McCarthy and McCarthyism stood for all that was held to be evil in American foreign policy and for much that was found to be disagreeable

in American life. In many places, McCarthy was looked upon as being, in and of himself, an instrumentality in the affairs of nations. The *Times* of London, a journal of almost spectacular sobriety, observed once that "the fears and suspicions which center around the personality of Senator McCarthy are now real enough to count as an essential factor in policy-making for the West." Therefore, it went on, with fierce British logic, "McCarthy has become the direct concern of the United States' allies." The *Times* made him sound as though he were nuclear fission or massive retaliation, and it was by no means alone in its estimate of him. Sir Winston Churchill became sufficiently exercised to write an eloquent anti-McCarthy passage into Elizabeth II's Coronation speech.

From a distance, McCarthy may have looked, by some odd reversal of optical principles, larger than life and of greater consequence than he ever really was. But he was large and consequential

---

[9] one who believes that reform can come about only through the destruction of all existing social, economic, and political institutions

enough in those years, and he was, in any case, the first American ever to be discussed and described as being himself a menace to the comity[10] of nations and the strength of alliances. He was the first American ever to be actively hated and feared by foreigners in large numbers. . . .

*I*t was a striking feature of McCarthy's victories, of the surrenders he collected, that they were mostly won in battles over matters of an almost comic insignificance. His *causes célèbres*[11] were *causes ridicules*.[12] The Secretary of the Army groveled before him and offered up General Zwicker as a sacrifice in the course of a lunatic controversy over whether an Army dentist named Irving Peress was properly raised from captain to major. It mattered not at all, except to the paymaster, what rank was held by this obscure jawsmith whose length of service had qualified him for a majority, but McCarthy claimed that in Peress's promotion he had found "the key to the deliberate Communist infiltration of our armed forces." Why was a chief of G-2 removed? Because of a bibliographical citation in a study of Siberian folkways, which the chief of G-2 had never seen. Why did heads roll in the International Information Administration and the Voice of America? Because a pair of callow, shallow youths named Cohn and Schine found on I.I.A. library shelves such items as detective stories by a pro-Communist writer and because a young woman employee of the Voice of America testified that she had received from a fellow employee a suggestion for a weekend's recreation that seemed to her not altogether wholesome.

Yet the antic[13] features of McCarthyism were essential ones. For McCarthyism was, among other things, but perhaps foremost among them, a headlong flight from reality. It elevated the ridiculous and ridiculed the important. It outraged common sense and held common sense to be outrageous. It confused the categories of form and value. It made sages of screwballs and accused wise men of being fools. It diverted attention from the moment and fixed it on the past, which it distorted almost beyond recognition.

[10] courtesy, civility
[11] literally, celebrated causes
[12] literally, ridiculous causes
[13] fantastic, ludicrous

The reality it fled, while madly professing to be the only doctrine that faced it, was a terrible one. Only a Communist or an idiot could have denied that the Communist threat to the United States was real and great. The whole Western world was imperiled, in those days as in these, by the thrust of Soviet power, which, just before McCarthy erupted, had been augmented by the emergence of China as an ally of the Soviet Union and by the Russian mastery of nuclear weapons. In the early part of the decade, the threat seemed more directly a military one than it does today, and within a few months of McCarthy's first appearance as a national figure, it was established by shellfire and tramping armies in Korea that Communism was willing to risk military aggression and war. Communist power in the world was the central reality for the United States in early 1950. The problem we faced, as the most powerful anti-Communist nation in the world, was to form and lead an alliance capable of resisting the Soviet thrust and to find strategies of resistance that would not lead to general war and universal destruction.

". . . McCarthy and McCarthyism stood for all that was held to be evil in American foreign policy and for much that was found to be disagreeable in American life."

McCarthyism ignored this reality and fostered the illusion that what was at most an aspect of it was the whole of reality. "There is only one real issue for the farmer, the laborer, and the businessman—the issue of Communism in government," McCarthy said in a campaign speech in 1952. He even insisted that the struggle against world Communism was a diversion from the struggle against the domestic conspiracy. Speaking, in 1951, of our intervention in Korea, he said, "So the administration which would not fight Communism at home undertook to prove to the American people that it was willing to fight Communism abroad." This sort of talk would have been nonsense at any time; in 1951 and 1952, it was asinine. In the thirties and early forties there had been a formidable Communist movement in this country and a Communist apparatus within the government. It was

> "... McCarthyism was, among other things, but perhaps foremost among them, a headlong flight from reality."

unquestionably the government's business to break up the apparatus and to combat the movement. By 1950, this had been fairly effectively done—if, in fact, it had not been overdone. Alger Hiss was convicted in 1950 for committing perjury about his activities thirteen years earlier. He had been out of the government since 1946. The atom spies had mostly been apprehended by the late forties. An employee-security system had been in operation since early in the war, and it had been considerably tightened up under the Truman administration. The FBI had just about abandoned its concern with bank robbers and white slavers to turn its full force on Communism. The Communist Party, moreover, was in an advanced state of disintegration—partly because of a spreading disillusionment among its members, partly because the government was locking up its leaders. If the conspiracy was still in any way effective, its effectiveness eluded McCarthy, who, with all his helpers in the FBI and his agents in G-2 and his Loyal American Underground, could find nothing more exciting than a Major Peress, a citation of Corliss Lamont in a bibliography, a girl who had heard talk of unwedded bliss in a propaganda agency, a novel by a Communist on a library shelf, and an ex-Communist here and there in some minor agency. He did no better than that. . . .

*B*ut even if McCarthy had done far better, McCarthyism would still have been trading in dangerous illusions. It was insisting, as Philip Rahv once pointed out, that Communism was a danger, not *to* the United States, but *in* the United States, when in truth it was just the other way about. It was focusing attention on the spy rather than on the power for whom the spy spies, on the Communist or ex-Communist dentist in the United States Army rather than on the Red Army, combat-ready and nuclear-armed. Indeed, most of its votaries[14] opposed all reasonable efforts to deal with these matters. Not Stalin and Khrushchev with their legions and their satellites and the billions of souls within their empires, not the gathering economic strength of Communism, not the devastating appeal of its propaganda in those parts of the world where bread is still scarce and there are no pop-up toasters at all—not any of this

were we to dread but Irving Peress and his promotion to major. At the time when 50 per cent of the American people were said to look upon him with favor, his rallying cry was "Who Promoted Peress?"

It had to be this way, for the demagogue, the seditionist, the master of the mob needs his enemy close at hand, familiar, manageable. McCarthyism could never have hoped to score off Stalin or Khrushchev, but it could stick pins into Major Peress, General Zwicker, and Robert Stevens. Hitler was once asked if he wished the destruction of the Jews. This was in the days before he succumbed utterly to desperation and madness. "No," he said, "it is essential to have a tangible enemy."

---

[14] dedicated followers

The New Immorality

JOSEPH WOOD KRUTCH

The provost of one of our largest and most honored institutions told me not long ago that a questionnaire was distributed to his undergraduates and that 40 per cent refused to acknowledge that they believed cheating on examinations to be reprehensible.[1]

Recently a reporter for a New York newspaper stopped six people on the street and asked them if they would consent to take part in a rigged television quiz for money. He reported that five of the six said yes. Yet most of these five, like most of the college cheaters, would probably profess a strong social consciousness. They may cheat, but they vote for foreign aid and for enlightened social measures.

These two examples exhibit a paradox of our age. It is often said, and my observation leads me to believe it true, that our seemingly great growth in social morality has oddly enough taken place in a world where private morality—a sense of the supreme importance of purely personal honor, honesty, and integrity—seems to be declining. Beneficent[2] and benevolent social institutions are administered by men who all too frequently turn out to be accepting "gifts." The world of popular entertainment is rocked by scandals. College students, put on their honor, cheat on examinations. Candidates for the Ph.D. hire ghost writers to prepare their theses.

But, one may object, haven't all these things always been true? Is there really any evidence that personal dishonesty is more prevalent than it always was?

[1] deserving blame
[2] bringing about good

"The New Immorality" by Joseph Wood Krutch from **Saturday Review.** Copyright 1960 Saturday Review, Inc. Reprinted by permission of Saturday Review and the author.

I have no way of making a historical measurement. Perhaps these things are not actually more prevalent. What I do know is that there is an increasing tendency to accept and take for granted such personal dishonesty. The bureaucrat and disk jockey say, "Well, yes, I took presents, but I assure you that I made just decisions anyway." The college student caught cheating does not even blush. He shrugs his shoulders and comments: "Everybody does it, and besides, I can't see that it really hurts anybody."

Jonathan Swift once said: "I have never been surprised to find men wicked, but I have often been surprised to find them not ashamed." It is my conviction that though men may be no more wicked than they always have been, they seem less likely to be ashamed. If everybody does it, it must be right. Honest, moral, decent mean only what is usual. This is not really a wicked world, because morality means mores[3] or manners and usual conduct is the only standard.

The second part of the defense, "it really doesn't hurt anybody," is equally revealing. "It doesn't hurt anybody" means it doesn't do that abstraction called society any harm. The harm it did the bribe-taker and the cheater isn't important; it is purely personal. And personal as opposed to social decency doesn't count for much. Sometimes I am inclined to blame sociology for part of this paradox. Sociology has tended to lay exclusive stress upon social morality, and tended too often to define good and evil as merely the "socially useful" or its reverse.

What social morality and social conscience leave out is the narrower but very significant concept of honor—as opposed to what is sometimes called merely "socially desirable conduct." The man of honor is not content to ask merely whether this or that will hurt society, or whether it is what most people would permit themselves to do. He asks, and he asks first of all, would it hurt him and his self-respect? Would it dishonor him personally?

It was a favorite and no doubt sound argument among early twentieth-century reformers that "playing the game" as the gentleman was supposed to play it was not enough to make a decent society. They were right: it is not enough. But the time has come to add that it is nevertheless indispensable. I hold that it is indeed inevitable that the so-called social conscience unsupported by

[3] accepted conventions or customs

the concept of personal honor will create a corrupt society. But suppose that it doesn't? Suppose that no one except the individual suffers from the fact that he sees nothing wrong in doing what everybody else does? Even so, I still insist that for the individual himself nothing is more important than this personal, interior sense of right and wrong and his determination to follow that rather than to be guided by what everybody does or merely the criterion of "social usefulness." It is impossible for me to imagine a good society composed of men without honor.

We hear it said frequently that what present-day men most desire is security. If that is so, then they have a wrong notion of what the real, the ultimate, security is. No one who is dependent on anything outside himself, upon money, power, fame, or whatnot, is or ever can be secure. Only he who possesses himself and is content with himself is actually secure. Too much is being said about the importance of adjustment and "participation in the group." Even co-operation, to give this thing its most favorable designation, is no more important than the ability to stand alone when the choice must be made between the sacrifice of one's own integrity and adjustment to or participation in group activity.

No matter how bad the world may become, no matter how much the mass man of the future may lose such of the virtues as he still has, one fact remains. If one person alone refuses to go along with him, if one person alone asserts his individual and inner right to believe in and be loyal to what his fellow men seem to have given up, then at least he will still retain what is perhaps the most important part of humanity.

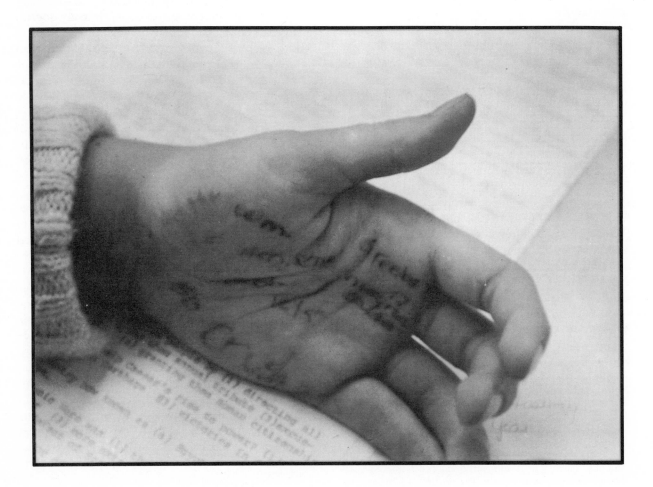

The Irresponsibles

ROBERT ELLIOT FITCH

"It's not my fault! it's not my fault! Nothing in this lousy world is my fault, don't you see that? I don't want it to be and it can't be and it won't be." This outcry comes from Kerouac's Sal Paradise, but it expresses the deep conviction of multitudes of irresponsibles in the age of self-pity. It is a curious paradox that, while the self is the center of all things, the self is never to blame for anything.

The fault is always the fault of someone or of something else. This is implicit in all the letters which are addressed to Abigail Van Buren. "Dear Abby: This is my problem . . . My husband . . ." "Dear Abby: Here is my problem . . . My wife . . ." Or it may be my son, my daughter, my mother-in-law, my neighbors. It is never Me.

Blame it on God, the girls, or the government, on heredity, or on environment, on the parents, on the siblings,[1] on the cold war, on the pressures toward conformity, on being unloved and unwanted. But don't blame it on me, the very center around which the whole universe revolves. This me is like the innocent and apparently unmenacing Dennis, who stands before an accusing mother, in the middle of the parlor, with his body twisted about as he looks back on the carpet at some curious mud tracks which lead right up to his heels. Says Dennis, in bewilderment, "I don't know what that stuff is . . . it just keeps following me."

One torment from which we all suffer is the stress and strain of modern life. In this connection the California State Department of Public Health has made a careful and scientific inquiry into the factors which tend to produce alcoholics. These factors, as reported in the San Francisco *Chronicle*, all come under the heading of "high stress." This "high stress," we are told, can be created by obvious irritations "such as a nagging wife, a bothersome mother-in-law, or an unbalanced family budget, as well as the vexations[2] of one-way streets, airplane noise and the accoutrements[3] of the atomic age," We also learn that "plenty of 'high stress' can also be brewed in the unconscious mind. The victim is troubled but doesn't know what troubles him."

In other words, it is enough simply to be alive today to be a neurotic. Nobody is likely to be subject to all of these strains, but surely anybody has enough of some of them—the airplane noise, the mother-in-law, the unbalanced budget—to be able to make out a good case for his loss of self-control. Of course the report says that the bottle is not the only means of escape from the torment of modern life. Others may do it by "attempting suicide, gambling, chasing women, over-eating, and otherwise over-indulging." At any rate, a tax-supported public agency fulfills its duty to the prejudices of the day by solemnly providing a set of scientific alibis for irresponsibility that can be appropriated by just about anyone.

*H*owever, the universal alibi of irresponsibility is centered in the family. The family can be regarded as a focal point for the forces both of heredity and of environment. Moreover, everybody has had, one way or another, a father and a mother. The father alone is a sufficient excuse for almost any irregularity of conduct—be he famous, or infamous, or mediocre, or non-functional. If the poor child has a famous father, then we know he must spend his life in a desperate effort to measure up to an impossible standard of excellence. If the poor child has an infamous father, then he must spend his life in a desperate effort to overcome the shameful heritage which is his own. If the poor child has an ordinary, average father, then he is bound to rebel against this example of mediocrity, and to strive for some kind of distinction whether by conventional or by unconventional means. If the poor child's father is out of

[1] brothers or sisters

From **Odyssey of the Self-Centered Self,** © 1960, 1961 by Robert Elliot Fitch. Reprinted by permission of Harcourt, Brace & World, Inc.

[2] irritations
[3] equipment, trappings

the picture after the time of conception, then we have another set of complexes and fixations, all of which relate to the mother.

Ideally, no doubt, there would be a minimizing of risk if fathers could be eliminated altogether. This goal seems to be a little way off. But we take hope from the fact that the federal government, in collaboration with the University of Wisconsin's genetics department, has developed a revolutionary, fatherless potato. This potato has only half the chromosomes of the normal variety, and breeds truer to form. Unfortunately, it has poor survival value.

"The plain fact is that our world in the United States suffers, not from an excess of impersonality, but from an excess of the opposite. Our society is too self-centered in its concerns."

The nice thing about the parental alibi is that it can always be made to work in either of two opposite directions. If a young man is a poor student, he may complain that his parents were relative illiterates, and never taught him the love of good books and habits of steady reading. Or he may complain that his parents were excessive in their addiction to scholarship, that he was so much surrounded by learning from early childhood that he developed a revulsion against it and since then can't bear the sight of a book. If someone is always late to appointments, he may protest that he had strict, old-fashioned parents, who were so rigorous in their insistence on punctuality that he was compelled to adopt the principle of continual tardiness as an affirmation of the freedom of his personality. Or he may protest that his parents were singularly careless and indifferent concerning times and seasons, and that, having grown up in this atmosphere of delightful laxity, he is unable to bring himself around to more scrupulous behavior. In any case the blame rests on the parent, never on the offspring.

One can draw just as good alibis from his siblings, if he has some, or even if he has none. A careful study of Freud, Jung, Adler, and of modern psychologists makes it quite plain that brothers and sisters are among the very worst hazards in life. It is dangerous to be the oldest child; it is perilous to be the youngest; it is tough to be the one in the middle. It is upsetting to be the only boy with several sisters. It is disturbing to be the only girl with several brothers. It is ruinous to be one child among a dozen. It is dangerous to be an only child. It is dangerous to be a child. Perhaps the perfect arrangement would be to eliminate parents, to skip childhood, and to be incubated and hatched at an advanced age, all ready to wear the honorifics[4] of our society as "free, mature adults." Unfortunately, that would deprive us of all the alibis for irresponsibility, which are occasionally useful even to the most "mature mind."

A more strictly contemporary complaint would have it that we live in a "cold and impersonal world," and that this has disastrous effects on personality. One can imagine the Pilgrim Fathers' resorting to some such excuse for their shortcomings. Certainly their world was cold enough in the winter. And it was impersonal enough, with savages, a wilderness, and famine haunting their very doorsteps. Somehow they seem never to have thought of this excellent alibi. One can also imagine a citizen of some collectivist[5] society making such a protest. Nothing could be more cold and impersonal than collectivism—more lacking in warmth of feeling for the individual, more contemptuous of his rights as a person. Yet here, too, there seems to be no one with ingenuity enough to make the lament.

Where the complaint of a "cold and impersonal world" is warranted, the complaint is not made. Where the complaint of a "cold and impersonal world" is not warranted, it is made. The plain fact is that our world in the United States suffers, not from an excess of impersonality, but from an excess of the opposite. Our society is too self-centered in its concerns. It is at this moment one of the most egocentric societies in history. Once again we bestow the fee upon the foul disease. We insist upon having as a remedy a more generous application of that which is the source of our ailment—the emphasis on the individual person.

---

[4] titles, terms of respect

[5] a system in which the state or the people as a whole own and control the material and means of production and distribution

The Plight of the Pleasure Neurotic

NORMAN M. LOBSENZ

And pleasure brings as surely in her train Remorse, and Sorrow, and vindictive Pain.

WILLIAM COWPER, *The Progress of Error*

One of America's most prolific and successful writers has confessed that the quantity and scope of his literary output is not so much the result of creative drive as it is of the dread of pleasure. For twenty-five years, Jerome Weidman told an interviewer, he worked mornings on his best-selling novels and afternoons on his short stories. But his evenings were free, and this struck Mr. Weidman as a miscarriage of justice. After all, he reasoned, he relished his work, and it brought him substantial returns both of worldly goods and worldly fame. Did he also deserve to have time in which to enjoy himself?

In an effort to atone for the guilt he felt during the leisurely evenings, Weidman started work earlier and earlier in the day. But even when his self-imposed schedule brought him face to platen with his typewriter at six o'clock in the morning, the work-free nights still nibbled at his peace of mind. Weidman finally decided to write plays so that he would have a legitimate excuse to labor in the evenings. The results, so far, have been two Broadway hits, with a third in the making. This may have created additional problems for Weidman's tax accountants, but the writer's own dilemma was solved: He had escaped the opportunity for pleasure.

Mr. Weidman is not alone in his quandary. Pleasure is a threat to many Americans. They go to almost any lengths to avoid it. They abhor free time because it is necessary to fill it with fun. To paraphrase the Bard, out of this flower, leisure, they pluck this nettle, duty.

Psychiatrists have a predilection[1] for finding a skeleton in even the most proper mental closet; but there is nevertheless considerable weight of evidence to lend credence to the claim that there is a valid clinical syndrome[2] which may be called the "pleasure neurosis," and that the fear of pleasure can be one of the symptoms of psychiatric illness.

The "pleasure neurotic" may be defined as a person who suffers from a deep psychological fear of relaxation. He is equipped, often brilliantly, for all the workaday functions of life. But he is lost when work is over. So deep is his fear of leisure that he *must* remain in harness as long as possible. The pleasure neurotic is the man who brings home enough work from the office to carry him through the awful hiatus[3] of the evening. He is the man who can't stand Sunday. He is the man who, at the behest of his subconscious, fritters away the hours of the day so that he will have a legitimate excuse to work overtime at night. He is the slave to lists and systems and routines—devices all nicely calculated to protect him from having time on his hands. He is the man for whom pleasure is equated with the defiance of authority; this creates feelings of anxiety and guilt; the only way he can appease these feelings and that authority—which is in fact the conscience of his childhood—is by hard work. He cannot give himself permission to let down.

Faced with the threatened possibility of enjoyment, the pleasure neurotic becomes restless and irritable. Intolerant of *in*activity, he is equally unable to bear activity. To read, to watch television, to go to a movie, to hit golf balls at a driving range—these escapist recreations produce not relaxation but intense guilt feelings. Only if these pleasures can be somehow converted into *necessities*—to read for business or for self-improvement; to watch a program or a picture so that one can discuss it intelligently at the office next day; to hit golf balls to improve one's waistline—

[1] readiness or predisposition
[2] set of symptoms which characterize a disease
[3] gap, break in continuity

84

only then can they be indulged in without the penalty of penitence.

The pleasure neurotic, as a result, takes part in enjoyable activities only furtively or defiantly. Either avenue leads inevitably to a deeper guilt. On occasion the pleasure neurotic secretly savors the delicious possibility of not only *not* enjoying himself, but of simultaneously being able to delude himself about his true motives and thereby to feel martyred for having to "give up" the pleasures he does not want in the first place. . . .

America is the only country where pleasure is a problem, and where the problem is so solemnly debated. Most of the world is too busy, poor, hungry, sick, weary, or oppressed even to think of pleasure. The minority for whom a modicum[4] of enjoyment out of life is possible do not worry pleasure as a dog worries a bone; they do what comes naturally. Only in America is pleasure a matter for scrutiny and breast-beating. Scholars of Olympian repute spend days in earnest panel discussions about "meaningful values for the leisure revolution." Sociologists research pleasure; psychiatrists analyze it; foundations publish reports about it; the President of the United States,[5] when he is not busy with the Cold War or civil rights, expresses official concern regarding it; and at least four major national organizations exist to cope with it.

The Indian writer Santha Rama Rau once was inveigled[6] into taking part in a conference on the uses of leisure. She listened for many hours to speakers most of whom viewed with alarm the prospect of a nation with five billion leisure hours to fill every week. Her own comment provided perspective. "Surely nowhere else in the world," she said, "do people fuss so much about what to do in their spare time . . . What is wrong with lying on the beach?"

Yet there are many reasons why Americans dissect pleasure. For one thing, we are fascinated by social self-analysis. For another, we are growing to be a stuffy people who look upon leisure and pleasure not as delights to be accepted but as responsibilities to be discharged. Management fusses because proposals for a shorter working week are almost invariably coupled with proposals for a higher rate of pay. Labor unions fuss because workers are more interested in money,

---

[4] a small portion
[5] Lobsenz's reference is to the late President John F. Kennedy.
[6] lured

and what it will buy, than they are in more time off. Some people wonder whether the ratio of work to pleasure should not be a matter of national policy rather than personal preference in these critical times. If, they say, during the next ten years a total of two hours is subtracted from the average work-week, our Gross National Product will suffer by fifty billion dollars. Others point out with equal logic that what counts is not the *amount* of the GNP, but the kinds of goods and services it includes, and the uses to which they are put. Perhaps all of this—including our individual qualms and personal misgivings about fun —stems from the root fact that we are *nouveau riche*[7] when it comes to leisure. Therefore we vacillate[8] between graceless uses and boorish displays of pleasure at one extreme, and self-conscious concern about it at the other.

"Pleasure is a threat to many Americans. They go to almost any lengths to avoid it. They abhor free time because it is necessary to fill it with fun."

Some of us suffer from well-ordered boredom; William Faulkner once described this thorn in the side of leisure. "One of the saddest things," he said, "is that the only thing a man can do for eight hours a day is work. You can't eat eight hours a day nor drink eight hours a day nor make love eight hours a day—all you can do for eight hours is work. Which is why man makes himself and everybody else so miserable and unhappy."

Others suffer from impatience; they demand *immediate* satisfaction from a pleasurable activity. Sophocles observed that one must wait until the evening to see how splendid the day was. Yet many people cannot wait for a long-term reward. Most of us, however, suffer from a surfeit[9] of potential pleasures. The sociologist Gunnar Myrdal in his study of the American Negro pointed out that the Negro had so little time free from labor, and was cut off by segregation from so many forms of recreation available to white

people, that he perforce learned to enjoy whatever simple pleasures were available to him. Americans today—to an increasing degree regardless of color—have so many divertisements[10] at hand that we can afford to be eternally disenchanted. We need not enjoy *this* because there is always *that*; we need not take pleasure in *that*, because there is always something else.

The Utopian assumptions[11] about pleasures have crumbled beneath the dead weight of the facts. Thomas More, predicting a society with a six-hour working day, took it for granted that all men would find their joys in tending gardens, in conversation, in leisurely travel, in the cultivation of the mind. Other romantics envisioned the liberated working class strolling through the fields at eventide discussing literature and philosophy.

Do not smile. These visionaries were not so far wrong in attributing to man the desire for such pleasures. Where the Utopians erred was in expecting that men would actually do what they said they wanted to do. When interviewers ask people today what they want to do for pleasure that they are *not* doing, the answers are much along Utopian lines: they want to read good books, to travel, study, quietly commune with loved ones. But what do these people actually do? They spend nearly four billion hours a week watching television and listening to the radio. And what would they do if they had an *extra* two hours every day all to themselves? Sociologist Alfred C. Clarke asked this question a few years ago of several thousand men whom he classified into "prestige levels" on the basis of their jobs. At the lower end of the scale—unskilled and semi-skilled workers—more than half would use this extra time to "loaf, sleep or work around the house." Even among small-business proprietors and white-collar workers these were the pleasure choices of 40 per cent. Only at the top level of executives and professional men was "reading and study" the first choice. And even among *them*, 25 per cent said they'd use two additional hours to loaf and sleep.

[10] diversions, entertainments.
[11] found in St. Thomas More's *Utopia*, a treatise on an imaginary, ideal society first published in 1516.

[7] the newly rich
[8] hesitate in choice of opinions or courses; waver
[9] oversupply

Playboy's Doctrine of Male

HARVEY COX

Sometime this month over one million American young men will place sixty cents[1] on a counter somewhere and walk away with a copy of *Playboy,* one of the most spectacular successes in the entire history of American journalism. When one remembers that every copy will probably be seen by several other people in college dormitories and suburban rumpus rooms, the total readership in any one month easily exceeds that of all the independent religious magazines, serious political and cultural journals, and literary periodicals put together.

What accounts for this uncanny reception? What factors in American life have combined to allow *Playboy's* ambitious young publisher, Hugh Hefner, to pyramid his jackpot into a chain of night clubs, TV spectaculars, bachelor tours to Europe and special discount cards? What impact does *Playboy* really have?

Clearly *Playboy's* astonishing popularity is not attributable solely to pin-up girls. For sheer nudity its pictorial art cannot compete with such would-be competitors as *Dude* and *Escapade.* Rather, *Playboy* appeals to a highly mobile, increasingly affluent group of young readers, mostly between eighteen and thirty, who want much more from their drugstore reading than bosoms and thighs. They need a total image of what it means to be a man. And Mr. Hefner's *Playboy* has no hesitancy about telling them.

Why should such a need arise? David Riesman has argued that the responsibility for character formation in our society has shifted from the family to the peer group and to the mass media peer group surrogates.[2] Things are changing so rapidly that one who is equipped by his family with inflexible, highly internalized values becomes unable to deal with the accelerated pace of change and with the varying contexts in which he is called upon to function. This is especially true in the area of consumer values toward which the "other-directed person" is increasingly oriented.

Within the confusing plethora[3] of mass media signals and peer group values, *Playboy* fills a special need. For the insecure young man with newly acquired time and money on his hands who still feels uncertain about his consumer skills, *Playboy* supplies a comprehensive and authoritative guidebook to this foreboding new world to which he now has access. It tells him not only who to be; it tells him *how* to be it, and even provides consolation outlets for those who secretly feel that they have not quite made it.

In supplying for the other-directed consumer of leisure both the normative[4] identity image and the means for achieving it, *Playboy* relies on a careful integration of copy and advertising material. The comic book that appeals to a younger generation with an analogous problem skillfully intersperses illustrations of incredibly muscled men and excessively mammalian[5] women with advertisements for body-building gimmicks and foam rubber brassiere supplements. Thus the thin-chested comic book readers of both sexes are thoughtfully supplied with both the ends and the means for attaining a spurious[6] brand of maturity. *Playboy* merely continues the comic book tactic for the next age group. Since within every identity crisis, whether in 'teens or twenties, there is usually a sexual identity problem, *Playboy* speaks to those who desperately want to know what it means to be a *man,* and more specifically a *male,* in today's world.

Both the image of man and the means for its attainment exhibit a remarkable consistency in *Playboy.* The skilled consumer is cool and unruffled. He savors sports cars, liquor, high fidelity and book club selections with a casual, unhurried aplomb. Though he must certainly *have* and *use* the latest consumption item, he must not permit

---

[1] Since this article was written the price of *Playboy* has increased to $1.00 per issue.

Reprinted from **Christianity and Crisis** April 17, 1961.

[2] substitutes
[3] excess, superabundance
[4] establishing a norm or pattern
[5] breasted
[6] false, illegitimate

himself to get too attached to it. The style will change and he must always be ready to adjust. His persistent anxiety that he may mix a drink incorrectly, enjoy a jazz group that is passé, or wear last year's necktie style is comforted by an authoritative tone in *Playboy* beside which papal encyclicals sound irresolute.

"Don't hesitate," he is told, "this assertive, self-assured weskit is what every man of taste wants for the fall season." Lingering doubts about his masculinity are extirpated[7] by the firm assurance that "real men demand this ruggedly masculine smoke" (cigar ad). Though "the ladies will swoon for you, no matter that they promise, don't give them a puff. This cigar is for men only." A fur-lined canvas field jacket is described as "the most masculine thing since the cave man." What to be and how to be it are both made unambiguously clear.

But since being a male necessitates some kind of relationship to females, *Playboy* fearlessly confronts this problem too, and solves it by the consistent application of the same formula. Sex becomes one of the items of leisure activity that the knowledgeable consumer of leisure handles with his characteristic skill and detachment. The girl becomes a desirable, indeed an indispensable "Playboy accessory."

In a question-answering column entitled: "The Playboy Advisor," queries about smoking equipment (how to break in a meerschaum pipe), cocktail preparation (how to mix a "Yellow Fever") and whether or not to wear suspenders with a vest, alternate with questions about what to do with girls who complicate the cardinal principle of casualness, either by suggesting marriage or by some other impulsive gesture toward permanent relationship. The infallible answer from this oracle never varies: sex must be contained, at all costs, within the entertainment-recreation area. Don't let her get "serious."

After all, the most famous feature of the magazine is its monthly fold-out photo of a *play*mate. She is the symbol par excellence of recreational sex. When play time is over, the playmate's function ceases, so she must be made to understand the rules of the game. As the crew-cut young man in a *Playboy* cartoon says to the rumpled and disarrayed girl he is passionately embracing, "Why speak of love at a time like this?"

The magazine's fiction purveys the same kind of severely departmentalized sex. Although the editors have recently dressed up the contents of *Playboy* with contributions by Hemingway, Bemelmans and even a Chekhov translation, the regular run of stories relies on a repetitious and predictable formula. A successful young man, either single or somewhat less than ideally married—a figure with whom readers have no difficulty identifying—encounters a gorgeous and seductive woman who makes no demands on him except sex. She is the prose duplication of the cool-eyed but hot-blooded playmate of the fold-out page.

"For Playboy's *man, others— especially women—are for him. They are his leisure accessories, his playthings."*

Drawing heavily on the phantasy life of all young Americans, the writers utilize for their stereotyped heroines the hero's school teacher, his secretary, an old girl friend, or the girl who brings her car into the garage where he works. The happy issue is always a casual but satisfying sexual experience with no entangling alliances whatever. Unlike the women he knows in real life, the *Playboy* reader's fictional girl friends know their place and ask for nothing more. They present no danger of permanent involvement. Like any good accessory, they are detachable and disposable.

Many of the advertisements reinforce the sex-accessory identification in another way by attributing female characteristics to the items they sell. Thus a full page ad for the MG assures us that this car is not only "the smoothest pleasure machine" on the road and that having one is a "love-affair," but most importantly, "you drive it—it doesn't drive you." The ad ends with the equivocal question, "is it a date?"

Playboy insists that its message is one of liberation. Its gospel frees us from captivity to the puritanical "high-hat brigade." It solemnly crusades for "frankness" and publishes scores of letters congratulating it for its unblushing "candor." Yet the whole phenomenon of which *Playboy* is only a part vividly illustrates the awful fact of a new kind of tyranny.

---

[7] destroyed, wiped out

88   Those liberated by technology and increased prosperity to new worlds of leisure now become the anxious slaves of dictatorial taste-makers. Obsequiously[8] waiting for the latest signal on what is cool and what is awkward, they are paralyzed by the fear that they may hear pronounced on them that dread sentence occasionally intoned by "The Playboy Advisor": "you goofed!" Leisure is thus swallowed up in apprehensive competitiveness, its liberating potential transformed into a self-destructive compulsion to consume only what is *au courant*.[9] *Playboy* mediates the Word of the most high into one section of the consumer world, but it is a word of bondage, not of freedom.

Nor will *Playboy's* synthetic doctrine of man stand the test of scrutiny. Psychoanalysts constantly remind us how deeply seated sexuality is in the human self. But if they didn't remind us, we would soon discover it anyway in our own experience. As much as the human male might like to terminate his relationship with a woman as he snaps off the stereo, or store her for special purposes like a camel's hair jacket, it really can't be done. And anyone with a modicum[10] of experience with women knows it can't be done. Perhaps this is the reason why *Playboy's* readership drops off so sharply after the age of thirty.

Playboy really feeds on the presence of a repressed fear of involvement with women, which for various reasons is still present in many otherwise adult Americans. So *Playboy's* version of sexuality grows increasingly irrelevant as authentic sexual maturity is achieved.

The male identity crisis to which *Playboy* speaks has as its roots a deep-set fear of sex, a fear that is uncomfortably combined with fascination. *Playboy* strives to resolve this antinomy[11] by reducing the terrible proportions of sexuality, its power and its passion, to a packageable consumption item. Thus in *Playboy's* iconography,[12] the nude woman symbolizes total sexual accessibility, but demands nothing from the observer. "You drive it—it doesn't drive you." The terror of sex, which cannot be separated from its ecstasy, is dissolved. But this futile attempt to reduce the *mysterium tremendum* of the sexual fails to solve the problem of being a man. For sexuality is the basic form of all human relationship, and therein lies its terror and its power.

Karl Barth has called this basic relational form of man's life *Mitmensch*, co-humanity. This means that becoming fully human, in this case a human male, necessitates not having the other totally exposed to me and my purposes—while I remain uncommitted—but exposing myself to the risk of encounter with the other by reciprocal self-exposure. The story of man's refusal to be so exposed goes back to the story of Eden and is expressed by man's desire to control the other rather than to *be with* the other. It is basically the fear to be one's self, a lack of the "courage to be."

Thus any theological critique of *Playboy* that focuses on its "lewdness" will misfire completely. *Playboy* and its less successful imitators are not "sex magazines" at all. They are basically antisexual. They dilute and dissipate authentic sexuality by reducing it to an accessory, by keeping it at a safe distance.

It is precisely because these magazines are antisexual that they deserve the most searching kind of theological criticism. They foster a heretical doctrine of man, one at radical variance with the biblical view. For *Playboy's* man, others—especially women—are *for* him. They are his leisure accessories, his playthings. For the Bible, man only becomes fully man by being *for* the other.

Moralistic criticisms of *Playboy* fail because its anti-moralism is one of the few places in which *Playboy* is right. But if Christians bear the name of One who was truly man because he was totally *for* the other, and if it is in him that we know who God is and what human life is for, then we must see in *Playboy* the latest and slickest episode in man's continuing refusal to be fully human.

---

[8] slavishly, submissively
[9] up to date, "with it"
[10] a moderate or small amount
[11] paradox, self-contradiction
[12] illustration by means of pictures, images, or symbols

What's American About America?

JOHN A. KOUWENHOVEN

student to know which accounts to trust? Especially since most of the explorers seem to have found not one but two or more antipodal[1] and irreconcilable Americas. The Americans, we are convincingly told, are the most materialistic of peoples, and, on the other hand, they are the most idealistic; the most revolutionary, and, conversely, the most conservative; the most rampantly individualistic, and, simultaneously, the most gregarious[2] and herd-like; the most irreverent toward

[1] diametrically opposed
[2] sociable

The discovery of America has never been a more popular pastime than it is today. Scarcely a week goes by without someone's publishing a new book of travels in the bright continent. The anthropologists, native and foreign, have discovered that the natives of Middletown and Plainville, U. S. A. are as amazing and as interesting as the natives of such better known communities as the Trobriand Islands and Samoa. Magazines here and abroad provide a steady flow of articles by journalists, historians, sociologists, and philosophers who want to explain America to itself, or to themselves, or to others.

The discoverers of America have, of course, been describing their experiences ever since Captain John Smith wrote his first book about America almost 350 years ago. But as Smith himself noted, not everyone "who hath bin at Virginia, understandeth or knowes what Virginia is." Indeed, just a couple of years ago the Carnegie Corporation, which supports a number of college programs in American Studies, entitled its Quarterly Report "Who Knows America?" and went on to imply that nobody does, not even "our lawmakers, journalists, civic leaders, diplomats, teachers, and others."

There is, of course, the possibility that some of the writers who have explored, vicariously or in person, this country's past and present may have come to understand or know what America really is. But how is the lay inquirer and the

their elders, and, contrariwise, the most abject worshipers of "Mom." They have an unbridled admiration of everything big, from bulldozers to bosoms; and they are in love with everything diminutive, from the "small hotel" in the song to the little woman in the kitchen.

Maybe, as Henry James thought when he wrote *The American Scene*, it is simply that the country is "too large for any human convenience," too diverse in geography and in blood strains to make sense as any sort of unit. Whatever the reason, the conflicting evidence turns up wherever you look, and the observer has to content himself with some sort of pluralistic conception. The philosopher Santayana's way out was to say that the American mind was split in half, one half symbolized by the skyscraper, the other by neat reproductions of Colonial mansions (with surreptitious modern conveniences).

"The American will," he concluded, "inhabits the skyscraper; the American intellect inherits the Colonial mansion." Mark Twain also defined the split in architectural terms, but more succinctly: American houses, he said, had Queen Anne fronts and Mary Ann behinds.

And yet, for all the contrarieties, there remains something which I think we all feel to be distinctively American, some quality or characteristic underlying the polarities[3] which—as Henry James himself went on to say—makes the American way of doing things differ more from any other nation's way than the ways of any two other Western nations differ from each other.

I am aware of the risks in generalizing. And yet it would be silly, I am convinced, to assert that there are not certain things which are more American than others. Take the New York City skyline, for example—that ragged man-made Sierra at the eastern edge of the continent. Clearly, in the minds of immigrants and returning travelers, in the iconography[4] of the ad-men who use it as a backdrop for the bourbon and airplane luggage they are selling, in the eyes of poets and of military strategists, it is one of the prime American symbols.

Let me start, then, with the Manhattan skyline and list a few things which occur to me as distinctively American. Then, when we have the list, let us see what, if anything, these things have in common. Here are a dozen items to consider:

1. The Manhattan skyline
2. The gridiron town plan
3. The skyscraper
4. The Model-T Ford
5. Jazz
6. The Constitution
7. Mark Twain's writing
8. Whitman's *Leaves of Grass*
9. Comic strips
10. Soap operas
11. Assembly-line production
12. Chewing gum

Here we have a round dozen artifacts which are, it seems to me, recognizably American, not likely to have been produced elsewhere. Granted that some of us take more pleasure in some of them than in others—that many people prefer soap opera to *Leaves of Grass* while others think Mark Twain's storytelling is less offensive than chewing gum—all twelve items are, I believe, widely held to be indigenous[5] to our culture. The fact that many people in other lands like them too, and that some of them are nearly as acceptable overseas as they are here at home, does not in any way detract from their obviously American character. It merely serves to remind us that to be American does not mean to be inhuman—a fact which, in certain moods of self-criticism, we are inclined to forget.

What, then, is the "American" quality which these dozen items share? And what can that quality tell us about the character of our culture, about the nature of our civilization?

Those engaged in discovering America often begin by discovering the Manhattan skyline, and here as well as elsewhere they discover apparently irreconcilable opposites. They notice at once that it doesn't make any sense, in human or aesthetic terms. It is the product of insane politics, greed, competitive ostentation, megalomania,[6] the worship of false gods. Its products, in turn, are traffic jams, bad ventilation, noise, and all the other ills that metropolitan flesh is heir to. And the net result is, illogically enough, one of the most exaltedly beautiful things man has ever made.

Perhaps this paradoxical result will be less bewildering if we look for a moment at the formal and structural principles which are involved in

[3] direct opposites
[4] illustration by means of pictures, images, or symbols
[5] native
[6] an obsessive concern with bigness

the skyline. It may be helpful to consider the skyline as we might consider a lyric poem, or a novel, if we were trying to analyze its aesthetic quality.

Looked at in this way, it is clear that the total effect which we call "the Manhattan skyline" is made up of almost innumerable buildings, each in competition (for height, or glamor, or efficiency, or respectability) with all of the others. Each goes its own way, as it were, in a carnival of rugged architectural individualism. And yet— as witness the universal feeling of exaltation and aspiration which the skyline as a whole evokes— out of this irrational, unplanned, and often infuriating chaos, an unforeseen unity has evolved. No building ever built in New York was placed where it was, or shaped as it was, because it would contribute to the aesthetic effect of the skyline—lifting it here, giving it mass there, or lending a needed emphasis. Each was built, all those now under construction are being built, with no thought for their subordination to any over-all effect.

What, then, makes possible the fluid and ever-changing unity which does, in fact, exist? Quite simply, there are two things, both simple in themselves, which do the job. If they were not simple, they would not work; but they are, and they do.

One is the gridiron pattern of the city's streets —the same basic pattern which accounts for Denver, Houston, Little Rock. Birmingham, and almost any American town you can name, and the same pattern which, in the form of square townships, sections, and quarter sections, was imposed by the Ordinance of 1785 on an almost continental scale. Whatever its shortcomings when compared with the "discontinuous street patterns" of modern planned communities, this artificial geometric grid—imposed upon the land without regard to contours or any preconceived pattern of social zoning—had at least the quality of rational simplicity. And it is this simple gridiron street pattern which, horizontally, controls the spacing and arrangement of the rectangular shafts which go to make up the skyline.

The other thing which holds the skyline's diversity together is the structural principle of the skyscraper. When we think of individual buildings, we tend to think of details of texture, color, and form, of surface ornamentation or the lack of it. But as elements in Manhattan's skyline, these

things are of little consequence. What matters there is the vertical thrust, the motion upward; and that is the product of cage or skeleton, construction in steel—a system of construction which is, in effect, merely a three-dimensional variant of the gridiron street plan, extending vertically instead of horizontally.

The aesthetics of cage, or skeleton, construction have never been fully analyzed, nor am I equipped to analyze them. But as a lay observer, I am struck by fundamental differences between the effect created by height in the RCA building at Radio City, for example, and the effect created by height in Chartres cathedral or in Giotto's campanile.[7] In both the latter (as in all the great architecture of the past) proportion and symmetry, the relation of height to width, are constituent to the effect. One can say of a Gothic cathedral, this tower is too high; of a Romanesque dome, this is top-heavy. But there is nothing inherent in cage construction which would invite such judgments. A true skyscraper like the RCA building could be eighteen or twenty stories taller, or ten or a dozen stories shorter without changing its essential aesthetic effect. Once steel cage construction has passed a certain height, the effect of transactive upward motion has been established; from there on, the point at which you cut it off is arbitrary and makes no difference.

"Our history is the process of motion . . . . a long, complex, and sometimes terrifyingly rapid sequence of consecutive change.

Those who are familiar with the history of the skyscraper will remember how slowly this fact was realized. Even Louis Sullivan—greatest of the early skyscraper architects—thought in terms of having to close off and climax the upward motion of the tall building with an "attic" or cornice. His lesser contemporaries worked for years on the blind assumption that the proportion and symmetry of masonry architecture must be preserved in the new technique. If with the

[7] a tower in Florence, Italy, designed in the 14th century by Giotto di Bondone. It stands 45 feet square by 275 feet high, rising sheer from the pavement without supporting buttresses.

steel cage one could go higher than with load-bearing masonry walls, the old aesthetic effects could be counterfeited by dressing the façade as if one or more buildings had been piled on top of another—each retaining the illusion of being complete in itself. You can still see such buildings in New York: the first five stories perhaps a Greco-Roman temple, the next ten a neuter warehouse, and the final five or six an Aztec pyramid. And that Aztec pyramid is simply a cheap and thoughtless equivalent of the more subtle Sullivan cornice. Both structures attempt to close and climax the upward thrust, to provide something similar to the *Katharsis* in Greek tragedy.

But the logic of cage construction requires no such climax. It has less to do with the inner logic of masonry forms than with that of the old Globe-Wernicke sectional bookcases, whose interchangeable units (with glass-flap fronts) anticipated by fifty years the modular unit systems of so-called modern furniture. Those bookcases were advertised in the 'nineties as "always complete but never finished"—a phrase which could with equal propriety have been applied to the Model-T Ford. Many of us remember with affection that admirably simple mechanism, forever susceptible to added gadgets or improved parts, each of which was interchangeable with what you already had.

Here, then, are the two things which serve to tie together the otherwise irrelevant components of the Manhattan skyline: the gridiron ground plan and the three-dimensional vertical grid of steel cage construction. And both of these are closely related to one another. Both are composed of simple and infinitely repeatable units.

*I*t was the French architect, Le Corbusier, who described New York's architecture as "hot jazz in stone and steel." At first glance this may sound as if it were merely a slick updating of Schelling's "Architecture . . . is frozen music," but it is more than that if one thinks in terms of the structural principles we have been discussing and the structural principles of jazz.

Let me begin by making clear that I am using the term jazz in its broadest significant application. There are circumstances in which it is important to define the term with considerable precision, as when you are involved in discussion with a disciple of one of the many cults, orthodox or progressive, which devote themselves to some particular subspecies of jazz. But in our present context we need to focus upon what all the subspecies (Dixieland, Bebop, Swing, or Cool Jazz) have in common; in other words, we must neglect the by no means uninteresting qualities which differentiate one from another, since it is what they have in common which can tell us most about the civilization which produced them.

There is no definition of jazz, academic or otherwise, which does not acknowledge that its essential ingredient is a particular kind of rhythm. Improvisation is also frequently mentioned as an essential; but even if it were true that jazz always involves improvisation, that would not distinguish it from a good deal of Western European music of the past. It is the distinctive rhythm which differentiates all types of jazz from all other music and which gives to all of its types a basic family resemblance.

It is not easy to define that distinctive rhythm. Winthrop Sargeant has described it as the product of two superimposed devices: syncopation and polyrhythm, both of which have the effect of constantly upsetting rhythmical expectations. André Hodeir, in his recent analysis of *Jazz: Its Evolution and Essence*, speaks of "an unending alternation" of syncopations and of notes played *on* the beat, which "gives rise to a kind of expectation that is one of jazz's subtlest effects."

As you can readily hear, if you listen to any jazz performance (whether of the Louis Armstrong, Benny Goodman, or Charlie Parker variety), the rhythmical effect depends upon there being a clearly defined basic rhythmic pattern which enforces the expectations which are to be upset. That basic pattern is the 4/4 or 2/4 beat which underlies all jazz. Hence the importance of the percussive instruments in jazz: the drums, the guitar or banjo, the bull fiddle, the piano. Hence too the insistent thump, thump, thump, thump which is so boring when you only half-hear jazz—either because you are too far away, across the lake or in the next room, or simply because you will not listen attentively. But hence also the delight, the subtle effects, which good jazz provides as the melodic phrases evade, anticipate, and return to, and then again

94 evade the steady basic four-beat pulse which persists, implicitly or explicitly, throughout the performance.

In other words, the structure of a jazz performance is, like that of the New York skyline, a tension of cross-purposes. In jazz at its characteristic best, each player seems to be—and has the sense of being—on his own. Each goes his own way, inventing rhythmic and melodic patterns which, superficially, seem to have as little relevance to one another as the United Nations building does to the Empire State. And yet the outcome is a dazzlingly precise creative unity.

In jazz that unity of effect is, of course, the result of the very thing which each of the players is flouting: namely, the basic 4/4 beat—that simple rhythmic gridiron of identical and infinitely extendible units which holds the performance together. As Louis Armstrong once wrote, you would expect that if every man in a band "had his own way and could play as he wanted, all you would get would be a lot of jumbled up, crazy noise." But, as he goes on to say, that does not happen, because the players know "by ear and sheer musical instinct" just when to leave the underlying pattern and when to get back on it.

What it adds up to, as I have argued elsewhere, is that jazz is the first art form to give full expression to Emerson's ideal of a union which is perfect only "when all the uniters are isolated." That Emerson's ideal is deeply rooted in our national experience need not be argued. Frederick Jackson Turner quotes a letter written by a frontier settler to friends back East, which in simple, unself-conscious words expresses the same reconciling of opposites. "It is a universal rule here," the frontiersman wrote, "to help one another, each one keeping an eye single to his own business."

One need only remember that the Constitution itself, by providing for a federation of separate units, became the infinitely extendible framework for the process of reconciling liberty and unity over vast areas and conflicting interests. Its seven brief articles, providing for checks and balances between interests, classes, and branches of the government establish, in effect, the underlying beat which gives momentum and direction to a political process which Richard Hofstadter has called "a harmonious system of mutual frustration"—a description which fits a jazz performance as well as it fits our politics.

The aesthetic effects of jazz, as Winthrop Sargeant long ago suggested, have as little to do with symmetry and proportion as have those of a skyscraper. Like the skyscraper, a jazz performance does not build to an organically required climax; it can simply cease. The "piece" which the musicians are playing may, and often does, have a rudimentary Aristotelian pattern of beginning, middle, and end; but the jazz performance need not. In traditional Western European music, themes are developed. In jazz they are toyed with and dismantled. There is no inherent reason why the jazz performance should not continue for another 12 or 16 or 24 or 32 measures (for these are the rhythmic cages which in jazz correspond to the cages of a steel skeleton in architecture). As in the skyscraper, the aesthetic effect is one of motion, in this case horizontal rather than vertical.

Jazz rhythms create what can only be called momentum. When the rhythm of one voice (say the trumpet, off on a rhythmic and melodic excursion) lags behind the underlying beat, its four-beat measure carries over beyond the end of the underlying beat's measure into the succeeding one, which has already begun. Conversely, when the trumpet anticipates the beat, it starts a new measure before the steady underlying beat has ended one. And the result is an exhilarating forward motion which the jazz trumpeter Wingy Manone once described as "feeling an increase in tempo though you're still playing at the same tempo." Hence the importance in jazz of timing, and hence the delight and amusement of the so-called "break," in which the basic 4/4 beat ceases and a soloist goes off on a flight of rhythmic and melodic fancy which nevertheless comes back surprisingly and unerringly to encounter the beat precisely where it would have been if it had kept going.

Once the momentum is established, it can continue until—after an interval dictated by some such external factor as the conventional length of phonograph records or the endurance of dancers—it stops. And as if to guard against any Aristotelian misconceptions about an end, it is likely to stop on an unresolved chord, so that harmonically as well as rhythmically everything is left up in the air. Even the various coda-like devices employed by jazz performers at dances, such as the corny old "without a shirt" phrase of blessed memory, are harmonically unresolved. They are merely conventional ways of saying "we quit," not, like Beethoven's insistent codas, ways of saying, "There now; that ties off all the loose ends; I'm going to stop now; done; finished; concluded; signed, sealed, delivered."

*T*hus far, in our discussion of distinctively "American" things, we have focused chiefly upon twentieth-century items. But the references to the rectangular grid pattern of cities and townships and to the Constitution should remind us that the underlying structural principles with which we are concerned are deeply embedded in our civilization. To shift the emphasis, therefore, let us look at item number 7 on our list: Mark Twain's writing.

Mark's writing was, of course, very largely the product of oral influences. He was a born story-teller, and he always insisted that the oral form of the humorous story was high art. Its essential tool (or weapon), he said, is the pause—which is to say, timing. "If the pause is too long the impressive point is passed," he wrote, "and the audience have had time to divine that a surprise is intended—and then you can't surprise them, of course." In other words, he saw the pause as a device for upsetting expectations, like the jazz "break."

Mark, as you know, was by no means a formal perfectionist. In fact he took delight in being irreverent about literary form. Take, for example, his account of the way *Pudd'nhead Wilson* came into being. It started out to be a story called "Those Extraordinary Twins," about a youthful freak consisting, as he said, of "a combination of two heads and four arms joined to a single body and a single pair of legs—and I thought I would write an extravagantly fantastic little story with this freak of nature for hero—or heroes—a silly young miss [named Rowena] for heroine, and two old ladies and two boys for the minor parts."

But as he got writing the tale, it kept spreading along and other people began intruding themselves—among them Pudd'nhead, and a woman named Roxana, and a young fellow named Tom Driscoll, who—before the book was half finished—had taken things almost entirely into their own hands and were "working the whole tale as a private venture of their own."

From this point, I want to quote Mark directly, because in the process of making fun of fiction's formal conventions he employs a technique which is the verbal equivalent of the jazz "break" —a technique of which he was a master.

When the book was finished, and I came to look round to see what had become of the team I had originally started out with—Aunt Patsy Cooper, Aunt Betsy Hale, the two boys, and Rowena the light-weight heroine—they were nowhere to be seen; they had disappeared from the story some time or other. I hunted about and found them—found them stranded, idle, forgotten, and permanently useless. It was very awkward. It was awkward all around; but more particularly in the case of Rowena, because there was a love match on, between her and one of the twins that constituted the freak, and I had worked it up to a blistering heat and thrown in a quite dramatic love quarrel [now watch Mark take off like a jazz trumpeter flying off on his own in a fantastic break] wherein Rowena scathingly denounced her betrothed for getting drunk, and scoffed at his explanation of how it had happened, and wouldn't listen to it, and had driven him from her in the usual "forever" way; and now here she sat crying and broken-hearted; for she had found that he had spoken only the truth; that it was not he but the other half of the freak, that had drunk the liquor that made him drunk; that her half was a prohibitionist and had never drunk a drop in his life, and, although tight as a brick three days in the week, was wholly innocent of blame; and, indeed, when sober was constantly doing all he could to reform his brother, the other half, who never got any satisfaction out of drinking anyway, because liquor never affected him. [Now he's going to get back on the basic beat again.] Yes, here she was, stranded with that deep injustice of hers torturing her poor heart.

Now I shall have to summarize again. Mark didn't know what to do with her. He couldn't just leave her there, of course, after making such a to-do over her; he'd have to account to the reader for her somehow. So he finally decided that all he could do was "give her the grand bounce." It grieved him, because he'd come to like her after a fashion, "notwithstanding she was such an ass and said such stupid, irritating things and was so nauseatingly sentimental"; but it had to be done. So he started Chapter Seventeen with: "Rowena went out in the back yard after supper to see the fireworks and fell down the well and got drowned."

It seemed abrupt, [Mark went on] but I thought maybe the reader wouldn't notice it, because I changed the subject right away to something else. Anyway, it loosened up Rowena from where she was stuck and got her out of the way, and that was the main thing. It seemed a prompt good way of weeding out people that had got stalled, and a plenty good enough way for those others; so I hunted up the two boys and said they went out back one night to stone the cat and fell down the well and got drowned. Next I searched around and found Aunt Patsy Cooper and Aunt Betsy Hale where they were aground, and said they went out back one night to visit the sick and fell down the well and got drowned. I was going to drown some of the others, but I gave up the idea, partly because I believed that if I kept that up it would arouse attention, . . . and partly because it was not a large well and would not hold any more anyway.

That was a long excursion—but it makes the point: that Mark didn't have much reverence for conventional story structure. Even his greatest book, which is perhaps also the greatest book written on this continent—*Huckleberry Finn*—is troublesome. One can scarcely find a criticism of the book which does not object, for instance, to the final episodes, in which Tom rejoins Huck and they go through that burlesque business of "freeing" the old Negro Jim—who is, it turns out, already free. But, as T. S. Eliot was, I think, the first to observe, the real structure of *Huck Finn* has nothing to do with the traditional form of the novel—with exposition, climax, and resolution. Its structure is like that of the great river itself—without beginning and without end. Its structural units, or "cages," are the episodes of which it is composed. Its momentum is that of the tension between the river's steady flow and the eccentric superimposed rhythms of Huck's flights from, and near recapture by, the restricting forces of routine and convention.

It is not a novel of escape; if it were, it would be Jim's novel, not Huck's. Huck is free at the start, and still free at the end. Looked at in this way, it is clear that *Huckleberry Finn* has as little need of a "conclusion" as has a skyscraper or a jazz performance. Questions of proportion and symmetry are as irrelevant to its structure as they are to the total effect of the New York skyline.

There is not room here for more than brief reference to the other "literary" items on our list: Whitman's *Leaves of Grass*, comic strips, and soap opera. Perhaps it is enough to remind you that *Leaves of Grass* has discomfited many a critic by its lack of symmetry and proportion, and that Whitman himself insisted: "I round and finish little, if anything; and could not, consistently with my scheme." As for the words of true poems, Whitman said in the "Song of the Answerer"—

They bring none to his or her terminus or to be
    content and full,
Whom they take they take into space to behold the
    birth of stars, to learn one of the meanings,
To launch off with absolute faith, to sweep through
    the ceaseless rings and never be quiet again.

Although this is not the place for a detailed analysis of Whitman's verse techniques, it is worth noting in passing how the rhythm of these lines reinforces their logical meaning. The basic rhythmical unit, throughout, is a three-beat phrase of which there are two in the first line (accents falling on *none, his,* and *term* . . . *be, tent,* and *full*), three in the second and in the third. Superimposed upon the basic three-beat measure there is a flexible, nonmetrical rhythm of colloquial phrasing. That rhythm is controlled in part by the visual effect of the arrangement in long lines, to each of which the reader tends to give equal duration, and in part by the punctuation within the lines.

It is the tension between the flexible, superimposed rhythms of the rhetorical patterns and the basic three-beat measure of the underlying framework which unites with the imagery and the logical meaning of the words to give the passage its restless, sweeping movement. It is this tension, and other analogous aspects of the structure of *Leaves of Grass* which give to the book that "vista" which Whitman himself claimed for it. If I may apply to it T. S. Eliot's idea about *Huckleberry Finn,* the structure of the *Leaves* is open at the end. Its key poem may well be, as D. H. Lawrence believed, the "Song of the Open Road."

As for the comics and soap opera, they too—on their own frequently humdrum level—have devised structures which provide for no ultimate climax, which come to no end demanded by symmetry or proportion. In them both there is a shift in interest away from the "How does it come out?" of traditional story telling to "How are things going?" In a typical installment of Harold Gray's *Orphan Annie*, the final panel shows Annie walking purposefully down a path with her dog, Sandy, saying: "But if we're goin', why horse around? It's a fine night for walkin' . . . C'mon, Sandy . . . Let's go . . ." (It doesn't even end with a period, or full stop, but with

was fascinated by the way "becoming somewhat else is the perpetual game of nature." And this preoccupation with process is, of course, basic to modern science. "Matter" itself is no longer to be thought of as something fixed, but fluid and ever-changing. Similarly, modern economic theory has abandoned the "static equilibrium" analysis of the neo-classic economists, and in philosophy John Dewey's instrumentalism abandoned the classic philosophical interest in final causes for a scientific interest in "the mechanism of occurrences"—that is, process.

the conventional three dots or suspension points, to indicate incompletion.) So too, in the soap operas, *Portia Faces Life*, in one form or another, day after day, over and over again. And the operative word is the verb *faces*. It is the process of facing that matters.

Here, I think, we are approaching the central quality which all the diverse items on our list have in common. That quality I would define as a concern with process rather than with product —or, to re-use Mark Twain's words, a concern with the manner of handling experience or materials rather than with the experience or materials themselves. Emerson, a century ago,

It is obvious, I think, that the American system of industrial mass production reflects this same focus of interest in its concern with production rather than products. And it is the mass-production system, *not* machinery, which has been America's contribution to industry.

In that system there is an emphasis different from that which was characteristic of handicraft production or even of machine manufacture. In both of these there was an almost total disregard of the means of production. The aristocratic ideal inevitably relegated interest in the means exclusively to anonymous peasants and slaves; what mattered to those who controlled and administered production was, quite simply, the finished product. In a mass-production system, on the other hand, it is the process of production itself which becomes the center of interest, rather than the product.

If we are aware of this fact, we usually regard it as a misfortune. We hear a lot, for instance, of the notion that our system "dehumanizes" the worker, turning him into a machine and depriving him of the satisfactions of finishing anything, since he performs only some repetitive operation. It is true that the unit of work in mass production is not a product but an operation. But the development of the system, in contrast with Charlie Chaplin's wonderful but wild fantasy of the assembly line, has shown the intermediacy of the stage in which the worker is doomed to frustrating boredom. Merely repetitive work, in the logic of mass production, can and must be done by machine. It is unskilled work which is doomed by it, not the worker. More and more skilled workers are needed to design products, analyze jobs, cut patterns, attend complicated machines, and co-ordinate the processes which comprise the productive system.

The skills required for these jobs are different, of course, from those required to make handmade boots or to carve stone ornament, but they are not in themselves less interesting or less human. Operating a crane in a steel mill, or a turret lathe, is an infinitely more varied and stimulating job than shaping boots day after day by hand. A recent study of a group of workers on an automobile assembly line makes it clear that many of the men object, for a variety of reasons, to those monotonous, repetitive jobs which (as we have already noted) should be—but in many cases are not yet—done by machine; but those who *like* such jobs like them because they enjoy the process. As one of them said: "Repeating the same thing you can catch up and keep ahead of yourself . . . you can get in the swing of it." The report of members of a team of British workers who visited twenty American steel foundries in 1949 includes this description of the technique of "snatching" a steel casting with a magnet, maneuvered by a gantry crane running on overhead rails:

In its operation, the crane approaches a pile of castings at high speed with the magnet hanging fairly near floor level. The crane comes to a stop somewhere short of the castings, while the magnet swings forward over the pile, is dropped on to it, current switched on, and the hoist begun, at the same moment as the crane starts on its return journey. [And then, in words which might equally be applied to a jazz musician, the report adds:] The whole operation requires timing of a high order, and the impression gained is that the crane drivers derive a good deal of satisfaction from the swinging rhythm of the process.

This fascination with process has possessed Americans ever since Oliver Evans in 1785 created the first wholly automatic factory: a flour mill in Delaware in which mechanical conveyors—belt conveyors, bucket conveyors, screw conveyors—are interlinked with machines in a continuous process of production. But even if there were no other visible sign of the national preoccupation with process, it would be enough to point out that it was an American who invented chewing gum (in 1869) and that it is the Americans who have spread it—in all senses of the verb—throughout the world. An absolutely non-consumable confection, its sole appeal is the process of chewing it.

The apprehensions which many people feel about a civilization absorbed with process—about its mobility and wastefulness as well as about the "dehumanizing" effects of its jobs—derive, I suppose, from old habit and the persistence of values and tastes which were indigenous to a very different social and economic system. Whitman pointed out in *Democratic Vistas* more than eighty years ago that America was a stranger in her own house, that many of our social institutions, like our theories of literature and art, had been taken over almost without change from a culture which was not, like ours, the product of political democracy and the machine. Those institutions and theories, and the values implicit in them, are still around, though some (like collegiate gothic, of both the architectural and intellectual variety) are less widely admired than formerly.

Change, or the process of consecutive occurrences, is, we tend to feel, a bewildering and confusing and lonely thing. All of us, in some moods, feel the "preference for the stable over the precarious and uncompleted" which, as John Dewey recognized, tempts philosophers to posit their absolutes. We talk fondly of the need for roots—as if man were a vegetable, not an animal with legs whose distinction it is that he can move and "get on with it." We would do well to make ourselves more familiar with the idea that the process of development is universal, that it is "the form and order of nature." As Lancelot Law Whyte has said, in *The Next Development in Man:*

Man shares the special form of the universal formative process which is common to all organisms, and herein lies the root of his unity with the rest of organic nature. While life is maintained, the component processes in man never attain the relative isolation and static perfection of inorganic processes. . . . The individual may seek, or believe that he seeks, independence, permanence, or perfection, but that is only through his failure to recognize and accept his actual situation.

As an "organic system" man cannot, of course, expect to achieve stability or permanent harmony, though he can create (and in the great arts of the past, has created) the illusion of them. What he can achieve is a continuing development in response to his environment. The factor which gives vitality to all the component processes in the individual and in society is "not permanence but development."

To say this is not to deny the past. It is simply to recognize that for a variety of reasons people living in America have, on the whole, been better able to relish process than those who have lived under the imposing shadow of the arts and institutions which Western man created in his tragic search for permanence and perfection— for a "closed system." They find it easy to understand what that very American philosopher William James meant when he told his sister that his house in Chocorua, New Hampshire, was "the most delightful house you ever saw; it has fourteen doors, all opening outwards." They are used to living in grid-patterned cities and towns whose streets, as Jean-Paul Sartre observed, are not, like those of European cities, "closed at both ends." As Sartre says in his essay on New York, the long straight streets and avenues of a grid-iron city do not permit the buildings to "cluster like sheep" and protect one against the sense of space. "They are not sober little walks closed in between houses, but national highways. The

moment you set foot on one of them, you understand that it has to go on to Boston or Chicago."

So, too, the past of those who live in the United States, like their future, is open-ended. It does not, like the past of most other people, extend downward into the soil out of which their immediate community or neighborhood has grown. It extends laterally backward across the plains, the mountains, or the sea to somewhere else, just as their future may at any moment lead them down the open road, the endless-vistaed street.

Our history is the process of motion into and out of cities; of westering and the counter-process of return; of motion up and down the social ladder—a long, complex, and sometimes terrifyingly rapid sequence of consecutive change. And it is this sequence, and the attitudes and habits and forms which it has bred, to which the term "America" really refers.

"America" is not a synonym for the United States. It is not an artifact. It is not a fixed and immutable[8] ideal toward which citizens of this nation strive. It has not order or proportion, but neither is it chaos except as that is chaotic whose components no single mind can comprehend or control. America is process. And in so far as people have been "American"—as distinguished from being (as most of us, in at least some of our activities, have been) mere carriers of transplanted cultural traditions—the concern with process has been reflected in the work of their heads and hearts and hands.

8 unchangeable

The New Language of Morals

MALCOLM BRADBURY

From time to time, the moral vocabulary of a society seems to alter substantially, in response to social changes and the conscious or unconscious election of new leaders of thought and opinion. In these times it is easy to tell what side of the fence people are on, not so much by the opinions they express as by the words they use to express them. There grows up an Elect of discourse,[1] using words in a new, a special, a group way, and using a language with its own honorific[2]· words and concepts. One interesting example of such a word is *Puritan*, which is used in many quarters to denote a suspicious and repressive attitude towards pleasurable indulgence, but which is esteemed in other quarters as meaning almost the exact opposite. The two groups encountered each other, with perceptible raising of eyebrows, at the *Lady Chatterley's Lover* trial, when Prosecuting Counsel, speaking with the voice of conventional educated culture, confronted Professor Hoggart, speaking with the voice of modern literary culture, and confusion ensued.

Another similar key-word, conveniently separating Elect from Mass, is *Life*. To most people, Life is what we get up and go to every day, however unwillingly; and it is hard to see how Being On the Side of Life is the property of some persons more than others. But this formulation, taken over apparently from the artists of the Decadence, has now a substantial vogue. The Life Enhancers and the Life Diminishers are seen as two contrary parties in society—seen, of course, by the self-confessed Life Enhancers.

The characteristic of moral vocabularies is that they have a way of praising those who use them. There is a modern formulation which divides people into Hips and Squares, but of course it is really only those who are, or think themselves, Hip that use it. The American formulation of Far In and Far Out is a distinction made by the Far Out. It is true that the word *bourgeois*[3] is largely a formulation of the bourgeois, but only because they had sufficient urbanity[4] to see themselves from outside, which meant that they ceased in fact to be bourgeois, in their own view at least. So it is with the Side of Lifers; it is rare to find anyone describing himself, or his friends, as being on the Side of Death.

There is nothing more dangerous than for a young man in our society to appear in public with the wrong mode of discourse. The honorific words of one group are the condemnatory words of another; hence the difficulty experienced by candidates for certain rather advanced departments in universities when they have the misfortune to be praised by their headmasters as *loyal*. One man's praise is another man's stigma.[5] In a recent *Observer* series on *Patriotism*, a number of eminent people presented themselves before us in poses of acute embarrassment, rather as a bishop might in being found in a brothel in the old days. Here they were, modern men, most of them, being asked to discourse in a traditional vocabulary which was hardly likely to be current among readers who had doubtless sucked in *A Farewell to Arms* with mother's milk:

I was always embarrassed by the words sacred, glorious, and sacrifice and the expression in vain. We had heard them, sometimes standing in the rain almost out of earshot, so that only the shouted words came through, and had read them, on proclamations that were slapped up by billposters over other proclamations, now for a long time, and I had seen nothing sacred, and things that were glorious had no glory and the sacrifices were like the stockyards at Chicago if nothing was done with the meat except bury it. There were many words you could not stand to hear and finally only the names of places had dignity. . . . Abstract words such as glory, honour, courage, or hallow were obscene. . . .

---

[1] talk, conversation
[2] implying honor or respect
[3] the middle class
[4] the polish and sophistication associated with people who live in large cities
[5] a stain or reproach, as on one's reputation

Reprinted by permission of the author.

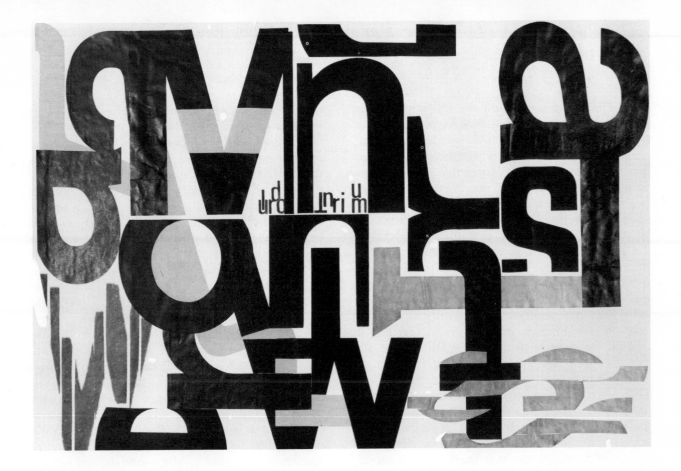

The fact of the matter is that the traditional discourse associated with the public virtues, made up of words like *patriotism, loyalty, courage* and *public spirit*, has tended to lapse, and indeed instead of attributing high motives to people who manifest them many of us are more than ready to be cynical about them. There used once to be a whole pattern of honorific words which described a happy correlation between a man's values and the aims and intentions of his society; but these are as unfashionable as the invocations to *thrift* and *self-help* that were current in Victorian society and have now disappeared in a time when we require people to spend rather than save, consume rather than produce. Most of the words that describe bridging motions between man and society have tended to vanish from the discourse of the moderns, though they remain solidly in the speech of those for whom a degree of social engagement seems impressive and worthy. Similarly many of the words that stigmatized[6] those who made a bad bridge between self and society have lost their force. There used once to be a wealth of words which manifested a general sense of the low repute in which evil and antisocial conduct was held. Nowadays, when we regard evil as a moral preference different from our own, we tend to turn to the neutral discourse of sociology or psychology. We likewise tend to suspect hierarchical[7] words, like *superior, refined* and so on. The preference today seems to be for apparently neutral and seemingly unhierarchical words without a public moral content. In this sense, the power of moral assertion in discourse would appear to be declining. In fact, of course, it is being reformed. New hierarchies and moral inferences emerge.

Words asserting a public standard of morality, roughly agreed on as a general direction for human aspiration, tend to be replaced by words asserting a relativistic and private conception. Linked with this is the discarding, in the newer vocabulary, of words seeming to imply a preference for fathers over sons. *Paternalism* is a case of a word now demoted and used pejoratively[8]—linguistically the fraternal society is already with us—and *educational* has suffered a similar

---

[6] branded as disgraceful or dishonorable

[7] ranking, or placing people into levels of prestige or authority
[8] used in a downgrading manner

"The characteristic of moral vocabularies is that they have a way of praising those who use them."

102   fate. The word *mature*, on the other hand, has undergone an interesting process of adaptation and reclamation, for it is now regarded as a moral quality almost exclusively the property of the young. This particular corrective process has struck particularly hard at Western religion, which has both a sense of the value of public moral consensus and a strong paternalistic symbolism. In consequence those aspects of religion which tend towards the fatherly, the authoritative or the social have been demoted, while those to do with the youthful and the private have been stressed of late. As more than one vicar has observed, Christianity is really a teenage religion; as others have suggested, it should never have become an institution at all, for this has set an organization intervening between man and his creator; as yet others have indicated, it never intended to become morally assertive, to take up that most unattractive of properties, a high moral tone. Religion thus tends to be de-moralized, and many of the clergy are at pains to point out that there is little moral consensus in the Church; it is the need to worship they are agreed on, though there are theologians without the clergy's degree of personal interest who hardly see the need for that. Thus in recent months we have heard a great deal about "religionless Christianity", which is, to put the matter crudely, Christianity divested of all the social apparatus which has enabled it to survive and be powerful. The new religionists—who, as a friend of mine once put it, believe in at the most one God and pray To Whom It May Concern—pay little attention to the superb sociology of the Church in the past. How cleverly, by means of great effectiveness and frequent undesirability, it kept alive the power of religion over the community! But for the new religionists it is the individual rather than the social implications of faith that matter; and the whole tone of their discourse reflects this fact, their pronouncements emphasizing contacts between man and creator, their words being personal, unabstract, tentative. As with the new philosophers the point of enquiry is the seeing eye and the thinking mind; and a logical consequence, already being reached in philosophy, is that discourse will in fact totally cease, other people lying beyond the self in a fearsome universe in whose reality one cannot for a moment trust.

Let me not suggest, however, that the Church is the stronghold of the new moral discourse—this is, on the whole, not so. Generally it is on the side of moral consensus and moral assertion, offering its positions almost as if they had some external authority. And thus it is the Church's words that are most suspect. In his Reith Lectures Professor Carstairs stigmatized Saint Paul as "an authoritarian character," a man who attempted to insist on a sexual morality remote from that of the Trobriand Islanders, and the tendency towards this sort of insistence is to be found extensively in the history of the Church. In his recent book on *The Family* the sociologist Ronald Fletcher collects together a veritable courtesy-book of old-style moral usages, most of them using the word *moral* itself. Many of the spokesmen he selects were Methodists who espoused a strict and traditional idea of public morality; they are here to be found complaining that the modern family has gone downhill, and in support of their impression they did not quote statistics but spoke rhetorically of the nation's "dire moral peril", of the "seedy dingy moral apathy of our time", "the moral failure of the home" and so on. Mr. Fletcher counters with the new mode of discourse; against moral decline he offers different behaviour. His tone is evidently more permissive but the interesting thing is that it is not without its prophetic note. He expresses "irritation" with the old manner (anger plays a substantial part in the new moral tone) and demands forward-looking thinking, better statistics, other words. So the point is not that the new prophets are without morality but that they have a different and a flatter style of moral speech to distinguish them. (In fact the word *moral* is central to the new discourse; but it means something rather different.)

What, then, we may perceive in the quiet linguistic changes that are taking place in our society at the moment is a tendency towards the heightening of private values at the expense of public ones, of the energization of words that tend to express this, and an opprobrious[9] weighting to certain traditional words which have been of evident value to public men of the past. The very overtones of the word *establishment* (i.e. that which is established is automatically to be suspected) suggests the fund of resources behind the new-style speakers, while the Conservative Party have long ceased defending the existence of anything on the grounds that it is traditional, though

[9] disgraceful or shameful

the test of time and the test of existence are as good tests as any. The gradual spreading of the new discourse naturally spreads the implied attitudes behind it (for one of the ways in which we acquire values is through acquiring an organized vocabulary—this is why vocabulary has power). And spreading it is, so that most of us now find that we straddle two linguistic worlds. The new language has extending currency. The ready acceptance of what it is conventional to call "satire" is the acceptance of the tone of voice, quizzical, demanding, informal, vernacular,[10] often faintly offensive and doctrinaire,[11] which is appropriate to the new language and which many writers have been exploring. The group of new-style speakers is thus spreading, and is leading to some gradual alienation of those who use the older tone of voice. One may examine this process in a number of conscious users of language, such as journalists or broadcasters. The formality of B.B.C.[12] official speech used to be one of our great reassurances; it spoke for order, like guards on trains. Now, in a wave of informality, even the news is changing. The names of contributors to newsreels are frequently mentioned (personal), announcers cough regularly and carefully do not, as they easily can, switch the cough out (informal), the opinions of people in the street are canvassed, though they frequently have none (democratic), and interviewers are aggressive and sometimes even offensive (vernacular). So, personal, informal, democratic and vernacular, comes the new common speech for all things.

However, the co-existence of the two modes of language can lead to confusion in these intermediate times, and it is not surprising that many people, caught between the two camps, feel now and then that a little assistance is needed. For most of us borrow our speech from all that is available, and these are hard days. One might take again the already mentioned instance of the word *moral*. In the old style of discourse (hereafter designated as OS) the word describes the obligation to choose between right and wrong; in new style (NS) it refers to the *difficulty* of choosing between right and wrong. It should be noted then that many words have diametrically

opposite meanings or intonations, and a short glossary here would not come amiss:

Youth = a person not yet fully mature (OS): a person fully mature (NS).
Mature = wise, responsible, capable of holding positions of power (OS); wise, conscious of difficulty, incapable of holding positions of power (NS).
Rebellious = out of touch with cultural experience (OS); in touch with cultural experience (NS).
Spontaneous = ill-considered, hasty (OS); imaginatively perceptive (NS).
Apathy = not being interested in taking on social duties and obligations (OS); being interested in taking on social duties and obligations (NS).
Paternal = taking an intelligent and encouraging interest in the young (OS); imposing upon and destroying the young (NS).
Culture = reading books, pursuing the arts (OS); doing anything (NS).
Commitment = an unfortunate obligation to a cause (OS); a necessary obligation to a cause (NS).
Hypocrisy = pretending to believe in what is self-evident (OS); believing in what pretends to be self-evident (NS).
Sinful = doing what everyone knows to be wrong (OS); knowing what everyone does to be wrong (NS).
Tradition = the proper preoccupation of the living with the dead (OS); the morbid preoccupation of the dead with the living (NS).

The list of course can be extended indefinitely.

A further problem emerges, however, when we find not the same word for different concepts, but different words for the same concept. Here, once again, a short list might give some guidance:

Guilt (OS) = *shame* (NS).
Puritan (OS) = *censor* (NS).
Libertine (OS) = *puritan* (NS).
Father (OS) = *brother* (NS).
Righteous indignation (OS) = *anger* or *hate* (NS).
Vulgar (OS) = *phoney* (NS).
Us (OS) = *them* (NS).
Them (OS) = *us* (NS).

There are many deductions that can be made from these slim and summary lists; it is outside my purpose here to make them. Studies are needed of the frequency with which each of these groups uses certain central words, and of particular interest are those words that appear frequently

---

[10] employing the ordinary, everyday language of a people
[11] authoritarian, dogmatic
[12] British Broadcasting Corporation, a government-controlled radio corporation

in the discourse of one group and never in the discourse of the other. In some cases they indicate the vanishing of certain concepts (*virginity* might for instance be one among NS-speakers) and the invention of others (*commitment* perhaps, totally irrelevant to OS-speakers.) My purpose here is simply to point out, to those who aspire to enter the arena of social discussion, that one's alliances may be determined by the very discourse one has acquired or chooses to espouse. The importance of a common language in establishing the free-masonry[13] of the Elect has been the theme of many modern novels, which frequently show private languages triumphing over public ones, the vernacular defeating the literary, the words of youth defeating the words of the aged. The idea of such an Elect, a central group of moral sophisticates who either triumph over or plunge more deeply into experience, whose private vision is higher than any public one, recurs frequently in fiction; it is present in Hemingway and Salinger, Lawrence and Sillitoe. It is present for that matter in Jane Austen. The logical development of the situation is to be found in the Beat Generation, an out group that distinguishes and selects its members largely by their language. What this means of course is that common discourse can both include and exclude, and in fact the Beat Generation is a very exclusive club, rather like our image of the traditional aristocracy. This sort of distinction by language has of course always existed, and it suggests that even in a classless society a hierarchy of discourse will survive. The assumption that those who are not *with it* are against it, that *them* is in no way a part of *us*, that the squares and the phoneys and the establishment—or the masses and the hoi polloi and the untutored—are by definition in another camp, means that language retains one of its essential functions. It reassures those who share our words with the warmth of phatic[14] communion; it separates those who do not into their rightful place—beyond the pale.[15]

In fact, of course, these two different languages represent two different functions of speech. The older language tends to be in character a language of idealism, of hortatory[16] and ennobling

concepts. It provides a range of discourse that is extensive and puts its users into touch with a history of language and thought. Its weakness is that it is apt to become detached from realities, to represent nothing but the will to speak. The second language tends, however, in the opposite direction. It is not a language of power, and is poor in abstract concepts. It tends to be anti-cultural. It is a language of uncertainty and scepticism to set off against the discourse of the confident. Its emphasis falls on realism rather than idealism, on descriptive rather than enlarging concepts. Its words for relations outside the self are often thin and indeterminate, and in some auditors it produces an impression akin to disturbed silence. Its best words are those which have to do with immediacy, spontaneity, and the presentation of disguised emotions and indignations. It stresses the value of being in touch and ready with a response. It closes off large areas of traditional thought and speech. Holden Caulfield, with all the resources of the English language behind him, can scarcely get beyond the word *phoney* to describe what he distrusts; we are invited to value him for his immediate touchstones, his vernacular of scepticism, though we tend to note too how narrow a discourse it is. It seems a thin discourse on which to pin a moral life; but the other discourse, with its heavily rhetorical note, its genial gestures toward meaning, can be a language quite as flat. The modern speaker needs to be quite as careful today as in the days when to use the word "notepaper" was enough to damn a man socially for life.

[13] fellowship
[14] revealing or sharing feelings or establishing an atmosphere of sociability rather than communicating ideas
[15] an idiom meaning beyond the limits within which one is protected and privileged
[16] urging or encouraging

The White Race and Its Heroes

ELDRIDGE CLEAVER

White people cannot, in the generality, be taken as models of how to live. Rather, the white man is himself in sore need of new standards, which will release him from his confusion and place him once again in fruitful communion with the depths of his own being.

JAMES BALDWIN, *The Fire Next Time*

Right from the go, let me make one thing absolutely clear: I am not now, nor have I ever been, a white man. Nor, I hasten to add, am I now a Black Muslim—although I used to be. But I *am* an Ofay[1] Watcher, a member of that unchartered, amorphous[2] league which has members on all continents and the islands of the seas. Ofay Watchers Anonymous, we might be called, because we exist concealed in the shadows wherever colored people have known oppression by whites, by white enslavers, colonizers, imperialists, and neo-colonialists.

Did it irritate you, compatriot, for me to string those epithets out like that? Tolerate me. My intention was not necessarily to sprinkle salt over anyone's wounds. I did it primarily to relieve a certain pressure on my brain. Do you cop that? If not, then we're in trouble, because we Ofay Watchers have a pronounced tendency to slip into that mood. If it is bothersome to you, it is quite a task for me because not too long ago it was my way of life to preach, as ardently as I could, that the white race is a race of devils, created by their maker to do evil, and make evil appear as good; that the white race is the natural, unchangeable enemy of the black man, who is the original man, owner, maker, cream of the planet Earth; that the white race was soon to be destroyed by Allah, and that the black man would then inherit the earth, which has always, in fact, been his.

I have, so to speak, washed my hands in the blood of the martyr, Malcolm X, whose retreat from the precipice of madness created new room for others to turn about in, and I am now caught up in that tiny space, attempting a maneuver of my own. Having renounced the teachings of Elijah Muhammad, I find that a rebirth does not follow automatically, of its own accord, that a void is left in one's vision, and this void seeks constantly to obliterate itself by pulling one back to one's former outlook. I have tried a tentative compromise by adopting a select vocabulary, so that now when I see the whites of *their* eyes, instead of saying "devil" or "beast" I say "imperialist" or "colonialist," and everyone seems to be happier.

[1] derogatory name for a white man
[2] shapeless

In silence, we have spent our years watching the ofays, trying to understand them, on the principle that you have a better chance coping with the known than with the unknown. Some of us have been, and some still are, interested in learning whether it is *ultimately* possible to live in the same territory with people who seem so disagreeable to live with; still others want to get as far away from ofays as possible. What we share in common is the desire to break the ofays' power over us.

*A*t times of fundamental social change, such as the era in which we live, it is easy to be deceived by the onrush of events, beguiled by the craving for social stability into mistaking transitory phenomena for enduring reality. The strength and permanence of "white backlash" in America is just such an illusion. However much this rearguard action might seem to grow in strength, the initiative, and the future, rest with those whites and blacks who have liberated themselves from the master/slave syndrome.[3] And these are to be found mainly among the youth.

Over the past twelve years there has surfaced a political conflict between the generations that is deeper, even, than the struggle between the races. Its first dramatic manifestation was within the ranks of the Negro people, when college students in the South, fed up with Uncle Tom's hat-in-hand approach to revolution, threw off the yoke of the NAACP. When these students initiated the first sit-ins, their spirit spread like a raging fire across the nation, and the technique of non-violent direct action, constantly refined and honed into a sharp cutting tool, swiftly matured. The older Negro "leaders," who are now all die-hard advocates of this tactic, scolded the students for sitting-in. The students rained down contempt upon their hoary heads. In the presit-in days, these conservative leaders had always succeeded in putting down insurgent[4] elements among the Negro people. (A measure of their power, prior to the students' rebellion, is shown by their success in isolating such great black men as the late W. E. B. DuBois and Paul Robeson, when these stalwarts, refusing to bite their tongues, lost favor with the U.S. government by their unstinting efforts to link up the Negro revolution with national liberation movements around the world.)

The "Negro leaders," and the whites who depended upon them to control their people, were outraged by the impudence of the students. Calling for a moratorium[5] on student initiative, they were greeted instead by an encore of sit-ins, and retired to their ivory towers to contemplate the new phenomenon. Others, less prudent because held on a tighter leash by the whites, had their careers brought to an abrupt end because they thought they could lead a black/white backlash against the students, only to find themselves in a kind of Bay of Pigs. Negro college presidents, who expelled students from all-Negro colleges in an attempt to quash the demonstrations, ended up losing their jobs; the victorious students would no longer allow them to preside over the campuses. The spontaneous protests on southern campuses over the repressive measures of their college administrations were an earnest of the Free Speech upheaval which years later was to shake the UC campus at Berkeley. In countless ways, the rebellion of the black students served as catalyst[6] for the brewing revolt of the whites.

What has suddenly happened is that the white race has lost its heroes. Worse, its heroes have been revealed as villains and its greatest heroes as the arch-villains. The new generations of whites, appalled by the sanguine[7] and despicable record carved over the face of the globe by their race in the last five hundred years, are rejecting the panoply[8] of white heroes, whose heroism consisted in erecting the inglorious edifice of colonialism and imperialism; heroes whose careers rested on a system of foreign and domestic exploitation, rooted in the myth of white supremacy and the manifest destiny of the white race. The emerging shape of a new world order, and the requisites for survival in such a world, are fostering in young whites a new outlook. They recoil in shame from the spectacle of cowboys and pioneers—their heroic forefathers whose exploits filled earlier generations with pride—galloping across a movie screen shooting down Indians like Coke bottles. Even Winston Churchill, who is looked upon by older whites as perhaps the greatest hero of the twentieth century—even he, because of the system of which he was a creature and which he served, is an arch-villain in the eyes of the young white rebels.

---

[3] a set of symptoms characterizing a disease
[4] rebellious
[5] temporary halt
[6] that which causes a reaction to take place
[7] bloody
[8] total array

At the close of World War Two, national liberation movements in the colonized world picked up new momentum and audacity, seeking to cash in on the democratic promises made by the Allies during the war. The Atlantic Charter, signed by President Roosevelt and Prime Minister Churchill in 1941, affirming "the right of all people to choose the form of government under which they may live," established the principle, although it took years of postwar struggle to give this piece of rhetoric even the appearance of reality. And just as world revolution has prompted the oppressed to re-evaluate their self-image in terms of the changing conditions, to slough off the servile attitudes inculcated by long years of subordination, the same dynamics of change have prompted the white people of the world to re-evaluate their self-image as well, to disabuse themselves of the Master Race psychology developed over centuries of imperial hegemony.[9]

". . . the initiative, and the future, rest with those whites and blacks who have liberated themselves from the master/slave syndrome. And these are to be found mainly among the youth."

It is among the white youth of the world that the greatest change is taking place. It is they who are experiencing the great psychic pain of waking into consciousness to find their inherited heroes turned by events into villains. Communication and understanding between the older and younger generations of whites has entered a crisis. The elders, who, in the tradition of privileged classes or races, genuinely do not understand the youth, trapped by old ways of thinking and blind to the future, have only just begun to be vexed—because the youth have only just begun to rebel. So thoroughgoing is the revolution in the psyches of white youth that the traditional tolerance which every older generation has found it necessary to display is quickly exhausted, leaving a gulf of fear, hostility, mutual misunderstanding, and contempt.

The rebellion of the oppressed peoples of the world, along with the Negro revolution in America, have opened the way to a new evaluation of history, a re-examination of the role played by the white race since the beginning of European expansion. The positive achievements are also there in the record, and future generations will applaud them. But there can be no applause now, not while the master still holds the whip in his hand! Not even the master's own children can find it possible to applaud him—he cannot even applaud himself! The negative rings too loudly. Slave-catchers, slaveowners, murderers, butchers, invaders, oppressors—the white heroes have acquired new names. The great white statesmen whom school children are taught to revere are revealed as the architects of systems of human exploitation and slavery. Religious leaders are exposed as condoners and justifiers of all these evil deeds. School-teachers and college professors are seen as a clique of brainwashers and whitewashers.

The white youth of today are coming to see, intuitively, that to escape the onus[10] of the history their fathers made they must face and admit the moral truth concerning the works of their fathers. That such venerated figures as George Washington and Thomas Jefferson owned hundreds of black slaves, that all the Presidents up to Lincoln presided over a slave state, and that every President since Lincoln connived politically and cynically with the issues affecting the human rights and general welfare of the broad masses of the American people—these facts weigh heavily upon the hearts of these young people.

The elders do not like to give these youngsters credit for being able to understand what is going on and what has gone on. When speaking of juvenile delinquency, or the rebellious attitude of today's youth, the elders employ a glib rhetoric. They speak of the "alienation of youth," the desire of the young to be independent, the problems of "the father image" and "the mother image" and their effect upon growing children who lack sound models upon which to pattern themselves. But they consider it bad form to connect the problems of the youth with the central event of our era—the national liberation movements abroad and the Negro revolution at home. The foundations of authority have been blasted to bits in America because the whole society has been indicted, tried, and convicted of injustice. To the youth, the elders are Ugly Americans; to the elders, the youth have gone mad.

---

[9] domination or leadership

[10] burden or responsibility

"In countless ways, the rebellion of the black students served as catalyst for the brewing revolt of the whites."

108   The rebellion of the white youth has gone through four broadly discernible stages. First there was an initial recoiling away, a rejection of the conformity which America expected, and had always received, sooner or later, from its youth. The disaffected youth were refusing to participate in the system, having discovered that America, far from helping the underdog, was up to its ears in the mud trying to hold the dog down. Because of the publicity and self-advertisements of the more vocal rebels, this period has come to be known as the beatnik era, although not all of the youth affected by these changes thought of themselves as beatniks. The howl of the beatniks and their scathing, outraged denunciation of the system—characterized by Ginsberg as Moloch, a bloodthirsty Semitic deity to which the ancient tribes sacrificed their firstborn children—was a serious, irrevocable declaration of war. It is revealing that the elders looked upon the beatniks as mere obscene misfits who were too lazy to take baths and too stingy to buy a haircut. The elders had eyes but couldn't see, ears but couldn't hear—not even when the message came through as clearly as in this remarkable passage from Jack Kerouac's *On the Road:*

At lilac evening I walked with every muscle aching among the lights of 27th and Welton in the Denver colored section, wishing I were a Negro, feeling that the best the white world had offered was not enough ecstasy for me, not enough life, joy, kicks, darkness, music, not enough night. I wished I were a Denver Mexican, or even a poor overworked Jap, anything but what I so drearily was, a "white man" disillusioned. All my life I'd had white ambitions. . . . I passed the dark porches of Mexican and Negro homes; soft voices were there, occasionally the dusky knee of some mysterious sensuous gal; the dark faces of the men behind rose arbors. Little children sat like sages in ancient rocking chairs.

The second stage arrived when these young people, having decided emphatically that the world, and particularly the U.S.A., was unacceptable to them in its present form, began an active search for roles they could play in changing the society. If many of these young people were content to lay up in their cool beat pads, smoking pot and listening to jazz in a perpetual orgy of esoteric[11] bliss, there were others, less crushed by the system, who

recognized the need for positive action. Moloch could not ask for anything more than to have its disaffected victims withdraw into safe, passive, apolitical little nonparticipatory islands, in an economy less and less able to provide jobs for the growing pool of unemployed. If all the unemployed had followed the lead of the beatniks, Moloch would gladly have legalized the use of euphoric drugs and marijuana, passed out free jazz albums and sleeping bags, to all those willing to sign affidavits promising to remain "beat." The non-beat disenchanted white youth were attracted magnetically to the Negro revolution, which had begun to take on a mass, insurrectionary tone. But they had difficulty understanding their relationship to the Negro, and what role "whites" could play in a "Negro revolution." For the time being they watched the Negro activists from afar.

The third stage, which is rapidly drawing to a close, emerged when white youth started joining Negro demonstrations in large numbers. The presence of whites among the demonstrators emboldened the Negro leaders and allowed them to use tactics they never would have been able to employ with all-black troops. The racist conscience of America is such that murder does not register as murder, really, unless the victim is white. And it was only when the newspapers and magazines started carrying pictures and stories of white demonstrators being beaten and maimed by mobs and police that the public began to protest. Negroes have become so used to this double standard that they, too, react differently to the death of a white. When white freedom riders were brutalized along with blacks, a sigh of relief went up from the black masses, because the blacks knew that white blood is the coin of freedom in a land where for four hundred years black blood has been shed unremarked and with impunity. America has never truly been outraged by the murder of a black man, woman, or child. White politicians may, if Negroes are aroused by a particular murder, say with their lips what they know with their minds they should feel with their hearts—but don't.

It is a measure of what the Negro feels that when the two white and one black civil rights workers were murdered in Mississippi in 1964, the event was welcomed by Negroes on a level of understanding beyond and deeper than the grief they felt for the victims and their families. This welcoming of violence and death to whites can

[11] understood by only a few

110 almost be heard—indeed it can be heard—in the inevitable words, oft repeated by Negroes, that those whites, and blacks, do not die in vain. So it was with Mrs. Viola Liuzzo.[12] And much of the anger which Negroes felt toward Martin Luther King during the Battle of Selma stemmed from the fact that he denied history a great moment, never to be recaptured, when he turned tail on the Edmund Pettus Bridge and refused to all those whites behind him what they had traveled thousands of miles to receive. If the police had turned them back by force, all those nuns, priests, rabbis, preachers, and distinguished ladies and gentlemen old and young—as they had done the Negroes a week earlier—the violence and brutality of the system would have been ruthlessly exposed. Or if, seeing King determined to lead them on to Montgomery, the troopers had stepped aside to avoid precisely the confrontation that Washington would not have tolerated, it would have signaled the capitulation of the militant white South. As it turned out, the March on Montgomery was a show of somewhat dim luster, stage-managed by the Establishment. But by this time the young whites were already active participants in the Negro revolution. In fact they had begun to transform it into something broader, with the potential of encompassing the whole of America in a radical reordering of society.

The fourth stage, now in its infancy, sees these white youth taking the initiative, using techniques learned in the Negro struggle to attack problems in the general society. The classic example of this new energy in action was the student battle on the UC campus at Berkeley, California—the Free Speech Movement. Leading the revolt were veterans of the civil rights movement, some of whom spent time on the firing line in the wilderness of Mississippi/Alabama. Flowing from the same momentum were student demonstrations against U.S. interference in the internal affairs of Vietnam, Cuba, and Dominican Republic, and the Congo and U.S. aid to apartheid in South Africa. The students even aroused the intellectual community to actions and positions unthinkable a few years ago: witness the teach-ins. But their revolt is deeper than single-issue protest. The characteristics of the white rebels which most alarm their elders—the long hair, the new dances,

their love for Negro music, their use of marijuana, their mystical attitude toward sex—are all tools of their rebellion. They have turned these tools against the totalitarian fabric of American society —and they mean to change it.

*F*rom the beginning, America has been a schizophrenic nation. Its two conflicting images of itself were never reconciled, because never before has the survival of its most cherished myths made a reconciliation mandatory. Once before, during the bitter struggle between North and South climaxed by the Civil War, the two images of America came into conflict, although whites North and South scarcely understood it. The image of America held by its most alienated citizens was advanced neither by the North nor by the South; it was perhaps best expressed by Frederick Douglass, who was born into slavery in 1817, escaped to the North, and became the greatest leader-spokesman for the blacks of his era. In words that can still, years later, arouse an audience of black Americans, Frederick Douglass delivered, in 1852, a scorching indictment in his Fourth of July oration in Rochester:

What to the American slave is your Fourth of July? I answer: a day that reveals to him, more than all other days in the year, the gross injustice and cruelty to which he is the constant victim. To him your celebration is a sham; your boasted liberty, an unholy licence; your national greatness, swelling vanity; your sounds of rejoicing are empty and heartless; your denunciation of tyrants, brass-fronted impudence; your shouts of liberty and equality, hollow mockery; your prayers and hymns, your sermons and thanksgivings, with all your religious parade and solemnity, are, to him, more bombast, fraud, deception, impiety and hypocrisy—a thin veil to cover up crimes which would disgrace a nation of savages. . . .

You boast of your love of liberty, your superior civilization, and your pure Christianity, while the whole political power of the nation (as embodied in the two great political parties) is solemnly pledged to support and perpetuate the enslavement of three millions of your countrymen. You hurl your anathemas[13] at the crown-headed tyrants of Russia and Austria and pride yourselves on your democratic institutions, while you yourselves consent to be the

---

[12] a white civil rights worker from Detroit who was murdered in Alabama in March, 1965

[13] curses

mere *tools* and *bodyguards* of the tyrants of Virginia and Carolina.

You invite to your shores fugitives of oppression from abroad, honor them with banquets, greet them with ovations, cheer them, toast them, salute them, protect them, and pour out your money to them like water; but the fugitive from your own land you advertise, hunt, arrest, shoot, and kill. You glory in your refinement and your universal education; yet you maintain a system as barbarous and dreadful as ever stained the character of a nation—a system begun in avarice, supported in pride, and perpetuated in cruelty.

You shed tears over fallen Hungary, and make the sad story of her wrongs the theme of your poets, statesmen and orators, till your gallant sons are ready to fly to arms to vindicate her cause against the oppressor; but, in regard to the ten thousand wrongs of the American slave, you would enforce the strictest silence, and would hail him as an enemy of the nation who dares to make these wrongs the subject of public discourse!

This most alienated view of America was preached by the Abolitionists, and by Harriet Beecher Stowe in her *Uncle Tom's Cabin*. But such a view of America was too distasteful to receive wide attention, and serious debate about America's image and her reality was engaged in only on the fringes of society. Even when confronted with overwhelming evidence to the contrary, most white Americans have found it possible, after steadying their rattled nerves, to settle comfortably back into their vaunted belief that America is dedicated to the proposition that all men are created equal and endowed by their Creator with certain inalienable rights—life, liberty and the pursuit of happiness. With the Constitution for a rudder and the Declaration of Independence as its guiding star, the ship of state is sailing always toward a brighter vision of freedom and justice for all.

Because there is no common ground between these two contradictory images of America, they had to be kept apart. But the moment the blacks were let into the white world—let out of the voiceless and faceless cages of their ghettos, singing, walking, talking, dancing, writing, and orating *their* image of America and of Americans—the white world was suddenly challenged to match its practice to its preachments. And this is why those whites who abandon the *white* image of America and adopt the *black* are greeted with such unmitigated[14] hostility by their elders.

For all these years whites have been taught to believe in the myth they preached, while Negroes have had to face the bitter reality of what America practiced. But without the lies and distortions, white Americans would not have been able to do the things they have done. When whites are forced to look honestly upon the objective proof of their deeds, the cement of mendacity[15] holding white society together swiftly disintegrates. On the other hand, the core of the black world's vision remains intact, and in fact begins to expand and spread into the psychological territory vacated by the non-viable[16] white lies, i.e., into the minds of young whites. It is remarkable how the system worked for so many years, how the majority of whites remained effectively unaware of any contradiction between their view of the world and that world itself. The mechanism by which this was rendered possible requires examination at this point.

"America has never truly been outraged by the murder of a black man, woman, or child."

Let us recall that the white man, in order to justify slavery and, later on, to justify segregation, elaborated a complex, all-pervasive myth which at one time classified the black man as a sub-human beast of burden. The myth was progressively modified, gradually elevating the blacks on the scale of evolution, following their slowly changing status, until the plateau of separate-but-equal was reached at the close of the nineteenth century. During slavery, the black was seen as a mindless Supermasculine Menial. Forced to do the backbreaking work, he was conceived in terms of his ability to do such work—"field niggers," etc. The white man administered the plantation, doing all the thinking, exercising omnipotent power over the slaves. He had little difficulty dissociating himself from the black slaves, and he could not conceive of their positions being reversed or even reversible.

[14] absolute
[15] dishonesty
[16] non-workable

"Look into a mirror! The cause is you, Mr. and Mrs. Yesterday, you with your forked tongues."

112   Blacks and whites being conceived as mutually exclusive types, those attributes imputed to the blacks could not also be imputed to the whites— at least not in equal degree—without blurring the line separating the races. These images were based upon the social function of the two races, the work they performed. The ideal white man was one who knew how to use his head, who knew how to manage and control things and get things done. Those whites who were not in a position to perform these functions nevertheless aspired to them. The ideal black man was one who did exactly as he was told, and did it efficiently and cheerfully. "Slaves," said Frederick Douglass, "are generally expected to sing as well as to work." As the black man's position and function became more varied, the images of white and black, having become stereotypes, lagged behind.

The separate-but-equal doctrine was promulgated by the Supreme Court in 1896. It had the same purpose domestically as the Open Door Policy toward China in the international arena: to stabilize a situation and subordinate a non-white population so that racist exploiters could manipulate those people according to their own selfish interests. These doctrines were foisted off as *the epitome of enlightened justice, the highest expression of morality.* Sanctified by religion, justified by philosophy and legalized by the Supreme Court, separate-but-equal was enforced by day by agencies of the law, and by the KKK & Co. under cover of night. Booker T. Washington, the Martin Luther King of his day, accepted separate-but-equal in the name of all Negroes. W. E. B. DuBois denounced it.

Separate-but-equal marked the last stage of the white man's flight into cultural neurosis, and the beginning of the black man's frantic striving to assert his humanity and equalize his position with the white. Blacks ventured into all fields of endeavor to which they could gain entrance. Their goal was to present in all fields a performance that would equal or surpass that of the whites. It was long axiomatic among blacks that a black had to be twice as competent as a white in any field in order to win grudging recognition from the whites. This produced a pathological motivation in the blacks to equal or surpass the whites, and a pathological motivation in the whites to maintain a distance from the blacks. This is the rack on which black and white Americans receive their delicious torture! At first there was the color bar, flatly denying the blacks entrance to certain spheres of activity. When this no longer worked, and blacks invaded sector after sector of American life and economy, the whites evolved other methods of keeping their distance. The illusion of the Negro's inferior nature had to be maintained.

One device evolved by the whites was to tab whatever the blacks did with the prefix "Negro." We had *Negro* literature, *Negro* athletes, *Negro* music, *Negro* doctors, *Negro* politicians, *Negro* workers. The malignant ingeniousness of this device is that although it accurately describes an objective biological fact—or, at least, a sociological fact in America—it concealed the paramount psychological fact: that to the white mind, prefixing anything with "Negro" automatically consigned it to an inferior category. A well-known example of the white necessity to deny due credit to blacks is in the realm of music. White musicians were famous for going to Harlem and other Negro cultural centers literally to steal the black man's music, carrying it back across the color line into the Great White World and passing off the watered-down loot as their own original creations. Blacks, meanwhile, were ridiculed as *Negro* musicians playing inferior coon music.

*T*he Negro revolution at home and national liberation movements abroad have unceremoniously shattered the world of fantasy in which the whites have been living. It is painful that many do not yet see that their fantasy world has been rendered uninhabitable in the last half of the twentieth century. But it is away from this world that the white youth of today are turning. The "paper tiger" hero, James Bond, offering the whites a triumphant image of themselves, is saying what many whites want desperately to hear reaffirmed: *I am still the White Man, lord of the land, licensed to kill, and the world is still an empire at my feet.* James Bond feeds on that secret little anxiety, the psychological white backlash, felt in some degree by most whites alive. It is exasperating to see little brown men and little yellow men from the mysterious Orient, and the opaque black men of Africa (to say nothing of these impudent American Negroes!) who come to the UN and talk smart to us, who are scurrying all over *our* globe in their strange modes of dress

—much as if they were new, unpleasant arrivals from another planet. Many whites believe in their ulcers that it is only a matter of time before the Marines get the signal to round up these truants and put them back securely in their cages. But it is away from this fantasy world that the white youth of today are turning.

In the world revolution now under way, the initiative rests with people of color. That growing numbers of white youth are repudiating their heritage of blood and taking people of color as their heroes and models is a tribute not only to their insight but to the resilience of the human spirit. For today the heroes of the initiative are people not usually thought of as white: Fidel Castro, Che Guevara, Kwame Nkrumah, Mao Tse-tung, Gamal Abdel Nasser, Robert F. Williams, Malcolm X, Ben Bella, John Lewis, Martin Luther King, Jr., Robert Parris Moses, Ho Chi Minh, Stokely Carmichael, W. E. B. DuBois, James Forman, Chou En-lai.

The white youth of today have begun to react to the fact that the "American Way of Life" is a fossil of history. What do they care if their old baldheaded and crew-cut elders don't dig their caveman mops? They couldn't care less about the old, stiffassed honkies[17] who don't like their new dances: Frug, Monkey, Jerk, Swim, Watusi. All they know is that it feels good to swing to way-out body-rhythms instead of dragassing across the dance floor like zombies to the dead beat of mind-smothered Mickey Mouse music. Is it any wonder that the youth have lost all respect for their elders, for law and order, when for as long as they can remember all they've witnessed is a monumental bickering over the Negro's place in American society and the right of people around the world to be left alone by outside powers? They have witnessed the law, both domestic and international, being spat upon by those who do not like its terms. Is it any wonder, then, that they feel justified, by sitting-in and freedom riding, in breaking laws made by lawless men? Old funny-styled, zipper-mouthed political night riders know nothing but to haul out an investigating committee *to look into the disturbance* to find the cause of the unrest among the youth. Look into a mirror! The cause is you, Mr. and Mrs. Yesterday, you with your forked tongues.

A young white today cannot help but recoil from the base deeds of his people. On every side, on every continent, he sees racial arrogance, savage brutality toward the conquered and subjugated people, genocide; he sees the human cargo of the slave trade; he sees the systematic extermination of American Indians; he sees the civilized nations of Europe fighting in imperial depravity over the lands of other people—and over possession of the very people themselves. There seems to be no end to the ghastly deeds of which his people are guilty. *GUILTY.* The slaughter of the Jews by the Germans, the dropping of atomic bombs on the Japanese people—these deeds weigh heavily upon the prostrate souls and tumultuous consciences of the white youth. The white heroes, their hands dripping with blood, are dead.

The young whites know that the colored people of the world, Afro-Americans included, do not seek revenge for their suffering. They seek the same things the white rebel wants: an end to war and exploitation. Black and white, the young rebels are free people, free in a way that Americans have never been before in the history of their country. And they are outraged.

*T*here is in America today a generation of white youth that is truly worthy of a black man's respect, and this is a rare event in the foul annals of American history. From the beginning of the contact between blacks and whites, there has been very little reason for a black man to respect a white, with such exceptions as John Brown and others lesser known. But respect commands itself and it can neither be given nor withheld when it is due. If a man like Malcolm X could change and repudiate racism, if I myself and other former Muslims can change, if young white can change, then there is hope for America. It was certainly strange to find myself, while steeped in the doctrine that all whites were devils by nature, commanded by the heart to applaud and acknowledge respect for these young whites—despite the fact that they are descendants of the masters and I the descendant of slave. The sins of the fathers are visited upon the heads of the children —but only if the children continue in the evil deeds of the fathers.

[17] derogatory term for white men

Salvation on the Campus: Why Existentialism Is Capturing the Students

J. GLENN GRAY

"Our Tom looked like a bum when he came home for Christmas. His clothes were filthy, he was wearing a mandarin[1] beard, and his hair hadn't been cut since September. Last fall we gave him permission to live alone off-campus and cook for himself. Now he has trench mouth, a bad case of athlete's foot, and some kind of mysterious virus."

Our neighbor was both exasperated and amused as she thus described her son, a senior at a famous Ivy League college. He is a superior student who had hitherto seemed anything but a beatnik. For years his parents have let him steer his own course and supported him financially at some sacrifice. What, then, is he rebelling against? Is this merely a ludicrous episode in his development or a sign of a severe disorder? His mother doesn't know.

Many other enlightened parents are equally perplexed by the bizarre actions of their college sons and daughters. Nor can professors and university administrators shed much light on the moods and motivations of students in the 'sixties. They have been baffled by the rioting at

[1] typical of a public official under the Chinese Empire

Berkeley last fall and other less publicized incidents elsewhere.

For today's student is a very different creature from his predecessors. In my own college days in the 'thirties, if I had come home at Christmas in Tom's condition, my parents would probably have had me committed to a different sort of institution. What lies behind the change?

For one thing, today's student is more affluent than we were, more comfortably housed, and better equipped with the materials of scholarship. But his college life is also more impersonal and competitive, less humane. It is harder for him to know his professors, the administration, or even his all too numerous fellow students. Learning is increasingly packaged and is sometimes referred to, shamelessly, as the "knowledge business." Knowledge itself expands at a rate that makes him feel like an impostor if he seeks to be broadly educated, and walls him off from others if he specializes. His professors are less attached to the institution where they teach and more to their disciplines. And they have less time to give him or the college. In this situation, the traditional college spirit—of either the rah-rah variety or the community of learners—may seem to the student as outmoded as the raccoon coat and the hip flask.

If he has reached the age of reflection, today's student is seeking above all to differentiate himself from the crowd. Thirty years ago it was distinctive merely to be a college man. Now he must struggle to be more than a grade-point average, an anonymous statistic with a college and home address. Often he expresses this yearning for uniqueness in ways that parents, administrators, professors, and other outsiders consider illegitimate. Well publicized are the bearded, sloppily dressed students, defiant of even minimal administrative regulations, studious enough, but incontinent[2] in their demands for alcoholic and sexual freedoms, fiercely insistent on leading their own lives.

Typical of this state of mind is a student's letter in a recent issue of our college newspaper. "The trouble is that they [administration and faculty] take it all as seriously as the rest of the piety we get about law and morality and the intellectual purpose of our existence. The most ironic thing on this campus is that they believe

[2] lacking in self-restraint

in their own hypocrisy. . . . One of the reasons that administration and much of the faculty alike draw grotesque pictures of students is that they probably have never talked with one, not that they'd listen if they did. For years the same situations occur, the same opinions are given, the same pleas are voiced, and the same nothing happens."

The desire for self-definition often goes hand in hand with an inner need—more or less conscious—for a compelling authority to make freedom meaningful. In the 'thirties, economic pressures for existence and our opposition to the fascist menace rescued us from this dilemma. In the 'forties there was the war and, afterward, the threat of the Bomb to distract attention from inner conflicts. For some students in the 'sixties the civil-rights struggle has become a Cause— a clear-cut issue on which to act and to argue. But as yet this movement has not reached anything like the numbers nor hit with anything like the impact that we experienced with fascism, communism, the war, and the Bomb.

Lacking an embracing cause and a fervent ideology, the student's search for a durable purpose is likely to become aggressive, extremist, at times despairing. It can easily turn into preoccupation with subjective feelings and plain egotism. As André Gide has put it, "Each human being who has only himself for aim suffers from a horrible void." Paradoxical as it sounds, the real problem of our college youth is to discover some authority, both private and public, that will make possible authentic individuality.

I have learned something about this search over the past fifteen years as one of the professors conducting a senior seminar called Freedom and Authority. Before generalizing, perhaps I should say a word about Colorado College, where I teach philosophy. It is a fairly typical small, private liberal-arts institution, founded in 1874 by New England Congregationalists before Colorado was a state. It has long since cut loose from church ties, drifting—like Grinnell, Carleton, Pomona, and others—into secularism.[3] Our students are drawn from many states; after Colorado, California and Illinois contribute the most.

We are not as selective as the Ivy League colleges nor as equalitarian as the state institutions. Since—like those of most private colleges—our costs are high, our students come largely from upper-middle-class families. (Some are shockingly rich. A few years back when we banned automobiles for freshmen, a Texas girl wired our admissions committee, requesting in good faith that she be permitted to bring her private airplane.)

I was originally lured out here by a dean who painted an enticing picture of Back Bay Boston accents mixed with Western ranch drawls. But the percentage of students from ranches, farms, and the working class has steadily declined, and drawls are now rare. In sum, our students and their families are, economically and socially, very much like you who are reading this magazine. They represent an important—if not typical—sample of American college students.

Our Freedom and Authority seminar is a very freewheeling, wide-ranging course. Though we constantly change the readings, a few books have remained by nearly unanimous consent from the beginning. The first of these is Plato's account of the trial, imprisonment, and death of Socrates in the *Apology, Crito,* and end of *Phaedo.* These short dialogues, conveniently grouped in one paperback, are probably exerting a profounder influence on the campus today than such bestsellers as Golding, Salinger, and Baldwin, which bloom and fade in campus popularity.

Why does Socrates appeal to contemporary students? They respond to his fearless assertion of his right to determine his own conduct despite powerful opposition from the majority of his fellow citizens. The conflict between individual freedom and sociopolitical authority which he dramatizes expresses their own central dilemma. These students have outgrown the discipline of parents. In college, various authorities—the college administration, campus mores, and student cliques—vie for their allegiance. They are also uneasily conscious of the different standards of the professional and business worlds they are about to enter. The sensitive student, confused by these uncertain values, is thrilled when Socrates, the original rebel who became the "father" of philosophy, tells his fellow Athenians that he loves and cherishes them, but chooses to obey only his own vision of the right and good. Socrates' example can still engender a revolutionary fervor in youthful hearts. It was hardly

[3] lack of concern for religion or religious matters

"Affluence, not religion, might be called the opiate of the 'sixties."

an accident that the campus rebellions at Berkeley and earlier at the University of Colorado were led by philosophy majors.*

Less acceptable to my students than Socrates' idea of freedom is his concept of authority, which leads him to refuse a proffered escape from prison after he has been sentenced to death. He likens the laws of Athens to parents, who must always be obeyed even if they chastise their children unjustly. At this point, my students begin to protest, and their identification with Socrates is broken. As one of them put it last fall, "I can't imagine anything less comparable to my parents than the U.S. government."

There are exceptions. One girl, for example, last November reconciled the seeming contradictions in Socrates' philosophy in this fashion: "In the *Apology* individual determination of conduct challenges and defeats all other values, including Athenian law. However, the reverse is not what happens in the *Crito*. Here, Athenian law is weighted *with* his personal laws of conduct *against* a solitary value, his life. His natural desire to flee for his life, not his individualism, is challenged here. . . . As part of his personal conduct code, Socrates could not destroy Athenian law simply because it was being used to destroy a less value, his life on earth. 'To injure in turn when ill-treated' was against his moral structure also, so that his personal conduct code forced him to abide by Athenian law. Of the three values considered in the *Apology* and the *Crito*, Socrates held individual determination of conduct most important, Athenian law second, and his own life least important."

All of us blessed her, a rank beginner in philosophy, for the kind of insight that an unburdened mind often brings to a complex issue. In the ensuing discussion, her classmates were intellectually persuaded that Socrates' freedom was sustained by his lifelong membership in the community of Athens. But how could his example be helpful today? Since patriotism is hardly an operable emotion among contemporary students, Socratic freedom, though intellectually appealing, does not in the end provide a satisfying answer. After all, Socrates was an old man with secure roots in a small community, a situation quite

opposite to that of young people in our huge, fast-changing, incredibly complex society.

As a contrast to Socrates, we study *The Death of Ivan Ilych*, Tolstoi's powerful short story in which a modern man must face an agonizing death with no resources save the polite conventions of an artificial society. Slowly dying, daily more isolated and desperate, Ivan asks:

"Then what does it mean? Why? It can't be that life is so senseless and horrible. But if it really has been so horrible and senseless, why must I die and die in agony? There is something wrong!

"Maybe I did not live as I ought to have done," it suddenly occurred to him. "But how could that be, when I did everything properly," he replied, and immediately dismissed from his mind this, the sole solution of all the riddles of life and death, as something quite impossible.

But he cannot dismiss these fears for long.

He lay on his back and began to pass his life in review in quite a new way. In the morning when he saw first his footman, then his wife, then his daughter, and then the doctor, their every word and movement confirmed to him the awful truth that had been revealed to him during the night. In them he saw himself—all that for which he had lived—and saw clearly that it was not real at all, but a terrible and huge deception which had hidden both life and death. This consciousness intensified his suffering tenfold.

In the end, Tolstoi rescues Ivan from utter meaninglessness and absurdity via his own (Tolstoi's) passionate faith in primitive Christianity. But this does little to alleviate the atmosphere of controlled terror and doom.

The story has a stunning impact on our students. If they find Socrates wholly admirable but a size larger than life, Ivan is all too human, the anonymous Everyman of our day, painfully contemporary. I have overheard more than one of my students breathe, "My God, he is just like my old man" They do not identify with him for he is too much like adults they know and dislike—a portrait of what modern life may force them eventually to become. Though they hardly aspire to be heroes like Socrates, they desperately want to escape being victims like Ivan.

Ivan's "inauthentic" life has become a rich source for the Existentialists in their indictment of modern society. On the campus Existential-

* Similarly, the unprecedented student demonstration at Yale in March was a protest against the administration's failure to give tenure to an admired philosophy teacher.

ism—which is both a mood and a metaphysics[4] —is compounded of anxiety about being lost in the crowd and the lack of closeness or intimacy with fellow students. Sometimes the despairing response to these feelings is sexual promiscuity; more often it is expressed in eccentric dress and flamboyant behavior. Such climates of opinion are contagious and often attract spurious reactions. These can be downright funny, as in the reported case of the student who used to telephone his girl friend and say, "Honey, I'm in the abyss again. How about going out for a beer?"

But in fact the underlying mood is quite different from the perennial depressions of late adolescence. These students are anxiously concerned with the problem of being themselves. Authenticity is the element of Existentialism that strikes the deepest note for them. The highest virtue is honesty with themselves and others while phoniness in whatever form is the greatest vice. "The thing that's wrong with this class," a senior burst out recently, "is that none of us is spontaneous. We're all trying to be so clever and to impress each other. I think we are simply

afraid to be ourselves. I'm sick of my own pretending."

To be a genuine or authentic person is not primarily a moral matter, in the sense that older Americans think of morality. For Existentialists authenticity means freely choosing what is one's own in behavior, attitude, and mode of living, however singular these may appear to others. The kind of society we are building—or that is being built around us—is, for them, a major obstacle to the attainment of authentic individuality.

The difficult art of becoming oneself can hardly be more than begun by the age of twenty-two or twenty-three. Hence the important question is: How long does the search continue? Graduates of our Freedom and Authority seminar often write to their old professors and many of them return to campus annually, from as far away as Pennsylvania and California. We hold an informal seminar with them at Homecoming, usually based on a book which we have assigned in advance.

Surprises about the future development of one's students are the rule for a college professor. But I am still disconcerted when the students I counted on fail me and the least promising prove to be "late bloomers."

[4] the branch of philosophy that deals with first principles and seeks to explain the nature of reality and of the origin and structure of the world

In the last category is a pretty Connecticut girl who seemed quite unremarkable when she left my seminar section a couple of years ago and proceeded to a government job in Washington. Soon afterward an FBI agent came to my office for a routine loyalty check and I gave him the expected replies. But meanwhile someone denounced her as an associate of Communists at college, and she was subjected to a thorough investigation. She secured help from the American Civil Liberties Union, an organization she had first heard of in our course. The investigation ended harmlessly at a hearing where one government agent testified that she was "an innocuous[5] person."

"Ironically, our technological society appears to widen the spheres of freedom while making it even harder to escape from the toils of 'the system'. . . ."

When she returned to campus last spring for a visit this characterization was much on her mind. "That agent was right," she told me. "Up till now I have been just that, an innocuous person, but I intend to be innocuous no longer." She asked me to support her application for law school, which she entered last fall. She had decided to become a defender of civil liberties in a private capacity, not to practice law. This winter she wrote me long letters displaying an unsuspected spirit and passion and marking her as a person who has attained security of mind. She has already resolved not to take the loyalty oath required of members of the bar in the state where she is studying, to make a court case of the matter. She has also become a militant pacifist. It was apparently the description of her as "innocuous" that triggered all these responses— all dormant in her college days.

The death of President Kennedy had a similar transforming effect on another unlikely student whose undistinguished college career included a troubled progress through my Freedom and Authority course. He married and went to work for a national soap company where he was rising rapidly. But the Kennedy assassination disrupted his world. Soon afterward he wrote to me asking for "a philosopher's point of view." "I felt a strong sense of identity with him," he wrote, expressing a feeling widespread at that time. "Perhaps this is because he was young, or because we shared similar political views (weak and irresolute as mine are) or because he was an 'intellectual' President, or because . . . I felt guilt because of his murder, and I feel dead because of his death."

He had tried, he said, to cope with the disaster, to reason it through, but in vain. "I usually end up saying 'God damn,' with an incredulous shake of the head. Surely there must be more grief written in people's hearts than what is written on their faces. Aside from a few hours at the funeral, all seems to be normal with the people I see and know. But for me this one act had made all other acts irrelevant and trivial; it has displaced time with paranoia,[6] good with evil, relative simplicity with incomprehensibility, an ideal with dirt."

He could no longer remain in the business world. Despite his wife and children, he decided to return to graduate school to prepare himself for work in international education. He is now immersed in the study of foreign languages and Existentialism. Wearing a heavy beard, he has lost all resemblance to the young executive of a year ago. For the first time in his life, he told me recently, he is truly "engaged" in discovering the meaning of existence through commitment to thought and action rather than middle-class drift.

These two cases are, of course, exceptions. Relatively few of our young alumni have made much progress toward attaining a distinctive individuality after leaving college. The demands of business and professional life on the men, of home-making and child-rearing on the women, tend either to halt the search or even to induce surrender to reigning values. It would seem that the very prosperity which permits college students to spend time pondering important issues of existence acts as a sedative in their early adulthood. Affluence, not religion, might be called the opiate of the 'sixties. The immediate requirements of making a living and getting ahead in

---

[5] harmless and insipid

[6] excessive suspiciousness and distrustfulness of others

the status race seem to dull the passions and despair which obsessed many of them in college. There is, of course, nothing surprising in this. Many of us escape the need to give meaning to our existence through the age-old expedient[7] of producing the next generation and letting them struggle with the problem.

*T*he Existentialist preoccupation with the Absurd, Nothingness, *Angst,* etc.—at least as metaphysical concepts—did not until recently have much of a grip on the English-speaking countries. When I first began teaching the leading Existentialists about 1950, interest in a Kierkegaard, Heidegger, or Sartre was likely to be a matter of either curiosity or fashion. Their very names were strange and most Americans had difficulty pronouncing the word Existentialism. In those years my colleagues frequently asked me to give a coffee-break explanation of the movement.

Now discussions are far more earnest and passionate. I conduct a Wednesday evening seminar on Existentialism at my home. Frequently I have to push the students out after several hours, if I am to simmer down and get any sleep that night. Often they continue heated arguments elsewhere till the small hours. In colleges all over America, courses dealing with Existentialists are currently very popular, to the disgust of the disciples of Language Analysis—an Oxford import—who once felt confident of dominating academic philosophy. The rapid availability of translations from German and French Existentialist writings and sales of large editions attest to the surprising new demand.

What accounts for it? Undeniably, there is a large element of the modish, for Americans have always been susceptible to philosophic imports from the Continent and England. (In philosophy, it has been said, we are still largely a colony of Europe.) I must also admit, rather shamefacedly, that even philosophy is not immune to the attraction of "the hottest thing in town." After the war it was Oxford Analysis, now it is Existentialism.

There is, however, much more to the matter. Existentialists draw their insights and inspiration from literature rather than science. They are concerned with the individual and with personal experience in an age that threatens to overwhelm individuality. This is why they attract so many American playwrights and novelists who have begun the process of Americanizing the European mood. Because the specific possibilities and frustrations of our everyday life are sharply different from those in France or Germany we were slow to accept the Existentialist mood and metaphysics. Now that our writers have succeeded in "translating" them into our American idiom, we are feeling their delayed impact.

The students I know best seem to have an intuitive grasp of what Heidegger and Sartre mean when they write of man's exposure to Nothingness. In a few extreme cases Nothingness means a profound feeling of disengagement with American culture, if not Western civilization itself. Other students who say in the privacy of my office, "I am at the end of my rope," are feeling only a temporary despair, perhaps little more than the romantic storm and stress of late adolescence. Sometimes I respond with a gentle joshing, and refuse to take them too seriously. With others I am far from sure.

The latter group includes students who often do superb work in my classes but who are quite as likely to be on academic probation as on the Dean's list. (One of them recently spent three semesters in the near-failing and three in the excellent category.)

These are brilliant, alienated young people. Generally, they do not care for Karl Jaspers, the Existentialist who identifies himself most closely with conventional philosophy. They respond to the philosophers radically at odds with the whole tradition of modern culture. They want Kierkegaard's either-or—the leap of faith or gross sensuality; Sartre's good faith or self-deception; Heidegger's nearness to Being or nihilism.[8]

The ablest student I ever taught at Colorado College was of this kind. He wrote better commentaries on these philosophers than are found in the published literature. His poems, which I alone was allowed to see, were also first-rate. But it was a trial to keep him in college from one semester to another. Again and again he would disappear into the mountains, by himself for days. My wife and I constantly feared his suicide. When he finally graduated I easily secured fellowships for him to three graduate schools. He turned down all of them and proceeded to wander over the

---

[7] doing what is of selfish interest rather than what is right or just

[8] the denial of the existence of any basis for knowledge or truth

country, supporting himself at odd jobs. In his college years I was, in effect, struggling with him for his very soul; it is now sadly clear that I lost.

*I*n an earlier day, before the disillusionment with communism, some such students found release in action, in attachment to a utopian[9] authority which gave them a feeling of belonging. For others, the crude menace of Hitler served to unite them with Western values. Today a few find a sense of belonging in Southern racism. Others in the civil-rights movement or in the Peace Corps with its opportunities for genuine service.

What these students need above all is action, not further study, yet how can I counsel them to give up their studies before the degree? To serve with any significance in our specialized society they will need more formal schooling than they have or want before they have "found" themselves. The plight of dropouts on the lower academic rungs is well known. Equally poignant is the problem of those at the top—often even in graduate school—who do not know where they are headed nor whether they should stay in college at all.

Ironically, our technological society appears to widen the spheres of freedom while making it even harder to escape from the toils of "the system" as students call it. Students today travel far more than we did in the 'thirties and 'forties; learn and see more and participate in a much larger range of activities. At an early stage the choice of many different careers is open to them. But once they have chosen anything specific, whether it be a "major" or marriage, they are soon past the point of no return.

In this situation Existentialism appeals. Its deepest conviction is that through his choices each individual makes himself. Its emphasis is not only on the absurd character of social reality, in some cases, of the world as a whole, but also on Possibility. In an inner sense everyone determines his own course. He can choose to lead an authentic existence or choose to be lost in the crowd. If the overwhelming majority opt[10] for the latter condition, this does not prevent the exceptional person from standing alone as an authentic "single one." To a man, Existentialists are against group activities. They never tire of reminding us that "existence" literally means to "stand out from."

"I have decided that I am simply different from all the others," a brilliant youth told me the other day, explaining how even his close friends saw no point whatever to his poetry. "I must think and write for myself from now on." Both resolution and pathos were in his voice.

I doubt that Existentialist philosophy can ultimately satisfy the search for authority. So far, few of these thinkers have provided guidelines for social or political action, though all of them stress the necessity for individual commitment. However, for students who are not yet able or ready to act, Existentialism offers a great deal. At the least it presents an escape from the morass[11] of conformity, *la dolce vita*, boredom, and the meaningless competitiveness in which they see so many of their elders caught.

Furthermore, those who go behind Sartre to the Danish and German originators of this movement discover a choice between an absurd or tragic view of human destiny. The absurd view is that existence is finally meaningless and futile, a defiant if admirable gesture in a void. The tragic conviction acknowledges the fragile and exposed character of individuality but discovers meaning and purpose in the individual's struggle to locate himself in nature and society. Though his personal life is of short duration, and subject to chance and misfortune while it lasts, his actions are of great importance in the moral sum of things. Tragedy links us to what has been in the history of our species and binds us in faith to the future. It teaches that there are things worth living and dying for, ideas, ancestors, and descendants.

On the other hand, the metaphysical idea that "life is a tale told by an idiot, full of sound and fury, signifying nothing" can do none of these things. The conviction of absurdity cuts all ties to history and nature and with them the nerve of meaningful action. Which version of Existentialism will be accepted by students in the rest of the 'sixties?

The answer will be important. It has been a favorite taunt of European critics that in America there are no tragedies, only mistakes. The quality of current experience is rapidly dissipating any remaining truth in this ancient charge. Yet young

[9] ideal
[10] make a choice

[11] difficult, perplexing state of affairs

people inevitably find it hard to learn the price of pain and suffering necessary to pay for the tragic vision. Falling into a persuasion of absurdity and meaninglessness is, on the surface at least, much easier. The polar choices again are between the life of Socrates and that of Ivan Ilych.

That the tragic and absurd should be competing for students' minds in the 'sixties is not surprising, when one remembers that many of their parents were fighting World War II while they were infants and that they have grown up in a world changing at an incredible pace. Indeed, were young people not constitutionally adaptable and preoccupied with the immediate present, they would be in a much worse plight than they are. The wonder is that so many are sane and resilient.[12]

Nevertheless, there has hardly been a time, in my experience, when students needed more attention and patient listening to by experienced professors than today. The pity is that so many of us retreat into research, government contracts, and sabbatical travel, leaving counsel and instruction to junior colleagues and graduate assistants. In so doing we deepen the rift between the generations and at the same time increase the sense of impersonality, discontinuity, and absence of community that makes college life less satisfactory in this decade than it used to be. What is needed are fewer books and articles by college professors and more cooperative search by teacher and taught for an authority upon which to base freedom and individuality.

After surviving so many turbulent decades of this century, some of us may feel a certain confidence that the present will prove no harder than the past has been. But we should remind ourselves that peace and affluence have their own perils as surely as do wars and depressions. Though our students increasingly come to us better prepared in the traditions of Western civilization, how many of them care more deeply about these traditions than did students in the bad old days? My pessimistic sense of catastrophe has lessened somewhat since 1960, but I find that deep uneasiness about the course of American higher education has grown. Nowadays nearly everyone looks to education for salvation as once we looked to

religion or to a political ideology. But before we succeed in building the great society, we shall need to resolve the doubt and bafflement about its validity and worth in the minds of those now in college who should serve as leaders. Many of the harassed young men and women I teach, at any rate, have not yet decided what sense, if any, their existence has.

121

---

[12] able to recover from shock or change

Are we living in particularly troubled times, or have Americans always been predisposed toward extremes of behavior? Can we discern in the American character a susceptibility toward violence, lawlessness, or injustice? Were things any different in the earlier days? The answer seems to be that we have had a long tradition of extremism and disaffection, and at least since the days of Thoreau, men have been harried by essentially the same problems that trouble them today. As Thoreau points out, generation gaps are nothing new. Over a century ago Dickens observed of us that we tended to distrust the strange or foreign, that we were ambivalent about our leaders, and that we loved "smart" dealing whether or not it was altogether honest or legal. Moreover, Grier and Cobbs tell us that between black and white men relations have not changed significantly since the infamous days of slavery.

Predispositions

Curiously, there are both positive and negative aspects to some American traits. Aggressiveness, acquisitiveness, and a belief in progress have accounted for varied positive accomplishments. They led to the great westward expansion, and today they are opening up the space frontier. As Hofstadter points out, they also led to the development of the great industrial empires of the last century. On the negative side, our material progress was achieved at a reckless waste of our resources and often meant ignoring human considerations. For a brief period not only the millionaire industrialists but also their victims and the public at large justified exploitation philosophically as "the survival of the fittest."

When economic prosperity and mass public education became a reality for the majority of Americans, we went to another extreme: instead of merely championing the common man we began to exalt him. As Krutch sees it, we passed into the Age of the Common Man and are still witnessing the Triumph of Mediocrity in our culture. Contradicting this view of sameness and conformity is Wakefield's more recent discovery, within the traditional framework of democratic process, that Americans are adopting diverse but often obsessive responses to the pressures of modern life.

The United States

E. M. FORSTER

America is rather like life. You can usually find in it what you look for. If you look for skyscrapers or cowboys or cocktail parties or gangsters or business connections or political problems or women's clubs, they will certainly be there. You can be very hot there or very cold. You can explore the America of your choice by plane or train, by hitch-hike or on foot. It will probably be interesting, and it is sure to be large.

I went there for the first time at the age of sixty-eight. By sixty-eight one is so to speak a pilgrim grandfather who knows very clearly what to look for when he disembarks. I had no doubt as to what I wanted to discover in America. It was to provide me with scenery and individuals. The scenery was to be of two sorts—gigantic and homely.[1] The individuals were not to be representative—I never could get on with representative individuals —but people who existed on their own account and with whom it might therefore be possible to be friends. That is the America I looked for and was to find. My visit was a complete success from my own point of view.

After a respectful glance at New York, I went a hundred miles north into the Berkshires. It was April. The trees were leafless—thousands and thousands of birch trees, their trunks whiter than the birch trees here,[2] milk white, ghost white in the sharp sunshine, covering the sides of the valley and the crests of the hills; and among the birches pushed pine and hemlock—which is like a not very dark green yew. Was I in England? Almost, but not quite. That was again and again to be my sensation, and in the Arizona Desert I was to feel I was almost but not quite in India, and in

[1] unpretentious; belonging to ordinary domestic life
[2] in England

the Yosemite Valley that it was not quite Switzerland. America is always throwing out these old-world hints, and then withdrawing them in favour of America. To return to the Berkshires: after a few days' quiet the snow descended and silence became absolute. The country became primeval[3] and polar—endless purity, underspreading motionless trees. I can never be grateful enough for those opening days of silence and snow. They imposed proportion. They made me realise that America is not all town: such a generalisation would be truer of England. It is country—controlled no doubt by mechanised gadgets, still it is country. I was glad I had not gaped too long at the New York skyscrapers. Exciting as they are, they mislead. They do not epitomise what lies behind them. Presently the snow melted. Where it had lain appeared dark brown earth and occasional pale lilac hepaticas, and the spring began— in double quick time compared to our spring.

The Berkshires are homely scenery. Gigantic scenery is more difficult to describe, but I will make an attempt. Suppose yourself walking on a Surrey common near Bagshot. There are a good many fir trees about, the soil is sandy, and the prospect rather dull. Suddenly the common stops, and you are standing without any warning on the brink of a precipice which is one mile deep. One mile into the tortured earth it goes, the other side of the chasm is miles away, and the chasm is filled with unbelievable deposits of rock which resemble sphinxes draped in crimson shawls. That, as far as I can get it into a single sentence, gives you my first impression of the Grand Canyon of the Colorado River, but the Grand Canyon would need many sentences to describe and many books. It is the most astounding natural object I have ever seen. It frightens. There are many colours in it besides crimson—strata[4] of black and of white, and rocks of ochre and pale lilac. And the Colorado River itself is, when one gets down to it, still more sinister, for it is muddy white and very swift, and it rages like an infuriated maggot between precipices of granite, gnawing at them and cutting the Canyon deeper. It was strange after two days amongst these marvels, and terrors, to return to the surface of the earth, and go bowling away in a 'bus between little fir trees.

The second item I sought in America was the human, the individual. My work lay mainly in

[3] belonging to the first ages before man appeared on earth
[4] layers or beds

universities, and there and elsewhere I found the individuals I sought. I had expected generosity and hospitality. I had not expected so much tact, charm and sensitiveness; here was the delightful surprise. Wherever I went I found delicate understanding of our troubles in Britain over food and clothing, and a desire to help that was never patronising.[5] This was not confined to the highly educated classes. I recall a cheap eating-house in Nevada where some strangers came up and asked what they could send. I remember the chambermaid in the hotel at Salt Lake City who when I offered her a tip replied, "I don't like to take your money, brother, you need it more than I do." That is the sort of remark which comes from the heart and goes to the heart, and in the light of it and the warmth of it I found difficulty in examining the defects of the American character. The defects are, I suspect, lack of discrimination, emotionalism, and a tendency to narrow the idea of freedom into freedom to make money. "What else have we fought the war for?" a business acquaintance enquired. But I cannot feel these defects are basic. My friends reassure me against this, and not only my friends; the faces of strangers lighting up everywhere, compassionate, respectful, anxious to help. The individuals I met were mostly of Anglo-Saxon stock; I also knew some Swedish and some Italian farming people, made some Oriental contacts, and had one or two Mexican friends. I did not have the good fortune to get to know any Negroes. On the whole I saw as much of the human landscape as an elderly traveller may reasonably expect, and I liked it.

But now comes a qualification. Although the Americans I encountered were full of charitable feelings towards Great Britain, I cannot say that they showed much interest in us otherwise. I have often been asked since my return home: "What do they think about us over there?" Indeed, it is often the only thing English people want to know. The answer, not very flattering to our pride, is that the Americans scarcely think about us at all. They are curious about our Royal Family, they are grateful and appreciative towards Mr. Churchill, they are —or were—enthusiastic over British films. That is all. They do not discuss our Empire. India, over which they have been so critical in the past, is now scarcely in the news and seems to bore them.

Even Palestine was seldom mentioned. An explanation of this indifference is that they concentrate, as we all do, on home affairs, and that when they do think of foreign affairs they think of Russia. China to some extent, but mostly Russia. Russia is always weighing on their minds. They are afraid of war, or that their standard of life may be lowered. I shall never forget a dinner party, supposedly given in my honour, at which one of the guests, a journalist, urged that atomic bombs should be dropped upon the Soviet Union without notice, and quoted with approval a remark which he inaccurately ascribed to Oliver Cromwell: "Stone dead hath no fellow." "That's good, isn't it, Tom?" he called to another journalist. "Stone dead hath no fellow." Tom agreed that it was very good, and they shouted; "Stone dead hath no fellow" in unison or antiphonically[6] for the rest of the evening. They were cultivated men, but as soon as the idea of Russia occurred to them, their faces became blood red; they ceased to be human. No one seemed appalled[7] by the display but myself, no one was surprised and our hostess congratulated herself afterwards on the success of her party. This obsession over Russia should be realised by all who would understand America, and it explains in part her lack of interest in us.

I did not encounter such hysteria elsewhere, and maybe did not frequent the circles where it is likeliest to occur. Most of the people I was with were not influential or highly placed: many of them were teachers, and some of them were young —students, or they practised music or painting or acting or the ballet, or they were doing small commercial jobs or working on the land. My general impression was of good temper and goodwill and hopefulness. I could darken the picture, no doubt. I do not take the Statue of Liberty in New York harbour as seriously as she takes herself. And I did encounter hints of oppression and of violence, and of snobbery. But the main verdict is favourable, and I do beg anyone who happens to have fallen into the habit of nagging at America to drop it. Nagging is so insidious.[8] It often resides not in what is said but in the tone of voice. It proceeds not from considered criticism but from envy and from discontent—and, of course, life out there is far more comfortable for the average man than it is here. The food is nicer, if dearer,

[5] condescending, lowering oneself (to do something)

[6] in response to each other
[7] horrified, made pale
[8] deceitful

the clothes are nicer and cheaper, the cold drinks are not lukewarm, and the railway carriages are not dirty. But these advantages over ourselves should not embitter us against the people who enjoy them. Nor should we charge it against all Americans that their politicians do what our politicians tell them, and tell us, they ought not to do.

I chanced to end my three months' visit in the same district of the Berkshires where it had begun. Now it was high summer. The little spring from which I fetched water every day had already begun to flag. The meadows were full of flowers—ox-eye daisies, black-eyed susans, orchids, and an under-carpet of creeping jenny; the meadows sloped down to a brook where the farm hands bathed. There were swallow-tail butterflies and fritillaries, and the bobolink, a very agreeable bird, skipped from post to post carolling, and another bird, the phoebe, repeated "phoebe, phoebe, phoebe," whence its name. At night there were fireflies to remind us that this was in the latitude of Madrid. Thunderstorms did not disconcert them, and I would watch their flash vanish in the superior brilliancy of lightning, and reappear. Some of them flew at the level of the grass, others across the curtain of birch trees. They were extraordinarily bright; it was a good year for fireflies, and the memory of them sparking in the warm rain and the thunder is the latest of my American impressions, and the loveliest.

The Shadow of the Past

WILLIAM H. GRIER and

PRICE M. COBBS

Americans characteristically are unwilling to think about the past. We are a future-oriented nation, and facing backward is an impediment[1] to progress. Although these attitudes may propel us to the moon, they are deficient when human conflict needs resolution. They bring white Americans to an impasse[2] when they claim to "understand" black people. After all, the thoughts begin, the Negro is also an American and if he is different it is only a matter of degree. Clichés are brought forth and there is a lengthy recitation of the names of famous Negroes. Long association has bred feelings of familiarity which masquerade as knowledge. But there remain puzzles about black people; all is not understood, something is missing.

For if the black American is to be truly understood, his history must be made intelligible. It is a history that is interwoven with that of this country, although it is rarely reported with candor. In recent years superficial studies of Negroes have been made. For those few who truly search, the past of the black man is seen reflected in his daily life.

It is evident in character structure and child-rearing. It can be heard on a Sunday morning in a Baptist church. It reveals itself in the temper of the ghetto and in the emerging rage now threatening to shatter this nation, a nation the black man helped to build. A few black people may hide their scars, but most harbor the wounds of yesterday.

The black man of today is at one end of a psychological continuum which reaches back in time to his enslaved ancestors. Observe closely a man on a Harlem street corner and it can be seen how little his life experience differs from that of his forebears. However much the eternals differ, their inner life is remarkably the same.

On a cold morning one of the authors sat watching a group of black men. They were standing outside an office for casual laborers in clusters of four or five. Some were talking and gesturing, but from a distance one could detect apathy in most.

These were the "hard-core" unemployed. Their difficulties could be blamed on lack of education, personal maladjustments, or just plain laziness and such a judgment would be partially correct. The greater truth was that they were black. Because of this fact, they had little chance of obtaining favorable or permanent work. They were doomed to spend endless gray mornings hoping to secure a day's work.

A truck drove up and they stiffened. There was a ripple of excitement as a white man leaned out of the cab and squinted. As he ran his eyes past the different men, one could almost hear his thoughts. *This one is too thin . . . that dark one looks smart-alecky and is probably slow . . . the boy way in the back there might do.*

No imagination is required to see this scene as a direct remnant of slavery. Move back in time and this could be an auction block. The manual labor is the same and so is the ritual of selection. The white man involved in the selection feels he is only securing a crew. But, then, so did his forefathers. In addition, the psychic structure of the black men being selected has altered little since slavery. To know this is deeply troubling—and frightening.

A city erupts in fury. Its residents are appalled and outraged. Biracial committees are appointed and scapegoats appear from everywhere. Instead of wretched housing and stifling unemployment, outside agitators and wily Communists are said to be the most important causes. Always the basic reasons are at best minimized and at worst denied. After three centuries of oppression the black man is still thought to need a provocateur to inflame him!

[1] handicap
[2] deadlocked situation

Chapter II of **Black Rage** by William H. Grier and Price M. Cobbs, © 1968 by William H. Grier and Price M. Cobbs, Basic Books, Inc., Publishers, New York.

History is forgotten. There is little record of the first Africans brought to this country. They were stripped of everything. A calculated cruelty was begun, designed to crush their spirit. After they were settled in the white man's land, the malice continued. When slavery ended and large-scale physical abuse was discontinued, it was supplanted by different but equally damaging abuse. The cruelty continued unabated in thoughts, feelings, intimidation and occasional lynching. Black people were consigned to a place outside the human family and the whip of the plantation was replaced by the boundaries of the ghetto.

The culture of slavery was never undone for either master or slave. The civilization that tolerated slavery dropped its slaveholding cloak but the inner feelings remained. The "peculiar institution" continues to exert its evil influence over the nation. The practice of slavery stopped over a hundred years ago, but the minds of our citizens have never been freed.

*"The practice of slavery
stopped over a hundred years ago,
but the minds of our citizens
have never been freed."*

To be a bondsman was to experience a psychological development very different from the master's. Slavery required the creation of a particular kind of person, one *compatible* with a life of involuntary servitude. The ideal slave had to be absolutely dependent and have a deep consciousness of personal inferiority. His color was made the badge of that degradation. And as a final precaution, he was instilled with a sense of the unlimited power of his master. Teachings so painstakingly applied do not disappear easily.

The white man tried to justify the lot of the slave in many ways. One explanation made the slave a simple child who needed the protective guardianship of a benevolent parent. For many whites this distortion has persisted to the present. A modern version holds that black people are little different from other citizens save for a paucity[3] of education and money. The reason for these deficiencies is left vague. The observer is left with the comfortable feeling that blacks are stunted in growth, have profligate[4] ways, and are uninterested in learning. This attitude obscures the multitude of wrongs and the ruthless oppression of blacks, from slavery to now.

The Negro man of eighty told a story. He was twelve and a playmate was tied in a cage waiting to be taken away and lynched. The shackled boy stood accused of raping a white woman.

The old man recalled the fright which caused him to run away the next day. From that time on he never knew a home. His years were spent roaming about the country. He became an itinerant[5] preacher, forever invoking God, but always too terrified to return to his place of birth. When asked why, he would reply: "The white folks down there are too mean."

For most of his life he was tortured by memories. Every place he stopped, he soon became frightened and moved on. Sometimes in the middle of a sermon he would cry out:

"How could they do that to a boy?"

This old man is even now living in one of our cities. He continues to preach in storefront churches. At times he may encounter whites who smile benevolently at his quaintness and apparent exaggerations. But his memories are real and his hatred, however masked, is a burning fire.

Because of an inattention to history, the present-day Negro is compared unfavorably with other racial and ethnic groups who have come to this country. Major differences in backgrounds are ignored. The black man was brought to this country forcibly and was completely cut off from his past. He was robbed of language and culture. He was forbidden to be an African and never allowed to be an American. After the first generation and with each new group of slaves, the black man had only his American experience to draw on. For most Negroes, the impact of the experience has been so great as to even now account for a lack of knowledge of their past.

This can be contrasted with the heritage of the American Indian. He truly has known the violence of white America, but his legacies are of a different sort. Now, decimated[6] and forlorn, survivors can nevertheless tell tales of past glories. At least in reliving the time when his people ruled the

---

[3] lack, insufficiency

[4] depraved or recklessly extravagant
[5] traveling
[6] largely destroyed

CONFRONTATION   A/p   Adeogla!

land, the Indian can vicariously achieve a measure of dignity.

Various groups that have come to these shores have been able to maintain some continuity of social institutions. In the process of Americanization, they have retained an identification with their homeland. The Chinese, who in many instances functioned virtually as slaves, were allowed to preserve a family structure. Other oppressed groups, notably the Irish and Italians, were never infused with the shame of color. In addition, they had the protection and support of the Roman Catholic Church. Except for the Negro, all sizable groups in America have been able to keep some old customs and traditions.

The black experience in this country has been of a different kind. It began with slavery and with a rupture of continuity and an annihilation of the past. *Even now each generation grows up alone.* Many individual blacks feel a desperate aloneness not readily explained. The authors have heard stories telling of each generation's isolation from every other. Non-black groups pass on proud traditions, conscious of the benefits they are conferring. For black people, values and rituals are shared and indeed transmitted, but with little acknowledgment of their worth. The Jew achieves a sense of ethnic cohesiveness through religion and a pride in background, while the black man stands in solitude.

There are other comparisons and Negroes participate in them. The white American has created a blindness for himself which has a peculiar effect on blacks. In psycho-therapeutic sessions Negroes are preoccupied with determining just how many of their difficulties are a consequence of the prejudice of whites. And while there is sometimes the tendency to attribute everything to white cruelty, there is often the opposite tendency—a determination not to see. They may insist that white oppression has never exerted any influence on their lives, even in the face of such realities as police brutality, job and housing discrimination, and a denial of educational opportunities. It is a powerful national trait, this willful blindness to the abuse of blacks in America. It is a blindness that includes the victim as well as the crime.

An eighty-seven-year-old woman was born in the deep South, the result of a union between one of the black "girls on the place" and the son of the white landowner. Years later she was told how, at her birth, the white mistress of the "big house" heard that her son had fathered a child. The young mother was summoned to bring the child for an audience with the grandmother.

The old lady admired the child, and noting her fairness suggested that she be taken and raised as white.

The mother objected: "She is my child and I'll keep her."

Even into old age, this Negro woman admired the courage of her mother. She spoke about the thin line separating the races. A flip of the coin could decide whether one was "colored" or "white."

The relationship between black and white is complex. This association has affected the white partner less than the black, but the effect on the white partner has had more significance since he has been the policy maker. An analysis of the relationship tells much about the American national character. Attitudes of the kind directed toward blacks, rooted deep in the fabric of this country, clearly have significant influence on many decisions. A nation which has made the despising of blacks a unique element of its identity is at a profound disadvantage when called upon to lock arms with people of other lands and form a brotherhood of nations.

A focus on the black partner yields information of a different sort. To be "colored" has meant far more than riding in the back of the bus. To be sure, there is great misery in being the last hired and first fired and relegated to decaying sections of town, but there is enduring grief in being made to feel inferior.

The old woman may have been fortunate in her awareness of that early choice. She is at least mindful of some of the factors in that selection. For most of her people, this is rarely the case. Their treatment is designed to impress them with their lowly position. The role of inferiority into which they have been cast has affected them deeply, but if the wounds are not physical, they are easily ignored.

The American black man is unique, but he has no special psychology or exceptional genetic determinants. His mental mechanisms are the same as other men. If he undergoes emotional conflict, he will respond as neurotically as his white brother. In understanding him we return to the same reference point, since all other explanations fail. We must conclude that much of the pathology[7] we see in black people had its genesis in slavery. The culture that was born in that experience of bondage has been passed from generation to generation. Constricting adaptations developed during some long-ago time continue as contemporary character traits. That they are so little altered attests to the fixity of the black-white relationship, which has seen little change since the birth of this country.

Long ago in the United States basic decisions were made. The most important of these made color the crucial variable. This began as the cornerstone of the system of black slavery. After refinements, it has remained to become imbedded in the national character. Persisting to this day is an attitude, shared by black and white alike, that blacks are inferior. This belief permeates every facet of this country and it is the etiological[8] agent from which has developed the national sickness.

The early farmers who migrated to this country were no more evil than other men. Many had fled from intolerable situations, caste systems, and religious warfare. They came filled with hope. A chance combination offered these early farmers fertile land and slaves. Initially, these slaves may have been black or white or, in the odd case, Indian. The country expanded and more and more land became available for cultivation. Supply and demand followed a predictable course and, with blacks available in large numbers, the African remained as the only bondsman.

Generations passed and the white master and the black slaves became more dependent on each

[7] here, psychological disorder
[8] causal

132 other economically and psychologically. Their lives took on a symbiotic[9] quality. When eventually the white assumed absolute power over the black, the psychology of each was changed. The reasoning which allowed these atrocities infused itself into the national thought. To hide and rationalize the barbarism, the justification became national in scope. All Americans were not slaveholders, but until a short while ago this was essentially a nation of farmers. A man working a harsh land knows that one uses whatever tools are available and he would not criticize his neighbor who held slaves.

The early white Americans were free of English common law. They were not a colony as was Brazil, subject to the laws of a European country with a long tradition of dealing with slaves. There were no powerful clerics, such as in the Catholic Church to insist that slaves had rights. And with a burgeoning[10] economy, everyone was willing to continue any practice which might bring more goods into the marketplace.

The nation became involved in a bizarre system of reasoning about slaves. No longer were they simply unfortunate beings caught up in an economic system which exploited their labor. Now they were to be subhuman—quasi[11]-humans who not only preferred slavery but felt it best for them. The American had to hide from himself and others his oppression of blacks. To be safe, the entire country had to share in the denial.

*I*n the second half of the twentieth century the posture of the nation generally is only slightly changed. Long after slavery, many whites are haunted by a vision of being oppressed, exposed to the whims of a powerful cruel *black* man. To dissipate the fantasy, increasing barriers have had to be erected. In reality it seems a remote possibility that blacks might overthrow their oppressors and enslave them. But all men have the capacity to deceive themselves, and the entire country has participated in devising humiliating laws and customs. Pseudo-scientific theories of racial superiority have been elaborated and unreasoning fears of blacks have become a part of the national character. How else to explain such massive preparations for such an unlikely attack?

An ex-serviceman recalled an incident. During World War II he was stationed in rural Montana. On a weekend he visited a nearby town. When he arrived he was the object of much wonder. No one in town had ever seen a black man before.

He went into a restaurant. The manager was polite and friendly. He passed the time of day and allowed as how this was the first Negro he had ever laid eyes on. He talked about the town and the generous nature of its people and then told the unfortunate brother that the restaurant had a policy against serving Negroes.

White citizens have grown up with the identity of an American and, with that, the unresolved conflicts of the slaveholder. White Americans are born into a culture which contains the hatred of blacks as an integral part.

Blacks are no longer the economic underpinnings of the nation. But they continue to be available as victims and therefore a ready object for the projection of hostile feelings. Throughout the country they are highly visible, by now. useless for exploitation, and demanding participation in the affairs of the country.

Because there has been so little change in attitudes, the children of bondage continue to suffer the effects of slavery. There is a timeless quality to the unconscious which transforms yesterday into today. The obsessions of slave and master continue. Both continue a deadly struggle of which neither is fully aware. It would seem that for most black people emancipation has yet to come.

A harried young mother, having exhausted the resources of several social agencies, turned to the psychiatrist as a last resort.

She had a pretty face but she was obese and wore frazzled clothes. As a result, she looked like a shapeless, middle-aged woman. On the first visit she wore an ill-fitting red wig which fell forward over her eyes. She made motions to right it, only to have it lodge over her ears.

She told of her difficulties by describing various crises. The younger children were sick and two older boys had disappeared the previous evening. A riot had broken out on that same evening and she feared for the safety of her sons.

She lived with her five children in a rat-infested apartment. She had never been married and most of her twenty-six years had been spent in public housing projects, living on welfare grants. With five

[9] depending on each other merely for mutual advantage, such as material benefits
[10] flourishing, growing
[11] superficially resembling but intrinsically different

children, she ran out of money near the middle of the month. Then her mother, who could scarcely afford it, would help her buy food. If the groceries were paid for, her roof would begin leaking, and once again she would call the housing office, only to be insulted.

The final blow involved problems with a "raunchy nigger." He had lived with her for several months and had disappeared when the last welfare check was late.

The most bitter outburst was reserved for the Welfare Department. It was headed by a "boss man" who, she believed, found delight in harassing black women. No one had any privacy. The woman next door awakened in the middle of the night, trembling with fright, to discover that the noise at the window was a social worker peering in to determine if a man was sleeping there.

The patient despised public charity, but having stopped school after the ninth grade, she found her meager skills of little use. Some of her neighbors worked as domestics, but only those with few or no children. If a woman had more than two young children, she could not earn enough to pay a sitter. On and on she went. Through most of her narrative she maintained her composure. But as she was relating an incident of little consequence, the tears came and, as she wept, her strength was revealed.

She continued to talk of her life and its burdens. In a short lifetime she had been subjected to great suffering, but she was not defeated. With genuine humor she could acknowledge and laugh at her shortcomings. In the midst of tears, she became warm and chuckled as she related an incident about her children. Hidden in despair was a distinctive vitality. It came out when she told of her church work or a meeting with a friend. As she spoke, her natural generosity was apparent.

At the end of the hour she dried her eyes, rearranged her wig, and strode out. As she moved, a particular style came through. She was depressed, upset, angry, and had her share of problems. She moved slowly, but her head was high. She disappeared down the hall. One knew that in the agony of her life was the beauty and torment of the black experience in this country.

If the resources and imperfections of this young woman were unique to her, her story would not assume such importance. Familiar concepts could adequately describe her intrapsychic conflict. We would search her past for early trauma, distorted relationships, and infantile conflicts. The social milieu[12] from which she came would be considered but would not be given much weight. Our youthful subject, however, is black and this one fact transcends all others.

She perceives herself and her surroundings in a manner deeply influenced by this fact. The dismal quality of her life shows how little society thinks of her. Six generations have passed since slavery, and her view of life's possibilities is the same as that of a slave on a Georgia plantation. The reluctant conclusion is that her assets and liabilities are the same as that slave's. She is wily, resourceful, and practiced in the art of survival. But, like her "soul sister" in bondage, she is a victim from the time of her birth. This society has placed her at a disadvantage from which she cannot recover. However visible her deficiencies, the true burdens are subtle and strike at her soul. For the more we become immersed in her problems, the more her life spells out a tragedy.

". . . along with their scars, black people have a secret. Their genius is that they have survived."

She meets her problems with ordinary defenses. But *her* difficulties have existed for hundreds of years. The pathology she shows is common to most Negroes. The curbing of her aggression began at an early age. It was in large measure determined by a society that is frightened of her. Beneath her passivity lies anger which might otherwise be directed at white people. As a consequence, we see the dependency about which so much has been written. This is another legacy of slavery. In the morning of her life, she saw her mother and other black adults vulnerable to the whim of white persons. From this it would seem logical that she could become as helpless in this society as her enslaved ancestors. To be prevented from growing and maturing is to be kept in a state of dependency.

The means by which she controls her anger have a direct link to the silent war between master and slave. She must be cautious. This may be why she speaks of the "boss man" with such bitterness. She sees him as free to hurt her, while she can never act on her hate for him. That they are both

12 environment

134 trapped in such an unequal contest is again a tribute to the unchanging nature of America.

In meeting the world, she seems defensive, as if protecting herself from a thousand slights. Her armor, however, guards against real danger. The suspiciousness may seem excessive, but to relax can be to invite disaster. If these types of character traits are seldom encountered in whites, it is because they do not face the same assaults or grow up in the same climate of hatred. As a result, this woman exhibits emotional weariness. The reality of being alternately attacked, ignored, then singled out for some cruel and undeserved punishment must extract its toll. That penalty may be a premature aging and an early death in some black people. To be regarded always as subhuman is a stultifying[13] experience.

*I*t is people like our patient whom the nation now fears. Some feel that she threatens the basic social structure. There is a dread that Negroes will impoverish the country by proliferating[14] on welfare rolls. Recently there has been a fear that they will gain political control of the cities now that whites are fleeing to the suburbs. No one can doubt that white America is afraid.

If our black woman could wipe away the tears, she would laugh. Reflect if you will: the most powerful nation on earth, afraid of the poorest, least educated, most leaderless ten percent of its population. Truly the white American projects his own hostility onto the latter-day slave. How else to understand his terror?

Our young patient weeps for good reason. She has seen her hopes soar only to be frustrated. But where her parents retreated into their black world, she is now demanding more of the white man's world. After three centuries of oppression, along with other black people, she has made a vow.

I will take it no longer.

We weep for the true victim, the black American. His wounds are deep. But along with their scars, black people have a secret. Their genius is that they have survived. In their adaptations they have developed a vigorous style of life. It has touched religion, music, and the broad canvas of creativity. The psyche of black men has been distorted, but out of that deformity has risen a majesty. It began in the chants of the first work song. It continues in the timelessness of the blues. For white America to understand the life of the black man, it must recognize that so much time has passed and so little has changed.

[13] giving the feeling of worthlessness
[14] occurring in increasing numbers

The Millionaire Industrialists

RICHARD HOFSTADTER

In the years from Appomattox to the end of the nineteenth century the American people settled half their continental domain, laid down a vast railroad system, and grew mighty in the world on their great resources in coal, metals, oil, and land. There is no other period in the nation's history when politics seems so completely dwarfed by economic changes, none in which the life of the country rests so completely in the hands of the industrial entrepreneur.[1]

The industrialists of the Gilded Age were such as one might expect to arise where great waste is permitted for great accomplishment, where many temptations are offered and few restraints imposed. For the most part they were parvenus,[2] and they behaved with becoming vulgarity; but they were also men of heroic audacity and magnificent exploitative talents—shrewd, energetic, aggressive, rapacious,[3] domineering, insatiable. They directed the proliferation[4] of the country's wealth, they seized its opportunities, they managed its corruption, and from them the era took its tone and color.

In business and politics the captains of industry did their work boldly, blandly, and cynically. Exploiting workers and milking farmers, bribing Congressmen, buying legislatures, spying upon competitors, hiring armed guards, dynamiting property, using threats and intrigue and force,

[1] one who organizes, manages, and assumes the risk of an enterprise or business
[2] upstarts, men who have risen above their beginnings or class
[3] seizing or plundering to satisfy greed
[4] rapid development

Reprinted by permission of the publisher from **The American Political Tradition** by Richard Hofstadter. Copyright, 1948 by Alfred A. Knopf, Inc.

they made a mockery of the ideals of the simple gentry who imagined that the nation's development could take place with dignity and restraint under the regime of laissez-faire. Their exploits created the moral atmosphere that caused such an honorable conservative of the old school as E. L. Godkin to say:

I came here fifty years ago with high and fond ideals about America. . . . They are now all shattered, and I have apparently to look elsewhere to keep even moderate hopes about the human race alive.

Yet it would be a mistake to assume that conscience had died among the business barons. What made it possible for them to operate in the proximate[5] spheres of politics and industry with such cheerful and unstinted rapacity was the fact that they had, in terms of those ultimate rationalizations upon which conscience rests, the most plausible, the profoundest reasons to believe that what they were doing would work to a final good. If they could buy Congressmen without making an apology, even to themselves, it was because they operated—or so they thought—in behalf of a benign transformation of tremendous magnitude. Because the abiding significance of their deeds would be so great and so good, they did not need to fret about their day-by-day knaveries.[6] Far from humble and apologetic, they were confident and arrogant. When Collis P. Huntington wrote to a political agent concerning some of his bribery for the Southern Pacific:

If you have to pay money to have the right thing done, it is only just and fair to do it. . . . If a man has the power to do great evil and won't do right unless he is bribed to do it, I think the time spent will be gained when it is a man's duty to go up and bribe the judge. A man that will cry out against them himself will also do these things himself. If there was none for it, I would not hesitate—

he was not being a sanctimonious[7] hypocrite; he was merely expressing his passionate American conviction that he had every honest right to come into his own, and it is doubtful that many tycoons of his time would have differed in principle. To imagine that such men did not sleep the sleep of the just would be romantic sentimentalism. In

[5] closely related; next in a line of relation
[6] tricky, deceitful acts; the acts of a knave, or rascal
[7] making a show of holiness

136 the Gilded Age even the angels sang for them.

The honest rationalizations of the captains of industry were manifold. Perhaps their primary defense was that they were building a great industrial empire; it was wasteful building, but their America thought it could afford waste. A few of their number—the name of Jay Gould stands out—were speculators, exploiters, and wreckers, pure and simple, but the majority could think of themselves as titans,[8] not merely of speculation and combination, but of industrial creativity on an epic scale.

"Those who emerged at the top were manifestly the fittest to survive and carry on."

Further, they stood squarely upon the American mythology of opportunity for the common man. The great industrial leaders had started life in the lower or lower-middle classes; most of them could point to early careers of privation, hard work, and frugality. When Andrew Carnegie declared at the close of the period that "the millionaires who are in active control started as poor boys and were trained in the sternest but most efficient of all schools—poverty," he could cite, besides his own case, over a dozen other eminent industrialists. Many biographies substantiate his opinion. Of course there were men like William Vanderbilt, whose fortune and properties had been left him by his father, the Commodore. There were others who had begun in comfortable circumstances, like Edward Harriman and Henry Villard, or had excellent family connections, like Henry Clay Frick, who was related on his mother's side to the Overholts of distillery fame. But Carnegie was the son of a painfully poor Scottish weaver; Philip Armour, Gustavus Swift, Daniel Drew, and Jay Gould had been children of humble farmers; Jim Fisk's father had been the proprietor of a little "travelling emporium," and John D. Rockefeller's an itinerant salesman of patent medicines. Jay Cooke and James J. Hill had begun their business careers as clerks on the frontier. Leland Stanford, although a product of the upper-middle class and the beneficiary of a fair education, had arrived in California almost penniless. Collis Huntington had been self-supporting at fourteen. Such men could tell themselves and the world that their riches and power were the results of hard work and special talents, could hold themselves up to the ambitious American middle class as exemplars[9] of an economy of magnificent opportunities. And, being successful only in the way everyone aspired to be, they enjoyed more freedom from moral condemnation than one can appreciate in the sickly retrospect of the twentieth century. They felt they had a good title to everything they could get. It was genuine indignation that could make a man like Hill say at the time of the Northern Securities anti-trust prosecution: "It really seems hard when we look back upon what we have done . . . that we should be compelled to fight for our lives against political adventurers who have never done anything but pose and draw a salary." Joseph Wharton, the Philadelphia nickel monopolist, resented an insinuation that his enterprises were "dependent" upon tariff favors:

I have supported and aided the Government more than it has supported and aided me. I am not a pauper nor a lawyer. . . . I am one of the men who create and maintain the prosperity of the nation and who enable it to survive even the affliction of wrongheaded and crank legislators.

Even Jay Gould, whose hand spoiled everything it touched, lashed back at Senators who presumed to inquire into his affairs: *"We* have made the country rich, *we* have developed the country." John D. Rockefeller said simply that "The good Lord gave me my money." Carnegie, when he observed of George Pullman that he "monopolized everything," added: "It was well that it should be so. The man had arisen who could manage and the tools belonged to him."

The ideas of the age were tailored to fit the rich barons. Economists, journalists, educators, and writers who rushed to do them honor found a strikingly plausible rationale in Darwinian biology and Spencerian philosophy, which were growing every year more popular. Since the publication of Darwin's *Origin of Species* in 1859, educated Americans had been learning eagerly of the new biological theory and constructing new cosmologies for themselves. From Darwin and his

---

[8] giants, with a suggestion of god-like strength and power

[9] models or patterns to be copied or imitated

popularizers they learned that life is a fierce and constant struggle which only the fittest survive. Confusing evolution with progress, as was natural to optimistic spokesmen of a rising class and a rising nation, they concluded that the bitter strife of competitive industry, which seemed to mirror so perfectly Darwin's natural world, was producing a slow but inevitable upward movement of civilization. Those who emerged at the top were manifestly the fittest to survive and carry on. Herbert Spencer, whose evolutionary philosophy glorified automatic progress, who threw all his authority into support of the thesis that natural economic processes must be allowed to go on without hindrance from reformers, was idolized in the United States as has been no other philosopher before or since. His visit in 1882 was practically an occasion of state; the intellectual and social leadership of the East turned out to do him honor, and reporters eagerly recounted how he hailed his great patron, Andrew Carnegie, as one of his closest friends.

It was natural, then, for a Rockefeller to say that "the growth of a large business is merely a survival of the fittest," and that the splendor of the American Beauty rose could be produced only by sacrificing the early buds that grow up around it. Or for James J. Hill to assert that "the fortunes of railroad companies are determined by the law of the survival of the fittest." Or for George Hearst, entering a Senate so filled with business magnates that it was popularly called "the Millionaire's Club," to declare:

I do not know much about books; I have not read very much; but I have travelled a good deal and observed men and things and I have made up my mind after all my experience that the members of the Senate are the survivors of the fittest.

For the most part the millionaires of the Gilded Age felt no immediate need of vindicating themselves by large-scale philanthropies.[10] Although fortunes made between 1865 and 1900 are the source of many great philanthropic foundations, in almost every case the foundations were created after 1910, when their originators were very old or had passed off the scene. Andrew Carnegie, who believed that "Amassing wealth is one of the worst species of idolatry," and that "Few millionaires are clear of the sin of having made beggars,"

was almost unique in feeling a sense of guilt during the earlier period. Assured by intellectuals of the progressive and civilizing value of their work, encouraged by their status as exemplars of the order of opportunity, and exhilarated by the thought that their energies were making the country rich, industrial millionaires felt secure in their exploitation and justified in their dominion.

[10] acts that show a love of mankind

The American Frontier Concept

WALTER PRESCOTT WEBB

The word *frontier* appears in similar form in nearly all the western European languages; and, as used in Europe, it means the boundary between two nations and is represented on maps by a thin line. It implies that the nations must not cross that line except by permission or at national peril; it is "the sharp edge of sovereignty," the door or bastion[1] of a neighbor, friendly or hostile as the case may be. There protocol[2] and diplomacy become important and a "frontier incident" may well become an international affair. In the United States the word *frontier* has an entirely different meaning, and carries a different set of implications and connotations. It becomes a concept with such wide ramifications[3] and so many shades of meaning that it cannot be wrapped up in a neat definition like a word whose growth has ceased and whose meaning has become frozen. It is something that lives, moves geographically, and eventually dies.

In America the word is hardly used at all to indicate the nation's limits. No American would refer to the line separating the United States from Canada or that from Mexico as the frontier, and to apply it to them in this sense would lead to misunderstanding.* The American thinks of the frontier as lying *within,* and not at the edge of, a country. It is not a line to stop at, but an *area* inviting entrance. Instead of having one dimension, length, as in Europe, the American frontier has two dimensions, length and breadth. In Europe the frontier is stationary and presumably permanent; in America it *was* transient and temporal.[4]†

The concept of a moving frontier is applicable where a civilized people are advancing into a wilderness, an unsettled area, or one sparsely populated by primitive people. It was the sort of land into which the Boers moved in South Africa, the English in Australia, and the Americans and Canadians in their progress westward across North America. The frontier movement is an invasion of a land assumed to be vacant as distinguished from an invasion of an occupied or civilized country, an advance against nature rather than against men. On a frontier the invaders often have immediate and exclusive possession whereas in a nonfrontier the invaders have to contend with the original inhabitants, whom they always find troublesome and frequently too much for them. Inherent in the American concept of a moving frontier is the idea of a body of free land which can be had for the taking.

This expanded concept of the frontier grew out of the American experience as the sole proprietor of an unsettled contiguous[5] territory. Always, for three centuries, to the west of the settlements there stretched an empty country inviting settlement, luring the venturesome toward the sunset. Of this territory the United States came piece by piece into undisputed possession. No foreign power contended for it; it therefore did not present a problem in sovereignty, and movement into it was civilian, not military.‡ The territory was adjacent to the settled area, and the journey there did not involve a sea voyage, a long trek, or any considerable outlay of capital. The settlers who went there were not colonists, and the land to

---

* The line separating the United States from Canada is generally referred to as the boundary; that separating the country from Mexico is likely to be called the border. The distinction is a nice one, and probably comes from the historic fact that there has been more friction between the United States and Mexico than between it and Canada. There has also been more lawlessness on both sides along the southern line, and the word *border* suggests that.

[1] fortified position
[2] rules of diplomatic ceremony and etiquette
[3] continuing logical consequences

From **The Great Frontier** by Walter Prescott Webb, University of Texas Press, 1964. Reprinted by permission of University of Texas Press.

† See Fulmer Mood, "Notes on the History of the Word *Frontier*," *Agricultural History,* XXII (April, 1948), 78–83. The evolution of the American meaning of the word is here traced from 1623 to recent times.

‡ I am ignoring the scattered Indian population who did present some resistance but were not a major problem except for the few people who were in contact with them on the farthest fringes of settlement. In the present area of the United States the Indian population was probably not more than 500,000, one Indian to about six square miles.

[4] temporary
[5] adjacent

140 which they went was in no sense a colony. The settlers were citizens moving into territory owned by the nation. The only thing that distinguished these citizens and this territory from the older region was the fact that the processes current were a step or two behind the processes of the older region, say in Virginia or Massachusetts.* It was understood on all sides that the status of the individual as a citizen was unchanged, and that within a short time the new territory would become automatically a state in the Union whose status would not differ from that of the oldest member. The absence of the military, the proximity of the new land to the old, the ease of migration, and the absence of any attempt on the part of government to regulate or control the process made the whole American situation the last word in simplicity, so simple that it amounted to chaos. In these respects the movement of the American people into the frontier after independence was unlike the movement of people from European nations into their overseas colonial possessions.

"Inherent in the American concept of a moving frontier is the idea of a body of free land which can be had for the taking."

American historians assume that the frontier process began with the English settlement at Jamestown, Virginia, in 1607. Since the process depended on the act of taking possession of new land, it would go on as long as there was new land to be taken. The year 1890 is usually accepted as marking the date when there was no more fron-

tier available, when the new land was no longer new. Though there is some quibbling about the date, 1890 does approximate the end of the frontier process in the United States, an experience of almost three centuries.†

It is the magnitude and the unbroken continuity of the experience that makes the frontier of major importance in American development. It made no difference what other tasks the Americans had on their hands at a given time, there was the additional, ever-present task of moving into and settling new country. They did it while they fought for independence, before and after; they did it while they hammered out the principles of a democratic government and that government was eventually shaped to the needs of frontier men; and they did not cease doing it in the period of civil strife. They rarely reached the limits of the vacancy they owned before they acquired another vacancy, the Louisiana territory by purchase, the Florida country by negotiation, Texas by treaty, and the southwestern quarter of the United States by conquest.‡ In every case the frontiersmen had infiltrated the country before the nation acquired it. Like locusts they swarmed, always to the west, and only the Pacific Ocean stopped them.

It would be strange indeed if such an experience as this should have had no effect on the people and the nation. Could people have as their main task for three centuries working with raw land without getting its dirt under their nails and deep under their skins? The effects were present everywhere, in democratic government, in boisterous politics, in exploitive agriculture, in mobility of population, in disregard for conventions, in rude manners, and in unbridled optimism. Though these effects were present everywhere, they were not understood anywhere by the people who felt and reflected them. The frontier lacked its philosopher, the thinker who could view the whole scene and the whole dramatic experience and tell what was its meaning. This philosopher arrived three years after the experience ended and told the

* The American method of expansion was simple and, for the people, highly impersonal. When new territory was acquired, it was understood that within a short time it would be cut up into states which would be admitted to the union. The process was as follows:

1. Acquisition of an area by purchase, conquest, or treaty.
2. Government of the area as unorganized territory.
3. Territorial organization of the prospective state or states.
4. Admission of the organized territory into the Union.

From the time of acquisition until admission, the territory, organized or unorganized, was governed by the United States Congress. After admission, state and local government was in the hands of the resident people. Any citizen of the United States could migrate to and become a legal resident of a territory without permit or formality of any sort. The land was never a colony nor the resident a colonist.

† The year 1890 is generally given as the date marking the close of the frontier. Actually the closing was gradual, covering the period from 1880 to 1910.
‡ The territorial expansion of the United States occurred in the following order: Louisiana territory, 1803; Florida, 1819; Texas, 1845; the Oregon country, 1846; the Southwestern territory, including all or part of seven present states, 1848. These acquisitions were all made in advance of the migratory horde that was moving west with the result that vacant land was available throughout the nineteenth century.

American people that from the beginning the American frontier had been the dominant force, the determining influence in their history.

It was in 1893 that a young and unknown historian appeared before the American Historical Association and read a paper entitled "The Significance of the Frontier in American History." That paper made him a scholar with honor in his own country, for, brief though his essay is, it is recognized as the most influential single piece of historical writing ever done in the United States. It altered the whole course of American historical scholarship. The young man was Frederick Jackson Turner of the University of Wisconsin. Following Turner's lead, there arose in the United States a whole school of frontier historians who have worked out in many directions the rich mine that Turner opened up. It is not necessary here to elaborate Turner's famous thesis except to reiterate that it expounded the overwhelming importance of the frontier as the dominant force in creating a democracy and making the individual free from Old World restrictions.*

What should be emphasized is that Turner confined his attention to *American* history. The frontier that he talked about was the new *American* land lying west of the *American* settlements. His disciples and followers have not greatly extended the scope of his investigation. Most of them have treated the frontier as if it were something exclusively American, as if the United States were the only nation that had felt the powerful influence of access to vacant land. As for historians in other countries,† in the New World or the Old World, they have with few exceptions ignored the frontier completely, have never become more than vaguely conscious of its existence.

I have often thought that each nation has something peculiar to itself that could be borrowed with advantage by its neighbors. If I could export one thing American to European scholars, something which, I believe, would help them to a better understanding of their troubled world, our troubled world, it would be an understanding of the frontier—not the American frontier, but their own —and its significance in their history and in their present lives. It is the American frontier concept that needs to be lifted out of its present national setting and applied on a much larger scale to all of Western civilization in modern times.

* The essay appears in various places but is most accessible in Frederick Jackson Turner, *The Frontier in American History* (New York: Henry Holt and Co., Inc., 1920), pp. 1–38. For the pros and cons of the Turner thesis see George Rogers Taylor, ed., *The Turner Thesis Concerning the Role of the Frontier in American History* (Boston: D. C. Heath and Co., 1949). A much quoted passage from the opening paragraph reads: "Up to our own day American history has been in a large degree the history of the colonization of the Great West. *The existence of an area of free land, its continuous recession, and the advance of American settlement westward, explain American development.*" (Italics supplied.)

Though Turner's interpretation has been challenged, it has continued to grow, and its influence has spread to literature, political science, philosophy, and even to psychiatry. It is today imbedded in the fabric of American thought, and is slowly invading other frontier societies.

† Canada is an exception. Its proximity to the United States has made it impossible for Canadian historians to escape the frontier hypothesis.

Space Flight and the Spirit of Man

ARTHUR C. CLARKE

It is exactly fifteen years since, at the October 1946 meeting of the British Interplanetary Society, I presented the first version of my paper *The Challenge of the Spaceship,* an inquiry into the cultural and philosophical implications of astronautics.* At the time, as the title indicates, I was somewhat under the influence of Professor Toynbee, having just attended a lecture he had given at the Senate House, University of London, on "The Unification of the World." He had opened my eyes to the highly parochial[1] view we Westerners take of human history, which is best summed up by our attitude that *we* discovered the rest of the world. Above all, however, I was struck by Toynbee's emphasis on "challenge and response" as shaping the rise and fall of civilizations, and it seemed to me that we would be presented with a classic example of this when the Space Age opened. Here without question was the greatest physical challenge that life on this planet had faced since the distant days when it emerged from the sea and invaded that other hostile environment, the arid, sun-scorched land.

As I went on to consider the possibilities opened up by this new field of exploration, my mind was inevitably drawn to the great voyages of discovery of the fifteenth and sixteenth centuries. These were not only voyages of discovery,

* The latest version is the opening essay in the book of the same name. (Harper & Brothers, 1959.)

[1] narrow, restricted

From **Astronautics & Aeronautics,** a publication of the American Institute of Aeronautics and Astronautics. Copyright © by Arthur C. Clarke. Reprinted by permission of the author and the author's agents, Scott Meredith Literary Agency, Inc., 580 Fifth Avenue, New York, N.Y. 10036.

but of escape; they liberated men's minds from the long trance of the Middle Ages, and fueled the fires of the Renaissance. Perhaps something similar would happen with space flight; looking toward a future which, in 1946, still seemed very distant, I wrote the following words:

With the expansion of the world's mental horizons may come one of the greatest outbursts of creative activity ever known. The parallel with the Renaissance, with its great flowering of the arts and sciences, is very suggestive. "In human records," wrote the anthropologist J. D. Unwin, "there is no trace of any display of productive energy that has not been preceded by a display of expansive energy. Although the two kinds of energy must be carefully distinguished, in the past they have been united in the sense that one has developed out of the other." Unwin continues with this quotation from Sir James Frazer: "Intellectual progress, which reveals itself in the growth of art and science . . . receives an immense impetus[2] from conquest and empire." Interplanetary travel is now the only form of "conquest and empire" compatible with civilization. Without it, the human mind, compelled to circle forever in its planetary goldfish bowl, must eventually stagnate.

Now that we are well into the space age, and achievements which in 1946 seemed to belong to the remote future are milestones in the past, it is time to ask if these predictions of a cultural revival can still be justified—and even if they already show signs of coming true.

*T*hat the world is now space conscious, to an extent which would have seemed unbelievable only a few years ago, is a statement that needs no proof. But it is not yet space *minded.* By this, I mean that the general public still thinks of space activities almost exclusively in terms of military strength and international prestige. These matters are, of course, vitally important; yet in the long run, if there is a long run, they will be merely the ephemeral concerns of our neurotic age. In the sane society which we have to build if we are to survive, we must forget spacemanship and concentrate on space.

Unfortunately, altogether too many educators, intellectuals and other molders of public opinion,

[2] stimulus

144 still regard space as a terrifying vacuum, instead of a frontier with infinite possibilities. Typical of this attitude, though seldom so clearly expressed, is the following passage from Professor Lewis Mumford's *The Transformation of Man:*

> Post-historic man's starvation of life would reach its culminating point in interplanetary travel. . . . Under such conditions, life would again narrow down to the physiological functions of breathing, eating and excretion. . . . By comparison, the Egyptian cult of the dead was overflowing with vitality; from a mummy in his tomb one can still gather more of the attributes of a full human being than from a spaceman.

The almost laughable falsehood of this passage was demonstrated by Commander Shepard's famous exclamation "What a beautiful sight!" as his Mercury capsule arced over the Caribbean. I would maintain that these words are enough to settle the matter, but it must be admitted that most people would prefer more substantial evidence for the benefits of manned space flight.

Let me first dispose of one argument for man in space that is frequently put forward, and which only confuses the issue. It is often suggested that the complexity and unreliability of automatic space probes will make it impossible to dispense with human astronauts, even if they merely serve as trouble shooters. This is a shortsighted view; in the not-too-distant future—perhaps only fifty years from now—we will have robots as good as any flesh-and-blood explorers. The frequent and predictable failures of the next decade's automatic astronauts must not blind us to the fact that they will be only clumsy, moronic toys compared with their successors half a century hence. The justification of man in space must depend not upon the deficiencies of his machines, but upon the positive advantages that he, personally, will gain from going there.

There is no point in exploring—still less colonizing—a hostile and dangerous environment unless it opens up new opportunities for experience and spiritual enrichment. Mere survival is not sufficient; there are already enough examples on this planet of societies that have been beaten down to subsistence level by the forces of nature. The questions which all protagonists[3] of space flight have to ask themselves, and answer

to their own satisfaction, are these: What can the other planets offer that we cannot find here on Earth? Can we do better, on Mars or Venus, than the Eskimos have done in the Arctic? And the Eskimos, it is worth reminding ourselves, have done very well indeed; a dispassionate observer might reasonably decide that they are the only really civilized people on this planet.

"The opening of the space frontier . . . . has saved us, perhaps in the nick of time, by providing an outlet for dangerously stifled energies."

The possible advantages of space can be best appreciated if we turn our backs upon it and return, in imagination, to the sea. Here is the perfect environment for life—the place where it originally evolved. In the sea, an all-pervading fluid medium carries oxygen and food to every organism; it need never hunt for either. The same medium neutralizes gravity, insures against temperature extremes, and prevents damage by too-intense solar radiation—which must have been lethal at the Earth's surface before the ozone layer was formed.

When we consider these facts, it seems incredible that life ever left the sea, for in some ways the dry land is almost as dangerous as space. Because we are accustomed to it, we forget the price we have had to pay in our daily battle against gravity. We seldom stop to think that we are still creatures of the sea, able to leave it only because, from birth to death, we wear the water-filled space suits of our skins.

Yet until life had invaded and conquered the land, it was trapped in an evolutionary cul-de-sac[4]—for intelligence cannot arise in the sea. The relative opacity of water, and its resistance to movement, were perhaps the chief factors limiting the mental progress of marine creatures. They had little incentive to develop keen vision (the most subtle of the senses, and the only long range one) or manual dexterity. It will be most interesting to see if there are any exceptions to this, elsewhere in the universe.

[3] here, advocates; spokesmen for

[4] dead end

Even if these obstacles do not prevent a low order of intelligence arising in the sea, the road to further development is blocked by an impassable barrier. The difference between man and animals lies not in the possession of tools, *but in the possession of fire.* A marine culture could never escape from the Stone Age and discover the use of metals; indeed, almost all branches of science and technology would be forever barred to it.

Perhaps we would have been happier had we remained in the sea (the porpoises seem glad enough to have returned, after sampling the delights of the dry land for a few million years) but I do not think that even the most cynical philosopher has ever suggested that we took the wrong road. The world beneath the waves is beautiful, but it is hopelessly limited, and the creatures who live there are crippled irremediably in mind and spirit. No fish can see the stars; but we will never be content until we have reached them.

There is one point, and a very important one, at which the evolutionary parallel breaks down. Life adapted itself to the land by unconscious, biological means, whereas the adaptation to space is conscious and deliberate, made not through biological but through engineering techniques of infinitely greater flexibility and power. At least, we think it is conscious and deliberate, but it is often hard to avoid the feeling that we are in the grip of some mysterious force or *Zeitgeist*[5] that is driving us out to the planets, whether we wish to go or not.

Though the analogy is obvious, it cannot be *proved*, at this moment of time, that expansion into space will produce a quantum jump in our development as great as that which took place when our ancestors left the sea. From the nature of things, we cannot predict the new forces, powers, and discoveries that will be disclosed to us when we reach the other planets or can set up laboratories in space. They are as much beyond our vision today as fire or electricity would be beyond the imagination of a fish.

Yet no one can doubt that the increasing flow of knowledge and sense impressions, and the wholly new types of experience and emotion, that will result from space travel will have a profoundly stimulating effect upon the human psyche. I have already referred to our age as a neurotic one; the "sick" jokes, the decadence of art forms, the flood of anxious self-improvement books, the etiolated[6] cadavers[7] posing in the fashion magazines—these are minor symptoms of a malaise[8] that has gripped at least the Western world, where it sometimes seems that we have reached *fin de siècle*[9] fifty years ahead of the calendar.

The opening of the space frontier will change all that, as the opening of any new frontier must do. It has saved us, perhaps in the nick of time, by providing an outlet for dangerously stifled energies. In William James's famous phrase, it is the perfect "moral equivalent of war."

*F*rom time to time, alarm has been expressed at the danger of "sensory deprivation" in space. Astronauts on long journeys, it has been suggested, will suffer the symptoms that afflict men who are cut off from their environment by being shut up in darkened, soundproofed rooms.

I would reverse this argument; our entire culture will suffer from sensory deprivation if it does *not* go out into space. There is striking evidence for this in what has already happened to the astronomers and physicists. As soon as they were able to rise above the atmosphere, a new and often surprising universe was opened up to them, far richer and more complex than had ever been suspected from ground observations. Even the most enthusiastic proponents of space research never imagined just how valuable satellites would actually turn out to be, and there is a profound symbolism in this.

But the facts and statistics of science, priceless though they are, tell only part of the story. Across the seas of space lie the new raw materials of the imagination, without which all forms of art must eventually sicken and die. Strangeness, wonder, mystery, adventure, magic—these things, which not long ago seemed lost forever, will soon return to the world. And with them, perhaps, will come again an age of sagas and epics such as Homer never knew.

Though we may welcome this, we may not enjoy it, for it is never easy to live in an age of

[5] the spirit of the time
[6] slender, puny; whitened as a plant kept from sunlight
[7] corpses
[8] feeling of vague discomfort
[9] end of the century

". . . if there are any gods whose chief concern is man,
they cannot be very important gods."

146 transition—indeed, of revolution. As the old Chinese curse has it: "May you live in interesting times," and the twentieth century is probably the most "interesting" period that mankind has ever known. The psychological stresses and strains produced by astronautics—upon the travelers and those who stay at home—will often be unpleasant, even though the ultimate outcome will be beneficial to the race as a whole.

The American public has already experienced some emotional highs and lows that give a slight foretaste of what is to come. To date, the ex-tremes are well represented by the explosion of the first Vanguard, and the success of the first manned sub-orbital shot, when the whole nation stopped its work and play to watch Cape Kennedy. But these are only pale shadows of such future triumphs and disasters as the landing on the Moon—or the impact of a Nova-class vehicle on Miami Beach.

We must also prepare ourselves for the probability—in fact, the virtual certainty—that the most painful and uncomfortable shocks will involve our philosophical and religious beliefs.

Many optimistic apologists[10] have tried to deny this, but the clear verdict of history is against them.

We now take it for granted that our planet is a tiny world in a remote corner of an infinite universe, and have forgotten how this discovery shattered the calm certainties of medieval faith. Even the echoes of the second great scientific revolution are now swiftly fading; today, except in a few backward regions, the theory of evolution arouses as little controversy as the statement that the Earth moves round the Sun. Yet it is only a hundred years since the best minds of the Victorian age tore themselves asunder because they could not face the facts of biology.

Space will, sooner or later, present us with facts that are much more stubborn, and even more disconcerting. There can be little reasonable doubt that, ultimately, we will come into contact with races more intelligent than our own. That contact may be one-way, through the discovery of ruins or artifacts; it may be two-way, over radio or laser circuits; it may even be face to face. But it will occur, and it may be the most devastating event in the history of mankind. The rash assertion that "God made man in His own image" is ticking like a time bomb at the foundations of many faiths, and as the hierarchy of the universe is disclosed to us, we may have to recognize this chilling truth: if there are any gods whose chief concern is man, they cannot be very important gods.

The best examination I have seen of the probable effects of space travel upon our philosophical-religious beliefs was made in a broadcast by Derek Lawden, well known for his work on interplanetary orbits. Because few people outside New Zealand will have heard his stimulating talk, it is worth giving Professor Lawden's conclusions at some length:

I think man will see himself as one agent by which the whole universe of matter is slowly becoming conscious of itself. He will cease to feel an alien creature in an indifferent world, but will sense within himself the pulse of the cosmos. He'll become familiar with the marvellous and varied forms which can be assumed by matter . . . and he's certain to develop a feeling of reverence for the awe-inspiring whole of which he's a very small part. I suggest to you that his reaction to these impressive experiences will find its expression in a pantheism[11] which will at last provide a philosophy of life and an attitude to existence which is in harmony with science. . . . It may be objected that the physical universe could never become the object of worship. I ask anyone who denies this possibility to turn his eyes skyward on a clear night. . . . Others may object that such a religion would possess little moral content. I would reply that this is by no means self-evident, but that, in any case, the conjunction of religion and ethics . . . is certainly not invariable; in fact, there's an excellent case for keeping the two separate. . . . Morality in the modern Western world has been greatly weakened because of its strong ties with Christianity, for as one decays, so does the other. . . .

These are hard sayings, which many will find unpalatable;[12] the truth may be yet harder. Perhaps if we knew all that lay ahead of us on the road to space—a hundred or a thousand or a million years in the future—no man alive would have the courage to make the first step. But that first step—and the second—has already been taken; to turn back now would be treason to the human spirit, even though our feet must some day carry us into realms no longer human.

The eyes of all the ages are upon us now, as we create the myths of the future at Cape Kennedy and Baikonur. No other generation has been given such powers, and such responsibilities. The impartial agents of our destiny stand on their launching pads, awaiting our commands. They can take us to that greater Renaissance whose signs and portents[13] we can already see, or they can make us one with the dinosaurs.

The choice is ours, it must be made soon, and it is irrevocable. If our wisdom fails to match our science, we will have no second chance. For there will be none to carry our dreams across another dark age, when the dust of all our cities incarnadines[14] the sunsets of the world.

[11] doctrine that every part of the universe is a manifestation of God
[12] of a disagreeable taste; unacceptable
[13] indications of what is to happen
[14] colors deep red

[10] persons who argue in defense of a cause

Spectator and Amateur Sports

MAX LERNER

Sports do for the popular culture of America what "circuses" did for the Roman culture at the height of the Empire. They let the populace take part in a crucial ritual that binds them to one another and to the culture. Every people, no matter how civilized, must have a chance to yell for blood. Americans express this barbarism daily in their gladiatorial arts—in acting as spectators and psychic participants while other men fight, wrestle, and race with one another, break through human walls to make a goal in football, on ice, or in basketball arenas, hit a ball hard and race out its return.

Compared with some other historical civilizations, the ritualized violence of the American gladiatorial arts is pretty thin. There are no Carthaginian or Aztec human sacrifices to watch, no Latin bullfights, no guillotinings such as once sickened Tolstoy in Paris, no public hangings such as the British once had, no cockfights or bear fights (except on the early frontier or as survivals in the mountain areas today), no battles to the death between Roman gladiators, no mangling of men by lions. What cruelty there is in American culture is reflected less in its spectator sports than in any other of the pugnacious[1] civilizations of history. Only wrestling, boxing, and (to some extent) football and ice hockey remain brutal, and the most ruthless of these—wrestling—has been converted into a TV buffoonery. The prize fights have had their murderousness muted since the days when frontier

[1] quarrelsome, inclined to fight

bullies fought catch-as-catch-can or two toughs pounded each other with bare knuckles for as many as fifty or sixty rounds. As the gladiatorial arts have become big industries the brutal in them has been diminished and the spectacle accented.

But these spectator sports are balanced in America by a network of participant sports in which people pursue their amateur skills actively and almost obsessively. This requires leisure, with whose development the history of American sports has been tied up. In earlier America, while work was still a life goal, fun was largely restricted to recreation at working-bees or the amenities of church socials, while on the frontier it took the form of heavy drinking and rough games. In a culture where farming exacted a round-the-clock attention to chores and factory hours were long, leisure for organized sports was rare. "Pastimes" imply that there is time to pass with them; spectator sports require purchasing power for admission—that is to say, a surplus after the necessities of life have been met. The increasing industrial productivity, by cutting down the working day and raising living standards, made both possible.

But before the big audience could find sports to watch, or the mass armies of amateurs could find sports to pursue, there had to be games carrying prestige that would furnish psychic pleasure. This happened when the American wealthy lost their sense of guilt about "conspicuous leisure" and began to develop horse racing, polo, yachting, and golf as the sports of aristocrats. One of the early games the rich took up was baseball. But they could not keep it long as their coteried[2] possession. By mid-nineteenth century baseball became a mania, by the 1880s a big business. The same thing happened to football, which started as the monopoly of the Eastern colleges. Fishing, hunting, bowling, lawn tennis, golf, all went through the sequence of being started by the fashionable and genteel, then becoming a diversion of the middle class, and finally a popular sport.

How far America has come away from sports as a leisure-class pursuit may be measured by the fact that Veblen's Theory of the Leisure Class, at the turn of the century, spoke of sports as an upper-class obsession, uncherished by the work-

[2] of or pertaining to a coterie, an exclusive group of persons sharing a common interest or purpose

ing class. His contention was that sports are a form of arrested emotional development, a survival of barbaric prowess, consisting of a "proximate[3] workmanship and an ultimate futility." The fact is that the gladiatorial arts have become more necessary to the middle and lower classes than to the rich. The rich still have their exclusive sports—fox hunting, yachting, polo. But the elite sports of yesterday are becoming the mass sports of today: golfers swarm over municipal links, tennis is played everywhere, horse racing and greyhound racing have been taken over by the pari-mutuel betting system, and even sailing has now been opened to a large middle class. As the lower and middle classes got money and leisure they used it on entertainment to get a direct or vicarious sense of bodily prowess. What they want in a spectator game is action, excitement, speed, and power. By these standards racing, basketball, and ice hockey are the sports moving up, and even the "national game" of baseball is stodgy by comparison.

*T*he change of scale in the mass spectator sports has brought with it also a change of phase. Much the same thing has happened to sports as to the big media: they have become adjuncts of Big Organization and the Big Money. It has proved difficult in games like football, basketball, and tennis to retain even the outward forms of amateurism. Whole industrial hierarchies[4] have been built around the national reputation of some tennis or football star—outfitting firms, sports equipment, auxiliary children's souvenirs, the newspaper sports pages, and the new profession of sports writing. In the case of college football, what was once a contest of prowess between young players has been transformed into a struggle of strategies between highly paid coaches who instruct their players on every possible move, leaving them only the refinements of execution. In professional baseball, what the "fans" regard as the triumph of particular stars is often the result of an elaborate system of baseball "farms" and a heavy money investment that makes the assemblage of talent possible. Thus the repetitive pennant and World Series triumphs of the New York Yankees [in the 1950s and early 60s] may be seen at least in part as the triumph of Big Busi-

ness organization applied to the task of developing pitching and hitting power.

The fun industries (not including betting) are estimated to cost about ten billion dollars a year, and the figure may be low. The amount spent on minor sports like golf and motorboating equals the box-office receipts of the movies. On bowling alone the estimates vary from a quarter to three quarters of a billion, spent by twenty million bowlers. As for horse racing, the important figures relate to betting. The estimate is that six billion dollars a year is bet on the races, and almost an equal amount on baseball, especially on the World Series. Clearly, this is a big jump from the little groups on the frontier that gathered around the bear pit or the cock pit, or the aristocratic spectators who gathered at their watering spas[5] or watched horse trotting. The sports themselves have become the narrow base of a top-heavy structure of the box-office and the betting industries.

The striking fact about this is that the commercialism of the spectator sports does little to trouble the American public, who take in their stride the fact that baseball, football, basketball, and boxing have become Big Business. In fact, they are the more inclined to value them for that reason and are pleasurably excited when a popular idol like DiMaggio receives a salary running into six figures.[6] This gave him a standing in the Pantheon, just as Eddie Arcaro got it by the purses he brought in as a jockey, or Joe Louis by his winning as a heavyweight fighter.

One of the instructive episodes in this connection is the history of the futile attempts to ban the "reserve clause" in baseball contracts as a vestige[7] of the preindustrial peonage[8] system on which baseball as a big business is built. In the Gardella case, which came to the U.S. Court of Appeals in 1949, Judge Jerome Frank commented wryly that "if players are regarded as quasi-peons, it is of no moment that they are well paid; only the totalitarian-minded will believe that higher pay excuses virtual slavery." But little emerged from the efforts to restrain

[3] very near or close to
[4] ruling bodies

[5] fashionable resorts; originally, resorts with mineral springs
[6] Salaries running into six figures are no longer exceptional, although it is still the "superstars" such as Willy Mays, Joe Namath, or Wilt Chamberlain who regularly command these salaries.
[7] a slight trace or remaining amount of something
[8] partial slavery effected by forcing people to pay off a debt or fulfill the terms of a contract

colors in a medieval tournament. Hence the hero symbolism in American sports and the impassioned hero worship which makes gods of mortals mediocre in every other respect, and gives them the place among the "Immortals" that the French reserve for their Academy intellectuals.

There is a stylized relation of artist to mass audience in the sports, especially in baseball. Each player develops a style of his own—the swagger as he steps to the plate, the unique wind-up a pitcher has, the clean-swinging and hard-driving hits, the precision quickness and grace of infield and outfield, the sense of surplus power behind whatever is done. There is the style of the spectator also: he becomes expert in the ritual of insult, provocation, and braggadocio; he boasts of the exaggerated prowess of his team and cries down the skill and courage of the other; he develops sustained feuds, carrying on a guerrilla war with the umpires and an organized badinage[10] with the players, while he consumes mountains of ritual hot dogs and drinks oceans of ritual soda pop.

Each sport develops its own legendry, woven around the "stars" who become folk heroes. The figures in baseball's Hall of Fame have their sagas told and retold in newspapers and biographies, and the Plutarchs who recount exploits become themselves notable figures in the culture. Some of these sports writers later become political

[10] playful remarks, banter

this throwback to a feudal system under the anti-trust laws—although in 1957 the Supreme Court, in a decision involving professional football, hinted that it might have second thoughts about the whole subject. The baseball fan does not seem shocked by the fact that his favorite sport rests on a system of chattel[9] contracts by which players lose their right to bargain in a free labor market, being "bought," "sold," and "swapped." Sometimes this even cuts the deeply ingrained loyalties of the fans, as in 1956 when Jackie Robinson was sold to the New York Giants and his devoted Brooklyn Dodger followers had to contemplate either abandoning him or transferring their allegiance to a hated enemy. When Ty Cobb appeared before the Celler Congressional Committee to defend peonage in baseball, no Congressman dared challenge him, for Cobb as hero symbol embodied the whole array of sentimental loyalties—of the players, the fans, and the bettors—which give the spectator sports their mass hold.

The psychic basis of American mass sports is tribal and feudal. Baseball is a good example of the modern totem symbols (Cubs, Tigers, Indians, Pirates, Dodgers, and Braves) and of sustained tribal animosities. The spectator is not *on* the team, but he can be *for* the team; he identifies himself with one team, sometimes with one player who becomes a jousting champion wearing his

[9] movable property

columnists, perhaps on the assumption that politics itself is only a sport riddled with greater hypocrisy and that it takes a salty and hard-hitting sports writer to expose the politicians. The sports heroes become national possessions, like the Grand Canyon and the gold in Fort Knox. It is hard for a people who in their childhood have treasured the sports legendry as a cherished illusion to surrender it when they grow up.

Each sport also forms a kind of subculture within itself, which a curious anthropologist could profitably study. The stars become life models for Americans who have played sand-lot baseball as kids and dreamed of striking out Babe Ruth or hitting like Ted Williams. This is important among the ethnic groups in slum areas where boxing and baseball give Irish, Jewish, Italian, Polish, and Negro boys a greater chance at a career, and where a boy who has made good in the ring or at Big League ball becomes the focus of the role-playing of all the neighborhood youngsters. The street-corner gangs in the tough neighborhoods serve as training and recruiting grounds for pugilists,[11] and boxing—and to some extent baseball and football —become not only ways of getting into the big money but also of channeling the emotional tensions of lower-status groups in the society. This is especially true of Negro players who have finally been admitted into Big League baseball and the bowling tournaments but are still kept

[11] prize fighters

out of golf and tennis tournaments.[12] Negro sports figures like Joe Louis and Jackie Robinson become not only national heroes but ethnic symbols of prowess and progress.

The point at which mass sports have violated the ingrained mores of the public is on the ques- of bribery. Americans have long been accustomed to the crookedness of the Yahoos of wrestling and have written it off as a serious sport. In the second decade of the century there were several scandals involving the "throwing" of games by bribed baseball players which led to a rigid supervision of the morals and public relations of the teams under Judge K. M. Landis as baseball "Czar." This system of internal policing enabled Big League baseball to survive and thrive. In the 1940s similar episodes developed in big-college basketball, with evidence that players had been bribed to rig games. Actually corruption of this kind is only marginal to the betting industries, which on the whole do best financially when the games are honest. But what is not marginal is the fact that even where everything is "straight" the fun and excitement of sports have been largely crowded out by commercialism. The capital investments not only in Big League professionalism but even in the college stadiums, the clinking of gate receipts, the noise the totalizers make, have all become too insistent to be ignored.

A realistic sports writer, hearing for the thousandth time about the "clean ideals" and "manly virtues" of sports, will reflect that even in the colleges the rhetoric of amateurism has given way under the steady pressures of "big-time" spectator performances. President Hutchins made a sardonic guess that his quarter-century tenure as head of the University of Chicago would be remembered chiefly by the fact that he banned college football. A number of colleges have a structure of hidden subsidies for recruiting their football players and maintaining and tutoring them while at college. When one former college president, Dexter Keezer of Reed, ironically proposed that the college convert the hidden subsidies into open ones and hire the best football team it could get, paying the players as well as the coaches, he was taken seriously and swamped by applications. There is a logical progression from these subsidies to the game-throwing episodes: if you are furtively recruited and bribed to play well, it is only a step to being bribed to play badly. What is striking is not that so many but that so few young Americans succumb. This is a tribute to the hold that amateur sports still have on the imagination of the young. After the pattern of Ring Lardner's biting short stories, the baseball player has been depicted in fiction chiefly as a zoological specimen whose brawn exceeds his intellect. What is more impressive, however, is the degree to which the player becomes emotionally involved in his pursuit, so that a loose collection of raw-boned young men is forged into a smoothly functioning team unit.

Moralists and psychologists have made too much of the passivity of spectator sports. America has been treated by them a little like a "condemned playground," doomed as Roman culture was doomed by the mass pursuit of pleasure for its own sake and by its passive spectator role. True, the people in modern societies preferred to seek external entertainment rather than to explore their inner resources. True also, the cult of American sports may delay maturity, keeping many of its devotees frozen as eternal juveniles. But there are few parallels in history to an American culture which was presented overnight with the gift of leisure, not just to one class but to almost the entire culture. Americans have found in sports a set of loyalties that in past cultures have been linked with more destructive pursuits. They have also found in it a kind of substitute for an urban culture's loss of relation to the natural environment.

One may argue, as Plato did, that the youth of any society carries on in its civic life the modes of behavior it learns in its sports. In that sense Americans have come to view politics and war as games after the image of competitive sports. The image of the team whose players work together under a captain or quarterback has been carried over into the popular thinking. One may assert, on the other hand, with Aristotle, that the

---

[12] It is no longer true that Negroes are kept out of golf and tennis tournaments. Althea Gibson became the first Negro Women's Singles Tennis Champion for the United States in 1957 and 1958. In 1968 Arthur Ashe was the Men's Singles Champion for the United States. In 1957 Charlie Sifford was the first Negro to win a professional golf tournament, but it wasn't until 1967 that he received official recognition as a winner of the Greater Hartford Connecticut open tournament. As of January, 1969, when Sifford won the Los Angeles open, there were eight Negro golfers on tour.

real function of sports is not emulative[13] but purgative.[14] It is a familiar theory that spectator sports strengthen American democracy by serving as a safety valve for tension and emotions that might otherwise have broken into flames of violence.

Beyond these theories is the fact that American sports express the energies of the culture as a whole and the will-to-youthfulness of its people. Sometimes this takes ugly forms of expression, as with bullying and bottle-tossing fans. Sometimes it is expressed in a manic ferocity, as with Branch Rickey's description of the ideal ball-player as one who "will break both your legs if you happen to be standing in his path to second base." Again it may take on the tinny values of the box office or the press agents. Sometimes it gets mixed up with gamblers, racketeers, and crooks, or with the fake heroics of what has been called the "grunt-and-groan business" in wrestling. Yet spectator sports are saved by a cultural vitality which both audience and players express.

The most hopeful fact about American sports is that they have reached their saturation point as passive spectacles, and that their growing point is now in the area of amateur participant sports. In sports, as also in writing, painting, photography, theater, carpentry, crafts, cooking, and dressmaking, America is becoming a nation of amateurs. The recruits for Rose Bowl football and for Big League baseball are taken from the sand-lot ball games of the kids and the skeleton football scrimmages at school and on the city streets. In the social climate of the mass sports, young Americans wrestle, race, swim, fight with their fists; in many localities high-school basketball has become a community passion. But beyond this recruiting base that the culture gives the spectator sports, there is also a new emphasis on direct participation of adults in forms of organized play and fun. The new leisure has made the beaches swarm with swimmers and sun worshipers; in winter the ski trains carry middle-class groups who never before had taken part in winter sports; golf has been largely transferred from the private links to municipal courses which make it available to almost any income group; with the automobile to transport them to formerly inaccessible streams, fishing has become

possible for many new millions; in terms of the numbers engaged, bowling has become the top American national sport, reaching into the factory and offices of the corporations, each of which has bowling teams belonging to the industrial bowling leagues.

This has given sports amateurism a new meaning, broader than the earlier sense which made an amateur a steady contestant who could afford not to sell his services. Amateurism in this older meaning has been declining rather than increasing in the commercial context of big American sports. The true amateurs have become the men and women who pursue sports in their leisure because they love them and find in them new accessions[15] of experience and a play of bodily skills which the machine culture fails to use. This may bring a psychic fulfillment more far-reaching than is involved in the theory of the spectator sports as a safety valve for tensions and frustrations. A people that finds an expressiveness at play too often denied on the job is less likely to be capturable by mass emotions. Thus the growth of sports amateurism acts as a counterforce to the more synthetic entertainments and hero worship engendered by the spectacle sports.

It is probably true that Americans will never develop in their sports the kind of ritual meaning and religious symbolism that makes the bull-fight in Spanish cultures express the tragic meaning of life. The genius of American sports is a different one. It expresses exuberant energies rather than a killer instinct or a death obsession. It is suited to a people who feel that careers are open for skill and resourcefulness, and that life with its unlimited possibilities yields both the big prizes to the professional and a quieter satisfaction to the amateur.

[15] acquisitions, increases gained by something added

[13] fostering competitiveness and rivalry
[14] inducing catharsis or release of tensions

Concluding Remarks from *American Notes*

CHARLES DICKENS

There are many passages in this book, where I have been at some pains to resist the temptation of troubling my readers with my own deductions and conclusions: preferring that they should judge for themselves, from such premises as I have laid before them. My only object in the outset, was, to carry them with me faithfully wheresoever I went: and that task I have discharged.

But I may be pardoned, if on such a theme as the general character of the American people, and the general character of their social system, as presented to a stranger's eyes, I desire to express my own opinions in a few words, before I bring these volumes to a close.

They are, by nature, frank, brave, cordial, hospitable, and affectionate. Cultivation and refinement seem but to enhance their warmth of heart and ardent enthusiasm; and it is the possession of these latter qualities in a most remarkable degree, which renders an educated American one of the most endearing and most generous of friends. I never was so won upon, as by this class; never yielded up my full confidence and esteem so readily and pleasurably, as to them; never can make again, in half a year, so many friends for whom I seem to entertain the regard of half a life.

These qualities are natural, I implicitly believe, to the whole people. That they are, however, sadly sapped and blighted in their growth among the mass; and that there are influences at work which endanger them still more, and give but little present promise of their healthy restoration; is a truth that ought to be told.

It is an essential part of every national character to pique[1] itself mightily upon its faults, and to deduce tokens of its virtue or its wisdom from their very exaggeration. One great blemish in the popular mind of America, and the prolific parent of an innumerable brood of evils, is Universal Distrust. Yet the American citizen plumes himself upon this spirit, even when he is sufficiently dispassionate to perceive the ruin it works; and will often adduce[2] it, in spite of his own reason, as an instance of the great sagacity[3] and acuteness of the people, and their superior shrewdness and independence.

"You carry," says the stranger, "this jealousy and distrust into every transaction of public life. By repelling worthy men from your legislative assemblies, it has bred up a class of candidates for the suffrage,[4] who, in their every act, disgrace your Institutions and your people's choice. It has rendered you so fickle, and so given to change, that your inconstancy has passed into a proverb; for you no sooner set up an idol firmly, than you are sure to pull it down and dash it into fragments: and this, because directly you reward a benefactor, or a public servant, you distrust him, merely because he *is* rewarded; and immediately apply yourselves to find out, either that you have been too bountiful in your acknowledgments, or he remiss in his deserts. Any man who attains a high place among you, from the President downwards, may date his downfall from that moment; for any printed lie that any notorious villain pens, although it militate directly against the character and conduct of a life, appeals at once to your distrust, and is believed. You will strain at a gnat in the way of trustfulness and confidence, however fairly won and well deserved; but you will swallow a whole caravan of camels, if they be laden with unworthy doubts and mean suspicions. Is this well, think you, or likely to elevate the character of the governors or the governed, among you?"

The answer is invariably the same: "There's freedom of opinion here, you know. Every man thinks for himself, and we are not to be easily overreached. That's how our people come to be suspicious."

Another prominent feature is the love of "smart" dealing: which gilds over many a swindle and gross breach of trust; many a defalcation,[5]

[1] excite or arouse by a provocation, challenge, or rebuff
[2] cite, allege
[3] wisdom
[4] voting privilege
[5] embezzlement

public and private; and enables many a knave[6] to hold his head up with the best, who well deserves a halter; though it has not been without its retributive operation, for this smartness has done more in a few years to impair the public credit, and to cripple the public resources, than dull honesty, however rash, could have effected in a century. The merits of a broken speculation, or a bankruptcy, or of a successful scoundrel, are not gauged by its or his observance of the golden rule, "Do as you would be done by," but are considered with reference to their smartness. I recollect, on both occasions of our passing that ill-fated Cairo on the Mississippi, remarking on the bad effects such gross deceits must have when they exploded, in generating a want of confidence abroad, and discouraging foreign investment: but I was given to understand that this was a very smart scheme by which a deal of money had been made: and that its smartest feature was, that they forgot these things abroad, in a very short time, and speculated again, as freely as ever. The following dialogue I have held a hundred times: "Is it not a very disgraceful circumstance that such a man as So-and-so should be acquiring a large property by the most infamous and odious[7] means, and notwithstanding all the crimes of which he has been guilty, should be tolerated and abetted by your Citizens? He is a public nuisance, is he not?" "Yes, Sir." "A convicted liar?" "Yes, Sir." "He has been kicked, and cuffed, and caned?" "Yes, Sir." "And he is utterly dishonourable, debased, and profligate?" "Yes, Sir." "In the name of wonder, then, what is his merit?" "Well, Sir, he is a smart man."

In like manner, all kinds of deficient and impolitic usages are referred to the national love of trade; though, oddly enough, it would be a weighty charge against a foreigner that he regarded the Americans as a trading people. The love of trade is assigned as a reason for that comfortless custom, so very prevalent in country towns, of married persons living in hotels, having no fireside of their own, and seldom meeting from early morning until late at night, but at the hasty public meals. The love of trade is a reason why the literature of America is to remain for ever unprotected: "For we are a trading people, and don't care for poetry:" though we *do*, by the way,

profess to be very proud of our poets: while healthful amusements, cheerful means of recreation, and wholesome fancies, must fade before the stern utilitarian joys of trade.

*T*hese three characteristics are strongly presented at every turn, full in the stranger's view. But, the foul growth of America has a more tangled root than this; and it strikes its fibres, deep in its licentious[8] Press.

Schools may be erected, East, West, North, and South; pupils be taught, and masters reared, by scores upon scores of thousands; colleges may thrive, churches may be crammed, temperance may be diffused, and advancing knowledge in all other forms walk through the land with giant strides: but while the newspaper press of America is in, or near, its present abject state, high moral improvement in that country is hopeless. Year by year, it must and will go back; year by year, the tone of public feeling must sink lower down; year by year, the Congress and the Senate must become of less account before all decent men; and year by year, the memory of the Great Fathers of the Revolution must be outraged more and more, in the bad life of their degenerate child.

Among the herd of journals which are published in the States, there are some, the reader scarcely need be told, of character and credit. From personal intercourse with accomplished gentlemen connected with publications of this class, I have derived both pleasure and profit. But the name of these is Few, and of Legion;[9] and the influence of the good, is powerless to counteract the moral poison of the bad.

Among the gentry of America; among the well-informed and moderate: in the learned professions; at the bar and on the bench: there is, as there can be, but one opinion, in reference to the vicious character of these infamous journals. It is sometimes contended——I will not say strangely, for it is natural to seek excuses for such a disgrace —that their influence is not so great as a visitor would suppose. I must be pardoned for saying that there is no warrant for this plea, and that every fact and circumstance tends directly to the opposite conclusion.

[6] rogue, rascal
[7] offensive, abhorrent

[8] lacking in moral restraint
[9] many; of a great multitude

156 When any man, of any grade of desert in intellect or character, can climb to any public distinction, no matter what, in America, without first grovelling down upon the earth, and bending the knee before this monster of depravity; when any private excellence is safe from its attacks; when any social confidence is left unbroken by it, or any tie of social decency and honour is held in the least regard; when any man in that free country has freedom of opinion, and presumes to think for himself, and speak for himself, without humble reference to a censorship which, for its rampant ignorance and base dishonesty, he utterly loathes and despises in his heart; when those who most acutely feel its infamy[10] and the reproach it casts upon the nation, and who most denounce it to each other, dare to set their heels upon, and crush it openly, in the sight of all men: then, I will believe that its influence is lessening, and men are returning to their manly senses. But while that Press has its evil eye in every house, and its black hand in every appointment in the state, from a president to a postman; while, with ribald[11] slander for its only stock-in-trade, it is the standard literature of an enormous class, who must find their reading in a newspaper, or they will not read at all; so long must its odium[12] be upon the country's head, and so long must the evil it works, be plainly visible in the Republic.

To those who are accustomed to the leading English journals, or to the respectable journals of the Continent of Europe; to those who are accustomed to anything else in print and paper; it would be impossible, without an amount of extract for which I have neither space nor inclination, to convey an adequate idea of this frightful engine in America. But if any man desire confirmation of my statement on this head, let him repair to any place in this city of London, where scattered numbers of these publications are to be found; and there, let him form his own opinion.*

It would be well, there can be no doubt, for the American people as a whole, if they loved the Real less, and the Ideal somewhat more. It would be well, if there were greater encouragement to lightness of heart and gaiety, and a wider cultivation of what is beautiful, without being eminently and directly useful. But here, I think the general remonstrance, "we are a new country," which is so often advanced as an excuse for defects which are quite unjustifiable, as being, of right, only the slow growth of an old one, may be very reasonably urged: and I yet hope to hear of there being some other national amusement in the United States, besides newspaper politics.

They certainly are not a humorous people, and their temperament always impressed me as being of a dull and gloomy character. In shrewdness of remark, and a certain cast-iron quaintness, the Yankees, or people of New England, unquestionably take the lead; as they do in most other evidences of intelligence. But in travelling about, out of the large cities—as I have remarked in former parts of these volumes—I was quite oppressed by the prevailing seriousness and melancholy air of business: which was so general and unvarying, that at every new town I came to, I seemed to meet the very same people whom I had left behind me, at the last. Such defects as are perceptible in the national manners, seem, to me, to be referable, in a great degree, to this cause: which has generated a dull, sullen persistence in coarse usages, and rejected the graces of life as undeserving of attention. There is no doubt that Washington, who was always most scrupulous and exact on points of ceremony, perceived the tendency towards this mistake, even in his time, and did his utmost to correct it.

I cannot hold with other writers on these subjects that the prevalence of various forms of dissent in America, is in any way attributable to the non-existence there of an established church: indeed, I think the temper of the people, if it admitted of such an Institution being founded amongst them, would lead them to desert it, as a matter of course, merely because it *was* established. But, supposing it to exist, I doubt its probable efficacy[13] in summoning the wandering sheep to one great fold, simply because of the immense amount of dissent which prevails at home; and because I do not find in America any one form of religion with

* NOTE TO THE ORIGINAL EDITION.—Or let him refer to an able, and perfectly truthful article, in *The Foreign Quarterly Review*, published in the present month of October [1842]; to which my attention has been attracted, since these sheets have been passing through the press. He will find some specimens there, by no means remarkable to any man who has been in America, but sufficiently striking to one who has not.

[10] bad reputation, public disgrace
[11] coarse, vulgar
[12] disgrace or reproach

[13] effectiveness

which we in Europe, or even in England, are unacquainted. Dissenters resort[14] thither in great numbers, as other people do, simply because it is a land of resort; and great settlements of them are founded, because ground can be purchased, and towns and villages reared, where there were none of the human creation before. But even the Shakers emigrated from England; our country is not unknown to Mr. Joseph Smith, the apostle of Mormonism, or to his benighted disciples; I have beheld religious scenes myself in some of our populous towns which can hardly be surpassed by an American camp-meeting; and I am not aware that any instance of superstitious imposture on the one hand, and superstitious credulity on the other, has had its origin in the United States, which we cannot more than parallel by the precedents of Mrs. Southcote, Mary Tofts the rabbit-breeder, or even Mr. Thom of Canterbury:[15] which latter case arose, some time after the dark ages had passed away.

*"It would be well,
there can be no doubt,
for the American people as a whole,
if they loved the Real less,
and the Ideal somewhat more."*

The Republican Institutions of America undoubtedly lead the people to assert their self-respect and their equality; but a traveller is bound to bear those Institutions in his mind, and not hastily to resent the near approach of a class of strangers, who, at home, would keep aloof. This characteristic, when it was tinctured with no foolish pride, and stopped short of no honest service, never offended me; and I very seldom, if ever, experienced its rude or unbecoming display. Once or twice it was comically developed, as in

[14] take refuge
[15] Dickens probably had in mind Joanna Southcott (1750–1814), a domestic servant who declared herself to be the woman mentioned in *Revelation* 12. She claimed she would be delivered of Shiloh, the second Messiah, on a particular date. She did not bear a child but she did write several books of religious interpretation. At her death from brain disease, her supporters numbered one hundred thousand. Dickens' other references, "Mary Tofts the rabbit-breeder" and "Mr. Thom of Canterbury," are undoubtedly specimens of the same kind of fanaticism.

the following case; but this was an amusing incident, and not the rule, or near it.

I wanted a pair of boots at a certain town, for I had none to travel in, but those with the memorable cork soles, which were much too hot for the fiery decks of a steamboat. I therefore sent a message to an artist in boots, importing, with my compliments, that I should be happy to see him, if he would do me the polite favour to call. He very kindly returned for answer, that he would "look round" at six o'clock that evening.

I was lying on the sofa, with a book and a wine-glass, at about that time, when the door opened, and a gentleman in a stiff cravat, within a year or two on either side of thirty, entered, in his hat and gloves; walked up to the looking-glass; arranged his hair; took off his gloves; slowly produced a measure from the uttermost depths of his coat-pocket; and requested me, in a languid tone, to "unfix" my straps. I complied, but looked with some curiosity at his hat, which was still upon his head. It might have been that, or it might have been the heat—but he took it off. Then, he sat himself down on a chair opposite to me; rested an arm on each knee; and, leaning forward very much, took from the ground, by a great effort, the specimen of metropolitan workmanship which I had just pulled off: whistling, pleasantly, as he did so. He turned it over and over; surveyed it with a contempt no language can express; and inquire if I wished him to fix me a boot like *that?* I courteously replied, that provided the boots were large enough, I would leave the rest to him; that if convenient and practicable, I should not object to their bearing some resemblance to the model then before him; but that I would be entirely guided by, and would beg to leave the whole subject to, his judgment and discretion. "You an't partickler, about this scoop in the heel, I suppose then?" says he: "we don't foller that, here." I repeated my last observation. He looked at himself in the glass again; went closer to it to dash a grain or two of dust out of the corner of his eye; and settled his cravat. All this time, my leg and foot were in the air. "Nearly ready, Sir?" I inquired. "Well, pretty nigh," he said; "keep steady." I kept as steady as I could, both in foot and face; and having by this time got the dust out, and found his pencil-case, he measured me, and made the necessary notes. When he had finished, he fell into his old attitude, and taking up the boot again, mused for some time. "And this," he said, at last, "is an English boot, is it? This is a London boot, eh?" "That, Sir," I replied, "is a London boot." He mused over it again, after the manner of Hamlet with Yorick's skull; nodded his head, as who should say, "I pity the Institutions that led to the production of this boot;" rose; put up his pencil, notes, and paper—glancing at himself in the glass, all the time—put on his hat; drew on his gloves very slowly; and finally walked out. When he had been gone about a minute, the door reopened, and his hat and his head reappeared. He looked round the room, and at the boot again, which was still lying on the floor; appeared thoughtful for a minute; and then said "Well, good arternoon." "Good afternoon, Sir," said I: and that was the end of the interview.

There is but one other head on which I wish to offer a remark; and that has reference to the public health. In so vast a country, where there are thousands of millions of acres of land yet unsettled and uncleared, and on every rood of which, vegetable decomposition is annually taking place; where there are so many great rivers, and such opposite varieties of climate; there cannot fail to be a great amount of sickness at certain seasons. But I may venture to say, after conversing with many members of the medical profession in America, that I am not singular in the opinion that much of the disease which does prevail, might be avoided, if a few common precautions were observed. Greater means of personal cleanliness, are indispensable to this end; the custom of hastily swallowing large quantities of animal food, three times a-day, and rushing back to sedentary pursuits after each meal, must be changed; the gentler sex must go more wisely clad, and take more healthful exercise; and in the latter clause, the males must be included also. Above all, in public institutions, and throughout the whole of every town and city, the system of ventilation, and drainage, and removal of impurities requires to be thoroughly revised. There is no local Legislature in America which may not study Mr. Chadwick's excellent Report upon the Sanitary Condition of our Labouring Classes, with immense advantage.

I have now arrived at the close of this book. I have little reason to believe, from certain warnings I have had since I returned to England, that it will be tenderly or favourably received by the American people; and as I have written the Truth in

relation to the mass of those who form their judgments and express their opinions, it will be seen that I have no desire to court, by any adventitious means, the popular applause.

It is enough for me, to know, that what I have set down in these pages, cannot cost me a single friend on the other side of the Atlantic, who is, in anything, deserving of the name. For the rest, I put my trust, implicitly, in the spirit in which they have been conceived and penned; and I can bide my time.

I have made no reference to my reception, nor have I suffered it to influence me in what I have written; for, in either case, I should have offered but a sorry acknowledgment, compared with that I bear within my breast, towards those partial readers of my former books, across the Water, who met me with an open hand, and not with one that closed upon an iron muzzle.

POSTSCRIPT

At a Public Dinner given to me on Saturday the 18th of April, 1868, in the City of New York, by two hundred representatives of the Press of the United States of America, I made the following observations among others:

"So much of my voice has lately been heard in the land, that I might have been contented with troubling you no further from my present standing-point, were it not a duty with which I henceforth charge myself, not only here but on every suitable occasion, whatsoever and wheresoever, to express my high and grateful sense of my second reception in America, and to bear my honest testimony to the national generosity and magnanimity. Also, to declare how astounded I have been by the amazing changes I have seen around me on every side,—changes moral, changes physical, changes in the amount of land subdued and peopled, changes in the rise of vast new cities, changes in the growth of older cities almost out of recognition, changes in the graces and amenities of life, changes in the Press, without whose advancement no advancement can take place anywhere. Nor am I, believe me, so arrogant as to suppose that in five-and-twenty years there have been no changes in me, and that I had nothing to learn and no extreme impressions to correct when I was here first. And this brings me to a point on which I have, ever since I landed in the United States last November, observed a strict silence, though sometimes tempted to break it, but in reference to which I will, with your good leave, take you into my confidence now. Even the Press, being human, may be sometimes mistaken or misinformed, and I rather think that I have in one or two rare instances observed its information to be not strictly accurate with reference to myself. Indeed, I have, now and again, been more surprised by printed news that I have read of myself, than by any printed news that I have ever read in my present state of existence. Thus, the vigour and perseverance with which I have for some months past been collecting materials for, and hammering away at, a new book on America has much astonished me; seeing that all that time my declaration has been perfectly well known to my publishers on both sides of the Atlantic, that no consideration on earth would induce me to write one. But what I have intended, what I have resolved upon (and this is the confidence I seek to place in you) is, on my return to England, in my own person, in my own Journal, to bear, for the behoof of my countrymen, such testimony to the gigantic changes in this country as I have hinted at tonight. Also, to record that wherever I have been, in the smallest places equally with the largest, I have been received with unsurpassable politeness, delicacy, sweet temper, hospitality, consideration, and with unsurpassable respect for the privacy daily enforced upon me by the nature of my avocation here and the state of my health. This testimony, so long as I live, and so long as my descendants have any legal right in my books. I shall cause to be republished, as an appendix to every copy of those two books of mine in which I have referred to America. And this I will do and cause to be done, not in mere love and thankfulness, but because I regard it as an act of plain justice and honour."

I said these words with the greatest earnestness that I could lay upon them, and I repeat them in print here with equal earnestness. So long as this book shall last, I hope that they will form a part of it, and will be fairly read as inseparable from my experiences and impressions of America.

May, 1868.

Supernation at Peace and War

DAN WAKEFIELD

Prologue

In which the author explains what he was doing, and what methods he used and did not use; why he encountered certain suspicions

I have just finished traveling for more than four months through a country that is fighting two wars, one at home in the streets of its cities, and the other 10,000 miles away in a tiny land whose people are of quite a different race and culture. The country through which I have traveled is regarded by most historians and experts as the most powerful nation of its planet and perhaps in the entire history of its planet. Many people regard this fact with satisfaction and awe, while others, even some within the supernation itself, find it a source of uneasiness, and even great fear. It of course is not for me to decide the proper attitude toward this great power, but simply to recount the findings of my journey and try to give you a sense of the life there during this crucial time in its history.

As with any great power involved in struggles at home and abroad, the situation is fluid, and by the time these papers will have reached you, there will have been certain changes, shifts of mood and emphasis and opinion, and yet it is doubtful that the basic life of the country will have drastically

altered; doubtful for instance that either of its two great wars will have ended (although the domestic one subsides each year during the winter solstice, for it is fought on a seasonal basis) or that it will have lost its supremacy among the nations. There is also, of course, the remote and yet very real chance that the nation overnight could cease to exist, ironically because of the power it pioneered and possesses in the form of superbombs. In that unhappy event, this report will be of interest only as a kind of curiosity.

At the end of my travels, I have come to the nation's capital, and secured modest but comfortable lodgings, where I will stay while preparing this report, and occasionally venture out to speak with some of the leaders and attend some of the functions and ceremonies of the government. My rooms are at the top of a small third-floor apartment in the capital city, and the window affords me a pleasant view of a street that one could find in an ordinary section of nearly any city in the country. The great shrines of the nation are all within walking distance, and yet they are not visible from my window. The stately dome of its Capitol building, the stark needle monument to the "Father" of the country (reflected in a long, clear pool), and the great rotunda where sits the stone statue of the man who reunited the nation in a time of civil war, all are nearby but beyond my immediate vision. I see only trees and small neat houses of two or three stories, and a large red-brick church with stained-glass windows. It is difficult for me now, as it is for most of the citizens here, to realize that the nation is at war, with itself and its enemies halfway around the globe. From here, as from most of the country's windows, there are no signs or sounds of power or conflict or fear. At the end of the block, children are playing in a small park. Several of the neighborhood dogs erupt into sporadic barking, then subside. A busload of high school students goes by, cheering and chanting, on the way to an athletic event. The chimes of the red-brick church peal the solemn, melancholy notes of a hymn. You see, it is difficult here, as it is in most places throughout the country, to remember that any wars are going on, or that the nation is living through a time of its greatest power and perhaps its greatest trouble.

Most people do not sit around discussing the war or debating the best means to halt the decay of the inner city. They go to work, watch television, have a beer, take an aspirin, talk about football or sex or cards; they sleep, pray, love, and mourn.

I have tried to convey some sense of this common life that is lived by most of the people, most of whom see the wars and internal revolts and crises only in magazines and newspapers and on television screens. I have also tried to touch upon some of the mores, myths, and customs of the society as well as its more immediate concerns. In going about my researches, I adopted the garb, appearance, and manner of the predominant social and ethnic group of the nation, in order to be as unobtrusive as possible. In some areas, of course, this was a handicap, and the fact that I appeared as an ordinary white male of middle height, weight, and age, wearing a standard suit, shirt, and tie, aroused deep suspicions and sometimes hostilities, as I will recount. In a sense, however, these reactions seemed useful to my purposes of studying the prevailing customs and attitudes, and I feel that I gained more than I lost by sticking to the standard attire. In recent times it has become a popular approach for some researchers of this land and its people to adopt the appearance of whatever particular group was being investigated, in an effort to "pass" as one of the group. With my limited time and lack of technical assistance, however, it did not seem to me worth the extra effort to dye my skin black before entering a Negro ghetto, or to decorate myself with feathers, earrings, and luminous paints before descending into the circle of the subculture known as *hippie*. I opted for the consistency offered by the more conventionally accepted costume.

I also attempted to be as straightforward as circumstances allowed in explaining to those natives I met and talked with that I was gathering materials for a report on their country, which also confused them. You must understand that in a supernation the gethering of information is usually carried on by vast networks and organizations; equipped with computers, recording machines, scientific questionnaires, and various other highly technical apparatus. Thus, I was often suspected either of being a secret emissary of one of those agencies or of being a poor misguided fellow who simply did not understand how things were done in a supernation. This attitude is not confined to academic circles, but is fairly prevalent throughout the whole society. While attending a dinner in one of the ghettos in a great city, a young member of the predominant local minority group asked me what I was doing, and when I told him, he said with obvious indignation, "You can't do that!" I asked him why I couldn't, and he said, "You need a research team for that."

Some writers nowadays travel in their own gaily colored buses or cars, but this again seemed too time-consuming for my mission, and so I went by commercial airlines, sipping my two-drink allowance and watching the aerovision movies just like all the other passengers.

Frankly, I was neither scientific enough nor colorful enough to have my mission seem acceptable or credible to many of the natives. Most of them, though, were kind enough to tolerate me and humor what seemed to some of them my mysterious enterprise. I am grateful to them, and to the hospitality that often was extended me. If this document should by chance fall into the hands of any of my hosts throughout this journey, I hope they will accept my real gratitude, and will not feel I have judged them or their country unfairly.

Large numbers of young people rebel against home, mother, country, school, and the affluent society which supports them anyway; subversion spreads to the hinterlands; collegians plan further guerrilla war on the colleges of their choice

---

An appeal is made for fresh fruit for the hippies; a tax-payer protests; prayer is proposed as an alternative to marijuana; Plastic Man substitutes love for nuclear vengeance

---

The citizens of supernation have a passion for investigating, studying, and trying to understand themselves and their society. Gatherings such as the "conference" and the "panel discussion" on topics of concern have the status of ritual, and are believed to bring about changes in the problems so dealt with. Such events also provide social diversion for the mounting number of educated citizens who thirst for what they think of as intellectual stimulation, which is believed by many to provide "meaning" and "fulfillment" to human existence.

The National Forum, sponsored by the National Council of Churches, is one of the many groups and organizations engaged in such good works. The Forum is divided into local chapters called "Town Meetings," a term borrowed from the early history of the nation when most of its people still lived in towns and determined their local affairs at meetings.

"The Town Meeting of Southern California," tackling one of the most troubling issues of the land, sponsored a panel discussion called "Parents Meet the Hippies," which had a rather ominous ring of confrontation, reminiscent of certain old horror movies such as *Frankenstein Meets the Wolf Man*. A crowd of more than a hundred people, including a scattering of hippies but mostly composed of parents and curious elders, gathered at 8 P.M. one Sunday evening for the show.

Leonard Harris, the coordinator of the Southern California Town Meeting, announced that the moderator would be a lady who was responsible for arranging the whole panel, and who had been working long and hard to establish a bridge between adults and one of the local hippie groups known as the Diggers.

Lily Weiner is a hydro-psychotherapist, who Harris said is "known for her pioneering work" in that field, a science which evidently seeks to improve mental health by techniques involving the use of a swimming pool. Miss Weiner was a robust-looking ·lady of middle years, who explained that progress had been made in the effort to establish adult communication with the Diggers: "After a period of testing we have come to trust and respect one another." It was not the hippies alone that Miss Weiner was concerned about, but also their families, whose mental and physical states had seemed to have been laid waste by their rebellious offspring. "These youths who have flown the nest have left in their wake heart attacks, ulcers, and nervous breakdowns."

Retribution, however, was not mentioned and Miss Weiner stressed that "our goal is reconciliation," a condition that sounded more perilous for the parents than the youth after the damage that had already been inflicted.

Such problems are attacked in supernation by what is sometimes known as an "interdisciplinary[1] approach," and thus the panel included not only representatives of the hippies but also experts from the fields of law, criminology, psychology, medicine, and religion.

The firm and yet tolerant attitude toward the problem maintained by the local police establishment was expressed by Lieutenant Onan Bomar, a Negro serving in the Community Relations Department of the sheriff's office.

"My appearance here," the Lieutenant was quick to explain, "doesn't mean that the sheriff's office supports the hippie community, but ours is not a blanket condemnation." He said his duty was to "serve mankind and to protect the peaceful against violence and disorder," regardless even of "dress or length of hair" as well as the more acceptable regardless of race-creed-and-color. Stressing again the police policy of equal prosecution of the law to all citizens, he noted that "though we don't approve of long hair and odd dress, that doesn't make such people criminals."

In spite of this enlightened attitude on the part of police, existing laws must be enforced, and the lieutenant warned that many of these kids are runaways, and older people who try to help them may be breaking the law. "Anyone who hides or abets a minor who is running away from home is guilty of a misdemeanor, for contributing to the delinquency of a minor."

This might have seemed technically to have made a criminal of another panelist, the Reverend Ross Greek, who is minister of the Hollywood Presbyterian Church. The Reverend Greek had opened his church to the summer influx of young hippies from all over the country, supplying them with food and allowing them to use one part of the church building as a "crash pad," which is hippie language for a temporary place to sleep. The Reverend explained that if the kids had run away from home, he tried to persuade them to call their parents, but did not notify parents without the child's permission. This practice seemed to adhere to more modern thinking, to which the letter of the law had not yet caught up. Anyway, his method was successful enough to have placed 143 girls, aged thirteen to seventeen, back at home in the past six months.

Lily Weiner praised the good works the Reverend was doing, and urged those in the audience to aid him in his ministry to the young. "Food is vital for Reverend Greek's work, especially fruit and vegetables. The church does feed them, as well as it can, but Reverend Greek is afraid they get too much starches."

[1] involving two or more branches of knowledge

Fortunately for the plight of these overstarched youths, the Hollywood Presbyterian Church was not the only agency contributing to their welfare. Also on the panel was Richard Pine, who was described as "the public relations man" for the hippie society known as the Diggers. The idea of the Diggers began in San Francisco, with some hippies banding together to help supply food and clothes for others, and several units sprang up in Los Angeles as well as many other hippie communities. One of the L.A. Diggers group was evidently having a hard time of it, and Mr. Pine came along and offered his services. He is not actually one of them, but at thirty-two feels he is able to serve as a go-between for them with the straight adult society, and he raises funds through lectures and appeals at public meetings and appearances before church and business groups. Pine said his Diggers in L.A. had helped house and feed about four thousand kids from all over the country.

"We know something's going on in this country. They come to us from Indiana, Montana, Nevada, all over."

A health problem that seemed more urgent than an unbalanced diet which also is besetting the young folks is the spread of venereal disease. Dr. Walter Smart, chief of the venereal disease division of the department of health in Los Angeles, first made clear that "I don't want to convey the idea that hippies are the only ones who have VD. We've had epidemics of it here since 1957, and we can hardly blame the hippies for what happened then."

The hippies had, however, brought a change in the type of VD that was most prevalent in

164 the area: "My own clinic in the Hollywood Wilshire area mainly dealt with syphilis among homosexuals. But due to the cooperation of the homosexuals, syphilis is coming under control. Most of the syphilis cases we have now are with people who have good jobs, and have lived in the area for more than six months."

The new problem, coincidental with the influx of hippies, is gonorrhea, which Dr. Smart said was up one third over last year. "Most of these cases are young adults, fifteen to nineteen."

A special problem of the treatment of these youths again seemed to indicate that the legal system was lagging behind the social reality. According to law, twenty-one is the "age of consent," and anyone younger must have parental consent to be treated for a venereal disease, the doctor explained. Also, they must live in or be residents of the county to be treated by the public health clinic. Both these factors made it difficult to treat the hippies, since most of them were not legal residents, most were under age, and many did not want to let their parents know where they were, much less that they had contracted a venereal disease and needed permission to have it treated.

When these and other problems had been brought to light by members of the panel, the floor was thrown open for discussion, and it developed that many of the members of the audience were not sympathetic to the burdens besetting the hippies.

A small silver-haired lady with a cane seemed most anxious to express herself, and she rose somewhat shakily but then stated her question with clear and firm passion: "Do you think our overburdened taxpayers who have struggled and slaved for years to pay for our little homes should be saddled with thousands of dollars to pay for these freeloaders?"

Richard Pine retorted that "a lot more of your tax money is being used to kill people in Vietnam, and we want the money used here."

"We don't approve of Vietnam either!" the lady shouted, and received surprised applause from some of the audience. "*But*," she continued, "we don't approve of freeloaders. I remember when they used to clean up skid row; if they made the drunks get out, the drunks would go home to their families and support them. They ought to do the same with you people."

"You tell 'em sister!"

This cry of approval came from directly behind me. It was uttered by a lady who had been muttering disapproval throughout most of the evening, and now her displeasure seemed to be growing. She was forty-five or so, and wore long magenta[2] gloves, a green and purple blouse, and from each ear dangled a long chain with a red ball at the end, creating an effect that was not so much exotic as jarring. Someone on the panel started telling how the Diggers held free art classes that encouraged young talent, and the lady behind me shouted derisively, "Yeh, I know, I bet it's that surrealistic junk."

There were boos, and other people started talking at once, and Lily Weiner took the microphone and said, "Now, this is supposed to be like a real old-fashioned town meeting, and we must all respect one another's views."

The silver-haired taxpaying lady wanted to be heard again, and Richard Pine said that the hippies would like to prove to her they were her friends, and would like her to come to the platform and speak. There was a quick huddle among the discussion leaders, but the lady was already toddling to the platform, and it would have been difficult to push her back down, cane and all. She took the mike and said:

"I am Mrs. Schuyler. I am of course an American citizen, an honorable American citizen. I am a member of a group called Truth Forum Unlimited. We believe only the truth can make you free, and that there's a right and a wrong. All these young people come here bringing VD and drugs and bad habits. Their idea of love is promiscuous sexual madness!"

There were boos and jeers, and a lady stood up and said, "We don't have to listen to this!"

Lily Weiner, finding it hard to maintain the old-town-meeting atmosphere of mutual respect, shouted back, "Well, then you can *leave*."

Mrs. Schuyler went on to say, "Last week a friend of mine was entertaining people, and hundreds of these hippies climbed over her fence, ruined her flower beds, and ate up all the food in the icebox."

There were cheers and applause. Lily told Mrs. Schuyler her time was up. The lady behind me said, "You can tell what nationality *she* is, the one running the meeting. She's a Jew—they want to keep control of everything."

[2] purplish red color

Someone asked a question about drugs, and Herb Porter, a well-known lawyer in the area who has defended a number of young people in narcotics cases, explained very calmly that while LSD sometimes has very harmful psychological effects and all of its effects are not known or understood yet, marijuana is not harmful and is not addicting. The lady behind me jumped up and yelled, "That's not true, I saw a woman on television who said her daughter was in terrible trouble because of marijuana!"

HIPPIES HAVE A QUIET HECKLER

Rep. Margaret Heckler (R.-Mass.) told the League of Republican Women yesterday that the bearded, rioting hippie generation of today is searching for "ideals," but has a tendency to place individual decisions above legitimate authority.

"It distresses me to see them this way, for so many of them are really fine people. They are just misguided, they've forgotten the Constitution," she said in a luncheon speech at the Mayflower.

the Washington *Post*

"Try to control yourself," Lily advised her.

Porter went on to say that in fact with the rise of marijuana use in California there had been a decrease in the use of heroin.

The lady behind me rose again and shrieked, "Why do we need any of that? Marijuana or heroin or anything?"

A bearded young man came down the aisle, and with a taunting smile, handed the agitated lady a yellow rose. She threw it to the floor, scattering the petals, and the bearded guy turned to the audience with a smile like a lawyer who has proved his case and said, "Behold!"

"Why don't he *pray?*" the lady shouted, and stretching a magenta arm into the air, she exclaimed, "I have been *healed* by prayer, I can prove it!"

Nobody asked for proof, and someone asked Lily Weiner, "Do hippies use hydropsychotherapy?"

"No," she said, "but I wish I had a pool and could get them into the water with me."

There were a few other questions, and then Len Harris, the chairman of the Town Meeting of Southern California, said that their time was up for using the auditorium, but that he had found the discussion so stimulating that he hated to end it, and if anyone in the audience wished to continue they were welcome to come to his house. Mr. Harris's faith in the town-meeting system seemed to me to border on masochism, but he actually announced his address, and I took it down.

After the meeting I got a ride over to Len Harris's house with a fellow wearing a graying T-shirt who introduced himself as Plastic Man. I had seen him come forward down one of the aisles during the meeting, asking to be heard, but no one would ever recognize him. It turned out that he was the leader of a rival Diggers group and felt that the panel was hardly representative without his being on it.

I met Plastic Man's sidekick, a quiet fellow named George who had recently left a theological seminary to try the hippie life, and also a quiet girl with long hair and glasses who was Plastic Man's wife (I never figured out whether I should call her Plastic Woman or Mrs. Plastic Man, but she rarely said anything so it wasn't a problem). The four of us drove over in Plastic Man's car, and he explained to me how in being a genuine Digger, he was just like a Mendicant in the Christian church of old, a person who was a beggar for alms but gave the proceeds to others. I thought but did not say that there were at least some superficial differences, as I had never heard of a Mendicant who drove a new red Dodge Dart, but then times change and there is no use splitting hairs. Plastic Man was no doubt frustrated from having been "silenced," as he called it, at the general meeting, and so he was voluble[3] at the gathering at Harris's house. Mrs. Schuyler was ensconced[4] in a big armchair, and perhaps

[3] talkative
[4] settled snugly

165

because she had already had her say or was less comfortable speaking in small groups, she was fairly quiet.

A nice lady of forty or so named Libby asked Plastic Man how he started into the hippie life, and that set him off.

He explained that he is thirty-one, and that only six months ago he had a filling station and a small furniture business on the side, and was quite successful and middle class. What turned him on was blowing grass and reading Marshall McLuhan and Mao Tse-tung. Becoming more immersed in the new world opened up by that heady trilogy, he started letting his business go to hell, and by the time he got his income tax form he just scrawled across it "I Refuse to Co-Operate With a Corrupt Government," and sent it back.

Mrs. Schuyler wondered if she could do the same thing, and did he get away with it?

He said he did, but shortly after mailing in the IRS form he left the town and the business and just started drifting around and not using his old name anymore.

Libby, the nice red-haired lady, leaned forward on the couch and asked, "What did you say your name was?"

"Plastic Man."

"Ah," she said, nodding, "Plastic Man."

After that Libby and Mr. Harris and everyone else simply addressed him as "Plastic Man," just as they would call a person Henry or Hamilton or Jeremy or any other name that a person has.

Now the center of attention, Plastic Man began holding forth about how "Youth today" feel on different subjects, and a clean-cut young insurance underwriter asked him, "How can you speak for the youth of today when you've said you're thirty-one, and I'm twenty-four and I don't agree with you and I'm younger?"

"Ah, but you can be old at twenty-four," Plastic Man retorted.

The underwriter fired back that he knew a lot about this stuff too: when he was in Vietnam he learned to smoke pot along with his buddies, and what was such a big deal about that?

Plastic Man was very interested in the use of pot among the servicemen over there, and the underwriter assured him it was very common, and that you could buy it from the Montagnards very cheap; in Vietnamese money it was something like five or ten piasters for a stick. Every-

one started to figure out how many piasters there were to a dollar, and it was agreed that this was a very good price.

I asked the underwiter how he felt now about the war in Vietnam, and he said, "It's funny. When I went over I was sort of buoyed up by the feeling that I was serving my country and all, and sort of a hero, but that was in '64. Just before I came home in '66, guys warned me I'd better expect to find that most people didn't support the war and would be against me. It was pretty much that way."

Plastic Man said all that was interesting, and that he was so much against the war that, "before I discovered Love, I mean the hippie ethic and all of it, I had a plan to put a small nuclear device in the Pentagon and blow the whole thing up. Now I see that's not the answer, but there may be some people who haven't learned about Love and might still do it."

Libby gasped at the idea, but the underwriter who was a veteran smiled, and said very politely, "You'll forgive me, Plastic Man, if I doubt your capacity to set off a small nuclear weapon."

Plastic Man only laughed.

After several hours this old-fashioned town meeting began to break up. When everyone was standing, Libby asked a quiet girl named Sharron what *she* did, and Sharron said she worked in the kitchen at the Hollywood Presbyterian Church crash pad, and that's how she got the scars on her face. That sort of got everyone's attention, and Sharron explained that she had had a fight with another girl who was to prepare dinner, and the other girl was jealous and went for her eyes, but luckily she only got her fingernails in Sharron's cheeks, and the scars would probably eventually go away.

Libby said, "My God, I was really jealous of you people having all that Love, but I guess you're no different than the rest of us."

Nobody answered, and then Libby put on her coat and said, "You know, I really am disillusioned," and she said it with real sadness.

Many people felt the same way after getting a first hand glimpse of the hippie scene.

Is Our Common Man Too Common?

JOSEPH WOOD KRUTCH

The age of the Common Man is not merely a phrase; it is also a fact. Already we are definitely entered upon it, and in all probability it is destined to continue for a long time to come, intensifying its characteristics as it develops in some of the directions which it has already begun to take.

Most people welcome the fact, but we have only begun to assess it or even to ask ourselves what choices are still open to us once the grand decision has been made, as by now it has. How common does the common man need to be? Does his dominance necessarily mean that the uncommon man will cease to be tolerated or that the world will become less suited to his needs, less favorable to the development of his talents, than it now is? Will excellence be looked upon as in itself unworthy or "undemocratic"? Can we have an Age of the Common Man without making it an Age of the Common Denominator? Do any dangers lie ahead?

One way to approach these questions is, of course, to ask what has happened already, what changes in attitudes have demonstrably taken place, how the culture of the first era of the Age of the Common Man differs from that which preceded it. What, in other words, is the culture of present-day America like, and are there aspects of it, directly traceable to the emphasis on the common man and his tastes, which are not wholly

reassuring? And if there are, then to what extent are the defects corrigible, to what extent are they necessary consequences of the premises we have already accepted?

Unfortunately, but not surprisingly, there is no general agreement concerning the real nature of the situation at the present moment, though it does seem clear enough that most Americans judge both the present and the future a good deal more favorably than many observers from the Old World do.

Thus, in his recent book *The Big Change*, Frederick Lewis Allen summed up very cogently the case for contemporary American culture. Hundreds of thousands read the selections of the book clubs; hundreds of thousands more attend concerts of serious music; millions listen to debates, symphonies, and operas on the radio. Never before in the history of the world has so large a proportion of any population been so interested in and so alert to intellectual and artistic activities. Ours is the most cultured nation which ever existed.

Compare this with any one of the typical fulminations[1] which proceed at regular intervals from European commentators and the result is both astonishing and disturbing. In Europe the prevalent opinion seems to be that this same civilization of ours constitutes a serious threat to the very existence of anything which can properly be called a culture.

We are told, in the first place, that for every American who does read the Book of the Month and attend a symphony concert there are a dozen who live in a vulgar dream-world induced by a perpetual diet of soap operas, comic books, torch songs, and "B" movies. Moreover, the material prosperity and political power of this majority of sick barbarians enable them to become, as no cultural proletariat ever was before, a threat to every civilized minority. They rule the roost, and they are becoming less and less tolerant of anyone or anything superior to them.

In the second place—and perhaps even more importantly—the culture or even the minority is described as largely an imitation. It consumes but does not produce art. The best of the books it reads and the music it listens to is imported. Its members are really only parasites feeding upon European culture, and their sterility will in time

[1] scathing verbal attacks

kill it completely. Even their power to "appreciate" is essentially shallow—the result of superficial education, propaganda, advertisement, and a general pro-cultural hoop-la, all of which produce something very different indeed from that deep, personal, demanding passion for Truth and Beauty which has always been the dynamic force in the production of any genuine culture.

Now it is easy enough to dismiss this European view as merely the product of ignorance, prejudice, and envy. But it is dangerous to do so. To look candidly at the two pictures is to perceive something recognizable in both of them. Nobody really knows what the American phenomenon means or what it portends. And the reason is that it is actually something genuinely new. Whether you call it the Dawn of the First Democratic Culture or call it the Triumph of Mediocrity, the fact remains that there is no obvious parallel in human history. Mr. Allen and those who agree with him are obviously right as far as they go. But the unique phenomenon which they describe can stand further analysis.

A college education for everybody and two cars in every garage are ideals not wholly unrelated. An even closer analogy can be drawn with the earlier, more modest ideal of universal literacy. America was the first country to teach nearly everybody to read. Whether we are quite aware of it or not, we are now embarked upon the pursuit of what is really an extension of the same ideal, namely, a minimum cultural literacy for all. There is a vast difference between being barely able to spell out a newspaper and being able to read in the full sense of what the term implies. There is a similar and probably no greater difference between, say, being able to get something out of the movie *The Great Caruso* or the latest volume dispatched to the members of a book club by editors who have trained themselves to understand the limitations of their average subscriber, and a genuine grasp of either music or literature. The term "literacy" covers a large area whether we are using it in its limited sense or extending it to include what I have called "cultural literacy." A few generations ago we pointed with pride to the fact that most Americans "could read"; we now point with pride to the fact that an astonishing proportion of them "read serious books" or "listen to serious music," and in both cases we take satisfaction in a mass capacity which exists only if we define it in minimum terms. In neither case does the phenomenon mean quite as much as those who celebrate it most enthusiastically sometimes seem to assume.

*B*ut, what, one may ask, is either disturbing or surprising about that? The minimum remains something more than any people as a whole ever before achieved. Is it likely that fewer people will read well just because a larger number can read a little? Is not, indeed, the opposite likely to be true? Is anything but good likely to come from the establishment of a broad base of even a minimum cultural literacy?

Any hesitation in answering "no" to the last question might seem at first sight to spring inevitably from nothing except arrogance, snobbishness, and a desire to preserve the privileges of an aristocracy. Yet a good many Europeans and an occasional American do seem inclined to take the negative position. The wide spread of our minimum culture does seem to them to constitute some sort of threat.

At least one fact or alleged fact they can cite as possible evidence on their side of the argument. So far, the number of recognized masterpieces produced by native-born Americans does seem disappointingly small when compared with the number of literate citizens we have produced. Is that because American art is inadequately recognized, or because we just haven't had time to mature? Or is it, perhaps, somehow connected —as some would say it is—with mass culture itself? Is the Good always the friend of the Best or is it sometimes and somehow the enemy? Is Excellence more likely to lose out to Mediocrity than it is to mere Ignorance or Nullity?[2]

The line being taken in Europe today has a good deal in common with that of the American intellectual of the Twenties. To some extent indeed it may have been learned from our post-World War I intellectuals; the disdainful European conception of American society is a good deal like Mencken's Boobocracy.[3] At the present moment, however, the current of opinion at home is running in the opposite direction, and it is no longer unusual for the confessed intellectual to defend the culture which his predecessor of a generation ago despised and rejected. But complacency has its dangers too, and it may be worth while to examine a little further what can be said in support of the European's thesis.

This, he hears us say, is the Age of the Common Man. But we as well as he are not quite certain what we mean by that. In so far as we mean only the age of universal opportunity, what was once called simply "the career open to talents," nothing but good could seem to come of it. But many people do, sometimes without being entirely aware of it, mean something more. When we make ourselves the champion of any particular group we almost inevitably begin to idealize that group. From defending the common man we pass on to exalting him, and we find ourselves beginning to imply, not merely that he is as good as anybody else, but that he is actually better. Instead of demanding only that the common man be given an opportunity to become as uncommon as possible, we make his commonness a virtue, and even in the case of candidates for high office, we sometimes praise them for being nearly indistinguishable from the average man in the street. Secretly, no doubt, we hope that they are somehow superior, but we feel at the same time that a kind of decency requires them to conceal the fact as completely as possible.

The logical extreme of this opinion would be the conviction that any deviation in either direction from the statistical average is unadmirable; even, to take a concrete example, that the ideal man or woman could best be represented, not by an artist's dream, but by a composite photograph of the entire population. And though few would explicitly acknowledge their acceptance of this extreme position, there is a very strong tendency to emphasize quantitative rather than

[2] that which lacks value, amounts to nothing

[3] H. L. Mencken, newspaperman and editor of the influential *American Mercury* magazine, relished his role as scourge of the stupidities and absurdities of American life. He was famous for coining words like "Boobocracy" (literally, "government by fools"), which conveyed his criticism of mass culture and government by the masses.

qualitative standards in estimating achievement. We are, for instance, more inclined to boast how many Americans go to college than to ask how much the average college education amounts to; how many people read books rather than how good the books are; how many listen to the radio rather than how good what they hear from it really is.

Argue, as I myself have argued, that more can be learned from almost any subject from ten minutes with printed page than from half an hour with even one of the better educational programs and you will be met with the reply: "Perhaps. But so many more people will listen to the radio." In a democracy quantity is important. But when the stress upon it becomes too nearly exclusive, then democracy itself threatens to lose its promise of moving on to higher levels. Thus the Good really can become the enemy of the Best if one insists upon exclusively quantitative standards.

Certainly one of the striking—some would say one of the inevitable—characteristics of our society is its penchant[4] for making widely and easily accessible either substitutes for, or inferior versions of, a vast number of good things, like the vile substitute for bread available at any grocer's. That bread can be come by without effort, and it may be true that fewer people are in want of bread of some kind than ever were in want of it in any society before. But that does not change the fact that it is a very inferior product.

Another and related tendency of this same society is its encouragement of passivity. A generation ago moralists viewed with alarm the popularity of "spectator sports": the fact that people gathered in stadia to watch others play games for them. But we have gone far beyond that and today the baseball fan who takes the trouble to make a journey to the Polo Grounds instead of watching the game on his TV set has almost earned the right to call himself an athlete. One wonders, sometimes, if the popularity of "discussion" programs does not mean very much the same thing; if most people have not now decided to let others hold remote conversations for them— as well as play remote games—even though the conversations are often no better than those they could hold for themselves.

As John Stuart Mill—certainly no anti-democrat—wrote a century ago:

Capacity for the noble feeling is in most natures a very tender plant. . . . Men lose their high aspirations as they lose their intellectual tastes, because they have not time or opportunity for indulging them; and they addict themselves to inferior pleasures, not because they deliberately prefer them, but because they are either the only ones to which they have access, or the only ones which they are any longer capable of enjoying.

In the history books of the future this age of ours may come to be known as the Age of Statistics. In the biological and physical as well as the sociological sciences, statistics have become, as they never were before, the most important tool of investigation. But as every philosophical scientist knows, the conclusions drawn by a science depend to a considerable extent upon the tools used. And it is in the nature of statistics not only that they deal with quantity but that they emphasize the significance of averages and medians. What usually exists or usually happens establishes The Law, and The Law is soon thought of as identical with the Truth. In all the arts, nevertheless, it is the exceptional and the unpredictable which really count. It is the excellent, not the average, which is really important. And there is, therefore, one aspect of the cultural condition of a civilization to which statistical study is curiously inappropriate.

No one, it may be said, needs to accept the inferior substitute or hold himself down to the average level. But simple and complete as that answer may seem to be, there are facts and forces which do tend to encourage an almost unconscious acceptance of mediocrity. One, of course, is that the inferior substitute—whether it be baker's bread or the movie show playing at the neighborhood house—is so readily accessible and so forced upon one's attention by all the arts of advertising as well as by the very way in which our lives have been organized. Another and more serious one is the tendency of the mass media to force out of the field every enterprise which is not based upon mass appeal. Whatever the reason may be, it is a generally recognized fact that it is becoming increasingly difficult, economically, to publish a book which is not a best seller or produce a play which is not a smash hit. More and more, therefore, artistic enterprise must be abandoned to the movies and to television where the mass audience is sufficient to defray the staggering cost.

---

[4] strong leaning, inclination

Besides these economic reasons why the new media tend to concern themselves only with mass appeals, there is the additional technical reason why the two newest of such media tend to confine themselves to it. Since TV and radio channels are limited in number, all the arguments in favor of democracy as it is sometimes defined justify the existing fact that these channels should be used to communicate what the greatest number of people seem to want. That is the argument of the great broadcasting chains, and on the premise assumed it is a valid one.

The only mechanical instrument of communication which can make a reasonable case for the claim that it has actually served to increase the popularity of the thing communicated on its highest level of excellence is the phonograph, and it is significant that the phonograph is the only such device for communication which—especially since the invention of tape recording and LP—has found it economically feasible to cater to relatively small minorities. The fact that it does not cost much to produce a record may well have an incalculably great effect upon American musical taste.

"What is most popular must be best. . . . 'Normality' has almost completely replaced 'Excellence' as an ideal."

What the question comes down to in the simplest possible terms is one of those which we asked at the very beginning of this discussion: Can we have an Age of the Common Man without having also an Age of the Common Denominator? That question has not been answered, probably cannot be convincingly answered, at the present moment. But it is a fateful question and the one with which this discussion is concerned.

One must not, of course, idealize the past to the extent of assuming that the best works were always, inevitably, and immediately the most popular. Two years ago James D. Hart's thorough and amusing *The Popular Book* (Oxford University Press) demonstrated conclusively that since colonial times there have always been absurd best sellers. The year that Hawthorne earned $144.09 royalty in six months was the year his

own publisher paid Susan Warner $4,500 for the same period and another publisher sold 70,000 copies of one of Fanny Fern's several works.[5]

Neither, I think, should it be supposed that any society ever has been or ever will be so organized as to favor exclusively the highest artistic excellence. As a system, aristocratic patronage is absurdly capricious; capitalistic democracy tends to favor vulgarity; Socialism would probably favor official mediocrity. The question here is not whether contemporary America provides ideal conditions for cultural developments on the highest level, but whether it renders such development unusually difficult instead of making it, as the optimists insist, almost inevitable.

Of the unfavorable influences which I have mentioned, it seems to me that the most serious is the tendency to confuse the Common Denominator with a standard of excellence. The mechanical and economic facts which tend to give the purveyors[6] of mediocrity a monopoly—highly developed in the case of radio and TV, probably growing in the publishing business—may possibly be changed by new developments, as they have already been changed in the case of the phonograph. But to confuse The Best with the most widely and the most generally acceptable is to reveal a spiritual confusion which is subtle and insidious as well as fundamental. It could easily nullify any solution of the mechanical and economic problems created by the age of mass production.

How real and how general does this confusion seem actually to be?

More than one sociologist has recently pointed out that as technology integrates larger and larger populations into tighter and tighter groups the members of these groups tend inevitably to work, live, and recreate themselves in the same way and in accordance with the standardized patterns which the facilities provided for these various activities lay down. For ill as well as for good, "community living" becomes more and more

[5] Susan Warner and Fanny Fern were two of a number of lady authors of domestic literature who were extremely popular in the middle of the 19th century. Typically they wrote sentimental accounts of orphan girls or widows whose lives are proof that happiness comes as a reward for suffering. The novels are characterized by trite philosophizing of a religious or moral nature. Susan Warner's *The Wide, Wide World* ranks second only to *Uncle Tom's Cabin* as the most widely read novel of the 19th century.
[6] suppliers or caterers

172 nearly inevitable and individual temperament or taste finds less and less opportunity to express itself.

One result of this is that the natural tendency of the adolescent to practice a desperate conformity is prolonged into adult life and the grown man continues to want what his neighbors have, to do what his neighbors do, to enjoy what his neighbors enjoy. This is one of the things which the European may have in mind when he calls us a nation of adolescents, and commercial interests take advantage of our adolescent characteristics by stressing, through all sorts of publicity, the fact that this is the kind of cigarette most people smoke, the kind of breakfast food most people eat, and the torch singer or crooner most people like. The best-selling book is not only the one easiest to buy, but it is also the one we must read unless we are willing to be made to seem somehow inferior. What is most popular must be best. As a broadcast official recently said, to call the most popular radio programs vulgar is to call the American people vulgar. And that, he seemed to imply, was not merely nonsense but pretty close to treason. The voice of the people is the voice of God. God loves the common man. If the common man loves Bob Hope then God must love Bob Hope also. In musical taste as in everything else the common man is divine.

It is this logic which, unfortunately, the purveyors to the mass audience are very prone to follow. Undoubtedly, it leads them to the line of least resistance at the same time that it provides them with a smug excuse for both inanity[7] and vulgarity. They are, they say, servants of the public and have no right to doubt that the people know not only what they want but what is good for them. The age of the common man has no place for any holier-than-thou attitude. It believes in government "by" as well as "for" the people. Totalitarianism is what you get when you accept the "for" but not the "by," and the attitude of, for example, the British Broadcasting Company, with its notorious Third Program,[8] merely demonstrates that England has not yet learned what democracy really means.

No doubt the questions involved are too complicated to be discussed here. A few years ago, Charles A. Siepmann in his *Radio, Television, and Society* fully and impartially reported on both the policies and the arguments as they affect the media with which he was dealing. But at least one conclusion seems obvious. If there is any such thing as responsibility on the part of those most powerful and best informed towards those whose appetites they feed, then no provider of movies or records or television programs can escape the minimal duty of giving his public the best rather than the worst it will stand for. Mr. Mencken once declared that no one had ever gone bankrupt by underestimating the taste of the American public, but there is an increasing tendency to believe that, by dint of long trying, certain commercial exploiters of the mass media have succeeded only too well in underestimating it considerably.

What is obviously called for is a public opinion less ready than it now is to excuse the failure to meet even minimal responsibilities; but that public opinion is not likely to arise unless those responsible for public thinking play their own parts, and there is a tendency for them to yield rather than protest. Unfortunately, the fanatical exaltation of the common denominator has been taken up not only by the common man himself and by those who hope to profit by his exploitation but also and increasingly by those who are supposed to be educators and intellectual leaders. Instead of asking "What would a good education consist of?" many professors of education are asking "What do most college students want?"; instead of asking "What books are wisest and best and most beautiful?" they conduct polls to determine which the largest number of students have read with least pain. Examination papers are marked, not in accordance with any fixed standard, but in accordance with a usual level of achievement; the amount of work required is fixed by the amount the average student does; even the words with which the average student is not familiar are edited out of the books he is given to read. How, granted such methods, is it other than inevitable both that the average will seldom be exceeded and that the average itself will gradually drop?

As David Reisman and his collaborators pointed out two years ago in their brilliant analysis called

---

[7] lack of sense or meaning, silliness
[8] an evening series offered by the British Broadcasting System. It was non-commercial and catered to small, special audiences. It did not adhere to a fixed time schedule in broadcasting live cultural events.

The Lonely Crowd (Yale University Press), the ideal now persistently held before the American citizen from the moment he enters kindergarten to the time when he is buried under the auspices of a recognized funeral parlor is a kind of conformity more or less disguised under the term "adjustment." "Normality" has almost completely replaced "Excellence" as an ideal. It has also rendered all but obsolescent such terms as "Righteousness," "Integrity," and "Truth." The question is no longer how a boy ought to behave but how most boys do behave; not how honest a man ought to be but how honest men usually are. Even the Robber Baron, who represented an evil manifestation of the determination to excel, gives way to the moneymaker who wants only to be rich according to the accepted standards of his group. Or, as Mr. Reisman sums it up, the American who used to be conspicuously "inner-directed" is now conspicuously "outer-directed."

According to the anthropologists, many primitive societies are based almost exclusively upon the idea of conformity and generate what are, in the anthropologist's meaning of the term, remarkable cultures. It may, of course, be argued that America and the whole world which follows in America's wake is evolving in the direction of this kind of culture. But if by "culture" we mean something more narrowly defined, if we mean a culture which is continuous with that of the Western world since the Renaissance, then it is my contention that it cannot flourish where the stress is as nearly exclusively as it threatens to become upon "adjustment," "normality," or any of the other concepts which, in the end, come down to mean that the Common Denominator is identical with the Ideal. Especially, it cannot flourish under those conditions if the result which they tend to produce is intensified by the fact that ingenious methods of mass production and mass propaganda help impose upon all the tyranny of the average.

Salvation, if salvation is possible, may be made so by technological developments like those in the phonograph industry which tend to break monopoly and permit the individual to assert his preferences and his tastes. But the possible will not become the actual if in the meantime the desire for excellence has been lost and those who should be leaders have willingly become followers instead. If the Age of the Common Man is not to become the Age of the Common Denominator rather than what is was originally intended to be —namely an age in which every man had the opportunity to become as superior as he could— then the cultural as well as the political rights of minorities must somehow be acknowledged. There is not really anything undemocratic about either the desire for, or the recognition of, excellence. To prove that ours is the most cultured nation which ever existed will constitute only a barren victory if we must, to prove our point, use nothing but quantitative standards and reconcile ourselves to the common denominator as a measure of excellence.

One might sum up the situation in a series of propositions. (1) The Age of the Common Man has begun. (2) Despite all the gains that it may legitimately claim, they are threatened by those confusions which arise when the common denominator is consciously or unconsciously allowed to function as a standard of excellence. (3) The dominance of mass media almost exclusively under the control of those who are little concerned with anything except immediate financial gain does tend to debase taste.

Ultimate responsibility for the future rests with the thinkers and the educators whose most important social task at the moment is to define democratic culture in some fashion which will both reserve a place for uncommon excellence and, even in connection with the largest masses, emphasize the highest rather than the lowest common denominator.

Selections from *Walden*

HENRY DAVID THOREAU

The mass of men lead lives of quiet desperation. What is called resignation is confirmed desperation. From the desperate city you go into the desperate country, and have to console yourself with the bravery of minks and muskrats. A stereotyped but unconscious despair is concealed even under what are called the games and amusements of mankind. There is no play in them, for this comes after work. But it is a characteristic of wisdom not to do desperate things.

When we consider what, to use the words of the catechism, is the chief end of man, and what are the true necessaries and means of life, it appears as if men had deliberately chosen the common mode of living because they preferred it to any other. Yet they honestly think there is no choice left. But alert and healthy natures remember that the sun rose clear. It is never too late to give up our prejudices. No way of thinking or doing, however ancient, can be trusted without proof. What everybody echoes or in silence passes by as true to-day may turn out to be falsehood to-morrow, mere smoke of opinion, which some had trusted for a cloud that would sprinkle fertilizing rain on their fields. What old people say you cannot do, you try and find that you can. Old deeds for old people, and new deeds for new. Old people did not know enough once, perchance, to fetch fresh fuel to keep the fire a-going; new people put a little dry wood under a pot, and are whirled round the globe with the speed of birds, in a way to kill old people, as the phrase is. Age is no better, hardly so well, qualified for an instructor as youth, for it has not profited so much as it has lost. One may almost doubt if the wisest man has learned anything of absolute value by living. Practically, the old have no very important advice to give the young, their own experience has been so partial, and their lives have been such miserable failures, for private reasons, as they must believe; and it may be that they have some faith left which belies that experience, and they are only less young than they were. I have lived some thirty years on this planet, and I have yet to hear the first syllable of valuable or even earnest advice from my seniors. They have told me nothing, and probably cannot tell me anything to the purpose. Here is life, an experiment to a great extent untried by me; but it does not avail[1] me that they have tried it. If I have any experience which I think valuable, I am sure to reflect that this my Mentors[2] said nothing about.

Some are dinning in our ears that we Americans, and moderns generally, are intellectual dwarfs compared with the ancients, or even the Elizabethan men. But what is that to the purpose? A living dog is better than a dead lion. Shall a man go and hang himself because he belongs to the race of pygmies, and not be the biggest pygmy that he can? Let every one mind his own business, and endeavor to be what he was made.

Why should we be in such desperate haste to succeed and in such desperate enterprises? If a man does not keep pace with his companions, perhaps it is because he hears a different drummer. Let him step to the music which he hears, however measured or far away. It is not important that he should mature as soon as an apple tree or an oak. Shall he turn his spring into summer? If the condition of things which we were made for is not yet, what were any reality which we can substitute? We will not be shipwrecked on a vain reality. Shall we with pains erect a heaven of blue glass over ourselves, though when it is done we shall be sure to gaze still at the true ethereal[3] heaven far above, as if the former were not?

[1] assist, help
[2] wise and trusted teachers or guides
[3] airy; not of the earth

To define a reasonable life in a mad world is the concern not only of Edman but of all the authors in this section. Their remedies are diverse, yet at least one strong theme recurs: personal integrity and spiritual independence are the essential foundations of a sane citizenry and a healthy society. Social limits, controls, and rules of action will be effective only insofar as they are paralleled by each person's capacity for self-regulation. But these authors are aware of how difficult it is to attain this capacity, how easy it is to be sidetracked by economic pressure, ambition, or frustration. Chase, in particular, presents a discouraging list of the pressures which deny most men the luxury of calling their souls fully their own. His message forces us to wonder how it is possible for a man to do only what he *wants* to do, a remedy which is Van Doren's prescription for happiness. Edman reviews, and rejects, some of the classical philosophies such as Epicureanism. His definition of

Prescriptions

the reasonable life is to make a stoic attempt to improve one's lot in the condition into which he was born, but only a few exceptional men would find his solution satisfactory. The goals of a liberal arts education as ten Hoor describes them seem much more attractive: learning to think, developing a moral philosophy, bringing our emotions under control, and living entertainingly with ourselves by practicing and appreciating the fine arts.

The concerns of Fischer and Bettelheim are to find satisfactory modes of behavior in what we may call a violent society. Bettelheim, a psychologist, believes that children should not be overprotected from violence but should be made aware of it as one method—but an inferior one—of human negotiation. Fischer maintains that if men are to live in peace and remain psychologically whole, they must find a "moral equivalent to war," a constructive method or a variety of methods of draining off normal aggressive impulses.

The conflict between private claims and social authority is responsible for many of the tensions in our society. Claiming that overpopulation, eventual food shortages, and increasing pollution of the environment are problems that can no longer be left to private conscience, Vidal makes the most specific recommendation of all. He asks for the immediate creation of a vast Authority which will have enormous powers to differentiate between private rights and the public welfare.

WE'RE A
SICK
SOCIETY. —

WE'RE A
SICK
SOCIETY. —

WE'RE A
SICK
SOCIETY. —

WE'RE A
SICK
SOCIETY. —

WE'RE A
SICK
SOCIETY. —

INSTEAD
OF
TALKING
ABOUT
IT WHY
DON'T
YOU DO
SOME-
THING
TO
CHANGE
IT?

WE'RE NOT
ALL THAT
BAD.

7-21

©1968 JULES FEIFFER

Know What You Want

MARK VAN DOREN

My brother Carl, the biographer of Benjamin Franklin, was famous for his generosity. Asked for anything, he was likely to give it. And nothing was more valuable than his advice, which he gave freely when asked. He was not one of those men who pull long faces and wonder whether you oughtn't to decide things for yourself. If you wanted his help, and said so, he never doubted that you did; nor did he foolishly assume that you were bound to take it; the final decision would of course be yours, but meanwhile he was happy to throw what light he could upon your problem.

I owe him more than I can say, and not merely in this one department of advice. Here, though, he was better than generous to me; he was prodigal,[1] he gave me every thought he had. Books to read, people to meet, trips to take, restaurants to try—he included me in his world, so that I lived doubly while he lived. He was nine years my senior, and when we were boys in Illinois he did not hesitate to counsel me sometimes as if I were his son. If I didn't know enough to ask, he told me.

But as I grew up, and later when I followed him to New York, this changed. Nothing, I think, interested him more than what I did or did not do, but he was never in my way. He took it for granted now that I knew enough to ask; and when I did, which was often enough, he held back nothing. I was never dependent upon him unless I chose to be. It was always my choice. And the wonderful thing—wonderful, I mean, about him, not me—

[1] extravagant

was that when I made it I felt stronger rather than weaker because I did. My problem immediately became his own; it excited him, it aroused his imagination; so that as we talked I could believe the alternatives to be his as well as mine, and the pleasure too of doing whatever thing would eventually be done, even though in the nature of the case I was to do that thing alone. There was the time, for example, when I begged him to tell me what I should write about for my doctor's dissertation at Columbia. He suggested a criticism of John Dryden's poetry; and within a few minutes was racing through the subject with such contagious zest that I caught fire and contributed a few ideas myself—to his work, as it were, though in the end it was entirely mine.

*T*he one great comprehensive piece of advice Carl gave me, however, came later than that, and I am sorry to say I do not precisely remember the occasion that called it forth—perhaps it was a teaching position I had doubts about, or a job of editing I was afraid I should not stop other work to do. But no matter, it was what he said that counted. I have never forgotten it, nor do I expect to while I live. It has made all the difference to me. And I gladly pass it on.

"The real question is," said Carl, "do you *want* to do it?" "Why," I said, "that's what I can't decide." He laughed. "It seems to me you have decided." "What?" "That you don't want to do it." "How can you tell?" "Why, by your doubt. In my own case this would be decisive." "But doubts are not decisions." "Yes, they are. I have made it a rule never to do anything I didn't want to do—immediately, that is, or else without much thought one way or the other. The longer I hesitate the better I know my answer must be negative." "But you do hesitate. You've even come to me and asked me what I thought you ought to decide."

He laughed again. "Well, then, I was weak. I didn't know the strength of my own inclinations—or disinclinations. Believe me, *they* are clear. And the thing to do is to be as clear yourself. Of course things get in the way—duty, obligation, the desire not to disappoint or offend, the wish always to be liked. But in the end, my boy, do only what you want to do. And do nothing you don't want to do. Now in this case you surely don't expect me to tell you what your inclination is—

or your disinclination. You are the only one in the world that knows. I think I understand you pretty well, but here is private ground. I'm keeping off."

Now in one sense this was not advice at all. But in the best sense it was the best; and I needed it the most. Not, of course, that it was easy to take. For it threw me back upon the question of who and what I was, and whether I had knowledge of this person. How far should I trust my doubts and my desires? How confident could I afford to be that even if I knew my feelings I should let them master me? Who was I to announce that I would never do anything I didn't want to do? It sounded arrogant. It sounded ruthless.

And the queer thing was, Carl qualified in neither of those roles. He was singularly unselfish; everyone said so, and I knew it for a fact. He was generous to a fault; he praised people to their faces and behind their backs; he gave incredible amounts of time and strength to helping others through hard places; he rejoiced in their successes; he was humane to the last ounce. Also, as I told him in our dialogue, he didn't find it easy to follow his own rule. He could be tortured by doubts as to what he should do next, and by misgivings over what he had done last. His large nature was at the same time extremely sensitive; which was why so many loved him, and why there were those who could take advantage of his kindness. I knew these things then, so what should I conclude?

What I concluded at that dramatic moment was less important for me than what I have concluded since. Without reservation, I now think Carl was right. His ideal—difficult for him, to be sure, but all the more an ideal because of that— still makes the clearest sense. Nothing else perhaps makes any sense at all.

Shall we consult the wishes of others? But what others? And if we could pick the right ones— whatever that means—how could we know that we would please them in the end? We would certainly fail in this if what we did was done unwillingly, unnaturally for us, and therefore against the grain. What they want is that *we* should want the same thing they do. When they invite us to their house they hope that it will give us happiness to come; and we hope they mean the invitation. Unwilling hosts and unwilling guests do not exactly mix; everybody has a poor time. My wife tells me I lean over backward with respect to this; she says I urge people to come only if they want to; she thinks I sound as if I weren't too eager to see them myself. Possibly so, but I defend the principle. There is only one guide through the labyrinth of choice: our own desire, if we know what that is. Sometimes, I grant, it is difficult to know. But I agree with Carl that ignorance is a serious matter. It causes others and ourselves no end of trouble.

The principle was stated recently by a man who I might have supposed was too young to understand it. But he had had, evidently, the necessary experience. He is a producer of plays, and I happened to ask him whether the interest he was expressing in a certain play had its origin in the sympathy and affection I knew he felt for the author.

"Are you being kind?" I asked. He looked at me in astonishment—I even thought, with pity. "Good Lord, no! I learned long ago that anything like that simply complicates everybody's life." He meant that false hope can produce more misery than no hope at all, that lack of frankness—about important things at any rate—has finally to be paid for by the innocent as well as by the guilty.

I remember being asked ten years ago whether I would consider accepting the presidency of a college whose aims I admired. The chairman of the trustees called me on the phone and put it to me in terms that were none too easy to ignore: I was the person they wanted, and I could do the college good. If I hesitated for as long as one minute it was because Carl's voice was for that minute farther away than the chairman's. But I heard it in time, and said what I really felt: this was not my kind of work, I would be unhappy with it, I wouldn't do it well, and therefore I would do the college harm.

"Let me come and see you anyway," he said. "But it wouldn't change my mind." "Then it will simply be a visit." "All right. You know I'd like that. But remember what I said. I'll never accept."

He did come—it was a day's train trip to my house in Connecticut where I was spending the winter—and when he left the next morning he assured me that he liked train trips because they gave him time to read. The presidency had been scarcely mentioned, and I still don't know if he was disappointed with respect to it. I do know, however, that his disappointment in me as president, supposing I had been weak enough to argue down my instinct, would have been enormous and woeful; beginning and ending with me, everybody concerned would have had his life complicated for nothing.

Ruthless? No, I am convinced it is the finest form of scruple. I have not been describing a curmudgeon.[2] The curmudgeon wants nothing, whereas the normal thing is to have many desires—and the ideal thing is to know which ones of them are strongest. The curmudgeon, presumably, wants neither work nor a wife, and does without them. The normal thing is to want a wife, and the ideal thing of course is to take (if you can) the one you want the most. What if you consulted her parents and her friends? What if you married her only because you promised to, and meanwhile you changed your mind? This has been done, but neither party could have benefited by the act. The truly ruthless thing is to do what you do because you believe you ought to, and for no gentler reason. That is invoking monsters you have no human right to invoke. It is being, in the crudest possible sense, impersonal. It will not merely complicate life, it will ruin it.

Why is it that we are flattered when an animal likes us—when, for instance, we are in somebody's house and the cat, after staring at us from across the room, comes over and jumps up on our lap? The mistress of the cat can say nothing better at that moment than: "Look! He doesn't do it to everybody." We may pretend otherwise, but we are deeply pleased; and surely the reason is that we know cats—particularly cats—to be devoid of the sense of duty. They do what they want to do, and cannot be forced to do anything else. So in this case the motive is pure. Which is to say, it is purely selfish. Which is to say, it is capable of giving pleasure unmixed with any other thing. The same is true of small children—those who are too small to have compromised with complication, the adult vice that will beset them later.

As a vice it has its uses in society, and sometimes its beauty too. But it is a vice. Which is why I have learned, when someone comes to me and asks for counsel, that the most helpful thing to do is to let him talk until he has told himself what his own choice is. He probably knew before he came,

but doubted that others would approve. Now, though, in an atmosphere free of disapproval, he convinces himself that at last he knows what he wants. He is lucky in the knowledge, and so will those be with whom he is to be concerned.

[2] gruff, irritable old man

The Luxury of Integrity

STUART CHASE

I Once upon a time I worked for the United States Government. In the course of my official duties I was directed to make a rather particular and painstaking analysis of the profits of certain mammoth corporations. The welcome of the mammoth corporations, needless to say, was not warm.

One of my subordinates in the investigation was continually getting into trouble. He was a likeable fellow, a good routine worker, always ready to do odd jobs after hours. I took a personal interest in his troubles; I loaned him money, patched up a quarrel between himself and his wife, gave him books to read, tried to help him slide a little more easily along his white-collar groove. That he was grateful, that he really respected and liked me, I do not doubt to this day. Yet here is what he did after two years of friendly association:

He ransacked my private files and turned over any evidence showing liberal political tendencies on my part to the aforesaid mammoth corporations. He came into my office late one evening—fortified by a drink or two—and said: "Chase, I'm a Bolshevik. I'm fed up with the whole damned capitalist system. I'd like to help kick it over. I'd like to join something. You know about these socialists and I.W.W's. I see you reading pieces about them. Tell me all about it, shoot the works, tell me what I ought to join. I'll pay the dues."

At first I thought the poor boy had really come to the end of his rope; that this was a last desperate gesture before the white-collar routine doomed him altogether. Then I began to realize that he was lying: that he was hoping to pick up some information from me which could be twisted in such a way as to discredit my work in the investigation. (Not that I had much to offer.) I went on with my columns of figures, and gradually his receptive attitude waned. "Aren't you going to tell me anything?" he whined. "No," I said. "And I guess you had better go."

He took his hat and went. As the door closed behind him, I knew that the man I had befriended could not afford the luxury of integrity. Someone was paying him to act as a spy. His government salary was little enough, while his wife had definite ideas about her proper position in the world. He had been bought. (I doubt if the vendee got his money's worth.) I was bitter at the time, but to-day that bitterness is tinged with pity. He is only one among many Americans who increasingly cannot afford the luxury of integrity. His case is more dramatic perhaps, but essentially on all fours with the plight of too many men you meet upon the street. They, like him, have betrayed their personal sense of decency and honor because forces are loose too powerful for ordinary clay to oppose.

In the custody and handling of transferable property Americans grow more dependable; but in that more subtle definition of integrity which bids a man play fair with his own soul, never, it seems to me, has the Republic sunk to lower levels. As the machine breeds increased specialization, increased technological unemployment, as mergers spread their threat to white-collar jobs, the case grows worse. The greater one's economic insecurity the greater the tendency to sacrifice spiritual independence and to chant in dreary unison the simple credo[1] of the yes man. It is my contention that for uncounted millions of Americans the price of integrity is more than they can

If I were writing this essay today, rather than many years ago, I should change the emphasis somewhat. For example, the independent farmer class, cited as an example of integrity, has suffered a great decline in relative numbers, and the so-called "service trades" have greatly increased. I should introduce some new cases where integrity is at a minimum, drawn from local, state and national officials, certain foundations, the communications industries. Along with these should go outstanding examples of individual integrity, often at great personal sacrifice. The main thesis of the essay is, I feel, unfortunately at least as sound as ever.

S. C.

Amended and edited by Stuart Chase and reprinted with his permission.

[1] statement of belief

184 afford. Nor should I be surprised if the ratio of growth in the process bore more than a casual relationship to the growth in urban as against rural population.

Even as the interlocking technical structure of industry makes for an increasing tenuousness[2] in the condition of the live nerves of transport, power, and communication which provide city dwellers with physical necessities, so the psychological condition of the inhabitants of Megalopolis[3] grows more precarious. Living in a crowd, it has become highly important to *fit in.* There are fewer square holes for square pegs; to make the close-locked wheels of industry turn, an employee must be as round as a ball-bearing. This smooth and oily quality that eases the friction of the highly organized machine is in a way more vital than professional training, ability, or energy. One may may be genial and tactful by nature, while nine have to achieve tact and geniality by effort. For the milk of human kindness the most obvious substitute is soft soap.

II The yes man had no place in the pioneer tradition. The pioneer had his faults and virtues. The faults included a prodigal[4] wastefulness, a disposition to befoul one nest and move on to the next, a certain laxity in respect to the social amenities.[5] The virtues included a sturdy independence, and the compulsion, if need arose, to look every man level in the eye and tell him to go to hell. Reasonably secure in the fruits of his own labor and thus economically independent, he could express in any company his honest opinions as forcibly as he pleased, and, subject to the local *mores*[6]—the base line from which all human behavior must stem—he could translate his beliefs into tangible performance. He could vote for candidates he respected, agitate for reforms he believed in, refuse to do jobs which galled his sense of decency or craftsmanship, come and go as the seasons dictated, but not at the bidding of any over-lord. His opinions may have been frequently deplorable, his acts often crude and peremptory,[7] but he was free to be true to the

best that he knew—and so, by the Eternal! a man, and not a rubber stamp.

His was not the gentleman's code of honor, but one less punctilious,[8] more democratic, more human, and probably in the long run superior. The gentleman has a divided responsibility; he must not only seek to be true to himself, but he must maintain a wide margin between himself and the herd. The pioneer was of the herd and proud of it, and could thus devote himself single-mindedly to the one responsibility. Compare, let us say, a thousand assorted pioneers of the Berkshire Hills in Massachusetts in 1800 with a thousand assorted New York bank clerks in 1930, and, unless the monumental history of the Berkshires which I have lately ingested is a tissue of falsehoods, you will find about as many no men in the former area as you will find yes men in the latter. The ratios, I should guess, have reversed themselves in one hundred and thirty years. With the no men will lie character, courage, individuality, saltiness. With the yes men will lie radios, automobiles, bathtubs, and a complete paralysis of the will to act in accordance with their fundamental inclinations. That Berkshire babies were fashioned of better stuff than bank-clerk babies, I absolutely deny. Opinion for opinion and belief for belief, it is probable that the New York thousand have a more civilized outlook, a better stock of human values in their heads, than had the Pittsfield thousand. But for the latter integrity was cheap and abundant, while for the former it is very dear. Like all luxuries, it can be bought, but few dare to pay the price. For the price may be the job, and the job means life or death.

If you object that most men and women are without a sense of honor, then call it early conditioning. From the cultural mulch[9] in which we are reared—compounded of the influences of parents, school, church, folkways, literature—our personalities are formed. We take and we reject; we give lip service to much that our hearts do not subscribe to. But certain principles we make our own. Integrity consists in living up to them. I am not here concerned with those broad principles of morality which now, as in the days of David and Solomon, move more or less *in vacuo*,[10] but rather with a far more concrete and personal standard. I ask only if your behavior squares with your con-

[2] weakness; flimsiness
[3] a very large urban unit
[4] extravagant
[5] acts of courtesy
[6] customs or standards of behavior
[7] absolute, intolerant of opposition

[8] exacting in forms of etiquette
[9] protective covering to assist growth and nourishment
[10] literally, in a vacuum

ception of what honest behavior should be, and care not twopence how lofty or low the original conception. A stream can rise no higher than its source.

The point is not that we traduce[11] our honor to climb up—such behavior has affected a fixed fraction of the race since the Cro-Magnon man—but that most of us to-day are forced to traduce our honor *to cling to what we've got;* aye, to exist at all. It would be easier if life were simpler, but the perspiring supersalesmen take excellent care that life shall never simplify. No more have we won to a standard of living held respectable by our fellows, than presto! a new and higher standard confronts us—two-cars-per-family, college-for-all-the-children, annual models in furniture, country club memberships—and this we must attain on pain of social disapprobation.[12] There is no level, but a steady ascending curve which tolerates little margin of saving, no dependable economic security. While jobs grow more uncertain, desires, built in by the high-pressure fraternity, grow more clamorous.[13] In this compound-pressure pump, the wayfaring man finds it almost impossible to be true to his innermost nature.

III Consider initially the simple and widespread practice of yesing the boss—to use the current phrase. The man with the strong jaw sits at the head of the conference table, his confreres gathered around him, each with pad and sharpened pencil. From the strong jaw comes the announcement of a certain policy—perhaps a wage reduction, perhaps a wage increase, perhaps a universal system of time clocks. He looks about him. The policy may be utterly repugnant to his staff, but, "I check with you, chief," "check," "check," "check"—the little threadbare word runs round the table. Not always, to be sure, but frequently enough to make our case. On any given business day, the number of such checks and yeses must be astronomical in magnitude. It would be interesting to chart their yearly curve superimposed upon a curve exhibiting the growth of mergers.

The psychological effect of continually pretending to agree with that with which one does not agree is disastrous. An internal conflict is set up

which tends to polarize[14] work into neutrality. Initiative, concentration, straight thinking evaporate, leaving only purposeless activity. Probably less damage is suffered by the individual who knows in advance the fire he must pass through and deliberately makes up his mind to prostitute his talents. He is tragic enough, but a less unhappy exhibit on the whole than the hordes who fool themselves into thinking that they are doing honest work, unaware of the conflict beneath the surface.

Next let us consider that very considerable fraction of the population engaged in making commodities which the maker knows to be evil, shoddy, adulterated, and a rank imposition upon the public. He may whistle cheerfully enough, say "What the hell?" and believe that the plight of the public troubles him hardly at all. But deep down inside the continued outrage to his instinct of workmanship troubles him considerably. It is contrary to the whole history of mankind to waste good hours of labor on worthless or evil products.

Not long ago I delivered an address on the Russian economic experiment. I told of the method whereby an oil pool was developed as a single geological unit without competitive drilling and its appalling waste. After the lecture an engineer came up to me. He seemed deeply stirred. "My God," he said, "do you suppose I could get a job in Russia? I'm sick of drilling wells in competitive fields, watching most of my work run to waste. I know how a pool ought to be organized, but with all this offset drilling we aren't allowed to organize it." In his excitement, it was only too plain that there was a tragic breach between his standard of workmanship and the work that he had to do.

Of the ten million factory employees in America in 1925, the two million in the building trades, and the two hundred thousand engineers, how many can hold up their hands and say that they take pride in what they make? Many of them, of course, are operating processes so specialized that they have no idea of what they are helping to produce, but the majority are probably still aware of it. The show of hands is not impressive. When one considers the weighted silks, the bulk of the patent-medicine traffic, jerry-built bungalows on Garden Crest developments (I have talked to the carpenters working on them), shoes that dissolve into their essential paper, rickety furniture brave

[11] slander
[12] disapproval, condemnation
[13] noisy

[14] split

in varnish—commodity after commodity, process after process, the reason is sufficiently clear.

Leaving the factory, we come out upon the market place. Here we find a group almost as numerous as the producers, pushing goods which they know to be inferior or useless. A salesman has no canons of workmanship to be outraged, but if he has to sell an inferior product, and knows it, his case is not much happier than that of his fellow in the shop. He has to lie blatantly,[15] loudly and continually. He has to tell the world that bad products are good. He becomes used to it, of course; he may even take a little pride in his sales charts. But that does not mean that somewhere behind the table pounding, door-bell ringing, and copy writing there is not a *man*, who, in the darkness of the night after an ill-advised dinner, does not sometimes wish to God he could earn his living doing something he believed in.

We now come to one of the saddest exhibits on the list. There may be more deplorable human behavior than the violation of hospitality practiced daily by uncounted thousands of house-to-house canvassers, but I am at a loss to know what it is. Since time out of mind it has been the kindly human custom to welcome the stranger at the gate. The reaction is doubtless tied up with a dim fear that, some day, you too may be a-wandering and need rest and welcome. On this ancient custom the up-and-coming canvasser is forced to trade. In company schools he is deliberately coached in ways and means for capitalizing the instinct of hospitality, for gaining admission, a chair, a respectful audience—only to outrage it in the end.

Here, to quote an actual case, is a woman canvasser who announces herself as a member of the local school committee—only she is not a member of the school committee but recites a name which induces the lady of the house to think that she is. The "committee," it appears, recommends a certain book to aid the children's education. The visitor mentions the children by name, their ages, their bright looks. The lady of the house is pleased. The cost of the book is five dollars. Her face falls. She cannot afford five dollars. Haltingly, ashamedly, she confesses it. The canvasser turns on her with the sure-fire line, "Mrs. Green, don't you care enough about the future of your children to pay five dollars?" What mother can resist such an accusation? Company statistics coldly demonstrate that seven times out of ten it consummates a sale. Yet what troubles me is not the plight of Mrs. Green with a worthless volume on the parlor table, but the utter abandonment of self-respect on the part of the lady canvasser. Had she hit Mrs. Green with a blackjack as she stood defenseless and welcoming on her own doorstep, the loss of personal integrity could hardly have been greater. Hospitality is a particularly precious custom in a civilization which drifts so rapidly to cities and apartment houses. By ruthless violation the canvassers have all but killed it.

Not content with the assault in person, enterprising vendors of commodities, particularly of certain types of securities, are lately using the telephone to effect a sale. In one day at my office I was called to the telephone five times by total strangers giving a Wall Street address, succulently outlining the profit to be made by an immediate purchase of American Consolidated International Class B. To the first man I tried to be polite, to the second I was curt, for the other three I simply hung up the receiver. But the day was ruined by a feeling of baffled rage, partly at my assailants, and partly at myself for having to crush the habit of years of being courteous to those who had taken the trouble to call me on the telephone.

IV This brings us to that growing army of "publicity men" and women who sometimes do not—but frequently do—give the best of their years and their vitality to pushing causes in which they have no faith, and to booming personalities whom privately they designate as stuffed shirts. Business being business, their shingle is normally out for any propaganda however worthless, and for any publicity seeker however shameless. As in the textile industry, there is overproduction in the publicity game, and a client is a client. How many nationalists at heart are writing purple copy for peace societies; how many socialists at heart lauding the benign activities of the power trust; how many intelligent judges of human character stirring the tom-toms for men they despise?

In this connection, the testimonial writer demands a note. If he—or she—really likes the product, well and good. But in many cases he or she has never tried it. A thumping lie is exchanged for

---

[15] obtrusively, obviously

a bag of gold. The flight of Lindbergh from America to France was a fine and stirring achievement. But also fine to my mind is the fact that he has never sold his honor to a manufacturer.

Consider the activities of the ghost writer. According to the rules of this flourishing profession, he writes the speech for somebody else to deliver or the article or book for somebody else to sign. In certain cases he endeavors to put into words the somebody else's general thoughts, but in other cases the somebody else has no general thoughts, and it is his function to supply them. Thus he foists on the public an entirely false picture of his client; he puts brains—his brains—into a man of straw; and far worse, he abuses the craft of letters which the Lord has given him by writing words in which he places no credence, while neatly dodging responsibility by placing his client's name above them. As a writer I have frequently been invited to "ghost" under such circumstances and once or twice have been sorely tempted by the size of the fee. Fortunately my economic circumstances at the time were such that I could afford to refuse. Heaven knows when, unfortunately, they will be such that I cannot afford to refuse. But when I fall, I shall know that my position as a responsible professional man—voicing his own thoughts and signing his own stuff—has come to an end.

I know a writer of newspaper editorials. Himself a liberal, he has to grind out a thousand words daily which reflect the ultra-conservative policy of the paper for which he works. He keeps a record like a batting average chart, noting the editorials to which he can subscribe against those to which he cannot. When he last showed it to me he was scoring about .150—say one out of seven.

Pot boiling is no new phenomenon. Many of the Humanists' greatest heroes were known to stoop to the practice from time to time. It may be defined as doing, for a cash consideration, work markedly below the level of the artist's best. In the past, stark necessity was its chief inspiration. To-day as I go about among novelists, poets, playwrights, painters, I find a new motive widely voiced. We will, they say, "ghost," write success stories, produce canned editorials and advertising copy, concoct synthetic drama (a new type of laboratory research), illustrate magnificent brochures, or what you will, in order that we may lay aside a cash reserve, and *then* watch us burn up Olympus. I am still watching. The formula in most cases is spurious.[16] A continued and calculated flow of second-rate work is more than likely to poison the original spring. One can cite names —a number of very promising names—but it would be too painful. Enough that American art and literature have lost some distinguished ornaments because integrity comes too high.

"In the custody and handling of transferable property Americans grow more dependable; but in that more subtle definition of integrity which bids a man play fair with his own soul, never, it seems to me, has the Republic sunk to lower levels."

Lastly we shall consider a usage almost as widespread as yesing the boss, one indeed that may be said to be an integral part of the folkways of a pecuniary[17] civilization. I refer to the art of backslapping in the interest of a profitable sale. Under the canons of this culture complex it is encumbent upon the vendor to welcome the prospective vendee with all the warmth and sympathy hitherto reserved for dear and chosen friends. He must be dined and wined, his most infantile pronouncements must be received with the highest respect, one's home must be thrown open to him, his lightest fancy instantly satisfied. The fact that the company pays the bills is entirely beside the point. The point is that the whole procedure, like the canvasser's behavior, makes a mockery of natural human intercourse. Friendship is one of the few compensations for a complex life. To shower upon strangers and upon people who never could be one's friends all the earnests of comradeship is to debase rare metal. The dismal panorama passes before us: Manufacturers' agents departing with suit cases of gin to dentists' conventions. . . . Rotary club luncheons with members roaring songs, embracing one another, "Jim" calling to "Joe" (and Jim hates Joe)—all in the hope of more business. . . . The hearty dinner at home to the chief buyer for the National Widget Corpo-

---

[16] false
[17] relating to money

ration, with one's wife in a new and alluring frock and carefully coached in the art of drawing out Mr. Blatterfein on his favorite topic—the postage stamps of the Hawaiian Islands. . . . The high and costly strategy employed by publisher B in weaning an author away from publisher A—the agent preferably to be an old college friend. . . . "Contact men" in dinner coats at week-end parties.

V We have but touched the surface of the phenomenon, and already most of us are in it up to the waist, if not indeed completely mired. Certain groups are less involved than others, and a rough appraisal of relative saturation might prove instructive.

The independent farmer, standing closest to the pioneer tradition, leads the list. Despite the steady encroachments of business motives upon his way of life—for agriculture is far more a way of life than a pecuniary pursuit—he still has the best chance among all classes of Americans to call his soul his own. Perhaps the independent storekeeper, surviving in those few remote neighborhoods where chain stores and full-line forcing have not rendered his life a burden, takes second place. I know a few still functioning in the White Mountains of New Hampshire. They are the sort of men who will not send a bill when the neighbor who owes it is ill or out of luck.

Next in line we might place the housewife. More remote from the commercial front than her spouse, she still frequently reserves the right to speak her mind freely, "to stand right up in meeting," as we New Englanders say. I recall the case of a brilliant young accountant who, shortly after winning his C.P.A., was given an opportunity to make a million dollars, more or less, in a few months' time. All he had to do was to approach certain corporations with an offer to split whatever rebates he might earn for them in their filed income tax returns. His share in turn was to be split with a government examiner who supplied the names of such corporations as had legitimate claims for rebates in past tax payments. He told his mother of the glittering opportunity. "Tom," she said, "you know when I come to wake you in the morning I shake you hard, and you don't stir?" "Yes," he said. "And then I shake you even harder, and you give a little moan?" "Yes." "And finally I shake as hard as I can, and you open one sleepy eye?" "Yes." "I'd hate to come in morning after morning and find you awake." He turned down the job and has been sleeping soundly ever since.

Reasonably high in the comparative scale would come the skilled manual worker affiliated with a strong trade union. One does not find an unduly grave percentage of yes men among locomotive engineers, machinists, or building trades workers. In the main they are utterly dependent on their jobs, but their jobs are objective and technical, while the backing of the union—sometimes with its benefit clause—stiffens their independence and self-respect.

Next we might place independent manufacturers and entrepreneurs.[18] The great corporations are fast undermining them, financially and spiritually; but many sturdily maintain the Forsyte tradition,[19] refuse to grow maudlin[20] about Service, honestly admit they are in business for profit and not for public welfare, and take pride in producing a sound article, honestly sold. Below them would stand professional men and women, with physicians at the head of the group and lawyers at the bottom. There was a time when this class topped the whole list, but that was before competition became so keen; before the days of split fees, ambulance chasing, and yesing the president of the university. Professors, like canvassers, must eat. If the gentle reader is of a professional persuasion, he is doubtless an exception, but as a journeyman member of his class, I know that all too frequently I am not an exception.

On a level with professional people would come the unskilled manual workers, with farm laborers at their head. They are largely a beaten lot, but many of them lose their jobs so often they get used to it, and accumulate, if not independence, at least a certain stoicism, a bitter crust against a bitter world. Not far below them we find the servant class—some two millions of them in America. Here we note a peculiar phenomenon. Servants are protected to a degree by their time-honored professional status. Nobody expects their work-a-day manners to reflect their real personalities, and thus they are enabled to preserve some semblance

---

[18] enterprisers; those who organize, manage, and assume the risk of an enterprise or business

[19] In three novels collectively known as *The Forsyte Saga*, John Galsworthy treats exhaustively of the possessive instinct, embodied to an exaggerated degree in Soames Forsyte, a man with a passion for acquiring all things desirable and for exercising his right of ownership to the utmost.

[20] overly sentimental or emotional

of integrity behind and remote from the frozen smiles and conventional obsequiousness[21] of their trade.

From servants it is a long drop downward to the salesman, though here again we note, or are beginning to note, a loss of human dignity which is freezing into a convention. It is the salesman's business to be hypocritical if necessary, just as it is the servant's business to be servile. We do not expect much from a salesman or a blurb-writer save words, and presently he may be able to save his soul by taking, in his business hours, some such conventionalized and definite status as the butler or the waiter takes.

Salesmen are low in the scale of integrity, but at least they are alive. They have even been known to tell the boss what they thought of him and throw the job in his face. Clerks and office workers, being all but dead, must stand still lower. They are the saddest group of yes men on the whole list.

As we feel for the bottom, we encounter in the murky gloom a large round object. Dragging it with some reluctance toward the light, we discover it to be a politician. To expect integrity from an elected public servant is almost to expect a miracle. When Mr. Dwight Morrow, running for senator in New Jersey, actually and honestly spoke his mind about prohibition the shock was almost too great for the country to bear. Editorial writers lost their heads completely at the wonder of it. The politician leads a harrowing economic life, granted; there are often sound reasons for his debasement, but this incident would seem to make it plain that it is not always good business, or good publicity, to flounder so persistently in the lower depths. Once and again the poor fellow might come up for air.

We would seem to have touched the bottom. Not quite. We have yet to deal with certain types of corporation executives. As a class, executives may be arranged up and down the scale, but enough of them at least to be identified as a subspecies are the least enviable exhibit in the whole national category, firmly anchored to the ocean floor. Their case is the more deplorable in that they have less excuse than most of us for being untrue to themselves. They have more economic security than all the rest of us combined. Instead of quaking for their jobs, they need quake only

for their balance sheets. They have sold themselves, not to inexorable[22] terms of livelihood, but to a legal abstraction, an almost mythical monster, in whose bowels is nothing more than a certificate of incorporation. They dare not open their mouths in public, put pen to paper, pronounce judgment on any social question, attend a banquet—almost take a bath—without first securing the received policy of the company for which they work. They move in a world of juggernauts[23] and spooks which pass under the name of unfavorable publicity. They cower before the dire warnings of counsels on public relations. Instead of honestly admitting they are in business for profit, they squirt atomizers filled with the rank perfumes of "service," "good will," "public duty" in all directions, until the atmosphere of the nation is choked with alien gases. They wriggle, this subspecies, into schools, universities, women's clubs, churches. They teach the teacher to teach the little children to wash their little hands with their little cakes of Banana Oil Soap. It is difficult to walk a block in Washington without bumping into one of their legislative agents. Even as the Russians substitute Communism for God, these gentlemen substitute their Corporation. It can do no wrong. Once I was walking the streets of Boston with the vice-president of a great financial institution. We came to a little decayed brick building near the docks. He stopped, with reverence in his every gesture, and all but took off his hat. "This," he said, "is where our Company first began to do business." We might have been visiting the birthplace of a saint.

I should like to see old Jolyon Forsyte at a few American directors' tables; I should like to hear him express his mind freely at a conference of Junior Executives. Here was a man who ransacked the world for tea, sold you only the finest, and took a good round profit on the transaction. He did not cower before sticks of type, cared not a damn about "unfavorable publicity," had no corporate god to serve, and could call his soul his own.

I have been perhaps unduly harsh with that fraction of corporate executives who have forsworn all canons[24] of personal integrity to serve a paper monster. But I should like them to know how their activities impress the outside public;

---

[21] submissiveness

[22] unalterable
[23] relentless and inflexible destructive forces
[24] rules, principles

and I would point out, furthermore, that the lesson taught the politicians by Mr. Morrow is equally applicable in their case. They could afford to substitute facts for propaganda far more frequently than they do.

Questionable morals as reflected in graft, peculation,[25] and legal crime lie quite outside the discussion. Such behavior is to be found in every civilization since Mesopotamia; whether the ratio is worse in modern America I do not know, and for the moment do not care. All I have tried to say is that you and I, and Americans generally, have each a personal standard of honorable conduct. Under prevailing conditions, largely economic, it is frequently impossible to live within striking distance of that standard. Dr. Paul S. Achilles of Columbia, professor of vocational psychology, estimates that over 50 per cent of Americans are not happy in their work. (The suicide rate per thousand has jumped fivefold in seventy years.) I am but pointing out a major reason for that unhappiness. There is better stuff in us than we are permitted to express, and callous as routine may have made us, the failure of self-expression still hurts.

[25] embezzlement

On Not Losing One's Cool About the Young

THE EDITORS of *TIME*

A Russian revolutionary once suggested that everyone over 25 should be shot. His proposal was not adopted, but he might feel reasonably comfortable in the U.S. today. Nearly half of all Americans are now 25 or under, and the rest of the population, while not yet in danger of being liquidated, appears rather nervous and definitely on the defensive.

The situation is not exactly new. The man who first said "I don't know what the younger generation is coming to" probably died several thousand years ago. But Americans in the mid-1960s seem to have more reason than ever to lose their cool about the young. FBI statistics tell them that youngsters under 25 account for 73.4% of the arrests for murders, rapes, larcenies and other major crimes, and cause 31.5% of all traffic fatalities. Youth stages demonstrations in support of the country's enemies. Youth parades with placards of four-letter words. Youth scandalizes proud suburbs with grass parties—grass being one of the hippiest synonyms for marijuana. The latest campus fad seems to be underground "anti-universities" with courses in such subjects as revolution, "Search for the Authentic Sexual Experience" and hallucinogenic drugs. Boys look like girls, girls look like boys, and the songs they sing are not of love and laughter, but sour, self-pitying whines about how awful things are in a culture that supplies them with about $12 billion worth of such essential equipment as cars, clothes, acne lotions and hair sprays. The blaring jukebox message to the adult world seems to be: "Get off of my cloud . . ."

Even liberal intellectuals can be shocked at the frequent failure of the young to take ideas seriously. Writes Critic Leslie Fiedler, 48: "Not only do they reject the Socratic adage[1] that the unexamined life is not worth living, since for them precisely the unexamined life is the only one worth enduring at all. But they also abjure[2] the Freudian one: 'Where id was, ego shall be,' since for them the true rallying cry is, 'Let id prevail over ego, impulse over order'—or 'Freud is a fink!' "

Freud is not the only fink. Marx and the Communists, at least in their Moscow incarnations, are just as Out with the new radicals, who prefer Peking and Havana. Complaining that the young are not really interested in ideology but only in protest for the sake of protest, Editor Irving Kristol, 42, notes that the same middle-aged critics like himself who so fervently condemned "the silent generation" of the '50s "are now considerably upset and puzzled at the way students are 'misbehaving' these days. One wants the young to be idealistic, perhaps even somewhat radical, possibly even a bit militant—but not like this! It used to be said that the revolution devours its children. It now appears that these children have devoured the revolution."

*T*his, of course, is a picture of a minority, and a noisy one at that; the majority of American youth would say, "Not me." But the youth that makes the noise sets the tone, and the tone remains significant—and unique in comparison with the rest of the world. The noisy, "alienated" young are an American monopoly at the moment.[3]

The youth of Britain and France have the same blue-jeaned bottoms and fright-wig haircuts as their U.S. contemporaries, and they dig the same big beat and atonal balladry. Still, the Teen-Age International is largely confined to matters of style; underneath, European youth today seems less discontented and considerably more cowed by the adult world. In Germany and Italy, the

[1] a saying embodying common observation
[2] literally, to swear off
[3] It has become evident that American youth are not unique in their protest and discontent, as European and Japanese students have demonstrated in dramatic fashion on numerous occasions.

Ages abound in accounts of pitched battles, rapes and homicides. A proclamation of 1269 denounced the scholars of Paris who "by day and night atrociously wound and slay many, carry off women, ravish virgins, and break into houses."

Britain's illustrious public schools suffered repeated student rebellions in the 18th and 19th centuries. At Winchester in 1793, after stoning the assistant headmaster with marbles, the boys locked him up overnight in the dining hall with the warden and a teacher. When the high sheriff was appealed to the next day, he refused help because the boys had firearms and were getting ready to defend the Outer Gate by flinging flagstones down on the police. Harvard and Princeton experienced numerous such episodes. In 1788 the situation at Harvard was so bad that Professor Eliphalet Pearson kept what he called a Journal of Disorders. "In the hall at breakfast this morning," he recorded on Dec. 9, "bisket, tea cups, saucers & a *knife* thrown at tutors. At evening prayers the lights were all extinguished by powder and lead." A partial list of college casualties during this period includes one undergraduate dead in a duel at South Carolina College and another at Dickinson, several students shot at Ohio's Miami University, a professor killed at the University of Virginia, and the president of Mississippi's Oakland College stabbed to death by a student.

All this past history suggests that Americans, in their tendency to idealize youth, often forget what it is really like.

Society's important political, moral and intellectual changes, according to U.C.L.A. Historian Eugen Weber, have always been brought about by that section of the population that was "most available." Sometimes it was the nobility, as in the curbing of absolute monarchy, sometimes the rich, as in the rise of mercantilism, sometimes the bourgeois intellectuals, as in the French Revolution. In recent times, Weber holds, the most available group for rebellion has been the young, with more time—and certainly more energy—than anyone else.

Before the industrial revolution, "youth" could hardly be said to exist at all. In primitive societies, children become full-fledged members of the tribe in one painful and often hazardous initiation, which compresses—and purges—the terror of entering adult life. In Europe until well into the 18th century, children were both indulged and ignored. Medieval artists even seemed ignorant

young are just too busy cashing in on their new prosperity to protest against much of anything. In Soviet Russia, while society is changing and the young show signs of restlessness, youth by and large remains earnestly conformist. In Japan, despite occasional student riots organized by the left, the students' competitive drudgery makes even the American race for college seem relaxed by comparison; a Japanese youngster who fails to get into a university is called a *ronin*, the term for the pathetic samurai[4] who wandered about without a master.

U.S. parents and teachers who may hanker for a bit more obedience and less obstreperousness[5] from their own young should take comfort in the recollection that things have been worse. Riot and rebellion are a student tradition in the Western world; university records from the Middle

[4] in feudal Japan, a member of the warrior class who generally worked for a lord in return for land, money, or rice
[5] stubborn defiance

of what a child looked like; they habitually painted them as small adults. A 12th century miniature illustrating Jesus' injunction to "suffer the little children to come unto me" shows Christ surrounded by eight undersized men. Before the 17th century, a child passed directly into the adult world between the ages of five and seven. Schoolchildren carried weapons, which they were supposed to check at the schoolroom door. Marriages often took place in childhood. Youngsters drank heavily and even wenched according to their abilities. Montaigne wrote that "A hundred scholars have caught the pox before getting to their Aristotle lesson."

At the same time, society firmly kept the young in their place. In times when life as well as education was far shorter than today, they often made history at an age when the modern young are still working for their degrees; Edward the Black Prince was 16 when he won the battle of Crécy, Joan of Arc was 17 when she took Orléans from the English, and Ivan the Terrible was the same age when he hounded the boyars[6] to death and had himself crowned czar. But for ordinary people, particularly under the long-prevalent guild system of apprentices and journeymen, life was a slow progression toward experience and eventual reward.

"The U.S. has alternated between taking the judgment of its children not seriously enough— and too seriously."

In the 17th century came the beginnings of the modern idea of the family with the child at its center. With greater concern for children and more schooling came a new stage of life between childhood and adulthood: adolescence, a new combination of weal and woe that has profoundly altered human institutions and attitudes.

If adolescence had an inventor, it was Rousseau, who was cynical about man in civilization: "At ten he is led by cakes, at twenty by a mistress, at thirty by amusements, at forty by ambition, and at fifty by avarice. When does he make wisdom

his sole pursuit?" Rousseau saw wisdom in nature. Against the traditional Christian notion that children, scarred at birth by original sin, must be civilized through education, he felt that they were really innocent and that they are best educated through the emotions. In *Emile*, in 1762, he advised: "Keep your child's mind idle as long as you can."

The young thus "educated" by the emotions took stage center in the romantic era, when the glorious dreams of the French Revolution—and their bloody, reactionary demise[7]—turned youth toward an eccentric sentimentality. "They found satisfaction in ideals," wrote Madame de Staël, "because reality offered them nothing to satisfy their imaginations." Goethe intended his *Werther* as a warning to this mooning generation, but the young character who committed suicide for unrequited love became the hero of romanticism. The dirty speech movement of that day was suicide. It was, as Princeton Historian James Billington points out, the first major appearance of alienated youth.

Just as Rousseau had provided the ideological basis for adolescence, the industrial revolution provided the practical one: the factories needed the young as workers. Compulsory education was sold to the House of Commons largely as a device to keep the growing number of unemployed agricultural workers under 15 from "idling in the streets and wynds; tumbling about in the gutters; selling matches, running errands; working in tobacco shops, cared for by no man." The time spent in school fitted them for jobs in the new industrial world, and the young acquired greater economic importance than ever before. On the Continent, they also began to perform an entirely new political role in the liberal revolutions of 1848. They manned the barricades—against Louis Philippe in France, against King Frederick William in Prussia, against Metternich in Austria. They set up a quasi-revolutionary government at the University of Vienna, issued proclamations and organized an Academic Legion uniformed in blue coats, red-black-and-gold sashes and scarlet-lined cloaks.

Although the young rebels were brought back into line quickly enough, the European student remained a political force that reached a climax in the youth movements, both Fascist and Commu-

193

[6] members of the old nobility of Russia, before rank was dependent upon service to the country

[7] death

194 nist, between the world wars. Yet throughout all this, Europe refused to take the young more seriously than absolutely necessary. Until after World War II, the European social pattern closely resembled the ancient Chinese formula, according to which a man married at 30 and continued his learning, was first appointed to office at 40, promoted, if successful, at 50, and retired at 70. Disraeli might proclaim that "almost everything that is great has been done by youth." But the vast majority agreed instead with Lord Chesterfield, who remarked, "Young men are apt to think themselves wise enough, as drunken men are apt to think themselves sober enough."

It was different in the U.S. From America's beginning, youth was not a shortcoming but a virtue, not a time of preparation to be got through but a glorious Eden to be prolonged and preserved. Americans do not really want to keep the young in their place; they expect that the young will stay there out of their own essentially good nature. America's alltime young hero is Huck Finn, but not in the role of the brave rebel which serious critics (including T. S. Eliot) have cast him in, but in the safe and comfortable role of a backwoods Penrod or Andy Hardy—the eternally lovable bad boy. Until very recently, the sheltered and privileged American young gladly went along with that role. Their hell-raising was equally far removed from Werther's despair and the political barricades. The U.S. was thus enabled to go on worshiping youth without really facing the traits of youth that all other civilizations have accepted as inevitable—rebelliousness, moodiness, shifting passions for shifting causes. Americans want to deny the basic conflict, not to say war, between youth and age. Thus when the young do flare up, their elders are surprised, hurt and disappointed.

In part, this situation was fostered by the immigrant nature of American society. The children of the immigrants were the pathfinders in a new world, and taught their elders its ways. This contributed to the child-centered—some say child-ridden—nature of American life. More recently, what has caused American youth to live increasingly in a separate enclave or "sub-culture" is the ever-lengthening education process. In no other civilization have so many of the young been kept so long from the responsibilities of adult life. This prolongation of the school years, argues British

Sociologist Frank Musgrove, is partly a ploy[8] by the adult world to keep the young out of competition as long as possible, for, he asserts, the "mature of Western society" regard the young "with hatred." With people living longer and retaining their vigor into advanced age, there is certainly less disposition by the mature to make way—although "hatred" seems overstating the case. Still, the diagnosis may yet prove accurate, unless the older generation keeps its cool about the young.

*E*very parent should know that his child judges him; but he should also know that the judgment is that of a child. The U.S. has alternated between taking the judgment of its children not seriously enough—and too seriously. What is regarded as today's youthful nihilism is undoubtedly much less alarming than it seems. Whatever political causes the apolitical American young managed to find before have virtually disappeared—hence the concentration on the few remaining ones, such as civil rights and Viet Nam. Among the young bored by prosperity and consensus government, some observers discern a special group, the "New Puritans," who may be toting a protest placard alongside an anti-everything beatnik, but with an entirely different attitude inside.

Sociologist David Riesman agrees; he finds that service careers—schoolteaching, social work, government—are increasingly popular with undergraduates, and many of them are working at them part time while still in college, "trying to show that they are capable of human concern," says Riesman, "even while they are competing for grades." And Harvard Professor Erik H. Erikson believes that youth's main virtue and need is "fidelity"—to a worthwhile cause. Until that object of fidelity is found and tested, rebelliousness may simply be "a period of delay, a moratorium."

It is difficult to do justice to the young without being alarmist about their failings, or sentimental about their charms, or condescending about their rawness. The dialogue between experience and naiveté, between "we-know-better" and "we-don't-care," is in a sense impossible, because it is eternally carried on in two different languages.

[8] tactic intended to embarrass or frustrate an opponent

In this dialogue, youth is bound to have the last word—but only by the time youth itself is no longer young. In the face of this ultimately common destiny, Robert Louis Stevenson struck perhaps the best note of loving humor when he said: "Prudence is not a deity to cultivate in youth. Youth is the time to go flashing from one end of the world to the other both in mind and body; to try the manners of different nations; to hear the chimes at midnight; to see sunrise in town and country; to be converted at a revival; to circumnavigate the metaphysics,[9] write halting verse, run a mile to see a fire."

But it still matters where the fire is, and who set it.

[9] speculative philosophy in general

Substitutes for Violence

JOHN FISCHER

Scoundrels and in some cases even ruffians
terrified the citizens. Young mothers had to take
their babies to Central Park in armored cars. Old
women went to the theater in tanks, and no pretty
woman would venture forth after dark unless
convoyed by a regiment of troops . . . the
police wore bullet-proof underwear and were
armed with mortars and fifteen-inch howitzers . . .
JAMES RESTON, *The New York Times*, Oct. 29, 1965

Like most fables, Mr. Reston's moral tale exaggerates a little. But not much; for all of us are uneasily aware that violence is becoming a central fact of American life. Year after year the official graph for crimes of violence—murder, rape, assault, robbery, and riot—inches a little higher.* Many of these crimes seem to be entirely senseless: a California sniper blazes away at random at passing motorists . . . Bronx youngsters pillage[1] the Botanical Garden and wreck their own schoolrooms . . . a subway rider suddenly pulls a knife and starts slashing at his fellow passengers . . . a gang of roaming teen-agers comes across an old man drowsing on a park bench; they club and burn him to death without even bothering to rifle his pockets.

It is hardly surprising, then, that violence is becoming a dominant concern in our politics, literature, and conversation. Every campaigning candidate promises to chase the hoodlums off the city streets. Murder and mayhem—usually aimless, inexplicable, "existential"—are a growing preoccupation of American novelists: witness the recent work of Norman Mailer, Nelson Algren, and a hundred less-publicized writers. And not only the novelists; one of the most memorable nonfiction books of the past year was Truman Capote's *In Cold Blood*, a factual account of the peculiarly brutal murder of the Clutter family by two young sadists. Significantly, the scene was not a city street but a Kansas farm.

Nor is the carnage limited to the United States. As *The Economist* of London pointed out in a recent article (reprinted in the November issue of *Harper's*), rioting and hooliganism are on the rise in nearly every country, including England, Sweden, and Russia. Bloodshed in the big cities naturally gets most of the headlines, but it seems to be almost as widespread in predominantly rural areas—the Sudan, for example, India, the Congo, and Colombia, where *la violencia* has taken

* According to the annual reports of the Federal Bureau of Investigation. But its figures are based on voluntary reports by more than eight thousand local law-enforcement agencies, using different definitions of crime and widely varying statistical methods; therefore the FBI does not vouch for their accuracy. In fact, nobody knows precisely how much crime is committed in the United States, or its rate of increase, if any.

[1] loot, plunder, rob

hundreds of thousands of lives during the last two decades.

Explanations for all this are easy to come by, from nearly every clergyman, sociologist, and politician. Unfortunately they are seldom consistent. Some blame the miseries of slum life, others the breakdown of the family, or religion, or our national moral fiber. Racial and religious frictions apparently account for much free-floating hostility —in Watts and Calcutta, Capetown and Hué, even in Moscow and Peking, where African students report a lot of rough treatment from their hosts. Marxists, naturally, explain it all in terms of bourgeois decadence (although that would hardly account for the outbreaks in Prague and Novocherkassk, where the wicked bourgeoisie were liquidated long ago). While the Black Muslims decry[2] police brutality, J. Edgar Hoover is prescribing more policemen, armed with wider powers. The Freudians suggest that sexual frustration may be the root of the trouble, while Billy Graham is just as sure that it is sexual laxity. Nearly everybody points an indignant finger at the dope peddlers, and William Buckley gets cheers whenever he proclaims that nothing will save us short of a universal moral regeneration.

Perhaps there is some truth in all these explanations. But I am beginning to wonder whether, far beneath them all, there may not lie another, more primordial[3] reason. Just possibly the global surge of antisocial violence may result from the fact that nearly all societies—especially those we describe as "advanced"—suddenly have been forced to change a key commandment in their traditional codes of behavior; and many people, particularly the young males, have not yet been able to adjust themselves to this reversal.

*T*hat commandment was simple: "Be a fighter." Ever since human beings began to emerge as a separate species, something over a million years ago, it has been our first law of survival. For the earliest men, life was an incessant battle: against the hostile Pleistocene environment, against other mammals for food, against their own kind for a sheltering cave, a water hole, a hunting range, a mate. The fiercest, wiliest, and strongest lived to raise children. The meek, weak, slow, and stupid made an early breakfast—for a local tiger or, per-

haps oftener, for a neighboring family, since archaeological evidence suggests that cannibalism was common among primeval man. The result was that "our ancestors have bred pugnacity[4] into our bone and marrow. . . ."*

As civilization began to dawn, fighting became more organized—a community enterprise rather than a family one. In addition to their daily skirmishes with wolves, cattle thieves, and passing strangers, the ablebodied men of the village (or polis, kingdom, or pueblo) normally banded together at least once a year for a joint killing venture. The convenient time for settled farming people was early fall, after the harvest was in; then they had both enough leisure and enough surplus food to mount an expedition. So it was about September when the Assyrian swept down like a wolf on the fold, when Gideon smote the Philistines, when Vikings ravaged the Kentish coast, when the Greeks shoved off for Troy, when the Dorians swept into the Argive plain, irresistibly armed with that first mass weapon, the iron sword. (Because iron ore was much more plentiful than copper, it could be used—once the secret of smelting it was learned—to equip every man in the ranks. The victims of the Dorians, still lingering in the Bronze Age, normally armed only their officers with metal blades; the rest carried flint-tipped spears and arrows.) Tribes in the preagricultural stage sometimes found other seasons more suitable for rapine.[5] The War Moon of the Great Plains Indians, for example, came in May —since the spring grass was then just high enough to graze the horses of a raiding party, and the full moon made it easy to travel fast at night. Regardless of timing, however, warfare was for centuries the main social enterprise, absorbing virtually all of the community's surplus time, energy, and resources. "History," as William James put it, "is a bath of blood . . . war for war's sake, all the citizens being warriors . . . To hunt a neighboring tribe, kill the males, loot the village, and possess the females was the most profitable, as well as the most exciting, way of living."

As soon as warfare became socialized, the premium on belligerence was redoubled. Always

* As William James put it in his classic essay, "The Moral Equivalent of War," published in 1910. His other comments on this grisly topic will be noted in a moment.

[2] condemn or disparage openly
[3] original, first in order of time

[4] disposition to fight or quarrel
[5] the taking of property by force, as in war; plundering

198 highly favored by the processes of natural selection, it was now celebrated as a prime civic virtue as well. The Great Fighter was enshrined as the universal hero. His name might be Hercules or Rustum, Beowulf or David, Kiyomori or Hiawatha, but his characteristics remained the same: physical strength, reckless courage, skill with weapons, and a bottomless appetite for bloodshed. From earliest boyhood the males of the community were taught to emulate him. Their training for combat began as soon as they could lift a spear, and by eighteen they normally would be full-fledged warriors—whether in Athens or Cuzco—equally ready to defend their city's walls or to pillage a weaker neighbor. Success in battle was the basic status symbol. The best fighters were feted[6] in victory celebrations, heaped with honors and plunder, endowed with the lushest women, both homegrown and captive. The weak and timid, on the other hand, were scorned by elders and girls alike, and in many societies cowardice was punished by death.

For nearly all of human history, then, the aggressive impulse—so deeply embedded in our genes—had no trouble in finding an outlet. This outlet was not only socially acceptable; it was encouraged and rewarded by every resource at society's disposal.

*T*his remained true until roughly a hundred years ago. (When my grandfathers were boys, the martial[7] virtues were still applauded about as much as ever, and both of them marched off to the Civil War with the joyous spirit of an Alcibiades bound for Syracuse.)

Then, with stunning abruptness, the rules changed. Within about a century—a mere eyeblink in terms of evolutionary development—the traditional outlet for violence closed up. Fighting, so long encouraged by society, suddenly became intolerable.

One reason, of course, was the industrialization of war. It not only made warfare ruinously expensive; it took all the fun out of it. Long before the invention of the atom bomb, farsighted men such as William James had come to see that war was no longer "the most profitable, as well as the most exciting, way of living"; and by 1918 the lesson was plain to nearly everyone. In retro-spect, our Civil War seems to have been the last in which physical strength, raw courage, and individual prowess[8] could be (sometimes, at least) decisive; perhaps that is why it is written about so much, and so nostalgically.

For there is a certain animal satisfaction (as every football player knows) in bopping another man over the head. By all accounts, our ancestors thoroughly enjoyed hammering at each other with sword and mace; it exercised the large muscles, burned up the adrenalin in the system, relieved pent-up frustrations, and demonstrated virility in the most elemental fashion. But nobody can get that kind of satisfaction out of pulling the lanyard on a cannon, pointed at an unseen enemy miles away; you might as well be pulling a light switch in a factory. Indeed, in a modern army not one man in ten ever gets near combat; the great majority of the troops are cranking mimeograph machines, driving trucks, and tending the PX far to the rear. As a consequence, warfare—aside from its other disadvantages—no longer satisfies the primitive instinct for violence as it did for uncountable thousands of years.

*A*t about the same time—that is, roughly a century ago—the other socially approved outlets for pugnacity also began to close up. For example, so long as our society was mostly rural and small-town, a good deal of purely personal, casual brawling was easily tolerated. When Lincoln was a young man, the main public amusement seemed to be watching (and often joining in) the donnybrooks[9] which boiled up regularly in the village street; and during his New Salem days, Abe more than held his own. Our literature of the last century, from *Huckleberry Finn* to the story of the OK Wagon Yard, is studded with this kind of spontaneous combat. And our chronicles memorialize the violent men (whether fur trappers, river boatmen, forty-niners, lumberjacks, or cowboys) in the same admiring tone as the sagas of Achilles and Roland. As recently as my own boyhood, fist-fighting was considered a normal after-school activity, like marbles and run-sheep-run; nobody thought of us as juvenile delinquents, in need of a corps of Youth Workers to hound us into docility. A tight-packed urban society, however,

---

[6] honored with festivities and celebrations
[7] pertaining to war or military life

[8] strength, skill, and courage, especially in battle
[9] free-for-alls (after Donnybrook Fair, an annual event, known for its brawls, held in Donnybrook, Ireland)

simply can't put up with this kind of random combat. It disturbs the peace, endangers bystanders, and obstructs traffic.

As we turned into a nation of city dwellers, we lost another traditional testing ground for masculine prowess: the struggle against nature. Since the beginning of history, when men weren't fighting each other they spent most of their time fighting the elements. To survive, they had to hack down forests, kill off predatory animals, battle with every ounce of strength and cunning against blizzards, droughts, deserts, and gales. When Richard Henry Dana came home after two years before the mast, he knew he was a man. So too with the striplings who rafted logs down rivers in a spate, drove a wagon over the Natchez Trace, pulled a fishing dory on the Grand Banks, or broke

sod on the Nebraska prairies. Not long after he started shaving, my father went off alone to homestead a farm in what eventually became the state of Oklahoma. If he had been bothered by an ''identity crisis''—something he couldn't even conceive—it would have evaporated long before he got his final papers.

Today of course the strenuous life, which Theodore Roosevelt thought essential for a healthy man, has all but vanished. Probably not 5 per cent of our youngsters grow up to outdoor work, in farming, forests, or fisheries; and even for them, although the work may be hard, it is rarely either exciting or dangerous. (The modern cowboy does most of his work in a pickup truck, while Captain Ahab's successor goes to sea in a floating oil factory.) This final conquest of nature has had

some results both comic and a little sad. Among the Masai tribesmen, for instance, when a boy comes of age it has always been customary for him to prove his manhood by killing a lion with a spear; but according to recent reports from Africa, there are no longer enough lions to go around.

*I*n our tamer culture, we have shown remarkable ingenuity in inventing lion-substitutes. The most fashionable surrogates[10] for violence are the strenuous and risky sports—skiing, skin diving, surfing, mountain climbing, drag racing, sailing small boats in rough weather—which have burgeoned so remarkably in recent years. When a middle-aged Cleveland copy editor crosses the Atlantic alone in a twelve-foot sloop, nobody accuses him of suicidal impulses; on the contrary, millions of sedentary[11] males understand all too well his yearning for at least one adventure in life, however self-imposed and unnecessary. (Women, of course, generally do not understand; most of the wives I've overheard discussing the Manry voyage wondered, not how he made it, but why Mrs. Manry ever let him try.)

But these devices serve only the middle class. For the poor, they ordinarily are too expensive. When Robert Benchley remarked that there was enough suffering in life without people tying boards on their feet and sliding down mountains, he missed the point; the real trouble with skiing is that slum kids can't afford it. Consequently, they try to get their kicks vicariously, by watching murder, football, boxing, and phony wrestling matches on television. When that palls, their next resort usually is reckless driving. That is why access to a car (his own, his family's, or a stolen one) is as precious to the adolescent male—rich or poor—in our culture as possession of a shield was in fifth-century Athens. It is a similar badge of manhood, the equipment necessary to demonstrate that he is a fearless and dashing fellow. (It also is the reason why insurance premiums are so high on autos driven by males under twenty-five years old.)

Such games are socially useful, because they absorb in a relatively harmless way some of our pent-up aggressions. But they all have one great drawback: they are merely games. They are contrived; they are artificial adjuncts to life, rather than the core of life itself. When our ancestors harpooned a whale, pillaged a city, or held the pass at Thermopylae, they knew they were playing for keeps. When our sons break their legs on a ski slope or play "chicken" on the highway, they know that the challenge is a made-up one, and therefore never wholly satisfying. They still yearn for a genuine challenge, a chance to prove their hardihood in a way that really means something.

Lacking anything better, some of them—a growing number, apparently—turn to crimes of violence. Gangs fights, vandalism, robbery are, in an important sense, more "real" than any game. And for large groups of disadvantaged people, any form of antisocial violence is a way of striking back, in blind fury, at the community which has condemned them to disappointment and frustration. This is equally true, I suspect, of the Negro rioters in Watts and the poor whites of the South, who take so readily to the murders, church burnings, and assorted barbarities of the Klan.

*T*his sort of thing may well continue, on a rising scale, until we can discover what James called a "moral equivalent for war." He thought he had found it. He wanted to draft "the whole youthful population" into a peacetime army to serve in "the immemorial human warfare against nature." What he had in mind was a sort of gigantic Civilian Conservation Corps, in which every youngster would spend a few years at hard and dangerous labor—consigned to "coal and iron mines, to freight trains, to fishing fleets in December . . . to road-building and tunnel-making." When he wrote, a half-century ago, this idea sounded plausible, because the need for such work seemed limitless.

Today, however, his prescription is harder to apply. In many parts of the globe, the war against nature has ended, with nature's unconditional surrender. Automation, moreover, has eliminated most dangerous and physically demanding jobs; our mines and freight trains are overmanned, our roads are now built with earth-moving machines rather than pick and shovel.

Nevertheless, so far as I can see James's idea is still our best starting point. And already an encouraging number of people are groping for ways to make it work, in the different and more difficult circumstances of our time.

A few have found personal, unofficial answers. The young people who join the civil-rights move-

[10] substitutes; specifically, artificial substitutes
[11] inactive, accustomed to sitting

ment in the South, for example, are encountering hardship, violence, and occasionally death in a cause that is obviously genuine; they aren't playing games. But The Movement can accommodate only a limited number of volunteers, and presumably it will go out of business eventually, when the white Southerners reconcile themselves to rejoining the United States. In the North, civil-rights work has often turned out to be less satisfying, emotionally, because The Enemy is harder to identify and the goals are less clear. As a result its young partisans sometimes have drifted into a kind of generalized protest, carrying placards for almost anything from SNCC to Free Speech to World Peace: that is, they have ended up with another form of game playing.

President Kennedy, who understood thoroughly the youthful need for struggle and self-sacrifice, had the Jamesian principle in mind when he started the Peace Corps. It remains the most successful official experiment in this direction, and it led to the Job Corps and several related experiments in the domestic Antipoverty Program. How they will work out is still an open question, as William Haddad pointed out last month in *Harper's*. At least they are a public recognition that the country has to do *something*. If we don't—if we continue to let millions of young men sit around, while the adrenalin bubbles and every muscle screams for action, with no outlet in sight but a desk job at best and an unemployment check at worst—then we are asking for bad trouble. Either we can find ways to give them action, in some useful fashion, or we can look forward to a rising surge of antisocial violence. In the latter case we may, a decade from now, remember the Fort Lauderdale beach riots as a mere boyish prank.

What I am suggesting, of course, is that all of us —especially our businessmen, sociologists, and political leaders—ought to invest a good deal more effort, ingenuity, and money in the search for acceptable substitutes for violence. How many industries have really tried to create interesting and physically demanding jobs for young people? Have the paper companies, for instance, figured out how many foresters they might use, if they were to develop their timber reserves for camping, hunting, and fishing, as well as for wood pulp? And are they sure such a venture would not be profitable?

To take care of the population explosion, we are going to have to duplicate all of our present college buildings within the next twenty years. Has any university looked into the possibility of using prospective students to do some of the building? Maybe every able-bodied boy should be required to labor on the campus for six months as a bricklayer or carpenter before he is admitted to classes?

Cleaning up our polluted rivers is a task worthy of Paul Bunyan, and one we can't postpone much longer. What governor has thought of mobilizing a state Youth Corps to do part of the job? Has Ladybird Johnson calculated how many husky youngsters might be deployed, axes in hand, to chop down billboards along our highways and replace them with trees?

The possibilities aren't as easy to spot as they were in William James's day, but even in our overcrowded and overdeveloped society some of them still exist. No single one of them will provide the kind of simple, large-scale panacea[12] that James had in mind—yet if we can discover a few hundred such projects, they might add up to a pretty fair Moral Equivalent. In any case, the search is worth a more serious try than anyone has made yet.

Why, my wife asks me, is all that necessary? Wouldn't it be simpler for you men to stop acting like savages? Since you realize that belligerence is no longer a socially useful trait, why don't you try to cultivate your gentler and more humane instincts? Are you saying that You Can't Change Human Nature?

No, that isn't quite what I'm saying. I recognize that human nature changes all the time. Cannibalism, for example, is now fairly rare, and polygamy (at least in its more open form) has been abandoned by a number of cultures. Someday (I hope and believe) the craving for violence will leach out of the human system. But the reversal of an evolutionary process takes a long time. For a good many generations, then, the Old Adam is likely to linger in our genes; and during that transitional period, probably the best we can hope for is to keep him reasonably quiet with some variant of William James's prescription.

[12] literally, a cure-all

A Reasonable Life in a Mad World

IRWIN EDMAN

That the world is mad has been the judgment of self-denominated sane philosophers from the Greeks to the present day. It is not a discovery of our own age that both the public and private lives of human beings are dominated by folly and stupidity. Philosophers pressing the point have brought such charges not against human nature only—that is, the world of human relations— but against that larger universe in which the world of human relations is set. As far back as the Book of Job and probably much further back, for there must have been at least gruntingly articulate Jobs in prehistory, it is not only men who have been declared mad: by any standards of rationality the universe itself has been called irrational, pointless, meaningless, with incidental, unintended overtones of cruelty and injustice.

With the provincialism[1] of each generation, ours imagines that the causes of cynicism and despair are new in our time. There have, of course, been modern improvements and refinements of stupidity and folly. No previous generation has been by way of organizing itself with insane efficiency for blowing the whole race to smithereens. It does not take a particularly logical mind at the present moment to discover that the world is quite mad, though a great many critics apparently think that the cruel absurdity of technical efficiency combined with moral bankruptcy is a discovery that it took great wit on their part to turn up.

Reputations are being made by reiterating, to the extent of four or five hundred pages, that collective modern man is a technical genius merged with a moral imbecile.

The first encouragement I can bring is the reminder that the kind of madness which we all realize to be the present state of the world is not something new. It is, just like everything else in the modern world, bigger and more streamlined, if not better. It is a pity some of the great satirists are dead; Swift and Voltaire would have given their eyeteeth for the present situation. And Aristophanes would scarcely have believed it. But the essential charges they would bring against the present time and the essential absurdities they would show up are not different in essence now from what they were.

Neither nature nor man appears reasonable by reasonable human standards. So acutely does this seem to many people to be true that in almost exuberant desperation they decide to march crazily in the insane procession. Existentialists make a cult of anxiety and despair and find a kind of wry comfort in saying, Since the world is absurd, let absurdity and irony be our standards. There are others who say—and the currency of an ersatz[2] theological literature shows how epidemic[3] they are—that since the world and mankind at present seem so palpably[4] absurd it simply can't be true, and history, as Toynbee* now assures us, moves delightfully and progressively to fulfillment in the Church of God—a kind of quiet, English Church incorporating the best features of Islam, Buddhism, Confucianism, and a little, even, of the Hebrew prophets and the secular sciences.

The excitements and confused urgencies of the present time may seem to make hysteria or mystical narcosis[5] or hedonistic[6] excitement tantamount[7] to a philosophy. But the still, small voice of rationality persists. And the question still remains the same as that propounded by the Greeks long ago: How, in a world certainly not at first acquaintance rational-appearing, is it possible to lead a rational life?

It seems mad now to say that anyone could believe, as the Fabians† did (including such un-

---

[1] indifference to things alien or unfamiliar (here, the history of man)

* Arnold J. Toynbee, contemporary English historian and author of *A Study of History*.
† English socialists who aimed to reform society gradually, avoiding revolutionary methods.

[2] based on a substitute, usually inferior; synthetic
[3] widespread; in all the people
[4] noticeably
[5] deep stupor produced by a drug
[6] based on the belief in the pursuit of pleasure as the chief activity of life
[7] almost the same as

sentimental people as George Bernard Shaw and Sidney and Beatrice Webb and Graham Wallas and later H. G. Wells), that the world could be transformed into a livable, beautiful, reasonable place by the co-operation of reasonable men. It is not simply that the violent external events of the past generation have revealed to us how precarious were security and comfort, and for how few it obtained at all.

But the psychological sciences have revealed to us the deep sources of violence, confusion, hysteria, and madness in ourselves. What perhaps a generation ago seemed a melodramatic aphorism[8] when Santayana uttered it seems now to be a hitting of the nail on the head: "The normal man holds a lunatic in leash." The definition needs to be amended. In the light of the past twenty-five years, the normal man no longer *does* hold a lunatic in leash. The fact that even talk about a third world war has become standard has practically made lunacy respectable. It is now become a stamp of madness to talk as if one seriously believed that a peaceful and just world were possible.

And yet the sentiment of rationality persists and the hope persists also that it is not impossible, at least in imagination, to dream and in organized effort to work for what seems "an ordered, coherent world society." The most ardent workers for such a world, however, realize that there is plenty of madness left, out of which a third world war may come.

II The persistence of power politics, the greed for privilege, the insane clutching of wealth, the pathological tribalisms of nations, of class, and of race; it is this world in which we are actually living, and the human problem for anyone in it is to discover what is a reasonable life in such a world.

Is it to forget as far as possible and to live only in the moment and to make that moment as brief and bright as possible? Is it to surrender any hope for pleasure or happiness now and give one's dedicated and ruthless devotion to work for a more reasonable world? Is it to seek Nirvana[9] or to seek some salvation in another world? There

[8] wise saying wittily expressed
[9] in Buddhism, the state of absolute felicity, characterized by freedom from pain, passion, suffering, etc., and attained through the annihilation of the self

seems to be some sense in each answer, but which answer one chooses will depend ultimately on how one answers a basic question: Is the world always and necessarily mad? Is it completely mad now, and is it possible even now to understand the madness and, through understanding, to endure or change it?

"It takes something like genius in folly to have millions starving in the midst of plenty, to have technological magic whose fruits are poverty, squalor, anarchy, and death. . . ."

Let us try as simply as possible to deal with some of these questions. First, is the world always and necessarily mad? By "the world," of course, one means both the processes of nature and the activities of human beings. For "world" in the first sense one had perhaps better use the word "universe." A thoroughly rational universe would be one which was achieving a purpose set down in advance, a purpose which in human terms made sense and which by human standards made moral sense. A rational universe might be one such as the Deists conceived in the eighteenth century, in which nature was simply reason incarnate or reason embodied in the vast machinery of things.

In one respect at least the advance of knowledge of the physical world has not made the world seem more irrational. It has made it seem orderly and regular. But in another respect an understanding of the causes and consequences of nature by conventional standards made nature seem wholly irrational. "I am what I am," said Jehovah in the Old Testament, as if that announcement were sufficient explanation of his wrathful ways. "It is what it is and it does what it does" may be said to be the conclusions of empirical[10] physical science. It is maddening to rational creatures to discover they were born into a world which is not particularly interested in human purposes, which perhaps permits and sustains these purposes but is innocent of any solicitude concerning them. The

[10] based on observation and experiment

*". . . human intelligence accompanied by human goodwill
may profoundly improve the life of mankind."*

204 rain notoriously falls on the just and the unjust, and the just feel highly put upon. Death is no respecter of persons; plagues fell the virtuous. The most generous and devoted enterprises are washed away by floods along with the conspiracies of the sinister and hateful.

Theologians have spent a good deal of time trying to gloss away the irrationalities of the universe, explaining that God moves in a mysterious or at least salutary[11] way, his morally therapeutic wonders to perform. Job was not greatly impressed by his comforters, and neither are we. But if exasperated humans have criticized the world in general, they have been especially critical of the madness of their fellow men. Voltaire found his greatest weapon of satire in treating cruelty, barbarism, and superstition not as evil but as absurd.

The most serious and damaging charge we can bring against civilization is that by the very standards of civilization it is a ridiculous failure. It takes a high degree of sophistication and technical resources to make such an international shambles as we seem fated to do. It takes something like genius in folly to have millions starving in the midst of plenty, to have technological magic whose fruits are poverty, squalor, anarchy, and death; it takes a refinement of absurdity to use the most generous aphorism of the highest religions to justify or rationalize intolerance, violence, and our established international disorder.

Now about the first irrationality: that of the universe itself. Perhaps the only reasonable attitude is that of resignation and endurance of it. Perhaps it is only the persistence of our childhood wishes and expectations that has led to an assumption that the universe must conform to human purposes and that it is shockingly unreasonable of it not so to conform. We can, within the limits of a world not made for us, make it conform to ideals and values which flower out of nature itself. Part of the life of reason is a contemplation of the unchanging and unchangeable elements in the world of nature; part of it is a sedulous[12] attempt to discover the ways of changing the world in the interest of human values.

With respect to the world of human activities there has been an accelerated desperation at the present time. In the old days when humor could

still flourish in Central Europe it used to be said that the difference between the temper of Berlin and Vienna could be stated as follows: In Berlin when things went wrong it was remarked: "The situation is serious but not hopeless"; in Vienna with smiling deprecation the Viennese used to say: "The situation is hopeless but not serious." The Berlin version seems of late more greatly to have impressed the world.

Though Existentialism may be said to describe the world as being both hopeless and trivial, if one so conceives the realm of human affairs the Epicurean[13] prescription for a reasonable life is perhaps the best that one can find. However clouded and uncertain the future, there is at least possible for the lucky and the prudent a brief, bright interval in which they may find luster and to which their refined sensibilities may give luster. In a world without meaning they may find exquisite nuances[14] of meaning in the arts, in friendship, in love.

The trouble with the Epicurean solution and abdication is that it is always haunted by a scruple of conscience and the shadow of despair. There is something already tarnished in a brightness that declares itself both ultimately meaningless and transient. Sorrow and inhibition and regret dog the footsteps of the Epicurean in a world where folly is no longer a joke but a terrifying threat to all mankind.

There are those, therefore, in our own age who jump to the other extreme. One insists that one *must* give up any hope for present happiness and give one's dedicated and ruthless devotion to work for a better world. I have friends, especially in social or government work or in the social sciences, who regard humor, irony, urbanity,[15] or relaxation with something of the same moral impatience with which a missionary might watch the natives of the Fiji Islands dance or lounge in the sun. There is so little time; it is later than you think; there is no time for comedy. Urbanity is a form of evasion, and laughter is a form of bourgeois or decadent callousness. Let us gird our loins and work together rapidly for the common good or we shall all in common be destroyed. The psychiatric departments of hospitals number among their patients a good many

[11] beneficial
[12] diligent in pursuit

[13] based on the pursuit of cultural interests, development of inner serenity, and temperance in sexual pleasure
[14] shades of difference
[15] refinement, polish

206 people who in their earnest haste to save the world from destruction ended up by destroying their equilibrium and almost themselves. The tension of moral earnestness, the refusal to permit the enjoyment of even such goods as are possible in a chaotic world, is one of the diseases of our civilization, not a sign of its health. If Epicureanism leads to dismay, unrelieved moral dedication leads to fanaticism. Neither the playboy nor the zealot is a true or adequate incarnation of the life of reason.

Those who recognize the disillusion of a pleasure philosophy or the destructiveness of a moral fanaticism have begun in our age, as they have in other ages, to turn to otherworldly philosophies. They have tried to seek an inward light unquenchable by external circumstances. They have tried in spirit to follow the Indian saint into the wilderness or the monk into his cell or the mystic into his remote meditation. They have sought Nirvana, or a Oneness with the One, or an Aloneness with the Alone. The follies of society are not cured by the incantations of pure mysticism, and the search for oblivion is really a pathological attempt simply to become oblivious to the actual and remediable conflicts and disorders in society.

There are still others than the pleasure-lovers, the Nirvana-seekers, the devotees of such mystics, who have sought to make a prescription for a reasonable life. Among those others now epidemic are followers of historians and zoologists who with the theological wave of a wand discover that a palpably absurd world is somehow moving toward a cozy fulfillment where, as I heard Mr. Toynbee say, "God is Love." It would seem a strange moment to detect the course of history as the operations of universal love when the world is being filled with universal hate.

No, I do not think any of these ersatz solutions will do. The pressure of events simply confirms again what the life of reason does consist in: a brave contemplation of what things are discoverably like and a resolute attempt to improve the lot of man in the conditions into which he finds himself born. The life of reason must always have a stoic element because there is no sign that either the follies of humanity or the uncaring order of nature will ever be magically transformed.

The life of reason must also contain an element of hope, for it is quite clear, as the history of every improvement in man's estate has shown us, that human intelligence accompanied by human goodwill may profoundly improve the life of mankind. The life of reason must include the pleasure principle also, for what else gives life meaning if not joy and delight of life, and what a folly it would be not to cherish and embrace, not to nourish then, even in a sick society, that which yields the fruit of a quickened, multiplied awareness, the substance of vision and of joy. The universe may be pointless, but there are many good points in it. Our urgencies may be intense, but the world does not end with us or even with our own civilization; nor, if we do not quench intelligence and generosity in ourselves, is it a foregone conclusion that our civilization must end. And the best insurance, perhaps, of maintaining both is to reaffirm the quality of life itself, of its possibility of beauty and its intimations[16] of order and of justice.

[16] hints

A Manifesto

GORE VIDAL

Ten percent of the human beings ever born are now alive and breeding like bacteria under optimum[1] conditions. As a result, millions live at famine level. Yet even with the fullest exploitation of the planet's arable[2] land—and a fair system of distribution—it will not be possible to feed the descendants of those now alive. Meanwhile, man-made waste is poisoning rivers and lakes, air and soil; the megalopolis[3] continues to engulf the earth, as unplanned as a melanoma[4] and ultimately as fatal to the host organism. Overcrowding in the cities is producing a collective madness in which irrational violence flourishes because man needs more space in which to *be* than the modern city allows.

But because the West's economy depends upon more and more consumers in need of more and more goods and services, nothing will be done to curb population or to restore in man's favor the ecological[5] balance. Present political and economic institutions are at best incapable of making changes; at worst, they are prime contributors to the spoiling of the planet and the blighting of human life. It could be said that, with almost the best will in the world, we have created a hell and called it The American Way of Life.

To preserve the human race, it is now necessary to reorganize society. To this end, an Authority must be created with the power to control human population, to redistribute food, to purify air, water, soil, to re-pattern the cities. Specifically:

[1] best, most favorable
[2] capable of being cultivated
[3] huge urban complex
[4] malignant tumor
[5] pertaining to the pattern of relationships between organisms and their environment

The Authority must have the power to limit births by law. All the usual means of exhortation will be used to convince the citizenry that it is not a good thing to create at random replicas of themselves when the present supply of human beings is already too great a burden for the earth's resources. Put bluntly: to bring into the world an unwanted human being is as antisocial an act as murder. The endlessly delicate problem of who should be allowed to have children might be entirely eliminated by the anonymous matching in laboratories of sperm and ova. If this were done, the raising of children could then be entrusted to those who show some talent for it, on the order of certain of the Israeli kibbutzim.[6]

The Authority must have the power to exploit the food resources of the nation in order to feed not only the 10,000,000 Americans currently at famine level but to use surplus food to assist the feeding of other countries, on condition that they, too, reduce population.

The Authority must have the power to divert waste from air and water, even though this will mean the sad banishment of the combustion engine from the automobile, and the placing of many factories underground.

The Authority must have the power to begin the systematic breaking up of the cities into smaller units. To avoid a re-creation of the present ghettos, living areas should be limited not only in size but, to avoid that deterioration which is due to poverty, each family entrusted with the raising of children should be given a minimum living allowance.

The Authority may *not* have the power or right to regulate the private lives of citizens.

It is a paradox of the acquisitive society in which we now live that although private morals are regulated by law, the entrepreneur[7] is allowed considerable freedom to use—and abuse—the public in order to make money. The American pursuit of happiness might be less desperate if the situation were reversed.

Since planned (and perhaps anonymous) breeding will eliminate the family as we now know it, those not engaged in bringing up the young would then be free to form whatever alliances they want, of long or short duration, in any mutually consenting arrangement with either sex, on

[6] collective farms in Israel
[7] one who organizes, manages, and assumes the risk of an enterprise or business

"It could be said that, with almost the best will in the world, we have created a hell and called it The American Way of Life."

208 the principle that each man has the right to do as he likes with his own body, including kill it with alcohol, cigarettes, drugs or a bullet. By drawing a line between what is private and of concern only to the individual and what is public and of concern to all, the Authority could begin to realize something of the spirit of this nation's early charters.

Finally, the Authority may not limit free speech in any form, including criticism of itself. In fact, the Authority's affairs should be under constant surveillance by watchful committees as well as by the press, though it might be advisable to deny the employees of the Authority any sort of personal public notice since love of glory has wrecked more human societies than all of history's plagues combined. Unsung managers constantly scrutinized by the wise: that is the ideal, partially achieved in another time (and for quite a different purpose) by the Venetian Republic.

These then are the things which must now be done if the race is to continue. Needless to say, every political and economic interest will oppose the setting up of such an Authority. Worse, those elements which delight in destroying human institutions will be morbidly drawn to a movement as radical as this one. But it cannot be helped. The alternative to a planned society is no society. If we do not act now, we shall perish through sheer numbers, like laboratory rats confined to too small a cage. The human race is plainly nothing in eternity but to us, in time, it is everything and ought not to die.

*E*ach of us contains a Private Self and a Public Self. When the two have not met, their host tends to be an average American, amiable, self-deluding and given to sudden attacks of melancholy whose origin he does not suspect. When the two selves openly disdain each other, the host is apt to be a strong-minded opportunist, equally at home in politics or advertising. When the selves wrangle and neither is for long dominant, the host is more a man of conscience than of action. When the two are in fierce and total conflict, the host is lunatic —or saint.

My own two selves wrangle endlessly. Hedonistic[8] and solipsistic,[9] my Private Self believes the making of literature is the whole self's only proper task. The Public Self, on the other hand, sees

world's end plainly and wants to avoid it, sacrificing, if necessary, art and private pleasure in order to be of use. *A Manifesto* has given the two selves a good deal to quarrel about, and in their endless dialogue some of the many questions *A Manifesto* is bound to raise are posed, if not always answered.

Private Self: It is typical of you to state what needs to be done and then not tell us how it should be done—whether it *ought* to be done I'll get to in a moment.

Public Self: And typical of you to dislike any kind of general statement (not to mention political action). One must first draw attention—in the broadest way imaginable—to the nature of the crisis. If the race is not to die of overpopulation, we must. . . .

Private Self: You've made your point. But first, do you really think anyone can change our present course? And, second, why not let the thing die? I find beautiful the vision of an empty planet, made glass by atomic fission, forever circling a cooling sun. . . .

Public Self: And you enjoy accusing *me* of rhetoric! I ignore your second question. The thing must not die. As for the first: it is possible to reduce population drastically in one generation. In two generations a viable[10] balance could be arrived at. . . .

Private Self: Could. Yes. But will it come to pass? Remember when we were in Egypt and Hassanein Heikal explained to us that even under Nasser—with all his power—the fellahin[11] could not be persuaded to practice birth control. . . .

Public Self: When persuasion fails, other means will be used.

Private Self: Yes! Force. That Authority of yours gives me the creeps. . . .

Public Self: I don't like it much myself but without it nothing will be done. The Authority must be absolute in certain areas.

Private Self: How does this square with your lofty guarantee of private freedom to everyone?

Public Self: There is only one limit to private freedom: no new citizen can be created without permission.

Private Self: And who will grant permission?

Public Self: Geneticists, biologists, anthropologists, politicians, poets, philosophers . . . in a year one could get some kind of general agreement as to *how* to proceed. Later, decisions would be made

---

[8] believing that pleasure or happiness is the highest good
[9] believing that only the self exists, that reality is subjective

[10] workable; physically fitted to live
[11] a native peasant or laborer in Syria, Egypt, etc.

as to which types should be perpetuated and which allowed to die out. . . .

Private Self: I must say, not even the Nazis. . . .

Public Self: None of that! No demagoguery.[12] The Authority's aim is to preserve and strengthen human types through planned breeding. Eugenically,[13] we have had enormous success with everything from cattle to hybrid corn. So why not people? A family in which the members are prone to die of cancer at an early age shoud probably not be allowed to continue. . . .

Private Self: That means that John Keats would not be reproduced because he had a weak chest which his descendants might inherit, along with his genius. . . .

Public Self: What strains are best worth preserving I'm willing to leave to science . . . with a good deal of overseeing from other disciplines. Anyway, since we descend from common ancestors, no seed can ever die: all men are cousins.

Private Self: Save that for television. Incidentally, it will be decades—if ever—before sperm and ova can be matched outside the human body. . . .

Public Self: One must think in terms of decades as well as of today. In any case, the early stages should be simple. A moratorium[14] on births for a year. Then an inquiry into who would *like* to have children . . . a smaller group than you might think, particularly if the tribe no longer exalts the idea of reproducing oneself. After the last war the Japanese realized that if they were to survive they would have to reduce population. They did so by making it, literally, unfashionable to have large families; overnight they reversed the trend of centuries. It can be done.

Private Self: But only in a disciplined society like Japan. It would be impossible in our country. The United States man is conditioned from birth to think only of himself. To think of any larger unit is to fall victim to the international menace of communism.

Public Self: I suspect we shall probably have to write off the generations now alive. They cannot be changed. But the newborn can be instilled with a sense of urgency.

Private Self: Oh, yes. The newborn! How do you plan to bring up the children?

Public Self: At first in the usual way through the family . . . even though the family as we have known it is ending due to the pressures of urban life. Incidentally, contrary to current tribal superstition, the family is not a biological unit. It is an economic one whose deterioration began the day it became possible for women to work and bring up their children without men.

Private Self: With men or without, in the family or in a commune, someone is going to have to look after those few children that you will allow us. Who is that someone?

Public Self: Those best suited.

Private Self: Their parents?

Public Self: Probably not. Very few people are good parents, a fact most are willing to admit—too late.

Private Self: But aren't children psychologically damaged by being brought up communally. . . .

Public Self: Not necessarily. The recent confrontation between a number of American psychiatrists and the products of an Israeli kibbutz was revelatory. The men and women who had been raised communally were alarmingly "healthy."

Private Self: I daresay the end of the family will benefit humanity, but it will destroy the novel. . . .

Public Self: Don't worry. Mythmaking is endemic[15] to our race. Neurosis will simply take new forms.

Private Self: To get back to the Authority. Just who and what is it? And in the United States is it to be achieved through constitutional means?

Public Self: Ideally, the Authority and the Constitutional establishment should exist side by side, each complementing the other. Shabby as our democracy is, I think it a good idea to retain it.

Private Self: But the world is not ideal. President and Congress will not suffer the existence of an Authority over which they have no control.

Public Self: What about the C.I.A., the F.B.I. . . .

Private Self: Flip liberal cant.[16] Congress and President would want control. And once they had it, nothing would be accomplished. Can you imagine those Senators who are in the pay of the oilmen allowing the combustion engine to be superseded?

Public Self: Ultimate power must reside in the Authority.

[12] appealing to prejudices and passions
[13] relating to the production of desirable physical specimens through selective breeding
[14] suspension; temporary cessation of action
[15] within or peculiar to a people
[16] insincere statements, especially conventional pretense of enthusiasm for high ideals

210

Private Self: Dictatorship?

Public Self: Yes. But involving only those things that affect the public at large: environment, food, population. . . .

Private Self: Do you really think it possible to order totally the economic and biological life of a country and yet not interfere in the private lives of its citizens?

Public Self: Why not?

Private Self: Because no dictatorship has ever confined itself to the public sector. Sooner or later the dictator. . . .

Public Self: The Authority is not a dictator but a changing group of men, representing the widest and most divergent interests. . . .

Private Self: Too wide and too divergent and it won't function. . . .

Public Self: All interests will be subordinate to the stated aims of the Authority. Those aims will not be open to dispute.

Private Self: Like "Marxism" in one-party states? I would think that whoever or whatever controls the public life of a society will automatically control the private sector.

Public Self: Obviously there will be a constant tension between public and private necessities. And it is possible that the private will lose. It usually does in authoritarian societies. But then it does not do very well in libertarian ones either. Witness the small-town American's terror of his neighbors' opinion. However, the one novelty I offer is a clear demarcation between public and private. The state may not intrude upon private lives as it does now. And private lives may not intrude upon the public welfare as they do now. And what is "good" and "bad" for the society's welfare will be set down with a minimum of ambiguity.

Private Self: I find your Authority a potential nightmare. The world is already shrinking. Soon there will be no escape from the managers with their Telexes and computers. No border to cross. No place to hide.

Public Self: I am as alarmed as you by a world in which it is altogether too easy for the managers to have their way. And not only through instant communications but through mind-altering drugs and genetic rearrangements of the unborn. . . .

Private Self: Genetic rearrangement! That ought to appeal to you: men bred to be gods, but *whose* gods?

Public Self: Something to brood on. Anyway, I do see the end of the *laissez-faire* society. Quasi-democracies like England and the United States are already moving toward totalitarianism—of Left or Right makes no difference. The result is the same: the control of the individual. Wanting to bolster currency, the British curtail travel and thus limit freedom. Our poor, needless to say, are quite as enslaved as they were when their ancestors built the Pyramids. In fact, they are worse off because technical means now exist for the state to control all its citizens simultaneously. The true nightmare is not the Authority. It is the popular television performer who will subvert the state simply for something to do. . . .

Private Self: That's you. Don't deny it!

Public Self: I confess that if it weren't for you, I might give it a try.

Private Self: I'll bet you would! And we'd both be shot down, probably on *The Tonight Show*.

Public Self: Since an authoritarian society is inevitable, I am for accepting it but only in order to achieve certain goals. Once they are achieved. . . .

Private Self: The Authority will wither away?

Public Self: Hopefully. But of course it will not. Something else will take its place. But that is far in the future.

Private Self: Exactly how is the Authority to come into existence?

Public Self: A Party for Human Survival must be formed in the United States, and elsewhere. Naturally—again ideally—it would be best if the Authority were voted into power by a majority. With proper education, through television, it could happen. . . .

Private Self: But if not?

Public Self: Then the Party will seize power and establish the Authority by force.

Private Self: You see yourself as Lenin?

Public Self: With you on my back, I am a natural victim. Anyway, if it does not happen, a *mindless* authority will come into being, one dedicated not to human survival but simply to its own aggrandizement,[17] and we shall perish.

Private Self: What is wrong with that? It is not written in stars that we endure for all eternity. So why not let it end? The way it does for each of us. I have known from birth that when I die the world ends, too.

Public Self: For us it ends. But there are others.

---

[17] increased power

Education for Privacy

MARTEN TEN HOOR

In view of the hundreds of conferences which have been held on liberal education, it would seem to be impossible to say anything new on the subject. Since there seems to be nothing new to say, one must, in order to be original, be contrary, eccentric or partisan. I have chosen to be partisan.[1] The proposition to be defended is, frankly, a half-truth. If it can be established, there will be some cause for satisfaction; for the establishment of a half-truth is not a bad average in this complex and confused world. There is the justification, moreover, that the other, and possibly the better, half has in our day had practically all of the attention.

Stated concretely, the proposition is this: Never in the history of the world have there been so many people occupied with the improvement of so few. To sharpen the point by a specific example: Never have there been so many people making a good living by showing the other fellow how to make a better one. If you are skeptical, I recommend that you try this exercise—add up, as of the current date, the social workers, planners and reformers; the college presidents, deans and professors; the editors of magazines, journals and newspapers (not forgetting college newspapers); almost everybody in Washington, D. C., during recent years; and the tens of thousands of miscellaneous social-minded folks who attend conferences, workshops and institutes organized for the improvement of the human race. Subtract that figure from the total population of this country, and compare this figure with a corresponding figure for, say, the year 1900. You will then see

what I mean when I say that this is the era of undiscriminating allegiance to good causes. To come nearer home, compute the sum of all college and university presidents, deans and professors who have in the last five years attended meetings devoted to the improvement of education. Compare that figure with the number of those who remained on the campus working and you will find proof even *in academia*.

As further evidence, and as a striking symptom, there is the recent popularity of educational surveys. Most states and many institutions have experienced several. I have lived through eleven, without noticeable improvement in myself or my neighbors. Note the procedure and the technique, for there you will find the moral. The surveyors are always from another state or another institution. This is in accordance with the well-known principle that an expert is an ordinary person who is away from home. These outsiders are brought in because of their objectivity, objectivity being the capacity for discovering faults abroad which you cannot recognize at home. To be a good educational surveyor—or any kind of social analyst, for that matter—you must have a sharp eye for foreign motes[2] but a dull one for domestic beams. You must be a contented extrovert, so that, after diagnosing the faults of others, you can continue to live in perfect comfort with your own.

I must confess that I view all this indiscriminate altruism[3] with a jaundiced eye. It does seem to me that these days there are too many leaders and too few followers; too many preachers and too few sinners—self-conscious sinners, that is. If this were an illustrated article, I would insert at this point a wonderful cartoon I saw not long ago. A little boy was asking an obviously astounded and embarrassed father, "But if we're here to help others, what are the others here for?" Nobody has time these days to improve himself, so busy is he with attempts to improve his neighbor. There is something wrong with that equation. It seems to me that it is time to try to balance it. I suggest that this can be done by shifting some weight from one side to the other, by shifting the emphasis from social improvement to self-improvement. I suggest that over the door of every academic cubicle there should hang the sign which Thoreau had over the door of his hut: "*My* destiny mended here, not yours." In

[1] supporting a cause

Originally published in **The American Scholar**, Volume 23, 1953–54. Reprinted by permission of Mrs. Marten ten Hoor.

[2] insignificant specks of dust
[3] selfless devotion to the welfare of others

short, I propose to make a plea for *education for privacy.*

Before undertaking to identify some of the elements of this type of education, I should like to offer some justification of my skepticism concerning the present emphasis on social-mindedness in education. To begin with, it is so easy to assume that your neighbor is much worse off than yourself. The universality of this tendency is undoubtedly accounted for psychologically by its attractive by-products. The assumption produces a feeling of comfort. If there is some slight suspicion that all is not well within, it is compensating to concentrate on the plight of one's neighbor. Since attention to him is distracting, it keeps the individual from worrying about himself. To do something about a neighbor's ignorance also makes one feel virtuous. This absorbing concern for the improvement of one's neighbor is undoubtedly a product of civilization. It is doubtful if primitive man worried much about it. The cannibal, in fact, represents the other extreme: he uses his neighbor solely for his own improvement.

"Nobody has time these days to improve himself, so busy is he with attempts to improve his neighbor."

In the second place, I doubt if the reformer always has the wisdom necessary to direct the lives of so many people—but this is certainly assumed. How many people are there who have demonstrated the capacity to prescribe for others? If an individual makes a mistake in trying to improve himself, this is not so serious; but consider the consequences if he has induced all his neighbors to do the same thing. History is filled with examples of self-confident leaders who led their followers straight to a common catastrophe. The fact is that we still know so little about human personality in the concrete. To be sure, there are excellent textbook pictures, with revealing analytical tables and graphs. But this is personality in the abstract. Any physician will tell you that he rarely finds a textbook picture in a patient. Not only is every human being a complex with variations, but there are the environment in which that complex functions and the accidental circumstances which confuse the vision and disrupt life.

Nor has the reformer too much reason for assuming that he has discerned the good life for his neighbors. Let us take as a familiar example the characteristic projection by parents into the lives of their children. This is something we can readily understand and, because it is suffused with parental affection, forgive. But how many parents are there who realize that each child is to some extent a new complex of elements and who can bring themselves to substitute that confounding reality for the fond subjective creation? Too often the recommendation of a way of life is nothing more than the advocacy of a personal preference.

From subjectivism in this sense of the term there is no complete escape. Even leadership is personalized in an individual. Hitler was an individual: he spun his fantastic and criminal notions out of his own warped private personality. It is therefore terribly important that everything shall be right in the reformer before he undertakes to reform others. "Nobody," says a character in Norman Douglas' *South Wind*, "has the right to call himself well disposed towards society until he has grasped the elementary fact that the only way to improve society is to improve oneself." And may I suggest in this connection that a major in the social sciences does not automatically qualify a student for social leadership?

Further reason for doubt is to be found in the characteristic reactions of the hypersocial-minded. They become so indignant when people resist their ministrations.[4] They are so determinedly selfish in their unselfishness. Ideas, particularly ideas designed for the improvement of others, so quickly become inflated. In extreme cases they devour themselves. How antagonistic even educators become over professional differences as to how the ignorant should be rendered less so! Note the bitterness between rival reform groups. Let us not forget that human beings have killed one another in the mass even on the authority of their religions. Note how political leaders fall out, quarrel, conspire, injure one another in their unselfish efforts to save the country. In the absence of sophistication and modesty, reform notions grow into delusions; their advocates become more and more autocratic; leadership becomes

4 help

pathological; the desire to help one's fellow-men is transformed into fanaticism and tyranny—and societies become authoritarian.

Here lies the explanation of the tendency of hypersocial-mindedness to suppress individualism and to produce too much uniformity. There are good reasons for doubting the wisdom of this lack of interest in the individual as a unique personality. There is, to begin with, the obvious and inescapable fact that everybody is an individual. The higher the scale of life, the more individuals differ and the greater their potentialities for differing. Society must make provision for individual differences. Authoritarianisms of the type of national socialism and communism are primitivistic, for they propose to turn back the course of social change and to establish societies in which individuals shall have a status more closely resembling that of ants, bees, or even of atoms or electrons than of human personalities. They have forgotten, or propose to ignore, the incontrovertible[5] fact that the great works of art, literature, music, philosophy, religion and science—that is, the world's great manifestations of excellence and leadership—were the products of intensely individual persons. Indeed, some of the world's great geniuses have been self-centered, unsocial and iconoclastic,[6] with little or no interest in the improvement of their fellow-men.

But society can well afford that. A regimented society will not only suppress and possibly ultimately breed out these "exaggerated" individuals, but will generally discourage the manifestations of the adventurous and original spirit. Government and education designed to do this will bring about a tragic cultural impoverishment in human life; for individual differences enrich life, they stimulate the intelligence and the imagination, and they invite comparison and criticism. They keep the individual alive *as an individual*, and not merely as a bearer of the racial genius or a servant of the state.

It is true that modern life requires a certain amount of regimentation. Individuals obviously cannot be permitted to run amuck. At least the great majority of persons must adapt themselves to other persons. Mechanical contrivances, such as traffic lights, must replace individual judgment; laws are to some extent substitutes for individual choice. But let us not forget that it is not the basic purpose of these substitutes to repress individuality, but rather to make possible a more general and richer realization of individuality. It is not the purpose of social organization to reduce man to the subhuman, but to create more favorable opportunities for the realization of what is uniquely human.

The need of complex societies for a high degree of organization is one reason why so much attention is focused on the improvement of the other fellow. Especially in a democracy, where everyone is more or less free to advocate schemes for the improvement of society, lively and self-confident minds are inclined to expend their intellectual and emotional potential on reform movements. The attention of the reformer is consequently drawn away from contemplation of the state of his own soul. Since he is so happily exercised in improving others, the habit of self-examination gradually atrophies.[7] How then can he be sure that he is the right person to prescribe for his neighbors? Should he not stop now and then to take an inventory of his resources? Does he in fact have these resources? It is because I have serious doubts of this sort, and because of the increasing neglect in education of attention to the accumulation of these resources, that I feel it time to make a plea for education for privacy.

What now are the essential elements of this education for privacy? In speaking of elements it is of course implied that the ideal construct of these elements constitutes an organized whole, a personality. It is this ideal at which we aim, though we know full well that in any concrete individual, no matter how well educated after the formula which we shall propose, one or the other desirable characteristic is certain to be under- or overemphasized.

The first requirement, clearly, is to learn how to think—not out loud or in print, but privately. The thinker himself, not his neighbor, is to be the beneficiary. To think does not mean to spend hours in idle daydreaming or in vagrant imaginings, or to make occasional impulsive sallies at ideas which happen to appear before the attention. The reference is certainly not to the semi-

[5] undeniable
[6] attacking cherished beliefs and institutions

[7] withers away

somnolent[8] and comfortable ruminations[9] which go on in the wandering mind of an inattentive student in the classroom. What is meant is systematic reflection, the constant purpose of which is to bring order out of the multiplicity and variety of things in which the human being is immersed.

To be sure, many people go through life with their senses alert, observing and savoring in generous measure the richness of the world about them. But what they experience they retain only in the form of materials for recollection. The mind gradually accumulates a rich inventory of goods, which can be brought out on display when there is social opportunity for it. But the relationship of these resources in the mind is one of mere contiguity,[10] like that of goods in a department store. Experience has not resulted in an over-all understanding because it has not been systematically thought about. Such individuals

> . . . see all sights from pole to pole,
>   And glance, and nod, and bustle by,
> And never once possess [their] soul
>   Before [they] die.

To possess one's soul in an intellectual sense means to have found some answer, or partial

8 sleepy
9 meditations
10 nearness

answer, to the questions: What is the nature of this world in which I find myself, what is my place in it, and what must be my attitude toward it? The problem is one of intellectual and spiritual orientation.

The benefits of such intellectual and spiritual adaptation have been extolled by the wise men of all ages and all countries. A "view of life" prepares us for what life brings us, for what happens to us in our physical environment, and most important of all, for what people turn out to be and for what they do. To be spiritually and intellectually lost in the world, on the contrary, is to be unarmed and helpless. A disorganized mind is unprepared for reality and easily frustrated. The fate that awaits the individual so afflicted is to be always a stranger and a wanderer in the world. The "lost soul" of literature, the ultimate in tragic creation, suffers from this great spiritual illness.

It may be unfortunate, but it is a fact that the sharper and livelier the intelligence and the more sensitive the spirit, the more serious the danger of disorientation. The simple-minded find life simple. Plants find themselves easy to live with, no doubt; for it cannot be difficult to vegetate successfully. It is not likely that the cow's ruminations are philosophical. Man, for better or worse, is a rational animal. The more he thinks, the greater the need of organization among his ideas. The more subjects a student studies in college, the more extensive the potential disorder of his mind. It is not surprising that the scholarly mind, lost in a Babel of learning, seeks escape into a clearly defined speciality, and the practical mind, as soon as its owner has permission, into the comforts of a business, a profession, or domesticity. To be sure, we must integrate the curriculum. But what good is this if the professor's mind remains perched on its gaunt pinnacle or secluded in the laboratory?

*T*he systematic way to the attainment of the organization of ideas is through philosophy and religion. It is true that the great intellectual constructions of the metaphysicians[11] are not available to all men, and that even to the initiated they sometimes offer but poor comfort. Moreover, all of us have known individuals of great simplicity and humbleness of mind, quite untutored in dia-

11 loosely, all speculative philosophers

lectic,[12] who somehow and in the simplest terms have securely located themselves in the cosmos.[13] Especially in the realm of religious experience do we find examples of this. The spirit seems to have found peace in terms of some all-embracing conviction or great renunciation. But this is not often possible for the inquisitive and analytical mind. To cast all burdens upon the Lord in one grand resolve sometimes implies ignorance of the nature of those burdens. There is only consciousness of their oppressive weight, but no understanding of their nature or causes. To be sure, the critical intelligence may also come ultimately to make this renunciation, but it will not feel justified in doing so until it has reflected upon causes and relationships and seen the problem of human trouble and sorrow *whole*. The solution must be a conquest, not an escape.

For this, the mind certainly needs philosophy, sacred or secular. No learned profession, however, can offer the inquiring mind an official formula which every man need only apply in order to be permanently on understanding terms with the world. To be sure, there are systems of metaphysics, sacred and secular, from which the troubled spirit can choose a ready-made synthesis. But this does not make the chosen system of ideas an integral part of the inner personality. Intellectual orientation to the world must be something more than an acquisition; it must be an organic growth. The student should by all means seek out the great religious and philosophical thinkers, study their systems, and add their insights to his own. But in the last analysis he must work out his own solution, for such a solution must be the end product of his *own* reflection in the context of his *own* experience. Only through the alchemy[14] of private reflection do philosophical ideas become private resources. Only then will they be available in time of crisis. When the normal course of existence is interrupted by conflict and frustration, it is a bit late to begin developing fundamental guiding ideas; that is the time to apply them.

A dramatic example of the saving grace of such resources is related by Admiral Byrd in his book on his expedition to the South Pole, entitled *Alone*. He had been left behind by the expedition in a dugout located several feet below the surface of the icecap. From this he periodically emerged through a vertical tunnel to make scientific observations. It happened that the heater in his subterranean shelter developed a leak of which he was not aware. Before he realized it, he had been dangerously poisoned and he became seriously ill. During his convalescence he found himself struggling to overcome not only the physical damage done to his body, but also a deep spiritual depression, an obstinate conviction of the meaninglessness of life, which threatened to overwhelm him. There was no physician or psychoanalyst or cleric available. His fellow-explorers would not return for months. He was absolutely *alone*. He had to guide himself out of this slough of despair. This he did, after many agonizing days, by steady thinking, by "digging down into" his intellectual resources. And it was then, to use his own homely but vivid phrase, that he "uncovered the pay-dirt of philosophy." He did not then collect the materials of his readjustment; he used them to recover his sanity. In this crisis, what would he have done without these resources?

But periods of crisis are not the only time when man needs an orderly mind. If a ship is to hold its course it needs a steady helm in good weather as well as in bad. I hasten to remark that this figure of speech has serious limitations, for a navigator has his chart prepared when he begins his voyage. Man, on the contrary, is faced with the problem of making a chart as he goes along. As a matter of fact, the plan of life is for every man to some extent an unconscious precipitate[15] of his experience. We are not completely free agents: compulsion and fate, in the form of the physical world, our fellow-men and social institutions, push the individual this way and that. What happens to him and what he becomes are clearly the result of a complex of inner and outer compulsions, over many of which he has no control.

We are not here primarily concerned with action, however, but with interpretation. In philosophical reflection, the individual to some extent plays the part of the Greek chorus. He observes himself as actor in a cosmic setting. If he does so systematically, he will gradually discern not only his own role, but the direction of the whole drama. Only when he understands the meaning of the

[12] logical argument
[13] the universe considered as an orderly system
[14] loosely, transformation

[15] product, result, or outcome

play can he orient himself in it. Such an understanding, vague and incomplete though it may be, will enable him to achieve his own view of life. If he is so fortunate as to see (what seems to him) the truth and to see it whole, he will thenceforth have a vision of the future as well as an understanding of the present and the past. If a rational man does not do that, why should he consider himself the crown of creation? If he does accomplish this, he can exult with poet Dyer:

> My mind to me a kingdom is;
> Such present joys therein I find
> As far exceeds all earthly bliss
>
> .   .   .
>
> Look, what I lack my mind supplies.
> Lo, thus I triumph like a king,
> Content with that my mind doth bring.

*I*n education for privacy, however, more is involved than philosophical orientation to the cosmos. There is equally urgent need for education in the establishment and maintenance of moral harmony. From the days of primitive religion, through Greek tragedy, the Christian epic of sin and salvation, and modern psychology, Freudian and non-Freudian, to contemporary existentialism, there runs the theme of the uneasy conscience. The dramatic specter[16] of moral guilt is the principal character in many of the greatest creations of literary genius. No matter what the learned explanation, the psychological state is one of inner moral disharmony. Though it may have outer causes, it is a private affliction and must be cured privately. In moments of despair or periods of cynicism we may doubt the existence or discernibility of moral meaning in the universe; but such a conclusion does not relieve the individual of the necessity for solving his personal moral problem. Even complete moral negativism, if not itself a moral philosophy, leaves the individual no recourse but to establish a private moral order in his life of action and reflection.

Here again, the more sensitive the individual, the greater the potentiality for disorganization. It is the sensitive who are the most deeply wounded by moral indifference, disorder and brutality. The predisposing causes of moral disorganization may be in the people and the things we love, in the institutions which demand that

---

[16] ghost or apparition

we conform to their customs and taboos, in the great world which so often mocks our need for moral significance and order. But a vision of the good life, the spirit must have; for devoid of it, the imagination is without moral perspective, conduct without guiding principles, and action without trustworthy habits. For an individual so unprepared for life, confusion will efface meaning and create frustration, with the onset in the case of the unusually sensitive spirit of pathological disturbances which may for a period or for a lifetime destroy happiness. Education for privacy must therefore include the education of the moral personality, the gradual acquisition by the self of moral resources. Here, too, there are available to the student in generous measure the works of the great philosophical and religious thinkers, for probably no one of the persistent problems of life has had more of their systematic and concentrated attention. It is relevant here to note that the previously discussed philosophical orientation to the world is sometimes the foundation for moral orientation.

A third requirement in the education of the personality is the development of emotional stability. Of all the immediate causes of unhappiness, emotional disorder is unquestionably the most serious and the most common. Currently there is a feeling that under the pressures of modern life its incidence is steadily increasing. Unfortunately, emotions are the component of the personality about which we know the least, as modern science has come to realize. Our ignorance is largely a consequence of the fact that traditionally the emotions have been considered to be effects rather than causes. Preoccupation with the flattering conviction that man is a rational animal has been attended with the assumption that therefore our emotions are under the domination of the reason. This assumption has been one of the basic tenets of formal education, though puzzled parents and self-conscious adults no doubt have all along had their suspicions. In our day, educators are being enlightened by psychology and the medical sciences on the subject of the devastating power of the emotions. Moreover, the modern conception of the integrated personality has redirected our approach to this subject, so that now we hypothesize and investigate in terms of interrelations and interactions. The simple classical vision of the reason enthroned in the psyche, making judgments, issuing commands, and directing the conscious life of the individual, is difficult to maintain in the face of the past record and the current spectacle of human behavior.

Let us grant that the contemporary individual lives in an age in which, as Goethe put it, "humanity twists and turns like a person on a sickbed trying to find a comfortable position." To offset this, however, he has the advantage of a better understanding of the compulsive and disruptive power of the emotions. He is aware of their insidious tendency to direct his thinking and affect his judgment. He knows that they feed on themselves and that, if they are of the destructive kind, they can bring him to the verge of despair. He knows that they can completely disorient him, isolating him from the friendship and sympathy of his fellow-men and estranging him from the beauty and utility of the world. He must learn that there is little he can do to remove the external causes, the irritants in his social and physical environment. In order to maintain or restore emotional stability *within* himself, he must learn to control the effects of these irritants *on* himself. Education of the emotions is education in self-control, in equanimity[17] and serenity.

To these three objectives of education for privacy—the attainment of a philosophical point of view, a steady vision of the good life, and serenity of spirit—I should like to add one more: the individual should be able to live entertainingly with himself. He should accumulate resources on which he can draw when he is at leisure. The universal symptom of the absence of such resources is the homely but hapless[18] state of boredom. It is an anomalous[19] condition of the spirit, a state of indifference lying between pain and pleasure. Neither the mind nor the hands can find anything interesting to do. In contrast with the other troubles of the spirit which have been mentioned, there is little excuse for this great emptiness. For there is a marvelous cure for boredom, universally available, readily tapped and virtually inexhaustible: the fine arts.

This claim hardly needs defense. Nor is it necessary to enumerate the arts and to identify their respective potentialities for beguiling the mind and the heart. For illustrative purposes, however,

[17] composure or calmness
[18] unfortunate
[19] abnormal

let us consider one form of art enjoyment which is available to virtually every normal human being, young or old, learned or simple, saint or sinner—reading. Its great virtue for education for privacy is that it is a strictly private experience. No other human being is necessary to the reader at the moment of reading. He can take his book with him to the jungle or the desert, on the ocean or the mountain top. He can select his company at will, and rid himself of it by a turn of the hand. It is potentially an inexhaustible resource: all ages of history; all countries; all varieties of human beings, and even of animals and plants and physical things; the entire range of human thoughts and feelings, hopes and fears, conquests and failures, victories and defeats; the real and the ideal—all are available at the turn of a page for the reader's contemplation and understanding.

When we measure the impoverishment of him to whom this world is literally and figuratively a closed book, whose ear is deaf to music and whose eye blind to the glories of painting and sculpture, we come to realize the responsibility of liberal education for instruction in the arts. I say instruction purposely, because I believe that the presentation of opportunities for enjoyment and training in appreciation are not enough: there should also be instruction and encouragement in the production of art. As even the bungling amateur knows, there is no greater source of pleasure than creative activity. The training of the most modest talent is an enrichment of a personality and develops another private resource for leisure hours. Even the unsuccessful attempt to create art, moreover, clarifies the understanding of art. To be sure, just as it is not necessary to trouble our friends with our thoughts, so it is not necessary to bore our friends with our productions. It is, after all, not the improvement of the neighbor but the improvement of oneself that is the immediate object of education for privacy.

> "To restore the individual to his former dignity as a human being is the urgent need of the day."

An understanding of the world, a vision of the good life, serenity of spirit, appreciation and practice of the fine arts—these, then, are the elements of the integrated personality, the development of which is the immediate object of liberal education. These are the resources which are accumulated in the course of education for privacy. Why, now, is it so important for every individual to possess these resources? In the first place, simply because he is going to need them. We never know when we are going to lose our external resources, our public possessions. Without private resources the individual has nothing to turn to when disappointment, frustration or misfortune become his lot. In the great depression which is still vivid in our memories, there were many individuals who possessed only external resources. When they lost these, life was over for them. They could not go on living with themselves because of their intellectual, moral, emotional and artistic poverty. He who possessed these resources, however, could exclaim with Thoreau: "Oh, how I laugh when I think of my vague, indefinite riches! No run on the bank can drain it, for my wealth is not possession but enjoyment."

Resources of the spirit are like savings: they must be accumulated before they are needed. When they are needed, there is no substitute for them. Sooner or later, the individual faces the world alone, and that moment may overwhelm him if he has no resources within himself. Distraction helps but little and betrays us when we least expect it. We can escape our physical environment and our neighbors, but we cannot escape ourselves. Everyone with any maturity of experience and self-knowledge knows that the loneliest moments are sometimes experienced in the midst of the greatest crowds and the most elaborate entertainments. "... the man at war with himself is at war, though he sits in a garden surrounded by flowers and singing birds," says the novelist Cloete in *Congo Song*.

And now, in conclusion, I wish again to pay my respects to the other half-truth, the improvement of others, which was so cavalierly dismissed in the beginning of this essay. That objective together with the other objective, self-improvement, compose the whole truth, which is the grand objective of liberal education. Education for privacy and education for public service constitute education of the whole personality. He who is not educated for privacy is hardly fit to educate others. The blind cannot lead the blind. The man who is not at peace with himself cannot be trusted to lead his fellow-men in the ways of peace. The unbalanced leader is certain to unbalance the society in which he functions. Even the leader who is in intent on the side of the good but who is a fanatic will stimulate fanaticism in his followers, arouse dogmatism and bigotry, and induce oppression and cruelty. When he is on the side of evil, he will lead his followers into such excesses and wickedness as will shame all humanity, and which even the innocent will wish to forget as soon as possible. Social pathology must in the last analysis be focused on the sickness of the individuals who compose the society. It is pure imagination, if not nonsense, to ascribe the ignorance, unbalance and wickedness of a collection of human beings to a mysterious social entity such as the group mind or the social organism. We might as well divorce the concept of an epidemic from the notion of the individuals who are ill, or ascribe hunger to a societal stomach. People mislead one another exactly as they infect one another. The psycho-pathic leader is potentially as dangerous as the carrier of an infectious disease.

The safe leader, in terms of the elements of education for privacy, is one who understands his place in the world and can thus envisage the place of his fellow-men; who can morally respect himself and can thus be respected by others; who has learned to control his emotions and can thus be trusted to exert control over others; who has learned to live in peace and contentment with himself and can thus with propriety urge others to do likewise.

We are living in a world and in a time when powerful leaders with millions of fanatical followers are committed to the forcible regimentation of their fellow-men, according to formulas which have no initial authority but that of their own private dogmatism. They not only refuse to recognize the right of private thought and personal conscience to be considered in the management of public affairs, but they have abolished the concept of the individual as a private personality and have reduced him to the level of the bee in the hive. To restore the individual to his former dignity as a human being is the urgent need of the day. This, in my opinion, should be the special objective of contemporary education.

But liberal education must so educate the individual that he is manifestly worthy of having his dignity recognized. If he wishes to lead his fellows, he must first learn to lead himself. Without education for privacy he will neither merit leadership nor learn to recognize it in others. He will strive in vain for happiness and success in private or public life until he has achieved understanding, goodness, serenity, and contentment within himself. That, according to my exegesis,[20] is in this connection the meaning of the Biblical text: "For what is a man profited, if he shall gain the whole world, and lose his own soul?" It is surely what Thomas Hardy meant when he wrote:

> He who is with himself dissatisfied,
> Though all the world find satisfaction in him,
> Is like a rainbow-coloured bird gone blind,
> That gives delight it shares not.

[20] interpretation

Violence:
A Neglected Mode
of Behavior

BRUNO BETTELHEIM

These violent delights have violent ends.

Romeo and Juliet

Aggression is by now a respectable object of study among students of human behavior. But in this paper I should like to refer to violence, which the same scholars tend to ignore or else treat with contempt. I may even share their contempt. But simply agreeing that violence is bad resolves nothing. To study aggression in detail while we close our eyes to its source is like wishing to clean out all filth without soiling our hands. If we are serious about understanding aggression and its role in society we have to start with a good look at the desire to do violence. Robert Ardrey, whose *African Genesis* found deservedly widespread attention,* makes the important point that Cain, and not Abel, is the father of man. If we are children of Cain, it behooves[1] us to know Cain well, to examine carefully his behavior and what causes it, and not to look away in disgust. The good friar of Verona knew that violent delights have violent ends. But if they were not delights, would we not shun them, since we all know they lead to disaster?

Man and society were born out of both: violence and gentle co-operation. To neglect either wellspring of life in our efforts to better human relations will be fruitless. In this paper I use aggres-

sion and violence as terms so closely related as to be interchangeable. I intend it as an invitation to study violence seriously, and not to stop short at its milder form, aggression.

VIOLENCE AND HEROES

One of our best literary critics, Robert Warshaw, wrote a defense of the Western movie, in particular of the gunfighter as moral hero.† This assertion is startling, since few of us would accept the cowboy in the Western as our moral hero, or gunfighting as an ideal way to solve moral problems. But let us remember that the sword-bearing Achilles stands as *the* moral hero at the beginning of Western civilization. Because of distance in time, the vast difference in settings, and our veneration[2] of *The Iliad*, it is often difficult to recognize what Simone Weil was the first to point out—that *The Iliad* is a poem of violence.‡ Violence there was before Homer. But with him appears the new civilizing Greek spirit, and this he casts into his poems. The new attitude he represents is that violence is the central problem to be dealt with in a world striving to be civilized and that nothing good ever comes of violent means. Paris, who broke violently the peace of Menelaus' home, has to perish. So does the greatest hero, Achilles, who tried to join the avenging party, not to speak of the fate of Agamemnon.

The human race, in *The Iliad*, is not divided into victorious heroes and victims. If there were conquering heroes, violence might even seem justified, at least to the victors. But in the course of *The Iliad*, if the Greeks win one day, the Trojans do the next, and in the end all of them perish. In this poem there is not a single man who does not, at one time or another, have to bow his neck to force. That the use of violence leads to retribution,[3] with almost geometric rigor—this was a main subject of Greek thought; it is the soul of *The Iliad*. Therefore, our first great epic impresses on us that we have to think seriously of what our inner and outer attitudes to violence should be. It may also explain the gunfighter of the Western film as a moral hero—why he has taken such hold of our

* Robert Ardrey, *African Genesis* (New York: Atheneum, 1961).

[1] is right or fitting

From **The Annals of the American Academy of Political and Social Science,** 1966. Reprinted by permission of the author and The American Academy of Political and Social Science.

† Robert Warshaw, *The Immediate Experience* (Garden City, N.Y.: Doubleday, 1962).

‡ Simone Weil, "The Iliad, or the Poem of Force," *Politics* (November 1945).

[2] respect or reverence for

[3] paying back

imagination, and not only among youngsters but also among grownups.

This condition exists, Warshaw thinks, chiefly because the Western

offers a serious orientation to the problem of violence such as can be found almost nowhere else in our culture. One of the well-known peculiarities of modern civilized opinion is its refusal to acknowledge the value of violence. . . . We train ourselves to be shocked or bored by cultural images of violence, and our very concept of heroism tends to be a passive one: we are less drawn to the brave young men who kill large numbers of our enemies than to the heroic prisoners who endure torture without capitulating.[4]

What we do seek in the Western is

the image of a single man who wears a gun on his thigh. The gun tells us that he lives in a world of violence, and even that he "believes in violence." But the drama is one of self-restraint: the moment of violence must come in its own time and according to its special laws, or else it is valueless. There is little cruelty in Western movies, and little sentimentality; our eyes are not focused on the sufferings of the defeated but on the deportment[5] of the hero.

Really, it is not violence at all which is the "point" of the Western movie, but a certain image of man, a style, which expresses itself most clearly in violence.

He is there to "suggest that even in killing or being killed we are not freed from the necessity of establishing satisfactory modes of behavior."

This, then, is our problem: to establish "satisfactory modes of behavior" though we live in a society where violence is rampant.[6] The gunfighter in the Western has found his solution to the problem. Obviously, it cannot be ours, but he at least, as Warshaw has shown, takes the problem seriously, and we ought to do the same.

VIOLENCE AND CHILD-REARING

Nowadays, parents receive a great deal of help in accepting their children's instinctual desires, as far as intake and elimination are concerned. Even about sexual behavior we tend to be more understanding, more accepting in our emotional attitudes. But as far as violence is concerned,

Freud might never have written *Civilization and its Discontents,* or have concluded it by saying:

The fateful question for the human species seems to me to be whether and to what extent their cultural development will succeed in mastering the disturbance of their communal life by the human instinct of aggression and self-destruction.

If this is the fateful question, and I certainly agree that it is, what measures are we taking to help our children do a better job of mastering the disturbance of their communal life that comes from the instinct of aggression? Freud certainly did not mean denial or suppression to be the answer, any more than he meant it for our sexual instincts. About these drives we have followed his teaching and try to be reasonable. We try to satisfy them within acceptable limits, so that they do not generate so much pressure as to cause explosive outbreaks or a crippling of the total personality. In regard to violence I find no such reasonable efforts.

Children are supposed neither to hit, nor to swear at their playmates. They are supposed to refrain from destroying their toys or other property—so far, so good. But what outlets for violence *do* we provide for them? As a matter of fact, in regard to violence, we are so unreasonable that here is where the parent is apt to resort to violence himself. Few children of the educated middle class are slapped for masturbating any more, though they are not exactly raised in sexual freedom. But let the same parent meet with violence in his youngster, and as likely as not he will slap the child or thunder at him, thus demonstrating that violence is all right if one is older and stronger, and makes use of it under the guise of suppressing it. So we end by using violence to suppress violence, and in doing so teach our children that, in our opinion, there is just no other reasonable or intelligent way to deal with it. Yet the same parents, at another moment, would agree that suppression is the worst way to deal with the instincts.

Unlike Wertham, who pleads for the suppression of vicious comics, I am convinced that neither comics nor television seduce the innocent.* It is high time that both the myth of original sin, and its opposite—that of original innocence—be dispatched to the land of the unicorns. Innocence is

---

[4] surrendering, giving up
[5] conduct or behavior
[6] widespread, unchecked

* F. Wertham, *Seduction of the Innocent* (New York: Rinehart, 1953).

221

neither an inborn characteristic nor a useful weapon; most of the time it is little more than an anxious clinging to ignorance.

Particularly in matters of violence is there no protection in ignorance. Elsewhere I have tried to point out that one's ignorance of the nature of violence, as during the Nazi regime, did not lead to bliss but to death.* Those under Hitler who wished to believe that all men are good, and that violence exists only in a few perverted men, took no realistic steps to protect themselves and soon perished. Violence exists, surely, and each of us is born with his potential for it. But we are also born with opposite tendencies, and these must be carefully nurtured if they are to counterbalance the violence. To nurture them, however, one must know the nature of the enemy, and this is not achieved by denying its existence.

What concerns me here is that, contrary to good therapy, Wertham attacks the symptom instead of the underlying disease. This error he did not make in *The Show of Violence*,† where he made exactly the opposite case: namely, that in the treatment of criminals it will not do to legislate against crime; that the only intelligent way to do away with crime is to do away with what breeds it. Comic books are apt to reinforce delinquent tendencies and to teach new and better ways of being delinquent. But then the basic issue is the delinquent tendencies, not the comics. And the case of the children merely reflects the pattern among adults.

Violence as normal behavior. We have abolished the red-light districts and outlawed prostitution. I am all for such progress, mainly because it offers the girls more protection from being exploited. But for those who cannot afford the call girl, we have closed off an easy way to discharge both sexual and violent tendencies. Worse, by asserting that there is no place for sex outside of marriage, and none for violence in our society, we force each individual to suppress his violent tendencies till they build up to a pitch where he can no longer deny them or control them. Then they suddenly erupt in isolated acts of explosive violence.

These outbursts are conspicuous. By their spectacular nature they even give the impression that ours is an age of violence. So we clamor for still greater suppression of even small eruptions of violence that could act as safety valves, draining off small amounts and leaving a balance that the individual could assimilate. Even among psychoanalysts, Freud's death instinct is not quite respectable, because we decree that what is supposed not to exist cannot and does not exist; all evidence to the contrary is simply disregarded as nonexistent.

What I believe is needed, instead, is an intelligent recognition of "the nature of the beast." We shall not be able to deal intelligently with violence unless we are first ready to see it as part of human nature, until we have gotten so well acquainted with it, by learning to live with it, that through a slow and tenuous process we may one day domesticate it successfully. In short, we cannot say that because violence *should* not exist, we might as well proceed as if it did not.

Violence is, of course, a short cut toward gaining an objective. It is so primitive in nature that it is generically[7] unsuitable to get for us those more subtle satisfactions we want. That is why it stands at the very beginning of man's becoming a socialized human being. It is not only the heroic sagas,[8] marking man's entry into the modern world, that are so dominated by themes of love and violence; it is true of our own entrance to life. The temper tantrum, so characteristic of the child about to become a complex human being, shows how the violent and destructive outburst heralds our coming ability to master inner drives and the external world.

Though we do not wish to acknowledge how normal this really is, many a birthday party of happy, normal children should teach us better. The birthday child, in his natural eagerness to get at the enticing present, will tear off the wrappings to get at the toy. And if the box he is ripping should be part of the game, so much the worse for the game. Thus desire begets violence, and violence may destroy the object desired. In this sense, as in many others, violence is both natural and ineffective. It rarely reaches its goal or else, in getting at it, destroys it. True, discharge itself is a

---

* B. Bettelheim, *The Informed Heart* (New York: Free Press, 1960).
† F. Wertham, *The Show of Violence* (Garden City, N.Y.: Doubleday, 1949).

[7] In this context he uses the word "generically" to mean that *by its nature* violence is too limited to be a suitable means of relating to men in a sophisticated, complex society.
[8] narratives of legendary or historical exploits

goal. But then we discharge the anger, and there is no further need to find out what caused it; it does nothing to prevent what enraged us from happening again.

To recount the evils of violence here is unnecessary. Having shown in my simple example that violence is a normal mode of human behavior, I shall say no more of its nature. Instead I shall consider whether our attitudes toward violence are reasonable, given our goal to contain it, and what ways might better serve our ends.

Gang warfare. Let me begin with the obvious, which is too often neglected when we think about violence. Whether or not it will be used or avoided depends entirely on what alternative solutions are known to a person facing a problem. Thus, violence is the behavior of someone who cannot visualize any other solution to a problem that besets him. It shows up clearest in gang warfare.

Today we are constantly bombarded by images of a life of ownership and consumption, but for a great number of people the means to consumership are slim. This is particularly true of many young people before they find a sure place in our economic system, and even more so for those from marginal or submarginal backgrounds. Yet they are told that without such things they cannot have a satisfying life. They feel helpless to provide themselves with what they feel is even a minimal satisfaction of the demands we create in them. But they see no alternative to reaching their goals except through violence, while the pressures of frustration only tempt them more to use it. Nothing in their education—and I shall return to this later—has equipped them to deal with violence, because in their whole educational life we have denied its existence.

Yablonsky, in an excellent analysis of what makes for the violent gang,[*] remarks with irony that their views and outlook, as in a nightmarish mirror, merely reflect back the official ethos.[9] The purpose of violence for the gang member is to achieve precisely what are the major values of respectable society: success and prestige in the eyes of one's peers. He quotes one homicidal youngster who explains his actions as follows: "I'm not going to let anybody be better than me

and steal my 'rep' (reputation). . . . When I go to a gangfight I punch, stomp and stab harder than anyone."

Yablonsky has correctly described what the violent act does for the doer. He says that the very fact that senseless, not premeditated violence is most respected by the gang shows the function that violence has for them. Despairing of alternative solutions, or, perhaps more correctly, convinced that for them no alternatives exist, they seek a quick, almost magical way to power and prestige. In a single act of unpremeditated intensity, they at once establish a sense of their own existence and forcefully impress this now valid existence on others.

Frustration and anxiety. Unfortunately, gang youth is merely one extreme of a situation that breeds violence, not only among gangs, but among normal, decent human beings. While similar situations exist all over the United States, I found the best account of it in Lewis' *Children of Sánchez*, the scene of which is laid in highly urban Mexico City. To understand fully what I mean, it will have to be read.[†]

Suffice it here to say that Jesus Sánchez, tied deep within himself to the communal ways of his old village life but wishing desperately to make a go of life in twentieth-century industrial society, is defeated again and again in his aspirations. Yet he is kept going, even driving himself beyond endurance, to see, at least, his children succeed in this world that is so alluring while it frustrates at every turn. Bewildering frustration and the fact that he can see no way out lead both him and his children to be violent, simply because they know of no alternative solution.

Nor is it only the lower-class world of the gang, or the children of Sánchez who share the feeling that no alternatives exist, no ways out. The whole of our society seems caught in a spirit of believing that we lack alternatives. "Red or dead" seems to be the slogan—either preparing for violence by creating weapons that are ever more destructive, or turning violence against the self: being ready to surrender without resistance to communism if it should knock at our door. And this anxiety about world affairs trickles down to college boards and grades and so on through the fabric of our lives.

---

[*] L. Yablonsky, "The Violent Gang," *Commentary*, XXX (August 1960), pp. 125–130.

[9] underlying and distinctive character or spirit

[†] O. Lewis, *The Children of Sánchez* (New York: Random House, 1961).

224 In the face of such persistent anxieties about success and survival, and by denying that violence is one way out, we fail to provide any safe or constructive channels for draining it off. Ours is by no means an age of greater violence than others—on the contrary. But the chances for discharging violent tendencies are now so severely curtailed that their regular and safe draining off is not possible any more. So the essential questions then are: How can violence be husbanded?[10] How can it be discharged in ways that are socially useful? Rural life before farming was mechanized offered the child at least a chance for vicarious discharge

[10] conserved, managed wisely

of violence. In my native Austria, slaughtering the pig was a distinct highlight in the lives of peasant children. But so were chopping wood and other forms of aggressive manipulation of nature which at least provided outlets that were socially useful and contributed to the well-being of the family. Moreover, such a discharge was safe; it aroused no counteraggression in the target.

Our competitive or spectator sports are no real substitute, because, in the first place, they raise the aggressive feelings of competition to the boiling point. And, secondly, for every time that one wins, one is likely to lose, and every lost game builds up more aggression than the player may have discharged in playing.

VIOLENCE AND EDUCATION

Having said this much, I must admit that I am at a loss to suggest what we should do. Maybe we should not go so far in suppressing violence in our children. Maybe we should let them experience—within safe limits—how damaging violence is, thus not denying them acquaintance with a tendency they must learn to control. But it is not the only way. If our experience at the Orthogenic School may serve as an example, children seem to want to learn *about* aggression, and not just to discharge it, though they want that too. Right now, the stories we teach them in class never contain any incidents of aggression. No child ever hits, becomes angry, or destroys things in an outburst. The worst they do is to tease or to pout. All of them live on Pleasant Street, in Friendly Town.

Maybe if our educational procedures were to acknowledge aggression, our children would not have to be glued to the television screen to see a bit of violence. Maybe there was some psychological wisdom to those old-fashioned readers where the child was told over and over what cruel fate befalls the evil-doer. While these stories scared the children, they allowed for some vicarious discharge of hostility, and, having discharged it, the children's positive tendencies could be freed for the learning process. We can do even better. We can tell children through stories that people are sometimes angry at each other and quarrel, but that they can make up, and that if they do they will have a better life together.

It is peculiar to our culture that, in pushing the competitive spirit to a pitch, we stress those aggressive emotions that power competition, though aggression itself is tabooed.[11] In a way we commit a parallel folly in our schools. But certainly one way to deal with anger is not to arouse it in the first place. Yet for quite a few children, our nice teaching materials do exactly that. Seeing pictures of the nice houses that other children have, when they themselves are living in slums, makes them angry.

How angry this makes some unfortunate children, so angry that they cannot learn, is taught us over and over by our children. One such child, who grew up in a variety of foster homes, was unable to learn and repeated first grade three times. While at the Orthogenic School, he finally was able to learn to read and print words as com-

plicated as *soldier, submarine, fireman* and *fighting* —all terms that were in line with his dominant feelings of hostility. But he still could not learn to read simple words like "come here," because no one had ever wanted him to come, or had lovingly called out to him.

Considering the number of adopted children who feel strongly about their natural parents having given them up, and considering also the number of children who have severe emotional difficulties with their parents, I wonder if the time has not come to add neutral stories to our primers. I mean stories where family relations are not touched upon, so that children who find them upsetting can learn to read more enjoyably without anger being aroused.

Once we do offer our children a chance to learn what is foremost in their minds, or I should say what is most deeply buried there, then they learn fast and furiously,* like the Maori children in Sylvia Ashton-Warner's novel, *Spinster*.† The heroine, a teacher, realized that these children wrote exciting stories of their own, only the titles of their stories were less apt to be "Fun With Dick and Jane" than "I Want You" or "I'm Scared." One of these Maori children, Tame, Wrote:

> I ran away from my
> mother and I hid
> away from my mother
> I hid in the Shed and
> I went home and
> got a hiding.

Having just read this, the teacher goes to the standard primer and turns curiously to the page from which this child was supposed to learn to read. There she finds the following story:

> Mother went to a shop.
> I want a cap, she said.
> I want a cap for John.
> She saw a brown cap.
> She saw a blue cap.
> I like the blue cap, she said.

---

11 forbidden as socially unacceptable

* This familiar construction, "learning fast and furiously," tells how well-known (though neglected) is the fact that we learn fast and well if, through the act of learning, we can also discharge fury, or "attack the problem," as we say.
† Sylvia Ashton-Warner, *Spinster, A Novel* (London: Secker & Warburg, 1958).

225

226 Irini, a six-year-old, asks the teacher to spell several words, and then writes with concentration. Finally she brings the teacher what she has written:

> Mummie said to Daddy
> give me that money else
> I will give you a hiding.
> Daddy swear ta Mummie
> Daddy gave the money
> to Mummie. We had
> a party. My father
> drank all the beer by
> hisself. He was drunk.

The teacher turns again to the primer and finds a story about parents:

> Look at the green house.
> Father is in it.
> It is father's home too.
>
> There is Mother
> She is in the green house.
> She can see us.
> Let us run to mother.

Compare the matter-of-fact acquaintance with aggression in these Maori tales with those in primers of the British dominions or our own up-to-date efforts.

Mrs. Ashton-Warner describes how she had to find what she calls "key words" in order to get her Maori children interested in reading and writing. Long before her, our children at the Orthogenic School forced us to similar conclusions. If we wanted them to learn, we, too, had to convince them that reading, writing, and spelling would help them with what concerned them most deeply. When we did that, children who for years had resisted learning even the simplest words, had been unable to learn to read from primers that pictured life in a single color—as all sweetness and light when their world was just as often drab and unhappy—these children were suddenly eager to read. Some of them who for years had not learned to read a single word then learned to recognize, read, and spell a hundred words or more in a couple of weeks' time.

When we felt they were ready for it—that is, when we felt that the resentment of learning built up through previous school experience had waned[12]—we introduced to them certain ideas, in

a short talk, in language they could understand. We told them that what is hardest to do—and the biggest problem in learning and living, but at the same time the most important one—is to master one's own scary ideas; that to learn words that help us separate the event of which we are afraid from what we only think about this event is greatly helpful. Because, while scary events that really happen are overpowering, our only thinking about them, or talking and reading about them, need not be. And in this way we come to understand them and learn to deal with them.

After such an explanation, three of our children picked as the first words they wanted to learn, *scary, fire,* and *hit*. To me it seems that in these three words our children, without knowing it, outlined a course on how to deal with aggression, at least in the classroom-learning situation. One word, *hit*, deals with animate aggression; the second, *fire*, with inanimate destruction; and the third, *scary*, with the outcome of aggression and destruction. If we permit them to state their aggressive tendencies, they can also come to recognize their scary character, and only this kind of recognition can lead to something better than denial and suppression. It can bring the conviction that in self-protection, and to avoid scary experiences, one must deal in constructive ways with the tendency to violence, both one's own and that of others.

A small sample of the emotionally charged words our children usually learn to read after seeing them once, and learn to spell and write after a few repetitions, are the following: *fire, knife, cut, crash, shoot, kill, hit, bite, teeth, cry, fight, jail, scream, yell.* Consider how much aggression they reveal, and the desire to learn about it. And compare these with what are generally considered easy words to learn.

It is just as enlightening to see how closely the words selected by our emotionally disturbed children compare with what Mrs. Ashton-Warner tells of her normal Maori children who were learning to read:

Rangi, who lives on love and kisses and thrashings and fights and fear of the police and who took four months to learn "come," "look," and "and," takes four minutes to learn: butcher-knife; gaol; police; sing; cry; kiss; Daddy; Mummie; Rangi; haka (a native word); fight.

Each of our children selected different words because what was emotionally significant to one

[12] diminished

was not so to the others. The interesting thing is that all children learned emotionally charged words, even ones not too meaningful to them, when they saw that they were charged words for another child. They shared not only learning but each other's emotions.

As we developed our method we realized that charged or scary words sometimes aroused too much emotion. We then devised many categories, only five of which I shall mention: scary words, not-nice words, nice words, warm words, and cold words. Maybe I should mention some of the nice words the children selected. They include things like *orange juice, milk, play,* and *hot dog.* And they tell us what experiences the children think are needed to counterbalance violence. In view of the fact that most primers concentrate on what we would call nice words, it might also be of interest that the children learn the not-nice and scary words much faster and more permanently than the nice words.

To make some comparison with "normal" learning: though our children do not, like Rangi in *The Spinster,* learn eleven words in four minutes, one of our boys who learned four nice words in one day, learned ten angry ones on the same day, including ones as difficult as *witch, tornado,* and *fighting.* Which shows how the wish to master what is important to us is a powerful motivating force for learning to read, whether important things happen to be pleasant or not. And that learning about violence makes for learning in general. Because learning what the world is really like means learning about emotions—and that includes violence and what it is really like. Mastery through understanding is still the best way to equip our children for dealing with their own tendencies to violence.

For this reason the recent heated discussions about Vietnam and related issues, pro and con, in public and at the dinner table, are a heartening sign. First, it brings into the open the ineffectiveness of violence as a way of ending our anxiety about nuclear war. And, second, it brings widespread attention to possible positive alternatives. In place of "red or dead," either one a defeat, it offers peace through compromise. And it documents how self-defeating a solution is force, since it can only bring a war in which nobody wins. "Thought," said a living British physicist,

is born of failure. Only when action fails to satisfy human needs is there ground for thought. To devote attention to any problem is to confess a lack of adjustment which we must stop to consider. And the greater the failure the more searching is the kind of thought which is necessary.*

It is good that we are thinking of alternatives to violence where our children can hear us.

* L. L. Whyte, *The Next Development in Man* (New York: New American Library, 1950).

In projecting into the future, it is natural to center attention on today's youth. Whether this influence will be for good or ill is hotly disputed, but among the writers represented here, the consensus is generally in favor of the young generation. When Faulkner delivered his address, the present rebelliousness had not surfaced, yet he acknowledged the same forces that grip youth today. The threat of annihilation is still a spectre. Indeed, Wald explains the turmoil among students as the result of a fear that there will be no future, that theirs may well be the last generation. The problems facing our country are not problems of youth but problems of all men. If we are to have a future, he says, we must rid ourselves of large standing armies and nuclear weapons.

Prognosis

Jack Newfield believes that the new young activists, particularly the New Left, will sting the conscience of the country until it rights the old wrongs. Goodman concurs that the influence of the young leaders generally is toward making a more decent society. But Boorstin sees today's activists and militants not as aristocrats or idealists but as new "barbarians" whose movements represent quests for power, not meaning. They are not true radicals, he argues, for their appeal to violence and direct action mask a lack of content or direction. They are self-centered, not community-centered, and their actions seem to him a withdrawal from society, not a shared concern for common human interests.

Finally, Harrington stands back and takes a wider view, bypassing many current issues and replacing them with what he feels is to become the most important fact of the future—abundance for all through fully automated production and cybernetic control. The elimination of work will have profound consequences. On the one hand, it can mean the destruction of a whole system of values and result in a totalitarian, dehumanizing social structure. On the other hand, if we adjust ourselves wisely to the new leisure, it could mean a liberating, utopian existence that will realize at last the goals of personal and social development.

230

YOU KNOW WHY **YOU'RE** ALWAYS SO **GLOOMY** AND **I'M** ALWAYS SO **CHEERFUL** — YOU KNOW THE **DIFFER- ENCE** BE- TWEEN US, CHARLIE?

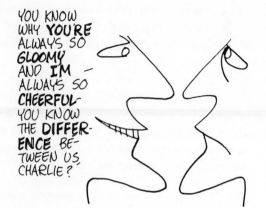

THE DIFFERENCE BETWEEN US IS **YOU** THINK EVERYTHING'S ROTTEN, MAN IS CORRUPT, SOCIETY IS MAD, AND THE WORLD COULD BLOW UP TOMORROW.

YOU'RE A PESSIMIST, CHARLIE.

I, ON THE OTHER HAND, THINK EVERYTHING'S ROTTEN, MAN IS CORRUPT, SOCIETY IS MAD, AND THE WORLD COULD BLOW UP TOMORROW —

BUT I **COULD** BE WRONG.

SEE? I'M AN OPTIMIST.

© 1966 JULES FEIFFER

9-4

Remarks on Accepting the Nobel Prize

WILLIAM FAULKNER

I feel that this award was not made to me as a man but to my work—a life's work in the agony and sweat of the human spirit, not for glory and least of all for profit, but to create out of the materials of the human spirit something which did not exist before. So this award is only mine in trust. It will not be difficult to find a dedication for the money part of it commensurate[1] with the purpose and significance of its origin. But I would like to do the same with the acclaim too, by using this moment as a pinnacle from which I might be listened to by the young men and women already dedicated to the same anguish and travail,[2] among whom is already that one who will some day stand here where I am standing.

Our tragedy today is a general and universal physical fear so long sustained by now that we can even bear it. There are no longer problems of the spirit. There is only the question: when will I be blown up? Because of this, the young man or woman writing today has forgotten the problems of the human heart in conflict with itself which alone can make good writing because only that is worth writing about, worth the agony and the sweat.

He must learn them again. He must teach himself that the basest of all things is to be afraid; and, teaching himself that, forget it forever, leaving no room in his workshop for anything but the old verities and truths of the heart, the old universal truths lacking which any story is ephemeral[3] and doomed—love and honor and pity and pride and compassion and sacrifice. Until he does so he labors under a curse. He writes not of love but of lust, of defeats in which nobody loses anything of value, of victories without hope and worst of all without pity or compassion. His griefs grieve on no universal bones, leaving no scars. He writes not of the heart but of the glands.

Until he relearns these things he will write as though he stood among and watched the end of man. I decline to accept the end of man. It is easy enough to say that man is immortal simply because he will endure; that when the last ding-dong of doom has clanged and faded from the last worthless rock hanging tideless in the last red and dying evening, that even then there will still be one more sound: that of his puny inexhaustible voice, still talking. I refuse to accept this. I believe that man will not merely endure: he will prevail. He is immortal, not because he alone among creatures has an inexhaustible voice, but because he has a soul, a spirit capable of compassion and sacrifice and endurance. The poet's, the writer's, duty is to write about these things. It is his privilege to help man endure by lifting his heart, by reminding him of the courage and honor and hope and pride and compassion and pity and sacrifice which have been the glory of his past. The poet's voice need not merely be the record of man, it can be one of the props, the pillars to help him endure and prevail.

[3] lasting a very short time; fleeting

[1] in proportion to
[2] work

The Future

JACK NEWFIELD

*Oh, deep in my heart, I do believe
we shall overcome, someday.*

FREEDOM SONG

Give flowers to the rebels failed.

ANARCHIST POEM

A prophetic minority creates each generation's legend. In the 1920's it was the expatriate[1] quest for personal expression. In the 1930's it was radical social action. In the 1940's it was the heroism of the trenches. In the 1950's it was the cultivation of the private self. Now, halfway through the decade, it is once again the ideal of social action that is *defining a generation.*

By this I mean specifically that in fifteen years Bob Dylan's poems will be taught in college classrooms, that Paul Booth, Julian Bond, and Stokely Carmichael will be the leaders of adult protest movements, that the Beatles movies will be revived in art houses, and that Tom Hayden, Norman Fruchter, Robb Burlage, Bob Parris, and Carl Oglesby will be major social critics. But I also mean to emphasize that the New Left has, and always will have, only a fraction of the whole truth, just as the Freudians, the Symbolists, Marxists and the Impressionists possessed only a fragment of the truth. But it is the fragment glimpsed by this generation.

The legend of the 1930's turned to ashes in Washington, Moscow, and Madrid before the decade was over. It is entirely possible that the New Left can meet such a tragic end as well. The possibility of political fissures exists in any movement. This one could split over tactics like the Bolsheviks or Mensheviks, or over morality like

[1] living in a foreign country

". . . the generators of dissent—
war, bureaucracy, guilt-producing affluence, racism, hypocrisy, moral rot—
are enduring in the fabric of American society."

234 Sartre and Camus. Black nationalism may yet poison it, and unfocused activism may exhaust it. But I doubt it.

In the immediate future, the impulse to rebel will continue to grow among marginal groups like students, Negroes, migrant farm workers, intellectuals, and white-collar workers. This will happen because the generators of dissent—war, bureaucracy, guilt-producing affluence, racism, hypocrisy, moral rot—are enduring in the fabric of American society. If the Vietnam war is settled, there will be another one in Thailand, or Angola, or Peru. If Bobby Baker is jailed, there will be another fast buck politician exposed. If the killers of Goodman, Chaney, and Schwerner are convicted, there will be other atrocities in the South.

All this means that the New Left—and the other sections of the society in motion—will grow and become even more uncomfortably radical. My own hunch is that SDS will be the chief repository[2] of this radical mood, that SNCC's time has passed, its gifts taken without adequate acknowledgment. I also suspect the Hereditary Left will not grow much, because it is too weighted down with the moral bankruptcy of Communism, and because it misses completely this generation's indictment of impersonal bureaucracies and the existential void of the middle class. Primarily, the New Left will become increasingly the umbrella under which indigenous,[3] decentralized movements will grow. Grass-roots insurgencies,[4] such as the grape strike in California, Berkeley's Vietnam Day Committee, the NCUP project in Newark, the Lowndes County Freedom Organization in Alabama, Dick Gregory's campaign for mayor of Chicago, independent community committees against the war in Vietnam, and campus protests against the draft like those at Chicago and CCNY, are the shadows of the future. National organizations are not the style of anarchists and improvisers.

Beneath this nation's gleaming surface of computers, Hilton hotels, and super-highways, there are latent volcanoes of violence. These volcanoes have erupted tragically in Birmingham, Mississippi, and Dallas in 1963; in Harlem and Rochester in 1964; in Watts and Selma in 1965; and in Watts and in Mississippi again in 1966. Riot and assassination are symptoms of the disease in our society below the Disneyland façade.[5] The New Radicals will rub these hidden sores until they bleed, or until the Great Society begins to heal the one in five who are poor, and the millions who are voteless, powerless, victimized, and mad.

But two yawning pitfalls stretch out before the New Left, diluting the chances of its growth. One is the rising tide of domestic McCarthyism, which is paralleling the escalation of the war in Vietnam. The other is the culture's spongelike genius for either absorbing or merchandizing all dissent.

If the Great Society becomes preoccupied by a narrow choice between "guns and butter," then it will become impossible even to hold up the alternate vision of "bread and roses." Already some social welfare and anti-poverty programs are not being funded, and New York's reform Congressman, William F. Ryan, has quipped, "Johnson is asking us to choose between guns and oleo."

There has always been a latent anti-intellectual strain to the American character, as Richard Hofstadter documented in his Pulitzer Prize-winning book, *Anti-intellectualism in American Life.* The country's repudiation of Adlai Stevenson and the upsurge of McCarthyism in the 1950's were the latest expression of attitudes that go back to the Alien and Sedition Acts and the Salem witch trials. Now, as the Vietnam war grows more bloody, the stalemate more frustrating, there seems to be a resurgence of paranoid know-nothing sentiment throughout the country. My fear is that if the war drags on, and there are 400,000 American troops in Vietnam at the start of 1967, then all of America will begin to close down, just as the nation turned in on itself during the Korean war, or as France became repressive during the last stages of its seven-year conflict with Algeria. If this happens, then all bets are off on the future of the New Left. Its elite will be drafted, its organizations pilloried[6] and red-baited,[7] its idealism shattered, its mentality turned underground.

The first smell of this new McCarthyism is already in the air, burning the nostrils and poisoning the lungs.

In October of 1965 Congress enacted a law that made the burning of a draft card punishable by

---

[2] place where something is stored or deposited
[3] produced, growing, or living in a particular environment; native
[4] rebellions carried out by people who rise up against the existing government but are not recognized as belligerents

[5] a false, superficial, or artificial appearance
[6] held up to public humiliation
[7] persecuted by charging with being Communist

five years in jail and a five-thousand-dollar fine. A few weeks later, Attorney General Katzenbach announced the Justice Department was investigating SDS. In January of 1966 the Georgia state legislature refused to seat the democratically elected Julian Bond because of his opposition to the Vietnam war. In February, Congressman Olin E. Teague of Texas introduced legislation making all anti-war protests illegal; he characterized the demonstrators as "beatnik types and pseudo-intellectuals." A few days later the Michigan state legislature adopted a resolution banning Communists from speaking on campuses in the state. On March 3rd, the Justice Department petitioned the Subversive Activities Control Board to order the Du Bois Clubs to register as a Communist-front organization. Within forty-eight hours the clubs' national headquarters was blown up, and its members beaten up on a Brooklyn street, and then arrested by police. On March 26th, anti-war marches in Oklahoma City and Boston were broken up by hooligans, and in New York, twenty thousand marchers were pelted with rotten eggs, and assailed by the *Daily News* as "dupes of the communists." On March 31st, four young draft-card burners were savagely beaten on the steps of a Boston courthouse by a mob of teen-agers, while police looked on, and newsreel photographers jostled each other for close-ups of the pummeling. On April 8th the VDC headquarters in Berkeley was bombed. On May 15th a crazed gunman killed a member of the YSA in Detroit. On June 5th, a sniper waiting in ambush shot James Meredith near Hernando, Mississippi.

*T*he other pitfall blocking the path of the New Left is the culture's skill at amiably absorbing all manner of rebels and turning them into celebrities. To be a radical in America today is like trying to punch your way out of a cage made of marshmallow. Every thrust at the jugular draws not blood, but sweet success; every hack at the roots draws not retaliation, but fame and affluence. The culture's insatiable thirst for novelty and titillation[8] insures LeRoi Jones television interviews, Norman Mailer million-dollar royalties, and Paul Goodman fat paychecks as a government consultant. Yesterday's underground becomes today's vaudeville and tomorrow's cliché. If the draft,

super-patriots, and the Justice Department don't wreck the New Left, masscult[9] may kill it with kindness and then deposit its carcass in the cemetery of celebrities, alongside of Baby Jane Holzer, Liberace, and Jack Kerouac.

Already there are signs that the middle class enjoys being flogged by the New Radicals, while ignoring their criticisms and ideas. Magazines like *Esquire, Mademoiselle,* and *Playboy* have printed glowing accounts of the New Left. Publishing houses have handed out thousands of dollars to the New Radicals for books they know will indict America root and branch—but will return a handsome profit. Government agencies like the Peace Corps and the Office of Economic Opportunity have offered several of the most gifted members of the New Left lucrative jobs.

The paradox of radical ideas creating celebrities can be an insidious[10] process. It is hard to nurse your anger if you're getting two thousand dollars to spill it out on national television. And it is hard to think creatively, or to organize effectively, if you are deluged with a stream of speaking engagements, interviews, and symposia.[11] The danger of becoming performers subsidized to goose a decadent middle class is a real one for the New Left.

Directly toward these twin pitfalls—escalating war in Vietnam and an endlessly absorptive culture—the New Radicals will march, just as they marched into Mississippi, Sproul Hall, and the urban slums of the North. They will continue to challenge the gods because they are cursed with the passion of Ahab and the innocence of Billy Budd. And because no one else is doing the marching.

The New Radicalism began with a request for a cup of coffee. In six years it has become a new way of looking at the world and a vision of a new kind of politics. It has given a whole generation what William James called "the moral equivalent of war."

To demand any more of this generation is to deny the responsibility of the last one—and the possibility of the next.

---

[8] pleasurable excitement

[9] mass culture; a coined word which indicates by the abbreviation and compression that the author is critical or even contemptuous of the concept
[10] harmful but enticing
[11] A symposium is a meeting at which several speakers deliver short speeches on a topic.

The New Aristocrats

PAUL GOODMAN

Predictions about the future of America during the next generation are likely to be in one of two sharply contrasting moods. On the one hand, the orthodox liberals foresee a Great Society in which all will live in suburban comfort or the equivalent; given a Head Start and Job Training, Negroes will go to college like everyone else, will be splendidly employed and live in integrated neighborhoods; billboards will be 200 yards off new highways, and the arts will flourish in many Lincoln Centers. On the other hand, gloomy social critics, and orthodox conservatives, see that we are headed straight for 1984, when everyone's life will be regimented from the cradle to the grave by the dictator in Washington; administrative double talk and Newspeak[1] will be the only language; Negroes will be kept at bay by the police (according to the social critics) or will be the pampered shock troops of demagogs[2] (according to the conservatives); we will all be serial numbers; civil liberties and independent enterprise will be no more.

Yet these predictions have much in common. They assume the continuation of the same trends and attitudes that are now in full sway. There will be increasing centralization in decision making, increasing mass education as we now know it, a stepped-up rate of technical growth and a growing Gross National Product, and more use of a technological style—of "planning" or "social engineering," depending on one's bias—with heavy use of computers. These same premises are seen by some as enriching and great, and by others as menacing and empty.

Oddly, however, both kinds of prediction describe the play and leave out Hamlet; namely, the next generation itself, the young people who are going to be the heirs to all this greatness or the slaves of this social engineering. I have not seen a single forecast that takes into account that present high school and college students will be of some importance in shaping society 20 years from now. Commencement speakers are eager to pass on the torch and they seem to be sure that there are ready hands to receive it. Yet the evidence is that students are not at all happy with the present trends and attitudes, whether the prediction is gloomy *or* rosy. For instance, in 1956, surveys showed that college students admired and wanted to work in big corporations, but last year (at Harvard) more seniors opted for the Peace Corps than for careers in business. Allow me a small personal example: My book *Growing Up Absurd* sells 1000 copies a week, of which the majority, my publisher guesses, are bought by high school students. This gives one pause; I wouldn't have thought they could read the words. Maybe they can't, but they get the message, that the conditions of our society are too inhuman to grow up in. For collegians that message is dated; they take it for granted.

I do not intend to predict what the future might look like if we take young people into account. I don't know (although I give plenty of advice, which they disregard). What I want to show, however, is that point by point, with remarkable precision, articulate students—and an indeterminate number of others—*live, feel and think in direct opposition to the premises on which both the rosy and the gloomy predictions are based.* It is so in their community life, their ethics and their politics. If only because of sheer numbers, the temper of young people must make a difference for the future. And it is whistling in the dark to think that their opposition is a "generational revolt" that will be absorbed as they grow older and wiser, for it is endemic[3] in our system of things. If the planners continue to treat this temper as if it did not exist, the result will be still deeper alienation and worse ultimate disruption. My experience in Washington, as a Fellow of the Institute of Policy Studies, is that social and educational planners have about as much information of what happens on college campuses as the State Department has about Vietnam.

Community: About 50 percent of all Americans are now under 26. Of the college-age group, nearly

[1] in George Orwell's novel *1984*, the official, "reduced" language used by the dictatorship to control the people
[2] mob leaders making use of popular prejudices and passions

[3] native to a people or country

40 percent go to college—there are 6,000,000 in 2000 institutions. Of the present collegians, it is estimated that five percent are in some activity of the radical youth movement, usually "left" but sometimes "right." This does not seem a big proportion, but it has increased at least tenfold in the last decade, and it and the number of its alumni will certainly increase even more rapidly in the next years. We are thus speaking of several million people.

More important, they are the leaders. Radical collegians are not only middle class but they are also disproportionately the best academically and from the most prestigious schools. Unlike Negro youth, who are now causing such turmoil, collegians are a major economic force, looming large among the indispensable inheritors of the dominant power in society. And although—or perhaps because—they do not share a common ideology but rather a common sentiment and style, in showdown situations like the troubles in Berkeley, they have shown a remarkable solidarity and a common detestation for the liberal center, crossing even the apparent chasm between extreme right and extreme left.

A chief reason for their solidarity and their increase in numbers is mass higher education itself. For most, going to college has little academic value—indeed, one of their shared sentiments is resistance to being academically processed for the goals of the "system." In my opinion, about 15 percent, instead of 40 percent, ought to be in colleges; the rest, including most of the bright, would be better educated in other environments. Nevertheless, *the major colleges and universities are, in fact, many hundreds of physical and social communities of young people, with populations of a few thousand to 25,000, sharing a subculture, propagandizing one another and learning to distrust anybody over 30. Such collections of youth are a phenomenon unique in history.*

Consider some details from San Francisco State College, where I was hired as a teacher by the Associated Students last spring. With 15,000 students, the Associated Students collect $300,000 annually in dues, more than half of which is free and clear and which they use for untraditional purposes. These purposes include organizing a tenants' league, helping delinquents in a reformatory, running a tutorial program for Negro and Mexican children (with 300 collegian tutors), sponsoring a weekly television program on KQED, running an "experimental college" with offbeat courses, and hiring their own professors. They apply on their own for institutional grants from the Ford Foundation and the Poverty Program. In the fall of 1966, the experimental college registered 1600 students!

Or consider the college press, with its fairly captive audience of a couple of million, many of them daily. In a few cases, e.g., Harvard and Columbia, publication has gone off campus and is not under the tutelage[4] of "faculty advisors."

[4] state of being under a guardian or tutor

237

*"If only because of sheer numbers,
the temper of young people must make a difference for the future. . . ."*

238 Increasingly, college papers subscribe to news services and print (and edit) national and international news; and they also use syndicated material, like Art Buchwald, Jules Feiffer, Russell Baker. Occasionally, the college paper is the chief daily of its town (e.g., the Cornell *Sun*). More important, there is a national student press service that could be a powerfully effective liaison[5] for mobilizing opinion on common issues. Last winter I wrote a fortnightly column on student matters for a tiny college in Vermont, which the enterprising editor at once syndicated to 50 other college papers. On this model there could spring up a system of direct support, and control, of students' "own" authors, just as, of course, they now indirectly support them through magazines whose main circulation is collegiate.

Nor are these young people properly called "youth." The exigencies[6] of the American system have kept them in tutelage, doing lessons, till 23 and 24 years of age, years past when young industrial workers used to walk union picket lines or when farmers carried angry pitchforks, or young men are now drafted into the Army. Thus, another cause of their shared resentment is the foolish attempt to arrest their maturation and regulate their social, sexual and political activity.

More than other middle-class generations, these young live a good deal by "interpersonal relations" and they are unusually careless, in their friendships, about status or getting ahead. I do not mean that they are especially affectionate or compassionate—they are averagely so—but they have been soaked in modern psychology, group therapy, sensitivity training; and as a style they go in for direct confrontation and sometimes brutal frankness. Add to this the lack of embarrassment due to animally uninhibited childhood, for their parents, by and large, were permissive about thumbsucking, toilet training, masturbation, informal dress, etc. They are the post-Freudian generation in this country—their parents were analyzed from 1920 to 1940. The effect of all this psychology—for example, long sessions of mutual analysis or jabber about LSD trips—can be tiresome, at least to me; but it is fatal to suburban squeamishness, race and moral prejudice, and to keeping up appearances. Still another cause of resentment at the colleges is the

5 close bond of connection
6 demands

impersonality and distance of the teachers and the big classes that make dialog impossible. Students are avid for dialog. Sometimes this looks like clamoring for "attention," as our statesmen say about the demonstrators, but it is really insisting on being taken seriously as troubled human beings.

Middle-class privacy also tends to vanish. An innovation of the Beats was the community use of one another's pads, and this spirit of sharing has persisted in off-campus university communities, which are very different from paternalistic dormitories or fraternity row. In big cities there are rapidly growing bohemian student neighborhoods, usually—if only for the cheaper rent—located in racially mixed sections. Such neighborhoods, with their own coffeehouses and headquarters for student political clubs, cannot be controlled by campus administration. In the famous insurrection of Berkeley, Telegraph Avenue could easily rally 3000 students, ex-students, wives and pals. (The response of the University of California administration has been, characteristically, to try to root up the student neighborhood with Federally financed urban renewal.)

Inevitably, sexual activity and taking drugs loom overlarge in the public picture: for, whereas unkempt hair, odd company and radical politics may be disapproved, sex and drugs rouse middle-class anxiety, a more animal reaction. The statistics seem to show, however, that quantitatively there are not many more sexual goings on than since the Twenties. The difference is that the climate has finally become more honest and unhypocritical. Sexuality is affirmed as a part of life rather than as the Saturday religion of fraternity gang bangs covered by being drunk. Since there is more community altogether, sex tends to revert to the normalcy of back rural areas, with the beautiful difference of middle-class prudence and contraceptives. (Probably, since there is less moralism, there are more homosexual acts, though not, of course, any increase of homosexuality as a trait of character.) In the more earnest meaning of sex, love and marriage, however, the radical young still seem averagely messed up, no better than their parents. There is no remarkable surge of joy or poetry—the chief progress of the sexual revolution, so far, has been the freer treatment of small children that I mentioned above. The conditions of American society do not encourage manly responsibility and moral courage in men, and we simply do not know how to use the tenderness and motherliness of women. The present disposition of the radical young is to treat males and females alike; in my observation, this means that the women become camp followers, the opposite of the suburban situation in which they are tyrannical dolls. I don't know the answer.

Certainly the slogan "Make love, not war"— carried mainly by the girls—is political wisdom, if only because it costs less in taxes.

The community meaning of the widespread use of hallucinogenic[7] drugs is ambiguous. (Few students use addictives; again, they are prudent.) I have heard students hotly defend the drugs as a means of spiritual and political freedom, or hotly condemn them as a quietist[8] opiate[9] of the people, or indifferently dismiss them as a matter of taste. I am myself not a hippie and I am unwilling to judge. It seems clear that the more they take pot, the less they get drunk, but I don't know if this is an advantage or a disadvantage. (I don't get drunk, either.) Certainly there is a difference between the quiet socializing of marijuana and the alcoholic socializing of the fraternities, suburbs and Washington. Also, being illegal and hard to procure, the drugs create conspiracy and a chasm between those who do and those who don't. As usual, the drug laws, like other moral laws, fail to eradicate the vice they intend to eradicate, but they produce disastrous secondary effects.

The LSD cult, especially, must be understood as part of a wave of religiosity in young persons that has included Zen, Christian and Jewish existentialism, a kind of psychoanalytic yoga, and the magic of the Book of Changes. On the campus, a young Protestant chaplain—or even a Catholic— is often the center of radical activity, which may include a forum for psychedelic theory as well as peace and Negro rights. Certainly the calculating rationalism of modern times is losing its self-evidence; and it is not the end of the world to flip. Personally, I don't like it when people flip, it is eerie; I like people to be in touch, and I think the heads are mistaken when they think they are communicating. Also, in our overtechnological society, I am intensely suspicious of Dr. Tim Leary's formula to "turn on, tune in and drop out" by

chemical means. Yet by and large, the public repression in this field is grossly disproportionate to the occasional damage that has been proved; and frankly, the burden of proof is the other way: If we do not want young people to live in harmless dreams, we have to provide something better than the settled arithmetical delusions of Mr. McNamara, not to speak of Herman Kahn, author of *On Thermonuclear War*.

The shagginess and chosen poverty of student communities have nuances[10] that might be immensely important for the future. We must remember that these are the young of the affluent society, used to a high standard of living and confident that, if and when they want, they can fit in and make good money. Having suffered little pressure of insecurity, they have little psychological need to climb; just as, coming from respectable homes, they feel no disgrace about sitting a few nights in jail. By confidence they are aristocrats—en masse. This, too, is unique in history. At the same time, the affluent standard of living that they have experienced at home is pretty synthetic and much of it useless and phony; whereas their chosen poverty is not degraded but decent, natural and in many ways more comfortable than their parents' standard, especially if they can always corral obvious goodies such as hi-fi equipment and motorcycles. Typically, they tour Europe on nothing, sleeping under bridges; but if they get really hungry, they can drop in at American Express to pick up their mail. Most of the major satisfactions of life—sex, paperback books, guitars, roaming, conversation, games and activist politics—in fact, cost little.

Thus, this is the first generation in America selective of its standard of living. If this attitude became general, it would be disastrous for the expanding Gross National Product. And there is obvious policy and defiance in their poverty and shagginess. They have been influenced by the voluntary poverty of the beat movement, which signified withdrawal from the trap of the affluent economy. Finally, by acquaintance they experience the harsher tone of the involuntary poverty of the Negroes and Spanish Americans whose neighborhoods they visit and with whom they are friends.

In a recent speech, Robert Hutchins pointed out that business can no longer recruit the bright

---

[7] causing hallucinations
[8] refusing to act because of the futility of action
[9] something that induces inaction or quiets uneasiness

[10] shades of difference

young. He explained this by the fact that the universities are rich and can offer competitive rewards. But I do not think this is the essence, for we have seen that at Harvard, business cannot compete even with the Peace Corps. The essence is that the old drive to make a *lot* of money has lost its magnetism. Yet this does not seem to mean settling for security, for the young are increasingly risky. The magnet is a way of life that has meaning. This is a luxury of an aristocratic community.

Ethics: The chief (conscious) drive of the radical young is their morality. As Michael Harrington, author of *The Other America*, has put it, "They drive you crazy with their morality," since for it they disregard prudence and politics, and they mercilessly condemn day-to-day casuistry[11] as if it were all utterly phony. When politically minded student leaders, like the Students for a Democratic Society, try to engage in "tactics" and "the art of the possible," they may temporarily gain in numbers, but they swiftly lose influence and begin to disintegrate. Yet indignation or a point of honor will rally the young in droves.

> *"There may be hope of bringing to life many of our routinized institutions if we surround them with humanly meaningful enterprises."*

Partly, the drive to morality is the natural ingenuousness[12] of youth, freed of the role playing and status seeking of our society. As aristocrats, not driven by material or ulterior motives, they will budge for ideals or not at all. Partly their absolutism[13] is a disgusted reaction to cynicism and the prevalent adult conviction that "Nothing can be done. You can't fight city hall. Modern life is too complex." But mostly, I think, it is the self-righteousness of an intelligent and innocent new generation in a world where my own generation has been patently stupid and incompetent. They have been brought up on a literature of devastat-

ing criticism that has gone unanswered because there is no answer.

The right comparison to them is the youth of the Reformation, of *Sturm und Drang*,[14] and of Russia of the Seventies and Eighties, who were brought up on their own dissenting theologians, *philosophes*[15] and intelligentsia. Let us remember that those students did, indeed, ultimately lead revolutions.

The philosophical words are "authenticity" and "commitment," from the existentialist vocabulary. And it cannot be denied that our dominant society is unusually inauthentic. Newspeak and double talk are the lingua franca[16] of administrators, politicians, advertisers and the mass media. These official people are not even lying; rather, there is an unbridgeable chasm between the statements made "on the record" for systemic[17] reasons or the image of the corporation, and what is intended and actually performed. I have seen mature graduate students crack up in giggles of anxiety listening to the Secretary of State expound our foreign policy; when I questioned them afterward, some said that he was like a mechanical man, others that he was demented. And most campus blowups have been finally caused by administrators' animal inability to speak plainly. The students have faithfully observed due process and manfully stated their case, but the administrators simply cannot talk like human beings. At this point it suddenly becomes clear that they are confronting not a few radical dissenters but a solid mass of the young, maybe a majority.

Two things seem to solidify dissent: administrative double talk and the singling out of "ringleaders" for exemplary[18] punishment. These make young people feel that they are not being taken seriously, and they are not.

In principle, "authenticity" is proved by "commitment." You must not merely talk but organize, collect money, burn your draft card, go South and be shot at, go to jail. And the young eagerly commit themselves. However, a lasting commitment is hard to achieve. There are a certain number of causes that are pretty authentic and warrant engaging in: Give Negroes the vote, desegregate a

---

[11] a method of dealing with cases of conscience and the resolution of questions of right and wrong in conduct
[12] straightforwardness, simplicity
[13] advocacy of a rule by absolute rules or principles

[14] a late 18th-century literary movement marked by a revolt against the French Enlightenment
[15] deistic or materialistic writers and thinkers of the 18th-century French Enlightenment
[16] something resembling a common language
[17] concerning the function and maintenance of the organization as a whole
[18] serving as a warning

hotel or a bus, commute Chessman's sentence to the gas chamber, abolish grading and get the CIA out of the university, abolish HUAC, get out of Vietnam, legalize marijuana and homosexuality, unionize the grapepickers. But it is rarely the case that any particular authentic cause can really occupy the thought and energy of more than a few for more than a while. Students cool off and hop from issue to issue, then some become angry at the backsliders; others foolishly try to prove that civil liberties, for instance, are not so "important" as Negro civil rights, for instance, or that university reform is not so "important" as stopping the bombing of Hanoi. Others, disillusioned, sink into despair of human nature. And committed causes distressingly vanish from view at the June vacation, when the community disperses.

Shrewder psychologists among the young advocate getting involved only in what you "enjoy" and gravitate to—e.g., don't tutor unless you like

kids—but this is a weak motive compared with indignation or justice.

The bother is that, except with a few political or religious personalities, the students' commitments do not spring from their own vocations and life ambitions; and they are not related in a coherent program for the reconstruction of society. This is not the fault of the students. Most of the present young have unusually little sense of vocation; perhaps 16 continuous years of doing lessons by compulsion has not been a good way to find one's identity. And there *is* no acceptable program of reconstruction—nobody has spelled it out—only vague criteria. Pathetically, much "definite commitment" is a self-deceptive way of filling the void of sense of vocation and utopian politics. Negroes, who are perforce really committed to their emancipation, notice this and say that their white allies are spiritually exploiting them.

It is a difficult period of history for the young to find vocation and identity. Most of the abiding human vocations and professions, arts and sciences, seem to them, and are (to a degree) corrupt or corrupted: law, business, the physical sciences, social work—these constitute the hated System. And higher education, both curriculum and professors, which ought to be helping them find themselves, also seems bought out by the System. Students know that something is wrong in their schooling and they agitate for university reform; but since they do not know what world they want to make, they do not know what to demand to be taught.

Politics: It is not the task of age 18 to 25 to devise a coherent program of social reconstruction; for instance, to rethink our uses of technology, our methods of management, our city planning and international relations. They rightly accuse us of not providing them a program to work for. A small minority—I think increasing—turns to Marxism, as in the Thirties; but the Marxist theorists have also not thought of anything new and relevant to overripe societies. Most radical students, in my observation, listen to Marxist ideological speeches with polite lack of interest—"they are empty, man, empty"—and they are appalled by Marxist political bullying. On the other hand, they are disgusted with official anticommunism. By an inevitable backlash, since they think all American official speech is double talk, they disbelieve that Communist states are worse than our own.

What the American young do know, being themselves pushed around, itemized and processed, is that they have a right to a say in what affects them. They believe in democracy, which they have to call "participatory democracy," to distinguish it from double-talk democracy. Poignantly, in their ignorance of American history, they do not recognize that they are Congregationalists, town-meeting democrats, Jeffersonians, populists.[19] But they know they want the opportunity to be responsible, to initiate and decide, instead of being mere personnel. Returning from their term overseas, the first thousand of the Peace Corps unanimously agreed that exercising responsibility and initiative had been the most

worthwhile part of their experience, and they complained that back home they did not have the opportunity.

The primary area for seeking democracy would be, one would imagine, the universities, for that is where the students are and are coerced. And the radical students, who, we have seen, are among the best academically, have campaigned for *Lernfreiheit*—freedom from grading, excessive examination, compulsory attendance at lectures and prescribed subjects—and also for the ancient privilege of a say in designing the curriculum and evaluating the teachers. But unfortunately, as we have also seen, the majority of students do not care about higher education as such and are willing to put up with it as it is. They are in college for a variety of extrinsic[20] reasons, from earning the degree as a union card to evading the draft. There is no mass base for university reform.

So instead of working in their own bailiwick,[21] activist students have mainly sought participatory democracy for poor people, organizing rent strikes, opposing bureaucratic welfare procedures, and so forth. But there is an inherent dilemma in this. Negroes claim, perhaps correctly, that middle-class whites cannot understand their problems; if Negroes are going to run their own show, they have to dispense with white helpers. The present policy of the Student Nonviolent Coordinating Committee is that Negroes must solve their own peculiar problems, which are the only ones they care about and know anything about, and let their young white friends attend to changing the majority society. There is something in this. Certainly one would have expected Northern students to get their heads broken in the cafeteria at Tulane or the University of Mississippi, where they could talk with their peers face to face, as well as on the streets of country towns. And white Southern liberals have desperately needed more support than they have gotten.

But pushed too far, the rift with the middle-class students consigns poor people to a second-class humanity. The young Negroes cannot do without the universities, for there, finally, is where the showdown, the reconstruction of society, will be—although that showdown is not yet. Consider: Some pressing problems are universal; the poor must care about them, e.g., the atom bomb. Many pressing problems are grossly misconceived if looked at at short range from a poor

---

[19] a United States political party formed in the late 19th century. It was a movement of the people, of short duration, which called attention to the growing power of private monopoly and the disadvantages from which agriculture suffered.

[20] external

[21] area of authority or domain

man's point of view; only a broad human point of view can save Negroes from agitating for exactly the wrong things, as they have agitated for educational parks, when what is needed in schooling is a small human scale. Also, there is something spurious[22] in Negro separatism, for a poor minority in a highly technological society will not engineer the housing and manufacture the cars that they intend to use. Finally, in fact, the Negroes are, perhaps unfortunately, much more American than Negro. Especially in the North, they are suckers for the whole American package, though it makes even less sense for them than for anybody else. The Negro subculture that is talked up has about the same value as the adolescent subculture; it has vitality and it does not add up to humanity.

As in other periods of moral change, only the young aristocrats and the intellectuals can *afford* to be disillusioned and profoundly radical. And in a high technology, only the students will be able to construct a program.

In their own action organizations, the young are almost fanatically opposed to top-down direction. In several remarkable cases, e.g., Tom Hayden, Bob Moses, Mario Savio, gifted and charismatic[23] leaders have stepped down because their influence had become too strong. By disposition, without benefit of history, they are reinventing anarchist federation and a kind of Rosa Luxemburgian[24] belief in spontaneous insurrection from below. In imitating Gandhian nonviolence, they do not like to submit to rigid discipline, but each one wants to make his own moral decision about getting his head broken. If the Army really gets around to drafting them, it will have its hands full.

All this, in my opinion, probably makes them immune to take-over by centralists like the Marxists. When Trotskyites, for instance, infiltrate an organization and try to control it, the rest go home and activity ceases. When left to their own improvisation, however, the students seem surprisingly able to mount quite massive efforts, using elaborate techniques of communication and expert sociology. By such means they will never get power. But, indeed, they do not want power, they want meaning.

[22] false, illegitimate
[23] with a personal magic of leadership arousing extraordinary enthusiasm or popular loyalty
[24] Rosa Luxemburg was a German socialist leader (1870–1910).

Parallel Institutions: The operative idea in participatory democracy is decentralizing, to multiply the number who are responsible, initiate and decide. In principle, there are two opposite ways of decentralizing: either by dividing over-centralized organizations where it can be shown that decentral organization is more efficient in economic, social and human costs, or at least not too inefficient; or by creating new small enterprises to fill needs that big organizations neglect or only pretend to fulfill.

Obviously, the first of these, to cut the present structures down to human size, is not in the power of the young. But it happens that it does require a vast amount of empirical research and academic analysis to find if, where and how decentralizing is feasible; and in current American academic style, there is no such research and analysis. So on 150 campuses, I have urged students to work on such problems. They seem fascinated, but I do not know if they are coming across. (To say it wryly, there is a fine organization called Students for a Democratic Society, but it is not enough evident that they are scholars for a democratic society.)

The other way of decentralizing, by creating parallel enterprises, better suits the student zeal for direct action, and they have applied it with energy and inventiveness. They have set up a dozen little "free universities" that I know about —probably there are many others—in or next to established institutions, to teach in a more personal way and to deal with contemporary subjects that are not yet standard curriculum, e.g., Castro's Cuba, Psychedelic Experience, Sensitivity Training, Theater of Participation. Some of these courses are action sociology, like organizing labor or community development. In poor neighborhoods, students have established a couple of radio stations, to broadcast local news and propaganda and to give poor people a chance to talk into a microphone. They have set up parallel community projects to combat the welfare bureaucracy and channelize needs and grievances. In the South, they have helped form "freedom" political machines, since the established machines are lily white. They have offered to organize international service projects as an alternative to serving in the Army. (I have not heard of any feasible attempts at productive cooperatives or planned urban communities of their own, and students do not seem at all interested in rural reconstruction, though they should be.)

Regarded coldly, such parallel projects are pitifully insignificant and doomed to pass away like so many little magazines. And, in fact, at present, the most intense discussions among student radicals, causing deep rifts, are on this theme. Some, following older thinkers like Michael Harrington and Bayard Rustin (director of a civil rights and poverty research institute) want to engage in "coalition politics," to become effective by combining with the labor unions and leftish liberals in the Democratic Party, to get control of some of the Federal money and to campaign for A. Philip Randolph's (president of the Brotherhood of Sleeping Car Porters) 185-billion-dollar budget to eliminate poverty. This involves, of course, soft-pedaling protests for peace, community action and university reform. Recent history, however, has certainly not favored this point of view. Federal money is drying up and radical coalition people who go to work for the Government get fired; nor is it evident that, if it were spent for liberal social engineering, Randolph's budget would make a better world —even if the money were voted.

Others, for example one wing of SDS, say that the use of participatory democracy and parallel institutions is not for themselves but to consolidate people into a political party; it is not to provide models for the reconstruction of society but, as a kind of initiation rite, to get into the big game of numbers and power. This seems to me to give up on the authenticity, meaning and beautiful spontaneous motivation that have, so far, been the real power of the radical young and the source of what influence they have had. And it presupposes that the young know where they want to go as a party, rather than in what direction they *are* going as a movement. But they don't know; they (and we) will have to find out by conflict.

In my opinion, it is better to regard the parallel institutions as a remarkable revival of a classical American movement, populism, that seemed to have been dead. It is now reviving on the streets and among citizens who storm city hall because they feel they have been pushed around; in such a movement, the young are natural leaders. The principle of populism, as in 1880, is to get out from under the thumb of the barons and do it yourself. And perhaps the important step is the first one, to prove that self-help is possible at all. There may be hope of bringing to life many of our routinized institutions if we surround them with humanly meaningful enterprises. The most

telling criticism of an overgrown institution is a simpler one that works better.

This was John Dewey's vision of the young 60 years ago: He thought of an industrial society continually and democratically renewed by its next generation, freely educated and learning by doing. Progressive education, free-spirited but practical, was a typical populist conception. And it is useful to regard the student movement as progressive education at the college and graduate-school level: for at this level, learning by doing begins to be indistinguishable from vocation, profession and politics. It is the opposite of the mandarin establishment[25] that now rules the country, and of the social engineering that is now called education. Maybe this time around, the populist movement will succeed and change what we mean by vocation, profession and politics.

So, describing radical students—and I do not know how many others—we have noticed their solidarity based on community rather than ideology, their style of direct and frank confrontation, their democratic inclusiveness and aristocratic carelessness of status, caste or getting ahead, their selectivity of the affluent standard of living, their effort to be authentic and committed to their causes rather than merely belonging, their determination to have a say and their refusal to be processed as standard items, their extreme distrust of top-down direction, their disposition to anarchist organization and direct action, their disillusion with the system of institutions, and their belief that they can carry on major social functions in improvised parallel enterprises.

Some of these traits, in my opinion, are natural to all unspoiled young people. All of them are certainly in contradiction to the dominant organization of American society. By and large, this is as yet the disposition of a minority, but it is the only articulate disposition that has emerged; and it has continually emerged for the past ten years. It is a response not merely to "issues," such as civil rights or Vietnam, but to deeply rooted defects in our present system, and it will have an influence in the future. It will make for a more decent society than the Great Society and it may well save us from 1984.

[25] intellectuals who are in the power structure, working in high government posts and offering intellectual solutions to the country's problems while ignoring the real needs of the masses. Like the Chinese mandarins of an earlier time, they are the ruling intelligentsia.

The New Barbarians

DANIEL J. BOORSTIN

For centuries, men here have been discovering new ways in which the happiness and prosperity of each individual revolves around that of the community. Now suddenly we are witnessing the explosive rebellion of small groups, who reject the American past, deny their relation to the community, and in a spiritual Ptolemaism[1] insist that the U.S.A. must revolve around each of them. This atavism,[2] this New Barbarism, cannot last, if the nation is to survive.

Because the New Barbarians seek the kudos[3] of old labels—"Nonviolence," "Pacifism," "Leftism," "Radicalism," etc.—we too readily assume that they really are just another expression of "good old American individualism," of "healthy dissent," of the red-blooded rambunctious spirit which has kept this country alive and kicking.

Nothing could be further from the truth. We are now seeing something new under the American sun. And we will be in still deeper trouble if we do not recognize what has really happened. The New Barbarism is not simply another expression of American vitality. It is not simply another expression of the utopianism[4] of youth. On the contrary. What it expresses, in tornado-potence, is a new view of America and of the world. It expresses a new notion of how the world should be grasped.

The Depression Decade beginning in 1929 saw in the United States a host of radicalisms, perhaps more numerous and more influential than at any earlier period of our history. Many of these were left-wing movements, which included large numbers of our academics, intellectuals, and men of public conscience, who became members or fellow travelers of groups dominated by Marxist ideas. They favored a reconstruction of American life on a base of socialism or communism. They had a great deal to do with promoting a new and wider American labor movement, with helping F.D.R. popularize the need for a welfare state, and with persuading Americans to join the war to stop Hitler. Although they fenced in American social scientists by new orthodoxies, they did have a generally tonic effect on American society. However misguided were many of the policies they advocated, these radicals did awaken and sensitize the American conscience. They confronted Americans with some facts of life which had been swept under the rug.

That was radicalism. And those of us who were part of it can attest to some of its features. It was radicalism in the familiar and traditional sense of the word. The word "radical" does, of course, come from the Latin "radix," meaning "root," and a radical, then, is a person trying to go to the root of matters.

Of course those radicals never were quite respectable. Their message was that things were not what they seemed, and that inevitably makes respectable people uncomfortable. But we would be mistaken if we assumed, as many do nowadays, that a radical is anybody who makes lots of other people uncomfortable.

What makes a radical radical is not *that* he discomfits others but *how* he does it. A drunk is not a radical, neither is a psychotic, though both can make us quite uncomfortable. Nor does mere rudeness or violence make a person a radical, though a rude or violent man can make everybody around him quite miserable. Nor is a man who is unjustly treated and resents it necessarily a radical. Caryl Chessman[5] may not have been guilty as charged—yet that did not make him a radical.

*T*he most vocal and most violent disrupters of American society today are not radicals at all, but a new species of barbarian. In the ancient world, "barbarian" was a synonym for foreigner, and meant an alien who came from some far-off savage land. He himself was "barbarous," wild, and uncivilized. He was a menace not because he wanted to reform or reshape the society he in-

[1] According to the Ptolemaic view, the earth was the center around which the sun and other elements revolved.
[2] throwback to primitive times
[3] glory or credit
[4] idealism; specifically, youthful visions of an ideal society

[5] Convicted in 1948 of robbery, kidnapping, and attempted rape, Caryl Chessman won eight stays of execution before being put to death at San Quentin in 1960.

vaded but because he did not understand or value that society, and he aimed to destroy it.

The New Barbarians in America today come not from without, but from within. While they are not numerous anywhere—comprising perhaps less than two percent of our two hundred million Americans—they pose a special threat precisely because they are diffuse, wild, and disorganized. They have no one or two headquarters to be surveyed, no one or two philosophies to be combated. But they are no less rude, wild, and uncivilized than if they had come from the land of the Visigoths or the Vandals. The fact that they come from within—and are somehow a product of—our society makes them peculiarly terrifying, but it does not make them any the less barbarians.

We must not be deceived by our own hypersensitive liberal consciences, nor by the familiar, respected labels under which the New Barbarians

like to travel. If American civilization is to survive, if we are to resist and defeat the New Barbarism, we must see it for what it is. Most important, we must see that in America the New Barbarism is something really new.

A first step in this direction is to cease to confuse the New Barbarians with the members of other, intellectually respectable groups which can and must claim tolerance in a free society. The New Barbarians are not radicals. This will be obvious if we recall the characteristics of the radicalisms that in one form or another have discomfited and awakened generations of Americans.

Radicalism in the United States has had several distinctive and interrelated characteristics:

1. Radicalism Is a Search for Meaning. The search for meaning is the search for significance, for what else something connotes. The socialist, for example, denies that the capitalist system of production and distribution makes sense; he wants to reorganize it to produce a new meaning in the institutions of property and in the economy of the whole society. The religious pacifist, if he is a Christian, seeks the meaning of society in the Christian vision of peace and the brotherhood of man. When the true radical criticizes society he demands that the society justify itself according to some new measure of meaning.

2. Radicalism Has a Specific Content. The radical is distinguished from the man who simply has a bad digestion by the fact that the radical's belief has some solid subject matter, while the other man is merely dyspeptic.[6] A stomachache or sheer anger or irritability cannot be the substance of radicalism. Thus, while a man can be ill-natured or irritable in general, he cannot be a radical in general. Every radicalism is a way of asserting *what* are the roots. Radicalism, therefore, involves affirmation. It is distinguished from conservatism precisely in that the conservative can be loose and vague about his affirmation. The conservative is in fact always tempted to let his affirmation become mere complacency. But the true radical cannot refuse to affirm, and to be specific, although of course he may be utopian. The radical must affirm that *this* is more fundamental than *that*. One great service of the radical,

[6] having bad digestion

then, is that by his experimental definitions he puts the conservative on the defensive and makes him discover, decide, and define what is really worth preserving. The radical does this by the specificity (sometimes also by the rashness) of his affirmation—of the dictatorship of the proletariat, of the Kingdom of God on earth, or of whatever else.

3. Radicalism Is an Affirmation of Community. It affirms that we all share the same root problems, that we are all in the same boat, though the radical may see the boat very differently than do others. For example, if he is a pacifist radical he insists that the whole society bears the blame for even a single man killed in war; if he is an anarchist radical he insists that the whole society bears the blame for the injustice of property and the violence of government. Radicalism, then, involves a commitment to the interdependence of men, and to the sharing of their concerns, which the radical feels with an especially urgent, personal intensity.

These are only general characteristics. Of course, there are borderline cases. We might be uncertain whether Henry George's Single Taxers or Tom Watson's Populists were real radicals. But a full-fledged radicalism, of the kind which can serve and has served as a tonic to the whole society, does have at least the three characteristics I have mentioned. There have been many such radicalisms in American History—from the Antinomians of Massachusetts Bay, through the Quakers of Pennsylvania, the Abolitionists and the Mormons down to the Jehovah's Witnesses and the Communists in our own day. But the most prominent, the most vocal, the most threatening, and the most characteristic disruptive movements in the United States within the last few years do not belong in this tradition. Whatever they or their uncritical observers may say to the contrary, they are not radicalisms. They do not exhibit the characteristics I have listed.

*I*t is characteristic of the Student Power and the Black Power "movements" that in them the quest for meaning has been displaced by the quest for power. Among students, the Bull Session tends to be displaced by the Strategy Session. The "discussions" of activist students are not explorations of the great questions that have troubled civi-

lized men as they come to manhood, since the days of the Old Testament and of Ancient Greece. They are not concerned with whether there is a God, with what is the true nature of art, or of civilization, or of morals. The Student Power Barbarians and the Black Power Barbarians pose not questions but answers. Or, as one of their recent slogans says: "Happiness Is Student Power." Their answer to everything is uncharmingly simple: Power. And to the more difficult questions their answer is: More Power.

"The most vocal and most violent disrupters of American society today are not radicals at all, but a new species of barbarian."

These New Barbarians offer no content, no ideology, hardly even a jargon. While dissident students thirty-five years ago spoke an esoteric[7] Marxist lingo, and debated "dialectical materialism," "the transformation of quantity into quality," etc., etc., the dissident students and Black Powerites today scream four-letter obscenities and expletives.[8] While the radicals explored an intricate ideology in the heavy volumes of Marx, the cumbersome paragraphs of Lenin, and the elaborate reinterpretations of Stalin and Trotsky, today's power-seekers are more than satisfied by the hate slogans of Mao Tse-tung, Che Guevara, or Malcolm X. They find nothing so enchanting as the sound of their own voices, and their bibliography consists mainly of the products of their own mimeographing. They seem to think they can be radicals without portfolio. If they call themselves "anarchists" they have not bothered to read their Thoreau or Proudhon, Bakunin or Tolstoy. If they call themselves "leftists" they have not bothered to read Marx or Engels, Lenin or Trotsky. If they call themselves Black Power Nationalists, they mistake the rattle of ancient chains for the sound of facts and ideas.

Having nothing to say, the New Barbarians cannot interest others by *what* they say. Therefore they must try to shock by *how* they say it. Traditionally, radicals have addressed their society

---

[7] understood only by a select few
[8] exclamations, often profane

248 with a question mark, but the new frustrates' favorite punctuation is the exclamation point! Having no new facts or ideas to offer, they strain at novelty with their latrine words. The Black Powerites, whose whole program is their own power, must wrap up their emptiness in vulgarisms and expletives. For racism is the perfect example of a dogma without content.

The appeal to violence and "direct action" as if they were ends rather than means is eloquent testimony of the New Barbarians' lack of subject matter. An act of violence may express hate or anger, but it communicates nothing precise or substantial. Throwing a rock, like hurling an epithet, proclaims that the thrower has given up trying to say anything.

These Student Powerites and Black Powerites are not *egalitarians*[9] seeking a just community; they are *egolitarians*, preening the egoism of the isolationist self. Students seek power for "students," Negroes seek power for "blacks"—and let the community take the hindmost! Unlike the radicalisms which affirm community and are preoccupied or obsessed by its problems, the Student Power and Black Power movements deny any substantial community—even among their own "members." A novel feature of S.N.C.C. and S.D.S., too little noted, is the fact that they are, strictly speaking, "nonmembership" organizations. Members do not carry cards, membership lists are said not to exist. A person does not "join" as a result of long and solemn deliberation, he is not trained and tested (as was the case in the Thirties with candidates for membership in the Communist Party). Instead the New Barbarian simply affiliates, and stays with the group as long as it pleases him. "I'm with you today, baby, but who knows where I'll be tomorrow?" A desperate infantinstantism reveals the uncertainty and vagrancy of these affiliations. The leader better act this afternoon, for maybe they won't be with him tomorrow morning!

All these unradical characteristics of the New Barbarians express a spiritual cataclysm.[10] This is what I mean by the Ptolemaic Revolution: a movement from the community-centered to the self-centered. While radicals see themselves and everything else revolving around the community and its idealized needs, each of these new frustrates tries to make the world revolve around himself. The depth and significance of this shift in focus have remained unnoticed. It has been the harder to grasp because it is in the nature of the New Barbarism that it should lack philosophers. Being closer to a dyspepsia than to an ideology, the New Barbarism has tried to generalize its stomachaches but has been unable to cast them into a philosophy. It is much easier, therefore, to describe the direction in which the chaotic groups comprising the New Barbarism are moving than to fix the precise position where they stand.

*T*he New Barbarism, in a word, is the social expression of a movement from Experience to Sensation. Experience, the dictionary tells us, means *actual observation of or practical acquaintance with facts or events; knowledge resulting from this.* A person's experience is what he has lived through. Generally speaking, experience is (a) cumulative, and (b) communicable. People add up their experiences to become wiser and more knowledgeable. We can learn from our own experience and, most important, we can learn from other people's experiences. Our publicly shared experience is history. Experience is distinguished, then, by the very fact that it can be shared. When we have an experience, we enter into the continuum of a society. But the dramatic shift now is away from Experience and toward Sensation.

Sensation is personal, private, confined, and incommunicable. Our sensations (hearing, seeing, touching, tasting, and smelling) are what we *receive.* Or, as the dictionary says, sensation is *consciousness of perceiving or seeming to perceive some state or affection of one's body or its parts or senses of one's mind or its emotions; the contents of such consciousness.* If an experience were totally incommunicable, if I could not describe it to anyone else, if I could not share it, it would not really be an experience. It would simply be a sensation, a message which came to me and to me alone. Sensations, from their very nature, then, are intimate and ineffable.[11] Experience takes us out of ourselves, sensation affirms and emphasizes the self.

What history is to the person in quest of experience, a "happening" is to the person in quest of sensation. For a "happening" is something totally

---

[9] people seeking to remove inequalities among men
[10] violent event characterized by overwhelming upheaval

[11] too overpowering to be expressed in words

discrete.[12] It adds to our sensations without increasing our experience.

Experience and Sensation, then, express attitudes to the world as opposite as the poles. The experience-oriented young person suffers Weltschmerz[13]—the discovery of the pain and suffering that are his portion of the world. The sensation-oriented suffers an "identity crisis": he is concerned mostly about defining the boundaries of that bundle of private messages which is himself. The experience-oriented seeks, and finds, continuity, and emphasizes what is shared and what is communicable. The sensation-oriented seeks the instantaneous, the egocentric, the inexpressible. The accumulation of *experience* produces the *expert*. Its cumulative produce is *expertise*—competence, the ability to handle situations by knowing what is tried and familiar about them. And the name for accumulated experience is knowledge.

While sensations can be more or less intense, they are not cumulative. A set of simultaneous, intense and melodramatic sensations is not instructive, but it is shocking: we say it is *sensational*. Experience is additive, it can be organized, classified, and rearranged; sensation is miscellaneous, random, and incapable of being generalized.

Everywhere in the United States nowadays—and not only among the New Barbarians—we see a desperate quest for sensation and a growing tendency to value sensation more than experience. We note this in what people seek, in what they find, in what they make, and in what they like to watch. We note a tendency in painting to produce works which do not appeal to a common, shareable fund of experience, but which, instead, set off each viewer on his own private path of sensation. In the theatre and in movies which lack a clear and intelligible story line, the spectators are offered sensations from which each is expected to make his own private inward adventure.

An example of the current quest for the indescribable, the ineffable, the transcendent[14]—aiming to maximize sensation rather than experience —is the current vogue for LSD and for other so-called "consciousness-expanding" drugs. Precisely speaking, they aim to expand not experience but *consciousness*. They aim somehow to increase the intensity and widen the range of the vivid, idiosyncratic[15] self.

The special appeal of an LSD "trip" is that it leads to the ineffable: what one person gets is as different as possible from what is obtained by another. And it is all quite individual and quite unpredictable. "Instead of a communion," one psychologist explains, "it [the LSD state] is a withdrawal into oneself. The *religio* (binding together) is not visible here." This is how Richard Alpert, the archbishop of LSD, explains the sensations under the drug:

" 'Nowhere' is Sidney's prediction of where the psychochemical (r)evolution is taking the 'young people' who are exploring inner space. I prefer to read that word as NowHere, and fervently hope he is right—that LSD is bringing man back 'to his senses'. . . . Do not be confused! The issue is not LSD. . . . Your control and access to your own brain is at stake."

LSD sensations, Alpert insists, are "eyewitness reports of what is, essentially, a private experience." "It was," in the words of a girl who had just been on an LSD trip, "like a shower on the inside."

The search for sensation is a search for some way of reminding oneself that one is alive—but without becoming entangled with others or with a community. "I have never felt so intense, alive, such a sense of well-being. . . . I have chosen to be

---

[12] not connected; individually distinct
[13] mental depression caused by a comparison of the actual world with the ideal world
[14] lying beyond the limits of ordinary experience
[15] having a characteristic peculiarity of habit

outside of society after having been very much inside. . . . My plans are unstructured in regards to anything but the immediate future. I believe in freedom, and must take the jump, I must take the chance of action." This is not the report of an LSD trip, but the explanation by a young white student of his sensations on joining S.N.C.C. The vocabulary of the Student Power movement reveals the same desperate quest for sensation. "Direct Action" is the name for spasmodic acts of self-affirmation. It is a way of making the senses scream. It matters not whether the "Direct Action" has a purpose, much less whether it can attain any purpose, since it gives satisfaction enough by intensifying the Direct Actor's sense of being alive and separate from others. "Direct Action" is to politics what the Frug or the Jerk is to the dance. It identifies and explodes the self without attaching the self to groups or to individuals outside. And now the "New Left" has become the LSD of the intellectuals.

The man who is pathologically experience-oriented will be timid, haunted by respectability. His motto is apt to be that posted over the desk of an English civil servant: "Never do anything for the first time!" On the other hand, the man pathologically obsessed by Sensation makes his motto: "Do everything only for the first time!"

*A*ll about us, and especially in the Student Power and Black Power movements of recent years, we see the pathology of the sensation-oriented. Contrary to popular belief, and to the legends which they would like to spread about themselves, they are not troubled by any excessive concern for others. Their feelings cannot accurately be described as a concern, and it is surely not for others. Their ailment might best be called *apathy*. For apathy is a feeling apart from others and, as the dictionary reminds us, *an indolence of mind*. The Direct Actionists, as President W. Allen Wallis of the University of Rochester has explained, "are the students who are truly apathetic." They do not care enough about the problems of their society to burn the midnight oil over them. Impatient to sate their egos with the sensations of "Direct Action," they are too indolent intellectually to do the hard work of exploring the problems to which they pretend a concern. Theirs is the egoism, the personal chauvinism[16] of the

isolationist self. Their "Direct Action" slogan means nothing but "Myself, Right or Wrong!"

These people I would call the *Apathetes*. Just as the Aesthetes of some decades ago believed in "Art for Art's Sake," so the Apathetes believe in "Me for My Own Sake." They try to make a virtue of their indolence of mind (by calling it "Direct Action") and they exult in their feeling-apartness (by calling it "Power"). Thus these Apathetes are at the opposite pole from the radicals of the past.

They abandon the quest for meaning, for fear it might entangle their thoughts and feelings with those of others, and they plunge into "Direct Action" for fear that second thoughts might deny them this satisfaction to their ego. Theirs is a mindless, obsessive quest for power. But they give up the very idea of man's need for quest. Instead they seek explosive affirmations of the self.

They deny the existence of subject matter, by denying the need for experience. How natural, then, that Youth should lord it over Age! For in youth, they say, the senses are most sensitive and most attuned. The accumulated experience of books or of teachers becomes absurdly irrelevant. There is no Knowledge, but only Sensation, and Power is its Handmaiden!

They deny the existence of time, since Sensation is instantaneous and not cumulative. They herald the age of Instant Everything! Since time can do nothing but accumulate experience and dull the senses, experience is said to be nothing but the debris which stifles our sensations! There must be no frustration. Every program must be instantaneous, every demand must be an ultimatum.

This movement from Experience to Sensation accelerates every day. Each little victory for Student Power or Black Power—or any other kind of Power—is a victory for the New Barbarism. Appropriately, the New Barbarism makes its first sallies and has its greatest initial successes against the universities, which are the repositories of Experience, and in the cause of Racism, which—whether it is Black or whether it is Aryan—is the emptiness to end all emptinesses.

[16] blind patriotism

A Generation in Search of a Future

GEORGE WALD

All of you know that in the last couple of years there has been student unrest, breaking at times into violence, in many parts of the world: in England, Germany, Italy, Spain, Mexico, Japan, and, needless to say, many parts of this country. There has been a great deal of discussion as to what it all means. Perfectly clearly, it means something different in Mexico from what it does in France, and something different in France from what it does in Tokyo, and something different in Tokyo from what it does in this country. Yet, unless we are to assume that students have gone crazy all over the world, or that they have just decided that it's the thing to do, it must have some common meaning.

I don't need to go so far afield to look for that meaning. I am a teacher, and at Harvard I have a class of about three hundred and fifty students—men and women—most of them freshmen and sophomores. Over these past few years, I have felt increasingly that something is terribly wrong—and this year ever so much more than last. Something has gone sour, in teaching and in learning. It's almost as though there were a widespread feeling that education has become irrelevant.

A lecture is much more of a dialogue than many of you probably realize. As you lecture, you keep

These remarks are the major portion of a speech given on March 4, 1969 by Dr. Wald, biologist at Harvard and a Nobel Prize winner. He spoke, extemporaneously, to a crowd of students and professors who had gathered at the Massachusetts Institute of Technology to protest the misuse of science.

watching the faces, and information keeps coming back to you all the time. I began to feel, particularly this year, that I was missing much of what was coming back. I tried asking the students, but they didn't or couldn't help me very much.

But I think I know what's the matter. I think that this whole generation of students is beset with a profound uneasiness, and I don't think that they have yet quite defined its source. I think I understand the reasons for their uneasiness even better than they do. What is more, I share their uneasiness.

What's bothering those students? Some of them tell you it's the Vietnam war. I think the Vietnam war is the most shameful episode in the whole of American history. The concept of war crimes is an American invention. We've committed many war crimes in Vietnam—but I'll tell you something interesting about that. We were committing war crimes in World War II, before the Nuremberg trials were held and the principle of war crimes was stated. The saturation bombing of German cities was a war crime. Dropping those atomic bombs on Hiroshima and Nagasaki was a war crime. If we had lost the war, it might have been *our* leaders who had to answer for such actions. I've gone through all that history lately, and I find that there's a gimmick in it. It isn't written out, but I think we established it by precedent. That gimmick is that if one can allege that one is repelling or retaliating for an aggression, after that everything goes.

And, you see, we are living in a world in which all wars are wars of defense. All War Departments are now Defense Departments. This is all part of the doubletalk of our time. The aggressor is always on the other side. I suppose this is why our ex-Secretary of State Dean Rusk went to such pains to insist, as he still insists, that in Vietnam we are repelling an aggression. And if that's what we are doing—so runs the doctrine—everything goes. If the concept of war crimes is ever to mean anything, they will have to be defined as categories of *acts,* regardless of alleged provocation. But that isn't so now.

I think we've lost that war, as a lot of other people think, too. The Vietnamese have a secret weapon. It's their willingness to die beyond our willingness to kill. In effect, they've been saying, You can kill us, but you'll have to kill a lot of us; you may have to kill all of us. And, thank heaven, we are not yet ready to do that.

Yet we have come a long way toward it—far enough to sicken many Americans, far enough to sicken even our fighting men. Far enough so that our national symbols have gone sour. How many of you can sing about "the rockets' red glare, the bombs bursting in air' without thinking, Those are *our* bombs and *our* rockets, bursting over South Vietnamese villages? When those words were written, we were a people struggling for freedom against oppression. Now we are supporting open or thinly disguised military dictatorships all over the world, helping them to control and repress peoples struggling for their freedom.

But the Vietnam war, shameful and terrible as it is, seems to me only an immediate incident in a much larger and more stubborn situation.

Part of my trouble with students is that almost all the students I teach were born after World War II. Just after World War II, a series of new and abnormal procedures came into American life. We regarded them at the time as temporary aberrations. We thought we would get back to normal American life someday.

But those procedures have stayed with us now for more than twenty years, and those students of mine have never known anything else. They think those things are normal. They think that we've always had a Pentagon, that we have always had a big Army, and that we have always had a draft. But those are all new things in American life, and I think that they are incompatible with what America meant before.

How many of you realize that just before World War II the entire American Army, including the Air Corps, numbered a hundred and thirty-nine thousand men? Then World War II started, but we weren't yet in it, and, seeing that there was great trouble in the world, we doubled this Army to two hundred and sixty-eight thousand men. Then, in World War II, it got to be eight million. And then World War II came to an end and we prepared to go back to a peacetime Army, somewhat as the American Army had always been before. And, indeed, in 1950—you think about 1950, our international commitments, the Cold War, the Truman Doctrine, and all the rest of it—in 1950, we got down to six hundred thousand men.

Now we have three and a half million men under arms: about six hundred thousand in Vietnam, about three hundred thousand more in 'support areas' elsewhere in the Pacific, about two hundred and fifty thousand in Germany. And there are a lot at home. Some months ago, we were told that three hundred thousand National Guardsmen and two hundred thousand reservists —so half a million men—had been specially trained for riot duty in the cities.

I say the Vietnam war is just an immediate incident because as long as we keep that big an Army, it will always find things to do. If the Vietnam war stopped tomorrow, the chances are that with that big a military establishment we would be in another such adventure, abroad or at home, before you knew it.

The thing to do about the draft is not to reform it but to get rid of it.

A peacetime draft is the most un-American thing I know. All the time I was growing up, I was told about oppressive Central European countries and Russia, where young men were forced into the Army, and I was told what they did about it. They chopped off a finger, or shot off a couple of toes, or, better still, if they could manage it, they came to this country. And we understood that, and sympathized, and were glad to welcome them.

"The only point of government is to safeguard and foster life. Our government has become preoccupied with death, with the business of killing and being killed."

Now, by present estimates, from four to six thousand Americans of draft age have left this country for Canada, two or three thousand more have gone to Europe, and it looks as though many more were preparing to emigrate.

A bill to stop the draft was recently introduced in the Senate (S. 503), sponsored by a group of senators that runs the gamut[1] from McGovern and Hatfield to Barry Goldwater. I hope it goes through. But I think that when we get rid of the draft we must also drastically cut back the size of the armed forces.

Yet there is something ever so much bigger and more important than the draft. That bigger thing,

of course, is the militarization of our country. Ex-President Eisenhower, in his farewell address, warned us of what he called the military-industrial complex. I am sad to say that we must begin to think of it now as the military-industrial-labor-union complex. What happened under the plea of the Cold War was not alone that we built up the first big peacetime Army in our history but that we institutionalized it. We built, I suppose, the biggest government building in our history to run it, and we institutionalized it.

I don't think we can live with the present military establishment, and its eighty-billion-dollar-a-year budget, and keep America anything like the America we have known in the past. It is corrupting the life of the whole country. It is buying up everything in sight: industries, banks, investors, scientists—and lately it seems also to have bought up the labor unions.

The Defense Department is always broke, but some of the things it does with that eighty billion dollars a year would make Buck Rogers envious. For example, the Rocky Mountain Arsenal, on the outskirts of Denver, was manufacturing a deadly nerve poison on such a scale that there was a problem of waste disposal. Nothing daunted,[2] the people there dug a tunnel two miles deep under Denver, into which they have injected so much poisoned water that, beginning a couple of years ago, Denver has experienced a series of earth tremors of increasing severity. Now there is grave fear of a major earthquake. An interesting debate is in progress as to whether Denver will be safer if that lake of poisoned water is removed or is left in place.

Perhaps you have read also of those six thousand sheep that suddenly died in Skull Valley, Utah, killed by another nerve poison—a strange and, I believe, still unexplained accident, since the nearest testing seems to have been thirty miles away.

As for Vietnam, the expenditure of firepower there has been frightening. Some of you may still remember Khe Sanh, a hamlet just south of the Demilitarized Zone, where a force of United States Marines was beleaguered[3] for a time. During that period, we dropped on the perimeter of Khe Sanh more explosives than fell on Japan throughout

[1] range

[2] intimidated
[3] surrounded

"I think that what we are up against is a generation that is by no means sure that it has a future."

World War II, and more than fell on the whole of Europe during the years 1942 and 1943.

One of the officers there was quoted as having said afterward, "It looks like the world caught smallpox and died."

The only point of government is to safeguard and foster life. Our government has become preoccupied with death, with the business of killing and being killed. So-called defense now absorbs sixty per cent of the national budget, and about twelve per cent of the Gross National Product.

A lively debate is beginning again on whether or not we should deploy[4] antiballistic missiles, the ABM. I don't have to talk about them—everyone else here is doing that. But I should like to mention a curious circumstance. In September, 1967, or about a year and a half ago, we had a meeting of M.I.T. and Harvard people, including experts on these matters, to talk about whether anything could be done to block the Sentinel system—the deployment of ABMs. Everyone present thought them undesirable, but a few of the most knowledgeable persons took what seemed to be the practical view: "Why fight about a dead issue? It has been decided, the funds have been appropriated. Let's go on from there."

Well, fortunately, it's not a dead issue.

An ABM is a nuclear weapon. It takes a nuclear weapon to stop a nuclear weapon. And our concern must be with the whole issue of nuclear weapons.

There is an entire semantics[5] ready to deal with the sort of thing I am about to say. It involves such phrases as "Those are the facts of life." No—these are the facts of death. I don't accept them, and I advise you not to accept them. We are under repeated pressure to accept things that are presented to us as settled—decisions that have been made. Always there is the thought: Let's go on from there. But this time we don't see how to go on. We will have to stick with these issues.

We are told that the United States and Russia, between them, by now have stockpiled nuclear weapons of approximately the explosive power of fifteen tons of TNT for every man, woman, and child on earth. And now it is suggested that we must make more. All very regrettable, of course, but "those are the facts of life." We really would like to disarm, but our new Secretary of Defense has made the ingenious proposal that now is the time to greatly increase our nuclear armaments, so that we can disarm from a position of strength.

I think all of you know there is no adequate defense against massive nuclear attack. It is both easier and cheaper to circumvent[6] any known nuclear-defense system than to provide it. It's all pretty crazy. At the very moment we talk of deploying ABMs, we are also building the MIRV, the weapon to circumvent ABMs.

As far as I know, the most conservative estimates of the number of Americans who would be killed in a major nuclear attack, with everything working as well as can be hoped and all foreseeable precautions taken, run to about fifty million. We have become callous to gruesome statistics, and this seems at first to be only another gruesome statistic. You think, Bang!—and next morning, if you're still there, you read in the newspapers that fifty million people were killed.

But that isn't the way it happens. When we killed close to two hundred thousand people with those first, little, old-fashioned uranium bombs that we dropped on Hiroshima and Nagasaki, about the same number of persons were maimed, blinded, burned, poisoned, and otherwise doomed. A lot of them took a long time to die.

That's the way it would be. Not a bang and a certain number of corpses to bury but a nation filled with millions of helpless, maimed, tortured, and doomed persons, and the survivors huddled with their families in shelters, with guns ready to fight off their neighbors trying to get some uncontaminated food and water.

A few months ago, Senator Richard Russell, of Georgia, ended a speech in the Senate with the words "If we have to start over again with another Adam and Eve, I want them to be Americans; and I want them on this continent and not in Europe." That was a United States senator making a patriotic speech. Well, here is a Nobel laureate who thinks that those words are criminally insane.

How real is the threat of full-scale nuclear war? I have my own very inexpert idea, but, realizing how little I know, and fearful that I may be a little paranoid[7] on this subject, I take every opportunity to ask reputed experts. I asked that question of a distinguished professor of government at Harvard about a month ago. I asked him what sort of odds

---

[4] extend; spread out or arrange, especially strategically
[5] code, or system of terms

[6] get around strategically; thwart
[7] suffering from delusions of persecution

he would lay on the possibility of full-scale nuclear war within the foreseeable future. "Oh," he said comfortably, "I think I can give you a pretty good answer to that question. I estimate the probability of full-scale nuclear war, provided that the situation remains about as it is now, at two per cent per year." Anybody can do the simple calculation that shows that two per cent per year means that the chance of having that full-scale nuclear war by 1990 is about one in three, and by 2000 it is about fifty-fifty.

I think I know what is bothering the students. I think that what we are up against is a generation that is by no means sure that it has a future.

I am growing old, and my future, so to speak, is already behind me. But there are those students of mine, who are in my mind always; and there are my children, the youngest of them now seven and nine, whose future is infinitely more precious to me than my own. So it isn't just their generation; it's mine, too. We're all in it together.

Are we to have a chance to live? We don't ask for prosperity, or security. Only for a reasonable chance to live, to work out our destiny in peace and decency. Not to go down in history as the apocalyptic[8] generation.

And it isn't only nuclear war. Another overwhelming threat is in the population explosion. That has not yet even begun to come under control. There is every indication that the world population will double before the year 2000, and there is a widespread expectation of famine on an unprecedented scale in many parts of the world. The experts tend to differ only in their estimates of when those famines will begin. Some think by 1980; others think they can be staved off until 1990; very few expect that they will not occur by the year 2000.

That is the problem. Unless we can be surer than we now are that this generation has a future, nothing else matters. It's not good enough to give it tender, loving care, to supply it with breakfast foods, to buy it expensive educations. Those things don't mean anything unless this generation has a future. And we're not sure that it does.

I don't think that there are problems of youth, or student problems. All the real problems I know about are grown-up problems.

Perhaps you will think me altogether absurd, or "academic," or hopelessly innocent—that is, until you think of the alternatives—if I say, as I do to you now: We have to get rid of those nuclear weapons. There is nothing worth having that can be obtained by nuclear war—nothing material or ideological—no tradition that it can defend. It is utterly self-defeating. Those atomic bombs represent an unusable weapon. The only use for an atomic bomb is to keep somebody else from using one. It can give us no protection—only the doubtful satisfaction of retaliation. Nuclear weapons offer us nothing but a balance of terror, and a balance of terror is still terror.

We have to get rid of those atomic weapons, here and everywhere. We cannot live with them.

I think we've reached a point of great decision, not just for our nation, not only for all humanity, but for life upon the earth. I tell my students, with a feeling of pride that I hope they will share, that the carbon, nitrogen, and oxygen that make up ninety-nine per cent of our living substance were cooked in the deep interiors of earlier generations of dying stars. Gathered up from the ends of the universe, over billions of years, eventually they came to form, in part, the substance of our sun, its planets, and ourselves. Three billion years ago, life arose upon the earth. It is the only life in the solar system.

About two million years ago, man appeared. He has become the dominant species of the earth. All other living things, animal and plant, live by his sufferance. He is the custodian of life on earth, and in the solar system. It's a big responsibility.

The thought that we're in competition with Russians or with Chinese is all a mistake, and trivial. We are one species, with a world to win. There's life all over this universe, but the only life in the solar system is on earth, and in the whole universe we are the only men.

Our business is with life, not death. Our challenge is to give what account we can of what becomes of life in the solar system, this corner of the universe that is our home; and, most of all, what becomes of men—all men, of all nations, colors, and creeds. This has become one world, a world for all men. It is only such a world that can now offer us life, and the chance to go on.

[8] the last, facing overwhelming destruction and breakdown

The Statues of Daedalus

MICHAEL HARRINGTON

There is only one condition in which we can imagine managers not needing subordinates, and masters not needing slaves. This condition would be that each (inanimate) instrument could do its own work, at the word of command or by intelligent anticipation, like the statues of Daedalus or the tripods made by Hephaestus,[1] of which Homer relates that

Of their own motion they entered the conclave of Gods on Olympus

as if a shuttle should weave of itself, and a plectrum should do its own harp playing.

ARISTOTLE, *The Politics,* 1253 B.C.

In the middle of the twentieth century, the statues of Daedalus, that "cunning craftsman" of Greek legend, are beginning to dance in the West.

Automation (i.e., self-correcting machines that feed back information and adjust themselves) and cybernation (i.e., making the automated machines capable of responding to a near infinity of contingencies by hooking them up to computers) possess the scientific capacity to accomplish the ancient myth.

As a result, the abolition of work, as Western man has defined the term, has become a technological possibility.

Aristotle understood that such a development would have the most profound consequences. His reference to the statues of Daedalus comes in the course of a defense of slavery. He realized that their discovery would shatter his own "natural" law: Managers would no longer need subordinates, masters could dispense with slaves. This is, happily, one of the options now open to technological man. But there are other, more complex and disturbing, possibilities if the statues of Daedalus are indeed coming to life in the twentieth century.

The modern West distinguished itself from other cultures by its Faustian[2] assault upon reality, its relentless ambition to remake the very world. In the matter of a few hundred years, this drive created an industrial civilization and a standard of living that became the envy, and model, of the entire globe. It also deeply marked the ethic, the religious values, the psychology, and social system of Europe and America. If the statues of Daedalus have indeed been found, it is clear that the moment signals the decadence of much that passed as wisdom and morality for hundreds of years. Ironically, the triumph of Faustian man could mean his suicide. For what will Faust do if,

[1] In Greek mythology, Daedalus and Hephaestus were the supreme craftsmen, the mechanical wizards who made wondrous contrivances for gods and kings. On command, the statues of Daedalus came to life and performed useful services. The tripods of Hephaestus, who excelled in metal work, were set on golden wheels and rolled of their own accord into the assembly of the gods.

[2] pertaining to Dr. Faustus, the hero of a 19th-century play by Goethe, who promises his soul to the devil in return for almost superhuman power and understanding. In his quest for significant experience, Faust completes a gigantic project of reclaiming land from the sea for the benefit of humanity.

as Paul Valéry once suggested, the world is to become "finished"? Or, to put the issue in American terms, if there are no more frontiers?

Such a happening is clearly in the far distance, though not so far as to be out of historical eyesight. Closer to the present, there are even now less ultimate, but extremely profound, results of the fact that work in the West is already being redefined.

The certitude that man must labor by the sweat of his brow was a weary, but consoling, knowledge. The machines are now lifting this burden from human shoulders and, in the doing, corrupting the central Western ethic of work. The stern necessities that drove Europe and America to secular[3] greatness are disappearing. In their place, there is a bewildering freedom. Thus, the machines are not simply a technological fact but the stuff of a spiritual crisis as well.

Then, there is another effect upon the inner man of the West. As Sigmund Freud understood it, work was essential both to society and to the self. At his most pessimistic, in *The Future of an Illusion* and *Civilization and Its Discontents*, Freud argued that civilization itself was based upon the repression of instinctual gratification, demanding that the individual sacrifice himself to the discipline and needs of the collective, to a large extent through hard labor. The majority, Freud said, were lazy and indolent. Without work and its attendant coercion, society would fall apart.

More positively, Freud believed that work was a means of linking man to reality and thus therapeutic. But taking either his dark or his optimistic theory, the disappearance of work could be a social and individual catastrophe, a psychological revolution.

Finally, that other recent Western giant, Karl Marx, argued that the coming of automation would destroy the very rationality of the Western capitalist system itself. Only, he said, in a society in which the exploitation of labor was the essential element in creating commodities could economic rewards and values be measured in terms of how much productive work a man did. Once machines and the practical application of science become the true source of wealth, he concluded, capitalism is a dangerous, unworkable anachronism.[4]

In each of these cases, and in many others, the same irony appears. The West, which more than any other part of the globe learned to cope with starvation and gradually to conquer it, faces the distinct possibility that abundance—its long-dreamed utopia,[5] its Cockaigne[6]—will be the decadence of some of its most cherished values and that it will take more ingenuity to live with freedom than it did to subsist under necessity.

I The contemporary statues of Daedalus can be described quite prosaically. With so many apocalypses[7] depending on their dance, it is well to start *sotto voce*,[8] empirically, statistically.

In a series of American Government documents in 1964, and most particularly in the Report of the Senate Subcommittee on Employment and Manpower, some trends of automation and cybernation were noted. Among them were changes in the increase of productivity per man-hour, an important shift in the quality of manpower needs, and chronic, high levels of unemployment.

Taken by themselves, these transformations were regarded as serious enough by the Senate Subcommittee to merit the title of a "manpower revolution." They demonstrate that at this very moment, without too many people noticing, the nature of work is being redefined. The figures do not yet show that work as it has been known is actually being abolished, but they certainly suggest this possibility in the middle historical distance.

The evidence presented here is exclusively American. There are considerable differences between Europe and the United States in this regard, most notably in the widespread acceptance of national planning on the Continent. Yet, there is every reason to believe that the Old World will soon experience the troubles of the New. The consumer boom that took place in the United States right after the war did not occur in Europe until the mid-fifties and is still in progress. That has provided a favorable context for the new technology. Once this trend plays itself out, there is no reason to believe that Europe can avoid the revolutionary consequences of its technology. These figures suggest, then, not sim-

---

[3] pertaining to things non-religious in nature
[4] something that does not fit the proper or natural time element

[5] ideal world
[6] imaginary country of luxury and idleness
[7] writings professing to reveal the future
[8] in an undertone

ply the American, but the European, future and, as industrialization proceeds around the globe, the fate of the world.

The American statues of Daedalus are visible in the prosaic statistics on the increase in output per man-hour in the private economy.

Between 1909 and 1962, American industry increased the worker's output by 2.4 percent a year. But then, this five-decade trend conceals a most significant shift. From 1909 to 1947, the productivity gain was only 2 percent a year. But between 1958 and 1963, productivity per man-hour went up 3.1 percent a year, and between 1960 and 1963, 3.6 percent a year. And it was, of course, in this period of accelerated productivity growth in the fifties and early sixties that automation and cybernation began to emerge as an important factor in the American economy.

Translate these gross quantities into some of their significant details. In 1964, ten men could produce as many automobile motor blocks as 400 men in 1954; two workers could make a thousand radios a day, a job that required 200 a few years before; 14 operators were tending the glass-blowing machines that manufactured 90 percent of all the glass bulbs in the United States of America. During the fifties, Bell Telephone increased its volume by 50 percent and its work force by only 10 percent.

This same trend also illumines an economic paradox: the coexistence, in the late fifties and early sixties, of prosperity and chronic unemployment. More unskilled and semiskilled jobs in private manufacture were destroyed than created, and joblessness persisted at over 5 percent of the work force despite the prosperity (this 5-percent figure is an understatement; it does not count those driven out of the labor market, possibly a million and a half workers, nor the underemployed; a "true" estimate of involuntary idleness would be in the neighborhood of 9 percent). At the same time, the machines were the source of enormous profit, and thus there was a deformed "prosperity," benign for corporations, malignant for millions of workers.

Curiously enough, this process stands out in even starker relief in American agriculture. There, productivity increases have recently hit a prodigious 6 percent a year. One result has been to cut the postwar farming population from 14 percent of the population to 7 percent. And even this statistic conceals the radical character of the change. Farming supports a tremendous amount of underemployment and hidden unemployment. A third of the American agricultural producers do not market crops but merely eke out an impoverished, miserable subsistence for themselves.

In short, less than 5 percent of the American people are able to produce more food than they can profitably sell to the other 95 percent under the present system. In order to satisfy these politically powerful farmers, the Government now pays them between $4 and $5 billion a year in subsidies. Here, then, is an anticipation of one of the strange logics of abundance: that American agriculture is so capable of plenty that nonproduction must be publicly supported. (The extreme irrationality of rewarding the rich farmer and penalizing the poor is not a deduction from technology but a conscious, and reactionary, political choice; yet the fundamental problem is there in any context.)

In private manufacturing, the decline in jobs has not been as spectacular as on the farm, but the trend is clearly present. Between 1957 and 1963, for instance, wage and salary employment in the nonagricultural, goods-producing sector dropped by 300,000 jobs—despite substantial increases in output, new products, and even new industries. In the ten years before this period, from 1947 to 1957, employment in the same sector had gone up at the rate of 250,000 new jobs a year.

In short, American industry broke through a technological barrier somewhere in the mid-fifties. Cybernation made it possible to expand production and contract the work force. Less labor produced more goods. Even so, the president of a corporation making automated equipment, John Snyder, remarked that his equipment was only at a "primitive" level, that an accentuation of the process was imminent.

At first, the new technology was most dramatically successful in reducing unskilled and semiskilled industrial jobs. But as time went on, other occupations began to be effected. In the financial services industry, machines took over more and more office work; transportation employment dropped; the increase in retail sales work slowed down (the automated department store will soon appear in the United States: machines will take orders, package goods, notify inventory of the sale, and keep instantaneous financial accounts).

But employment did grow in this period. And the areas where growth did take place indicate a significant change in the quality and meaning of work.

The largest single increase in jobs took place on the public payrolls, mainly through the hiring of teachers to handle the postwar baby boom. This category alone accounted for one-third of the new jobs in wage and salary employment, or 300,000 new places annually. Close behind was the personal service industry—hospitals, private schools, colleges and private social welfare organizations, hostelries[9]—with 250,000 additional jobs each year. As *The Wall Street Journal* noted in October, 1964, during the previous year there had been more new jobs for schoolteachers than for production workers.

So it was that in this time the most easily cybernated positions, routine, repetitive factory func-

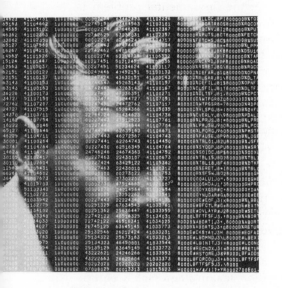

tions, declined; that the simpler office tasks declined or leveled off; that retail employment slowed down; and that real increases were achieved in those areas, such as teaching and hospitals, which required the human care of human beings. Given the revolutionary character of American technology, this pattern is likely to become even more accelerated in the immediate future. Even menial, miserably paid work, like much of that of migrant field hands, can be taken over by machines (and, with savage irony, probably will, not out of compassion for those who bend and stoop in the fields, but because those

workers will finally enforce minimal standards of decency for themselves and thus make it cheaper to enslave a machine than a man).

The striking aspect of this new pattern is that the job increases are in areas that are not "productive" in the lay sense of the term. Teaching and nursing do not make manufactured goods, or even help distribute them. The idea that the human care of human beings is an *economically* significant undertaking is a fairly new one. It was this significant change in American working life that led the Senate Subcommittee to speak of a "manpower revolution."

All of this takes place as a process, not as a sudden, definitive transformation. Millions of Americans still labor in fields and on assembly lines. But, as one scholarly vocabulary puts it, the trend is clearly away from primary employments like agriculture, to the secondary functions of industry, to the tertiary[10] of services, and now to a fourth level of training and human care. At each point, work is receding from the direct confrontation of man and nature. And, as time goes on, it is possible to conceive the abolition of entire sectors of economic activity, most obviously that of the factory worker.

Without even looking into the middle distance, however, these new patterns have already posed some massive social problems in America society.

One of the effects of automation and cybernation is to increase the skill "mix" in manufacturing. An airplane plant organized by the United Automobile Workers during World War II had 85 percent of its work force in organizable (blue-collar, generally speaking) occupations. By the sixties, that figure had been reduced to 35 percent, and the rest of the plant was filled with highly trained engineers and other management personnel. In a 1964 Department of Labor study of 3,440 plants, 11 percent had progressed to advanced stages of automation, and, of these, 84.1 percent had reported that their skill requirements had risen.

Left to itself, this trend could create a large increase in involuntary joblessness as a byproduct of abundance.

In the decade of the 1960's, according to the Government, 26 million new workers were entering the labor market. Of these, 7.6 million would be without high-school diplomas, 2.3 million

[9] lodging places

[10] third

without a grade-school education. At the same time, as Secretary of Labor Wirtz remarked, machines were being built with automated skills beyond the human reach of a high-school graduate. As a result, there were 730,000 youthful unemployed by October, 1963 (the figures neared a million in 1964), 350,000 young people were neither at school or work (and thus not "in the labor market" and not certified in the unemployment figures), and one million in the same age group were in what the Administration called "dead-end" jobs. Indeed, in the Selective Service examinations, fully a quarter of the young American males were declared unfit for military service by virtue of not being able to read up to seventh-grade levels.

For these young people—perhaps a third of their generation—the advance of American ingenuity is a catastrophe. Given their lack of skill and training, they are systematically misfitted for the economy which they are entering. Their future holds out chronic unemployment at worst, or at best laboring at tasks that are so menial they are beneath the dignity and education of machines. Part of their plight is already expressed in the explosive social conditions in the slums, the rise of juvenile delinquency, adult crime, and aimless violence.

Yet, under the American corporate system there are limits to this process. On the one hand, business can eliminate jobs in order to cheapen cost and maximize profit; on the other hand, it cannot abolish the consumer buying power needed to purchase the goods it produces, and this is still largely guaranteed through employment. Such a contradiction can, as will be seen, be resolved in many ways, not the least of them the transformation of the system itself. At this point, a few of the immediate American responses are relevant.

One answer, that of the Democratic Administrations of the sixties (theoretically stated by the Council of Economic Advisers), was to hold that technological unemployment was simply a temporary phenomenon. If money could be pumped into the economy by a cut in taxes, that would increase aggregate[11] effective demand and make it profitable to put people to work (the same tax cut, however, included a corporate bonus that could well be utilized to cybernate). In addition, the patchwork of American social insurance, wel-

[11] collected into a mass or sum

fare, and relief schemes was seen as adequate to handle those who fell out of the economy altogether. As the preceding analysis should make clear, this view simply does not meet the radical character of contemporary technological change.

> "The certitude that man must labor by the sweat of his brow was a weary, but consoling, knowledge. The machines are now lifting this burden from human shoulders and, in the doing, corrupting the central Western ethic of work."

A second response was somewhat more profound, involving redefinitions of work. In the discussion of the Senate Subcommittee on Employment and Manpower, there were demands for an expansion of the public sector in fulfilling the nation's unmet needs for housing, hospitals, schools, and transportation systems. While clearly leaving the corporate basis of the economy intact, this would amount to a modest political allocation of economic resources on the basis of social need. In addition, the Subcommittee urged the extension of universal free public education to two years beyond high school and Government support for those workers who were retired from the economy some years before they were eligible for Social Security.

Behind these suggestions were the beginnings of new ideas. First, they recognize that the public sector—where social personal services must be provided—takes on a new significance. Secondly, there is the emphasis on education and the recognition that it is probably no longer possible to train a young person for a lifetime skill, but necessary to give him a liberal education that would prepare him to change his skill several times according to the demands of technology. Thirdly, there is the advocacy of curtailing the working life of the citizen: through a later entry into the work force after prolonged education, and through an earlier exit by retirement. All of these ideas involve the intimation of new social principles: the importance of the public service sector of the economy; the recognition that going to school is

". . . at this very moment, without too many people noticing, the nature of work is being redefined."

262   an economically productive function; the realization that not working, for the young and the old, is becoming a social necessity.

These are only some of the changes which the reality of American life in the sixties has made into questions for discussion (there are also, of course, proposals to shorten the workweek itself to thirty hours). They indicate that a profound transformation in the character of work is taking place even now. But more than that, they point in the not-too-distant future to the appearance of the statues of Daedalus. The almost totally cybernated production of commodities and routine office services is not merely technologically possible; it is now probable.

In all of this, traditional wisdoms are being turned topsy-turvy. In a statement which would have been incomprehensible to the starving man of the past, John R. Bunting, a vice-president of the Federal Reserve Bank of Philadelphia, said in 1964, "I think on balance that the American economic system is threatened more by abundance than by scarcity."

And, well to the Left of Bunting on the political spectrum, the British scholar, Richard M. Titmuss, an important adviser to the Labor Party, wrote in the same year, "If the first phase of the so-called (industrial) revolution was to force men to work, the phase we are now entering may be to force many men not to work."

To a mankind which has been engaged in a grim struggle with hunger since the beginning of time, the idea that men would be forced not to work would, at first glance, seem a salvation. That could well be the case—so long as it is understood that this salvation would simultaneously portend[12] the decadence of some of the most fundamental economic, ethical, and even religious assumptions of Western life. It would therefore require a tremendous burst of freedom and imagination to fill up the void left by the disappearance of starvation.

II The capitalist West was built, in R. H. Tawney's phrase, by "practical ascetics."[13] This is to say that the West made hard labor into an ethical dictate, a guarantee of personal worth and even a path to God. In 1900, as remarked

earlier, Henry Adams contrasted the Virgin, as the spiritual principle of the medieval age, and the dynamo, the god of force presiding over the new industrialism. Forty years later, in keeping with Adams' own law of the acceleration of history, the dynamo, a source of energy, was ceding its Olympian position to the computer and its "intelligent anticipation." And just as the dynamo counterposed its social philosophy to the Virgin's theology, so the statues of Daedalus, the cybernated machines, mark the end of the practicality of asceticism.

The thesis that work took on a metaphysical[14] and even theological significance under Western capitalism is, of course, most identified with Max Weber's provocative study of the Protestant ethic. In Puritanism, Weber wrote, "The premiums were placed upon 'proving' oneself before God in the sense of attaining salvation—which is found in *all* Puritan denominations—and 'proving' oneself before men in the sense of socially holding one's own within the Puritan sects. Both aspects were mutually supplementary and operated in the same direction: they helped to deliver the 'spirit' of modern capitalism, its specific *ethos*:[15] the ethos of the modern *bourgeois middle classes.*"

Weber's analysis of the importance of the Calvinist idea of a "calling" to the rise of capitalism has been widely disputed. Some economic historians like Henri Pirenne have claimed to trace the capitalist spirit well back into the Middle Ages before the Reformation (and Marx once admitted in a letter to being puzzled as to why capitalism had not developed in Rome at the time of Christ, all of its preconditions having been fulfilled). Yet whatever the specific weight of the Protestant ethic in *determining* the rise of capitalism, there is little doubt that its distinctive spirit was part of the event. If Puritanism was not godfather to capitalism, then it was godson. As cause or effect, the ethical and religious importance of hard work became a constituent principle of the capitalist West.

Indeed, in the past four or five centuries, it was precisely this practical asceticism that drove the West to the most extraordinary material achievement history has known. Where Eastern philosophy, for instance, would accept reality as an illusion or a fate, and the cycles of suffering and

---

[12] point to a future development
[13] those whose lives were based on self-denial

[14] extending beyond the physical; in this context, the author is saying that work took on a spiritual significance.
[15] underlying and distinctive character of a people

starvation as events to be ignored or endured, the West was remaking the world. (Yeats understood this point when he limited tragedy, "the heroic cry," to the West.) In the mid-twentieth century, one of the great problems of the developing nations, with their feudal and tribal heritages, is to find a cultural basis for this Western attitude.

R. H. Tawney was a friendly critic of Weber's (some of their ideas converged). He stated the theological aspect of the work ethic this way: "For since conduct and action, though availing nothing to attain the free gift of salvation, are a proof that the gift has been accorded, what is rejected as means is resumed as a consequence and the Puritan flings himself into practical activities with the daemonic energy of one who, all doubts allayed, is conscious that he is a sealed and chosen vessel. Called by God to labor in his vineyard, he has within himself a principle at once of energy and order, which makes him irresistible both in war and in the struggle of commerce."

Tawney was writing of the origins of capitalism. Over time, the spirit which he described became less mystical, more secular, yet it persisted. Thorstein Veblen's *Theory of the Leisure Class* is primarily a description of the American *nouveau riche*[16] of the late nineteenth century. It chronicles an ethic of conspicuous consumption that is almost the exact opposite of the Protestant spirit. Yet even in this setting, he told of the continuing thrust of the earlier idea.

"The substantial canons[17] of the leisure class scheme of life," Veblen wrote, "are conspicuous waste of time and substance and a withdrawal from the industrial process; while the particular aptitudes here in question [essentially the Protestant ethic] assert themselves, on the economic side, in a deprecation[18] of waste and of a futile manner of life, and in an impulse to participation or in identification with the life process, whether it be on the economic side or in any other of its phases or aspects."

Veblen's leisure class did exist (even if more complexly than he imagined). In Europe, the aristocratic tradition of regarding work and commerce as degrading persisted even under capitalism. And those who actually did the backbreaking toil hardly regarded their daily toil as a spiritual value. "Certainly the workers in Hogarth's Gin

[16] newly rich people
[17] laws
[18] representing something as being of little worth

Alley," Daniel Bell has written, "or the people whom Melville's Redburn saw in the Liverpool slums, were little concerned with the scourging hand of God. What drove them to work was hunger, and much of the early movements of social protest can only be understood with that fact in mind."

But then, Western capitalism has not been aristocratic, proletarian, or leisured. It has been the bourgeois economic order. Without reducing all of its complexity to a single historic strand, one can say that it was dominated by the ethic, and even religion, of work. To this day, the West believes that a man establishes his worth in the eyes of his neighbor, and even before God, through industry and drudgery and saving: In its most acutely American form, as the poet William Carlos Williams once observed, this attitude asserts itself in the conversational opening, "What do you do?" This question follows immediately upon an exchange of names between strangers, it establishes much of the substance of their talk, it is the quickest means of identification. One is, it implies, what one does. One is one's work.

What, then, would happen if technology rendered work and the work ethic decadent?

Bread and circuses are an obvious, but hardly affirmative, substitute. In a series of Italian films of Antonioni and Fellini, there is a depiction of the empty, orgiastic lives of the leisure and celebrity class. They are tormented by their free time. Significantly, each of these movies contains a scene in which an anguished protagonist looks longlingly upon the vitality of working-class or peasant life, admiring its muscularity or simplicity. These particular cases are examples of what Empson defined as the "pastoral" theme in literature and art (the romantic courtier sings of the rustic swain; the middle-class novelist or movie director celebrates the noble proletarian). But they could also be the intimation of a possible nostalgia in the technological future. Will people then turn back to yearn for the working present and the even more hardworking past?

Were it possible to build a society on the principles of bread and circuses, the event would signify the decadence of central Western values. But it is doubtful whether such a society could exist at all. Here, Ortega's inaccurate charge against the twentieth century might apply to the twenty-first. The very existence of technological abundance presupposes a high level of science and

264 skill, at least on the part of the minority. A social order based upon orgy would destroy its own effortless prosperity by failing to reproduce its technological genius. (In terms of myth, Cockaigne, where there is only consumption, is impossible; utopia, which recognizes some form of work, is still conceivable.)

what decisions the machines will make. Indeed, a society split between the highly educated and sophisticated few on the one side, and the passive, consuming mass on the other, could hardly be democratic, since dialogue between the rulers and ruled would be impossible. Were this to happen, it would confirm the worst fears of soci-

There is another possible principle of the society that has eliminated work as it is now known: totalitarianism. In the past, hunger has been at least as important for the maintenance of order as for the fomenting of revolution. Out of necessity, millions "voluntarily" chose brutal toil in order to survive. If this indirect discipline were abolished, it might be replaced by the dictatorship of the programmers, of those who decide

ologists like Weber and Mills that the functional rationalization of life necessarily leads to the loss of substantive rationality for the majority of individuals.

Some of the positive options of a cybernated culture will be discussed shortly, others in the next chapter. For now, it is clear that the West is already approaching the decadence of the work ethic. Thomas Malthus said, "If our benevolence be indiscriminate . . . we shall raise the worthless above the worthy; we shall encourage indolence and check industry; and in the most marked manner subtract from the sum of human happiness. . . . The laws of nature say with Saint Paul, 'If a man will not work, neither shall he eat.'"

That law of nature, so basic to the recent history of the West, is now being abolished by machines. In 1964, the President of the United States intimated the new era when, in announcing the enactment of a cut in taxes, he urged Americans to spend and consume as a patriotic duty. Paradoxically, this decadence of the Protestant ethic comes at the very moment when it has finally conquered the world. As Sebastian de Grazia has pointed out, the UNESCO Declaration of Human Rights announces, "Everyone has the right to work."

So it is that at that point in history at which the Western work ethic is finally in sight of subverting[19] almost every remnant of tribalism, feudalism, and aristocracy on the globe, it ceases to be a practical guide for the culture that gave it birth.

III Sigmund Freud made two basic arguments for the necessity of work. With the coming of abundance, one of them will become obsolete and the other will constitute the most fundamental challenge of the future.

Freud's first analysis of the need for work rests upon a conservative view of the industrial masses and the assumption of scarcity as a fundamental condition of human life. "The masses," he wrote in *The Future of an Illusion*, "are lazy and unintelligent; they have no love for instinctual renunciation and they are not to be convinced by argument of its inevitability; and the individuals composing them support one another in giving free rein to their indiscipline. It is only through the influence of individuals who can set an example and whom the masses recognize as their leaders that they can be induced to perform the work and undergo the renunciations on which the existence of civilization depends. . . .

"To put it briefly," Freud continues, "there are two widespread characteristics which are responsible for the fact that the regulation of civilization can only be maintained by a certain degree of coercion—namely, that men are not spontaneously

fond of work and that arguments are of no avail against their passions."

Thus coercion, Freud makes clear, is essentially conservative in character. It aims "not only at affecting a certain distribution of wealth but at maintaining that distribution; indeed [it has] to protect everything that contributes to the conquest of nature and the production of wealth against men's hostile impulses." At the same time, this fact revolutionizes the majority. "In such conditions, an internalization of the cultural prohibitions among the suppressed people is not to be expected. On the contrary, they are not prepared to acknowledge their prohibitions, they are bent on destroying the culture itself, and possibly even on doing away with the postulates[20] on which it is based."

In part, this analysis is that of a conservative mind, and was wrong on the day it was made. For Freud, it was the very nature of the masses to shirk work. Yet, as he himself was to recognize in *Civilization and Its Discontents*, the work to which these people were driven was degrading and unfree. Under such circumstances, it is realism, and not laziness, to detest work. When those same masses saw real choices, they were anything but indolent. At great personal sacrifice, even of life itself, they organized a mighty and disciplined labor and socialist movement and contributed to the very reshaping of Western society.

With all his marvelous depth and a candor that shook a culture, Freud never fully escaped from the prejudices of a Viennese bourgeois.

The second element in Freud's analysis is much less capricious. He understood that culture had "not got beyond a point at which the satisfaction of one portion of its participants depends upon the suppression of another, and perhaps larger, portion . . ." Here, his social psychology is based on understanding that economic scarcity is a massive determinant of societal structure and the individual self. His point is historical, and not rooted in any assumptions about the "natural" habits of the mass.

But events are now destroying the historical conditions that gave Freud his context. As noted before, there are already Government proposals in the United States for contracting the individual's working life through a late entry into, and early withdrawal from, the labor force. And in a

[19] undermining

[20] self-evident truths

"The almost totally cybernated production of commodities and routine office services is not merely technologically possible; it is now probable."

time of cybernating technology, the coercive power of the Government under the neo-Keynesian ethic insists that the masses gratify their desires.[21] The consequences of such developments for the Freudian perspective are momentous.

Insofar as Freud's deep pessimism (most poignantly put in *Civilization and Its Discontents*) rests upon the assumption of economic scarcity, then abundance makes a psychic liberation possible. Freud had said that man becomes more neurotic as society becomes more complex. The more sophisticated the collective life, he argued, the more pervasive is the denial of instinctual gratification, for increasing renunciation is required to maintain such a vast community. In this tragic thesis, there is something pathological about progress.

But if onerous[22] work would no longer be necessary to the collective, then what function is there for coercion and repression? Under such conditions, the recent socialist interpretations of Freud by Herbert Marcuse and Norman Brown would become orthodox deductions from the master's premises. However, the matter is complicated because Freud, living through one world war, the rise of fascism, and the coming of the Second World War, also located an aggressive instinct in man's deepest self. If such a destructiveness is a "natural" human condition, then the elimination of scarcity would not mean the end of coercion but its irrational persistence. Then repression, having lost its economic function, would not express historical necessity but a basic human depravity. One hopes that Freud's dark thesis was an overgeneralization of post-1914 Europe in all of its violence. The possibility remains that it was not.

In any case, Freud's social psychology of work will be rendered obsolete if abundance, as threatened, does indeed come. Given the decadence of some of the basic assumptions of the Western psyche, the question will then be, what forms of repression or liberation will follow upon the event?

And it is here that Freud's second, and positive, argument on work becomes extremely relevant. "Laying stress upon the importance of work," he wrote in *Civilization and Its Discontents*, "has a greater effect than any other technique of living in the direction of binding the individual more closely to reality; in his work, he is at least attached to a part of reality, the human community. Work is no less valuable for the opportunity it and the human relations connected with it provide for a very considerable discharge of libidinal[23] component impulses, narcissistic,[24] aggressive and even erotic, than because it is indispensable for subsistence and justifies existence in society. The daily work of earning a livelihood affords particular satisfaction when it has been selected by free choice, i.e. when through sublimation[25] it enables use to be made of existing inclinations, of instinctual impulses that have retained their strength, or are more intense than usual for constitutional reasons. And yet as a path to happiness, work is not valued very highly by men. They do not run after it as they do after other opportunities of gratification. The great majority work only when forced by necessity, and this natural human aversion to work gives rise to the most difficult social problems."

In the last few sentences on the "natural human aversion to work," Freud is once again the Viennese bourgeois. His own definition of therapeutic, i.e., freely chosen, work has been denied the overwhelming majority of men in history. The only kind of work they have known is that imposed upon them in a struggle for survival. Abundance could completely change this situation. If all routine and repetitive chores can be done by machines, man can be freed for activity of his own choosing.

Freud's really profound point here is that such activity would still be necessary, even if not for subsistence. Work, he says, does not merely discharge narcissistic and aggressive impulses; it can, when freely chosen, even be erotic, a "path to happiness." There is, Freud would say with scientific rigor, a labor of love. In it, man is united

---

[21] John Maynard Keynes (1883–1946), a British economist, is credited with the modern theory of income analysis. He believed that the net national product consists of three parts: consumption expenditure, private net investment, and government expenditure on goods and services. When there is a large inflationary or deflationary gap between consumption expenditure and private net investment, the government can control the price rise or the widespread unemployment by a decrease or increase in its own expenditures. In this particular context, the author is saying that with the increased productivity of cybernated technology, the government must do what it can to place buying power in the hands of the people.
[22] burdensome

[23] characterized by the instinctual craving or drive behind all human activities
[24] showing self-love
[25] the act of deflecting sexual or other biological energies into socially constructive or creative channels

with reality and his fellowman, thus discovering some of his deepest satisfactions. And conversely, a man without any work at all would be shallow and sick and his narcissism, aggressiveness, and erotic energy could express themselves in sub-human and antisocial form.

In this psychological analysis of the meaning of work, one glimpses the extraordinary ambiguity of the present moment. Abundance could be the prelude to bread and circuses. A degrading leisure would be society's substitute for a degrading work. Some of these possibilities have already been outlined. On the other hand, there could be a new kind of leisure and a new kind of work, or more precisely, a range of activities that would partake of the nature of both leisure and work.

This latter development will not simply happen. If the decision is left to technology in its present context, then the first, and grim, possibility is more likely. A society with a cybernated revolution and a conservative mentality is not going to make new definitions of leisure and work. It is much simpler, and in keeping with the current wisdom, to vulgarize the neo-Keynesian ethic and to provide a market for the products of machines by simply injecting quantities of money into the economy, without any planning for the use of this productivity. Such a course would be defended in the name of allowing the individual freedom of choice. In reality, it would tend to constrict that freedom to its basest and most commercial options.

But on the other side there are enormous possibilities. Activities which are now regarded as hobbies, like photography, gardening, and fishing, could be seen as important human occupations in a society where machines did all the drudgery. So could the practice of the arts, of scientific research, of politics and education. To the Athenians, these latter employments were indeed the truly human work of man. But the Greek ideal rested, as Aristotle made so clear in the *Politics*, upon the degradation of the slaves. That fatal immorality of the Aristotelian scheme is no longer necessary—as Aristotle himself realized when he said that the appearance of the statues of Daedalus would obviate[26] the need for slaves. The machine slaves, the modern statues of Daedalus, are now coming into existence. Their appearance makes the Freudian notion of the

labor of love a possible choice, not simply for an elite, but for all mankind.

This varient requires the active and conscious intervention of man. Such a radical departure from present certitudes will take an act of the social imagination as fundamental as the one which, in the Neolithic Revolution, established the basis for society itself. But here again, in either case, some of the most obvious assumptions of the contemporary psychology are turned into illusions.

And the ambiguity is, one does not yet know whether these developments simply portend a decadence—or both a decadence and a marvelous birth.

IV In some notes which he never fully expanded, Karl Marx predicted that automation and cybernation would destroy the very basis of the capitalist system itself.

The analysis appears in *The Outline of the Critique of Political Economy* (*Grundrisse Der Kritik Der Politischen Oekonomie*), some "rough notes" dating from the late 1850's which have never been translated into English. In later years, Marx refined the vocabulary and argument of his outline but, to my knowledge, never returned to his remarkable anticipation of the statues of Daedalus. The intimations of 1857 and 1858 became the more prosaic theories of the change in the organic composition of capital (the substitution of machines for men) and the consequent tendency for the rate of profit to fall. Neither of these ideas is relevant here. The insights of the original notes, however, are utterly contemporary in the age of cybernation which began approximately one hundred years after Marx wrote.

These references are not made to document a historical curiosity, nor even to vindicate Marx as a seer. They are put forth because his words contain so much present truth.

Marx did not, of course, use terms like automation or cybernation, both of recent coinage. Yet he was unmistakably talking about these phenomena. "As large scale industry develops," he wrote, "the creation of real wealth depends less and less upon labor time and the quantity of labor expended, and more upon the might of the machines [Agentien] set in motion during labor time. The powerful effectiveness of these machines bears no relationship to the labor time

[26] make unnecessary

```
43434623  41104731  10000000  00002274  63462423  41102226  8000BXPALLOCJ8PI800000BXT
22465163  51104662  10000000  22745150  23464563  41103101  80000BXABORTR80S8000BXRQC
50314565  41103102  10000000  00002274  47646331  41102367  80000BXRQINVJ8I2800000BXF
47646362  41102363  10000000  22742625  63233031  41102357  800000BXPUTSJ8CT8000BXFET
63233062  41102353  10000000  00002274  62646247  41104717  8000BXFETCHSJ8CS800000BXS
74465127  51107560  10000000  00227443  47474446  41111034  8000000BXQRGR8=+80000BXLF
51416267  41104210  10000000  22742462  64010600  41105206  800000BXRJSXJ8K8800BXDSU
47514563  41101526  10000000  00002274  63214725  41106332  800000BXPRNTJ8:F800000BXT
23215124  41101447  10000000  00227451  50212451  41105036  800000BXCARDJ8oP800000BXRQ
50512563  41105037  10000000  00227451  50234624  41100117  80000BXRQRETJ8Q\80000BXRG
25262151  41100127  10000000  00247446  47452151  51100133  80000D%DEFARJ81G80000DXOF
43622151  41100137  10000000  00247424  43632151  41100143  80000D%RLSARJ81\80000D%DL
25263143  41100153  10000000  24744647  45263143  41100157  80000D%DEFILJ81$8000D%OPN
62263143  41100163  10000000  24742443  63263143  41100167  8000D%CLSFILJ81T8000D%DLT
43636226  41100173  10000000  00227423  47236351  41100271  80000D%DLTSFJ81,80000BXCP
66634727  51107150  10000000  00002474  51244727  51107051  800000D%WTPGR8ZQ800000D%F
63472762  51107207  10000000  00247451  24472762  51107117  80000D%WTPGSR8+780000D%RD
43624762  41107515  10000000  00227446  65264366  41105035  80000D%RLSPGJ8=:80000BXOV
25514370  41103711  10000000  22744724  21434623  41104736  8000BXOVERLYJ8\980000BXPDA
47514162  41107754  10000000  00227443  47512523  41107761  80000BXLPRJSJ8!*80000BXLP
51416222  41110046  10000000  00227443  47234644  41107704  8000BXLPRJSBJ90080000BXLP
47465127  41110646  10000000  22744444  62635163  41106671  80000BXLPORGJ9608000BXPMS
21646225  41104711  10000000  00227443  46272567  41104743  80000BXPAUSEJ8P980000BXLO
22430001  41100264  10000000  00227441  62264743  41104450  80000BXTBL01J82U80000BXJS
70462747  41104764  10000000  00227430  62516345  41104764  80000BXSYOGPJ8PU80000BXHS
46314623  41104753  10000000  24746246  24674363  41104752  80000D%SOIOCJ8P$8000D%SOD
22430105  41102417  10000000  00227463  22430107  41100673  80000BXTBL15J8D?80000BXTB
22430110  41102604  10000000  00227424  63425122  41105362  80000BXTBL18J8F480000BXDT
25512563  41105431  10000000  00227463  22430010  41100312  800000BXERETJ8*I80000BXTB
62266266  41104602  10000000  00000000  00273022  41011753  800000BXSFSWJ8028000000000
21436401  41007673  10000000  00000000  27302202  41013727  80000000ALU1J0",80000000G
27302421  41015703  10000000  00002730  47514663  41020007  80000000GHDAJ1'3800000GHP
70672762  51132340  10000000  00000070  24214564  51132654  80000000YXGSR#C+8000000YD
45642421  51132721  10000000  00000025  13252262  51133541  8000000YNUDAR#GA8000000E#
13254626  41033542  10000000  00227443  22224342  51134131  8000000E#EOFJ3(K80000BXLB
26236343  51132775  10000000  00251325  67634543  41033761  80000E#BFCTLR#G=80000E#EX
65432170  51134102  10000000  00251362  25636447  41033555  80000E#OVLAYR#J280000E#SE
63266226  41033340  10000000  22742122  46516325  51134031  80000LBFTFSFJ3.+8000BXABO
46516331  41034033  10000000  22742122  46516341  41034025  8000BXABORTIJ3*,8000BXABO
46516362  41034027  10000000  22745125  63645145  41033773  8000BXABORTSJ3*G8000BXRET
62632163  41033020  10000000  25132546  26212424  41033231  8000E#CKSTATJ3H 8000E#EOF
24444524  41033743  10000000  25134322  25673163  41033213  8000E#LBDMNDJ3\L8000E#LBE
31433163  41033575  10000000  25134323  46450001  41033544  8000E#LBINITJ3(=8000E#LCO
23452467  41033554  10000000  25135125  63645145  41033773  8000E#RECNDXJ3(*8000E#RET
63465125  41033211  10000000  43222621  24246266  41033553  8000E#RSTOREJ3&98000LBFAD
51234664  41034021  10000000  43222663  26622604  41033373  8000LBFORCOUJ3*A8000LBFTF
26622605  41033337  10000000  20202020  20202020  20202020  8000LBFTFSF5J3.\8000
32615634  17607051  00000002  07008025  00013313  10015623  W00001W/&/1]?+YR0002700E0
```

which it cost to produce them. Their power, rather, derives from the general level of science and the progress of technology . . ."

Then Marx, in some remarkably prophetic phrases, notes how this changes the very character of work. "Man's labor no longer appears as incorporated in [eingeschlossen] the production process. Rather, the worker relates himself to production as a supervisor and regulator [Wachter und Regulator] . . . He watches over the production process rather than being its chief agent." Clearly, Marx did not have mystical, advance knowledge of inventions that were to take place after his death. But just as he derived the tendency of capital to concentrate in larger and larger units from the limited evidence on hand in the mid-nineteenth century, so also did he understand the direction of largescale production, science, and technology.

Actually, the factory in which the worker became "supervisor and regulator" was not built until 1939, when Standard Oil of New Jersey and the M. W. Kellogg Company erected the first fluid-catalytic crackers. Today, in such plants, the work cycle is leisurely (a man repeats his routine only four times a day in one typical case, as compared to the assembly line on which he might perform the same task several times in the course of a minute). Since the complex system does most of the work by itself, management is content to have the workers "watch over the production process" and even loaf openly. In such factories, the main function of the work force is to be ready when the costly machines break down.

This development, Marx continues, means that the very basis of wealth has been transformed. Now, "neither the actual labor expended by man, nor the length of time during which he works, is the great pillar of production and wealth. That pillar is now the appropriation of man's own universal productivity." And, a little later Marx comments that this demonstrates "the degree to which society's general store of knowledge has become the main factor in increasing productivity."

For Marx, this eventuality does not simply transform the character of work and the source of wealth. It reveals a basic contradiction of the capitalist system itself.

In its earlier stages, Marx argues, capitalism was based upon the fact that riches were derived from poverty. The labor—and suffering—of the mass was the source of surplus production (that

is to say, after the capitalist deducted from his output the cost of paying his workers, that output, produced by those workers, was still much larger than what they received, directly or indirectly, in pay). This surplus constituted the profit of the few, and it was either reinvested to begin the process anew or consumed in luxuries for the few. There was thus a conflict between the demands of the people for more consumer's goods and the money to buy them and those of the entrepreneur for more producer's goods and profits (in another form, this contradiction is constantly plaguing the developing countries of the world today). But as production became more and more sophisticated, as it depended less and less upon the exploitation of brute labor and more upon the application of science to technology, this conflict no longer was necessary. An ever large part of production can be devoted to new machines without sacrificing the immediate enjoyment of the producers.

Up to this point, Marx's argument resembles Freud's analysis of the way in which the collective represses the instinctual gratification of the many in order to forward the common good as defined, and enjoyed, by the few. It might even win the support of some of the more educated celebrants of the corporation who would be willing to admit that capitalism vastly increased the productive basis of society while simultaneously raising the standard of living. But Marx, of course, went well beyond this point.

"On the one hand," he says, "capital uses every power of science and nature . . . to make the creation of riches independent of the labor time spent in production." The great stimulus to replacing men with machines is to cheapen the cost of production and to maximize profit. "But on the other hand," he continues, "capital measures this growing and achieved social power of production in terms of labor time . . ." As a producer, the capitalist wishes to reduce the number of workers to cheapen costs; but as a seller, he looks to an expanding work force as the source of a growing marketable to buy his goods. But once technology demonstrates itself capable of restricting employment while creating abundance, the system breaks down.

In simplified terms, Marx's insight could be illustrated by a (probably imaginary) conversation of the 1950's in America. Henry Ford III was said to have shown Walter Reuther of the United

Automobile Workers a completely automated engine block plant. Pointing to the assembly line, on which there were no workers, the corporate chief taunted the trade unionist, "How will you organize workers here?" To which Reuther is said to have replied, "And what workers here will buy your cars?"

In a more complex case, Daniel Bell (who is a sympathetic, but determined, critic of Marx) tells of how the new technology has perhaps already outmoded the old labor-time system of production accounting. "Most important perhaps, there may be an end, too, to the measurement of work. Modern industry began not with the factory but with the measurement of work. *When the worth of the product was defined in production units, the worth of the worker was similarly gauged.* Under the unit concept, the time-study engineers calculated that a worker could produce more units for more money. This was the assumption of the wage-incentive schemes (which actually are output-incentive schemes) and the engineering morality of a 'fair day's pay for a fair day's work.'

"But under automation, with continuous flow, *a worker's worth can no longer be evaluated in production units.* Hence, output-incentive plans, with their involved measurement techniques, may vanish. In their place, as Adam Arbuzzi foretells, may arise a new work morality. Work will be defined not in terms of a 'one best way,' not by the slide rule and the stop-watch, not in terms of fractioned time or units of production, but on the basis of planning and organizing and the continuously smooth functioning of the operation" (emphasis added).

Bell has an important point. In the cybernated factory where the machine, whose production- and tending-cost stands in little relation to its ability to produce goods, is the main source of wealth, how can the worker's worth be evaluated in production units? When the amount of human muscle expended in making an item was an essential element of its value, both the muscle and the product could be computed in terms of labor time (the wages of the muscle and the price of the product). But if that is no longer the case, how can income, the right to consume, be tied to a labor time that is less and less relevant?

As a result of this contradiction, Marx held, "the laboring mass must consume its own surplus product." This consumption is not a grudging necessity of diverting scarce resources to keeping the body and soul of the work force together. It is a precondition of the functioning of the economy, for the people must have the capacity to consume what is made or else there will be over-production and the crisis of glut. In a moderate form, this notion has become a basic principle of neo-Keynesian economics, recognized by the Western labor movement and the welfare state governments of most of the advanced countries. But it does not stop there.

Under such conditions, Marx concluded, "It is then no longer labor time but disposable time which is the measure of wealth." Now, precisely in order to expand productivity, there must be a vast expansion of consumption. Leisure, which robbed society of resources in a time of scarcity, goads society into activity in a time of abundance.

> *"As technology takes over more and more occupations, as the working day, week, year, and life are contracted, [Marx's] ultimate prophecy could come true: that it is the economic responsibility of the citizen to be free, leisured, to develop his own individual bents and proclivities, to consume, not simply manufactured goods, but freedom itself."*

In short, from Marx's point of view, the decadence of the old principles of scarcity would mark a decisive moment in the liberation of man. Production would no longer rest upon the hard, sweaty labor of the mass but rather upon free time and enjoyment. Where Malthus feared that raising up the poor would degrade the worth and dignity of the few, the modern technological economy of abundance must be frightened of the exact opposite: that not abolishing poverty will destroy prosperity.

Marx's description of the change in the nature of work is now beginning to take place in the West. In the automated factory, the worker is indeed one who "watches over" the production process rather than being its chief agent. His theory that increasing consumption would become an economic necessity has been modestly recognized within the welfare state as a practical reform but not as a revolutionary principle of a new life. As technology takes over more and more occupations, as the working day, week, year, and life are contracted, his ultimate prophecy could come true: that it is the economic responsibility of the citizen to be free, leisured, to develop his own individual bents and proclivities,[27] to consume, not simply manufactured goods, but freedom itself.

And yet, paradoxically, Marx did not realize one possible consequence of his own vision of cybernation and automation. He had assumed that a working-class revolution would transform the ownership of large-scale industry before the process which he described had reached its ultimate limits. The decadence of capitalism under conditions of abundance was not simply a decadence, since the system had created the historical agency for resolving its contradictions in a new way: the proletariat. The humane possibilities of the new development would be made practical by a social class, by those who had learned how to live joyously in the future out of the sufferings and miseries of the past.

But what if the working class in the Marxist sense is abolished before, or simultaneously with, the emergence of the fatal capitalist contradictions of abundance? That now seems quite possible.

V When Aristotle imagined the statues of Daedalus, he drew one main conclusion from their discovery: that there would no longer be any necessity for slavery and subordination.

Here I suggest that the situation is more complex than the Greek philosopher imagined. Abundance has not really yet arrived in the West, but its possibility—and the abolition of work as it has traditionally been defined in Europe and America—is within the range of commonsensible speculation. Even within the most prosaic Government statistics, one can note that the statues of Daedalus have begun to dance in our midst.

The coming of abundance will unquestionably mean a decadence. Much of the social wisdom of scarcity, that is to say much of man's history, will become irrelevant to the future.

What will replace the conviction that it is through arduous, unfree labor that man realizes himself? A void? Bread and circuses? The dictatorship of the programmers? Or new definitions of freely chosen work, work as creativity, the labor of love?

Will the ending of the economic compulsion to work allow each individual to discover reality in his own way and thus obviate the whole system of social discipline required by the struggle against scarcity? Or will it simply strip away all the extraneous historical guises from the innate destructiveness of man?

Will cybernation force the West to some kind of social humanity, providing practical reasons for making social and personal development the end of collective life? Or will the infinitely capable machines create surplus products and surplus people?

The options are of an extreme range, more so than Aristotle thought. Abundance could actually produce new slaveries, new subordinations. Or, as John Maynard Keynes once said, under such conditions, ". . . we shall be able to rid ourselves of many of the pseudo-moral principles which have hag-ridden us for 200 years, by which we have exalted some of the most distasteful of human qualities into the position of the highest virtues."

[27] leanings

Illustration Credits